REPUBLICAN GOMORRAH

REPUBLICAN GOMORRAH

INSIDE THE MOVEMENT THAT SHATTERED THE PARTY

MAX BLUMENTHAL

NATION
BOOKS

NEW YORK

Published by Nation Books,
A Member of the Perseus Books Group
116 East 16th Street, 8th Floor
New York, NY 10003

Nation Books is a co-publishing venture of the
Nation Institute and the Perseus Books Group

Books published by Nation Books are available at special discounts for bulk purchases in the United States by corporations, institutions, and other organizations. For more information, please contact the Special Markets Department at the Perseus Books Group, 2300 Chestnut Street, Suite 200, Philadelphia, PA 19103, or call (800) 810-4145, ext. 5000, or e-mail special.markets@perseusbooks.com.

Designed by Trish Wilkinson
Set in 11.5-point Minion

Library of Congress Cataloging-in-Publication Data

Blumenthal, Max.
    Republican Gomorrah : inside the movement that shattered the party / Max Blumenthal.
        p.   cm.
    Includes bibliographical references and index.
    ISBN 978-1-56858-398-3 (alk. paper)
    1. Republican Party (U.S. : 1854–) 2. Conservatism—United States—History—20th century. 3. Conservatives—United States—History—20th century. 4. United States—Politics and government—2001– I. Title.
JK2356.B68 2009
324.2734—dc22   2009019826

10 9 8 7 6 5 4 3

For my mother and father

The great difference between people in this world is not between the rich and the poor or the good and the evil. The biggest of all differences in this world is between the ones that had or have pleasure in love and those that haven't and hadn't any pleasure in love, but just watched it with envy, sick envy.

Tennessee Williams,
Sweet Bird of Youth, Act 1

Take, Lord Jesus Christ, and receive all my freedom, my memory, my understanding, and my will.

Saint Ignatius Loyola,
THE PRAYER OF ABANDONMENT

CONTENTS

———————————————————— PART THREE —

REPUBLICAN
GOMORRAH

INTRODUCTION
ESCAPE FROM FREEDOM

"*Home run! Home run! Home run! Home run!*"

A phalanx of young men in red baseball caps and polo shirts ran up and down the aisles of St. Paul, Minnesota's Excel Center pumping their fists and chanting boisterously.

"*Home run! Home run! Home run!*"

The chant quickly spread throughout the crowd.

Suddenly, the floor of the 2008 Republican National Convention is in rapture, having just heard vice-presidential nominee Sarah Palin taunt Barack Obama as an unqualified elitist, assail the liberal media, and bill herself as "an average hockey mom." The man at the top of the ticket, John McCain, would speak the following night, but Palin, a charismatic culture warrior, was the spark that ignited the party base.

When the chant finally died down, three country music stars stepped to the stage to perform a patriotic musical mash-up. John Rich and Gretchen Wilson stared deeply into one another's eyes, singing the national anthem, while Cowboy Troy, an African American singer known as the "king of hick-hop," stood off to the side, reciting lines from the pledge of allegiance. Gales of spontaneous cheers rose from the crowd when Cowboy Troy proclaimed, "One nation under God." From my position to the immediate left of the stage, standing next to the Pennsylvania delegation, Cowboy Troy was the only African American I could see among a sea of gray hair and white faces. After the pledge of allegiance, as Rich broke into "Raisin' McCain," a honky-tonk campaign anthem that extols Mc-Cain "goin' down in Vietnam town," a handsome middle-aged black man in a suit brushed by me, heading rapidly toward the arena exit. He was Lynn Swann, the Hall of Fame National Football League wide receiver and failed Republican gubernatorial candidate in Pennsylvania in 2006.

"Mr. Swann, where are the rest of the black people?" I asked him.

He paused, shrugged his shoulders, and kept walking. Then, before disappearing into the crowd, he turned and blurted out, "We need to do more."

Earlier that day, I milled around the convention floor and walked the arena hallways, chatting with party leaders and delegates. "These are the real people," Louisiana GOP chairman Roger Villere told me, echoing an emerging theme of the McCain–Palin campaign. "This is real America." When I asked Villere the whereabouts of his state's junior senator, David Vitter, he said he did not know. And when I asked about Vitter's confession to hiring several high-priced prostitutes, Villere shot back, "David is a moral man, a great senator, and we support him totally." Vitter, still a religious right favorite, was planning to run for reelection in 2010.

Near the press box, I ran into Ralph Reed, a Christian right operative once hailed by *Time* magazine as "God's Right Hand." Reed had harbored presidential ambitions, but his campaign for Georgia lieutenant governor ended in humiliating defeat when his role was disclosed in lobbyist Jack Abramoff's scheme to trick evangelical leaders into pressuring the Bush administration's Department of Interior to shut down Indian casinos that Abramoff's clients considered business competitors. I asked Reed whether he still had a political future. "What do you mean? I never left politics!" he chirped, beaming at me with a pearly smile. Reed and Abramoff's former friend and ally, ex–House Majority Leader Tom DeLay, hosted a private party that evening for Republican bigwigs. DeLay, who stood accused by the Texas attorney general of money laundering, had charged McCain with "betraying" the conservative movement. (One of the DeLay party's high-profile attendees, Representative John Mica, head-butted an ABC cameraman when a reporter asked him if he was happy to see his disgraced friend.)

Then I made my way to the far corner of the convention floor to mingle with the Idaho delegation. I asked delegates where the state's outgoing senior senator, Larry Craig, was. Craig, rated the third most conservative senator in Congress, had barely eluded criminal charges after soliciting sex with an undercover cop in an airport bathroom stall. "We'd rather not go back and revisit all that," Governor Jim Risch, running to replace Craig, told me. "I'm really here to talk about our party's plan for keeping the tax rate low."

From the Idaho delegation, I pushed through a gaggle of reporters and cameramen surrounding the Alaska delegation to meet some of Palin's constituents. When I approached a young man, the only delegate from the state who appeared to be under the age of fifty, he snapped, "You're not going to ask about Bristol, are you?" referring to Palin's pregnant sixteen-year-old daughter, who sat nearby with her fiancé, eighteen-year-old self-proclaimed "fuckin' redneck" Levi Johnston. I asked about Palin's support for laws banning abortion even in cases of rape, incest, or when the mother's life is in danger. "There's no reason to kill a baby, whether you consider him unborn or born," the delegate replied. Another delegate, a middle-aged woman, explained to me how her husband took their two daughters on "dates" to "talk about keeping themselves pure until marriage." (Two days later, the same woman, dressed in a construction worker's outfit like one of the Village People, bellowed on the convention floor in favor of offshore drilling: "Drill, baby, drill!")

This was a portrait of the Republican Party fully in the grip of its right wing: almost exclusively white, overwhelmingly evangelical, fixated on abortion, homosexuality, and abstinence education; resentful and angry; and unable to discuss how and why it had become this way. Noticeably absent from the convention were moderate Republicans. Senator Lincoln Chafee, legatee of the moderate Republican tradition in Rhode Island, was defeated in the 2006 midterms, and he was endorsing Obama. The last Republican House member from New England, Representative Chris Shays of Connecticut, would lose his seat in two months. None of the great Republican families of the past, from the Rockefellers to the Eisenhowers, were there either. Both of Ronald Reagan's natural children, Ron and Patti, endorsed Obama. President Dwight Eisenhower's granddaughter, Susan, addressed the Democratic National Convention in Denver just moments before Barack Obama appeared to accept his party's nomination.

How did a party once known for its "big tent" philosophy become a one-ring circus? How did a Republican Party that had dominated American politics for over twenty-five years become so marginalized?

■ ■ ■

During the 1952 presidential campaign, the Republican nominee and former Supreme Commander of Allied Forces in Europe Dwight D. Eisenhower silently observed the attacks on the patriotism of a man he knew was a great American, General George C. Marshall, then serving as secretary of state. His assailant was Senator Joseph McCarthy of Wisconsin, as opportunistic and sloppy as he was vicious. Eisenhower seethed while McCarthy smeared Marshall as "a man steeped in falsehood," who supposedly harbored at least fifty-seven active Communists within the State Department. Eisenhower loathed everything about McCarthy, regarding him as a dangerous and petty demagogue, but he shrank from attacking him or defending Marshall, fearing that McCarthy's influence among the Republican Party right-wing base might upset his campaign.

Only later, when McCarthy initiated a witch hunt of a phantom Communist Fifth Column within the top command of the U.S. Army in 1954, did Eisenhower strike back. He did so by sleight of hand. "I will not get into the gutter with this guy," he told aides. He instructed his staff to leak damaging information about the senator's ethical breaches and invoked executive privilege to stifle McCarthy's request for notes on the president's meetings with army officers. McCarthy's show trial quickly degenerated into a farce, leading to his rebuke by the army's attorney Joseph Welch ("Have you no sense of decency, sir, at long last?") and censure by the Senate for "vulgar and insulting" conduct. Eisenhower had guarded his party against the far right, defended its essentially moderate temper, and ensured the preservation of its national appeal.

By the time McCarthy drank himself to death in 1957, what the historian Richard Hofstadter had called "the paranoid style of politics" had spread into new and growing grassroots conservative groups that sought influence within the Republican Party. These groups cohered into the movement that enabled Barry Goldwater to seize the presidential nomination in 1964, would gain genuine power with the administration of President Ronald Reagan, and would reach their apotheosis under President George W. Bush.

Eisenhower observed the early development of the modern American right with anxiety. His experience in Europe had taught him that the rise of extreme movements could be explained only by the psychological yearnings and social needs of their supporters. He understood that these movements were not unique to any place or time. Authoritarianism could take root anywhere, even in America. Eisenhower did not believe that an American exceptionalism immunized the country against the spores of extremism.

Eisenhower, famous as a golfer and reader of Zane Grey western novels, was criticized for lacking an intellectual framework or even an interest in ideas. But throughout his presidency, Eisenhower clung to a short book that informed his view of the danger of extremist movements. He referred to this book in the first televised presidential press conference ever, distributed it to his friends and top aides, and cited its wisdom to a terminally ill World War II veteran, Robert Biggs, who had written him a letter saying he "felt from your recent speeches the feeling of hedging and a little uncertainty. We wait for someone to speak for us and back him completely if the statement is made in truth."

Eisenhower could have tossed Biggs's missive in the heap of unread letters his secretary discarded each day, or he could have allowed a perfunctory and canned response, but he was eager for an opportunity to expound on his vision of the open society. "I doubt that citizens like yourself could ever, under our democratic system, be provided with the universal degree of certainty, the confidence in their understanding of our problems, and the clear guidance from higher authority that you believe needed," Eisenhower wrote Biggs on February 10, 1959. "Such unity is not only logical but indeed indispensable in a successful military organization, but in a democracy debate is the breath of life."

The president then opined that free societies do not necessarily perpetuate freedom; many citizens would be far more comfortable under a structure that provides rigid order and certainty about all aspects of life. "The mental stress and burden which this form of government imposes has been particularly well recognized in a little book about which I have spoken on several occasions," Eisenhower wrote. "It is 'The True Believer,' by Eric Hoffer; you might find it of interest. In it, he points out that dictatorial systems make one contribution to their people which leads them to tend to support such systems—freedom from the necessity of informing themselves and making up their own minds concerning these tremendous complex and difficult questions."

Eisenhower's tone was one of humility and responsibility. He blamed himself for "purely an error of an expression" if his purposes were misunderstood. And he pointed out that fears of national security during the Cold War were distorted and exploited for political advantage. "It is difficult indeed to maintain a reasoned and accurately informed understanding of our defense situation on the part of our citizenry when many prominent officials, possessing no standing or expertness except as they themselves claim it, attempt to further their own ideas or interests by resorting to statements more distinguished by stridency than by accuracy." Eisenhower closed his letter praising the dying man for his "fortitude in pondering these problems despite your deep personal adversity." He made no reference to God.

Hoffer seemed the most unlikely of figures to influence the president. A self-educated itinerant worker, Hoffer toiled on San Francisco's Embarcadero, earning the nickname "the stevedore-philosopher" for the voracious reading and writing he did away from the job. On the docks, Hoffer encountered droves of tramps drifting in search of work.

When the Great Depression set in, some of the most bedraggled misfits he knew morphed suddenly into loyal foot soldiers for strikes led by militant longshoreman union leader Harry Bridges and his allies in the Communist Party. At the same time, when Hoffer looked across the ocean to Germany, he saw a revolution led by failed artists and frustrated intellectuals stirring the rabble with dreams of a transcendent dictatorial order.

Hoffer's experiences at this historical fulcrum provided the basis for his seminal work *The True Believer*, published in 1951. "A rising mass movement attracts and holds a following not by its doctrine and promises," he wrote, "but by the refuge it offers from the anxieties, barrenness and meaninglessness of an individual existence." The true believer was at his core an ineffectual man with no capacity for self-fulfillment. Only the drama provided by a mass movement gave him purpose. "Faith in a holy cause," Hoffer wrote, "is to a considerable extent a substitute for the lost faith in ourselves."

Hoffer's analysis of the political fanatic earned him national cult status, gaining the approval not only of Eisenhower but also of serious intellectuals such as the British philosopher Bertrand Russell. Hoffer's analysis, however, was limited for the same reason it resonated so widely. By positioning himself as a non-ideological voice of the American everyman, the ultimate individual standing alone against a rising tide of extremism, Hoffer conflated the underlying motives of all mass movements together. According to Hoffer, fascists, Communists, black nationalists, fanatical "Mohammadens," and Southern racists equally shared an extreme sensibility, and therefore he insisted, "All mass movements are interchangeable." But were they really?

Ten years before Hoffer published his book, a social psychologist and psychoanalyst named Erich Fromm identified and analyzed the character structure of people "eager to surrender their freedom," who sought personal transcendence through authoritarian causes and figureheads. Unlike Hoffer, whose theories were inspired exclusively by his rollicking American adventures and didactic but distant perspective on world affairs, Fromm was able to draw on the psychological atmosphere of Nazi Germany, where millions of ordinary Germans "instead of wanting freedom . . . sought for ways of escape from it." Although Fromm reached many of the same conclusions as Hoffer about the nature of fanaticism, he limited his analysis to the behavior of those who adhered to right-wing authoritarian movements, which he pinpointed as hothouses of individual dysfunction.

Born in 1900 in Germany, Fromm descended from a long line of rabbis. After studying to be a rabbi himself, he switched to the law, sociology, and the new field of psychoanalysis. He joined the famed Frankfurt School for Social Research but fled the country after Hitler's assumption of power, eventually making his way to New York. In 1941, Fromm published *Escape from Freedom*, a book illuminating the danger of rising authoritarian movements with penetrating psychoanalytical insight.

Writing after the Nazis had overrun Europe but before the entrance of the United States into World War II, Fromm warned, "there is no greater mistake and no graver danger than not to see that in our own society we are faced with the same phenomenon that is fertile soil for the rise of Fascism anywhere: the insignificance and powerlessness of the individual." Those who could not endure the vertiginous new social, political, and personal freedoms of the modern age, those who craved "security and a feeling of belonging and of being rooted somewhere" might be susceptible to the siren song of fascism. For the fascist, the struggle for a utopian future was more than politics and even war—it was an effort to attain salvation through self-medication. When radical extremists sought to cleanse society of sin and evil, what they really desired was the cleansing of their souls.

Fromm's understanding of the psychological character of authoritarianism was not only penetrating but also prophetic. He described how submission to the authority of a higher power to escape the complexities of personal freedom would lead not to order and harmony but ultimately to destructiveness. Movements that evangelized among the crisis-stricken and desperate, promising redemption through a holy crusade, ultimately assumed the dysfunctional characteristics of their followers. After sowing destruction all around it,

Fromm predicted that such a movement would turn on itself. Dramatic self-immolation was the inevitable fate of movements composed of conflicted individuals who sought above all the destruction of their blemished selves.

"The function of an authoritarian ideology and practice can be compared to the function of neurotic symptoms," Fromm wrote. "Such symptoms result from unbearable psychological conditions and at the same time offer a solution that makes life possible. Yet they are not a solution that leads to happiness or growth of personality. They leave unchanged the conditions that necessitate the neurotic solution."

■ ■ ■

Fromm's analysis in *Escape from Freedom* provides an eerie but prescient description of the authoritarian mindset driving the movement that has substantially taken over the modern Republican Party: the Christian right. Over the last five years, I interviewed hundreds of the Christian right's leaders and activists, attended dozens of its rallies and conferences, listened to countless hours of its radio programs, and sat in movement-oriented houses of worship where no journalists were permitted. As I explored the contours of the movement, I discovered a culture of personal crisis lurking behind the histrionics and expressions of social resentment. This culture is the mortar that bonds leaders and followers together.

Inside the movement initiates refer to it cryptically as "The Family," an exclusive sect. The Christian right as a whole is called "the pro-Family" movement, and movement allies are known as "friends of The Family." In an actual family, blood ties are required; however, joining the Christian right requires little more than becoming "born-again," a process of confession, conversion, and submission to a strict father figure.

The movement's Jesus is the opposite of the prince of peace. He is a stern, overtly masculine patriarch charging into the fray with his sword raised against secular foes; he is "the head of a dreadful company, mounted on a white horse, with a double-edged sword, his robe dipped in blood," according to movement propagandist Steve Arterburn. Mark Driscoll, a pastor who operates an alternative Christian rock venue from his church, stirs the souls of twenty-something evangelical males with visions of "Ultimate Fighting Jesus." This same musclebound god-man starred in Mel Gibson's blood-drenched *The Passion of the Christ*, enduring bone-crushing punishment at the hands of Jews and pagans for two hours of unrelieved pornographic masochism.

A portrait of virility and violence, the movement's omnipotent macho Jesus represents the mirror inversion of the weak men who necessitated his creation. As Fromm explained, "*the lust for power is not rooted in strength but in weakness* [italics in original]. It is the expression of the individual self to stand alone and live. It is the desperate attempt to gain secondary strength where genuine strength is lacking."

The movement's macho Jesus provided purpose to Tom DeLay, a dallying, alcoholic Texas legislator transformed through evangelical religion from "Hot Tub Tommy" into a dictatorial House majority leader known as "The Hammer." Macho Jesus was the god of Ted Haggard, a closet homosexual born-again and charismatic megachurch leader, risen to head of the National Association of Evangelicals, preaching the gospel of spiritual warfare and anti-gay crusades. And he was the god of Howard F. Ahmanson Jr., an eccentric millionaire whose inheritance of massive wealth literally drove him mad, prompting his institutionalization, who found relief as one of the far right's most reliable financial angels. Macho Jesus even transformed the serial killer Ted Bundy, murderer and rapist of dozens of women, who became a poster child for anti-pornography activists with his nationally televised death row confessional.

The movement's most powerful leader embodied the most severe qualities of his followers' god. James Dobson is a quintessential strict father whose influence has been compared by journalistic observers to that of a cult leader. Unlike most of his peers, Dobson had no theological credentials or religious training. He was a child psychologist who burst onto the scene with a best-selling book that urged beating children into submission in order to restore the respect for God and government that America's youth had lost during the 1960s. Dobson leveraged his fame and wealth to build a kingdom of crisis that counseled the trauma-wracked Middle American masses with Christian-oriented solutions to their personal problems. Then he marshaled them into apocalyptic morality crusades against abortion and homosexuality. When his Christian army reached critical mass, Dobson set them against the Republican establishment, flexing his grassroots muscle to destroy the ambitions of moderates such as Bob Dole and Colin Powell, and propelling movement figures such as DeLay and George W. Bush into ascendancy.

As Dobson consolidated his status as Republican kingmaker, the destructive tendencies of his closest allies began exploding, plunging the party into Gomorrah-like revelations of bizarre sex scandals and criminality. Ranging from DeLay's misadventures with the felonious super-lobbyist Jack Abramoff and Christian right operative Ralph Reed to Haggard's gay tryst with a male escort to Senator Larry Craig's bathroom stall come-on to an undercover cop, the scandals never ceased to surprise people who had once envisioned the Grand Old Party as a bastion of "family values." Piled atop the Republicans' disastrously handled occupation of Iraq and response to Hurricane Katrina, these sordid scandals ended the twelve-year experiment with Republican rule of the Congress in 2006.

In the chaotic 2008 Republican presidential primary, the Republican base split its vote between Mitt Romney, the economic conservative, and Mike Huckabee, the social conservative, creating space for John McCain, distrusted by all factions, to emerge. McCain wished to have as his running mate an independent-minded politician who could garner votes outside the Republicans' increasingly narrow sphere of influence. His intention was to name Senator Joseph Lieberman of Connecticut, who had been the Democratic candidate for vice president in 2000. But the movement rejected his appeal to pragmatism, threatened a full-scale revolt, and demanded to vet his running mate as a condition for support. From the Last Frontier of Alaska, a self-proclaimed "hardcore pro-lifer" and "prayer warrior," Governor

Sarah Palin, was summoned to deliver to McCain the political elements he had once labeled "agents of intolerance."

Through Palin, archetype of the right-wing woman, the movement's influence over the party reached its zenith. As a direct result, however, the party sank to its nadir, suffering crushing defeats in the presidential and congressional races. Palin's candidacy mobilized the Christian right elements that McCain alienated, but she repelled independents and moderate Republicans in droves, winnowing away the party's constituency in every region of the country except the Deep South. Palin fatally tarnished McCain's image while laying the groundwork for her potential resurrection—and that of the movement—in the presidential contest of 2012.

The Christian right reached the mountaintop with the presidency of George W. Bush, shrouding science and reason in the shadow of the cross and the flag. But even at the height of Bush's glory, in his 2004 campaign, a few isolated moderate Republicans warned that the Republican Party was in danger of collapse. Of course their jeremiads were ignored. That year, Christie Todd Whitman published a book titled *It's My Party Too*, decrying the takeover by what she called the "social fundamentalists." A member of a distinguished and wealthy eastern Republican family, with deep ties to the party, she had been governor of New Jersey and head of the Environmental Protection Agency under Bush, only to quit when fundamentalist ideologues substituted right-wing doctrine for science in its studies. After the 2008 Republican debacle, Whitman pointed out that even though McCain was not considered a champion of the religious right, his percentage of so-called "values voters" increased by 3 percent over Bush's in 2004. McCain, the last Republican moderate on the national stage, had lost among "moderate voters" by 21 points to Obama.

As soon as Obama took office, the movement camped in the wilderness prepared to take political advantage of the worst economic troubles since the Great Depression by injecting a renewed sense of anti-government resentment. As most people agonized and even panicked over the sudden economic collapse, the Christian right's peddlers of crisis lifted their hands to the heavens. They had a whole new world of trauma to exploit, more desperate and embittered followers to manipulate, and maybe—just maybe—another chance at power.

Republican Gomorrah is an intimate portrayal of a political, social, and religious movement defined by an "escape from freedom." As Erich Fromm explained, those who join the ranks of an authoritarian cause to resolve inner turmoil and self-doubt are always its most fervent, rigidly ideological, and loyal members. They are often its most politically influential members as well. President Eisenhower described the "mental stress and burden" that animates such movements. His admonition to beware the danger posed to democracy by those who seek "freedom from the necessity of informing themselves and making up their own minds concerning these tremendous complex and difficult questions" should be as memorable in history as his caution about the "military-industrial complex" in his farewell address.

The characters I have profiled may not represent a majority in terms of sheer numbers, but through their combined power, they reflect the dominant character of the movement—and, by extension, of the Republican Party they have subsumed. That party has ignored Eisenhower's warning and realized his darkest fears.

Brooklyn, New York
January 2009

PART ONE

"Yes, march against Babylon, the land of rebels, a land that I will judge! Pursue, kill, and completely destroy them, as I have commanded you," says the Lord. "Let the battle cry be heard in the land, a shout of great destruction."

JEREMIAH 50:21–22

CHAPTER 1

GOD'S GOVERNMENT

In April 1915, the snow had just begun to melt from the peaks of Mount Ararat and run into the villages nestled in its valleys. In the shadow of the mountain lay the idyllic town of Van, which the Rushdoony clan had called home for nearly 2,000 years. That spring brought catastrophe for the Rushdoonys. The Ottoman army laid siege to their town, hoping to quash the only fortress of resistance against its military crusade to eradicate the Armenian race. When the Ottoman cannons opened fire, Y. K. Rushdoony and his wife fled for the hills, embarking on a harrowing horseback trek westward through Europe, a voyage across the Atlantic, and a trip from one end of the American continent to the other, finally to begin a new life in California.

In 1916, the year of their arrival in the United States, Y. K.'s wife gave birth to their second son, Rousas John "R. J." Rushdoony. (R. J.'s older brother had been one of the 1.5 million who perished in the Armenian genocide.) As a descendant of a line of aristocratic priests reaching back to the year 315, and as a son of survivors of a recent genocide, the young Rushdoony was raised on tales of the slaughter that uprooted his family's ancient Christian heritage. He studied divinity, enrolling at the Pacific School of Religion in Berkeley, California, and plunged headfirst into the works of conservative theological authorities such as John Calvin, Abraham Kuyper, and Cornelius Van Til, which appealed to him as a way to revive the ruptured religious traditions of his aristocratic ancestors. Upon graduation, Rushdoony

17

entered the clergy as a minister in the ultraconservative Orthodox Presbyterian Church and immediately began mapping out a system to restore purity and order to the fallen world that surrounded him. His inspiration was the alternative Christian legal system that evolved in the shadow of the Roman Empire, a system that the Romans often turned to and the only legal system that survived the collapse of the empire. Rushdoony invoked the apostle Paul's defiance of civil court authority. "Don't go to the civil courts," Rushdoony said. "They're ungodly. Create your own courts."

Rushdoony's radical worldview intensified when the Red Scare swept across America in the 1950s. During the peak of anti-Communist Senator Joseph McCarthy's show trials, Rushdoony befriended a retired candy manufacturer named Robert Welch, who shared his visceral hatred of political subversives. Welch had leveraged his fortune into creating in 1958 a right-wing fringe group, the John Birch Society, and had gained notoriety by red-baiting prominent public figures such as President Truman, President Eisenhower, and Allen Dulles, director of the CIA—all covert Soviet agents in his mind. His hysteria reached a crescendo with his explanation of a "Master Conspiracy," a scenario in which the Rothschilds and the Council on Foreign Relations secretly controlled the Soviet Union and the Communist movement and, by extension, the United States. By 1961, the John Birch Society had more than 100,000 tightly organized and highly motivated members and had taken over sections of the Republican Party in California, Texas, and Arizona. After the 1964 presidential campaign in which the right seized control of the party through the candidacy of Senator Barry Goldwater of Arizona, who lost in a landslide, the Society became a divisive issue among conservatives. William F. Buckley Jr., the influential editor of the *National Review*, who had been close to the Society, denounced it as an impediment to the legitimacy of the conservative movement. But while Buckley's harsh attack isolated the Society as extremist, Rushdoony's admiration only grew.

Rushdoony marveled at the Leninist organizational model the John Birch Society had adopted from the Communist Party. Welch had divided Birch members into small cell groups (when a chapter grew larger than two dozen, it was split in half) with four-letter code names. Secrecy was of the essence; Welch believed that operating in the light of day might alert Communist secret agents to Bircher activities. Cells were deployed for acts of harassment and disruption that included sending to members of Congress postcards detailing a supposed Communist plot to erect a "Negro Soviet Republic" in the South, infiltrating ACLU meetings to shout down perceived Communist sympathizers (the ACLU, in fact, was hostile to Communism), and ensuring that local newsstands were stocked with copies of the right-wing weekly *Human Events*. On the fateful day that President John F. Kennedy visited Dallas, November 22, 1963, Birchers welcomed him by mounting posters around the city showing the president's head at the center of rifle crosshairs. Rushdoony was mightily impressed by the Society's actions. "The key to the John Birch Society's effectiveness has been a plan of operation which has a strong resemblance to the early church," he wrote.

Rushdoony, however, never became a card-carrying Bircher. "Welch always saw things in terms of conspiracy," he mused, "and I always see things in terms of sin." For Rushdoony, defeating the Red Menace was a noble cause, but an effort that would remove only one of the many malignant elements that lurked within what he called the "humanistic spectrum." He became actively involved in issues concerning home schooling and Christian schools. He took part in seminars on creationism at "evangelical convocations." He urged evangelicals to cast off their insular perspective and begin a process of taking dominion over the land as the Bible commanded them to do. His work dovetailed with the emerging conservative counterculture.

The Reverend Billy Graham had railed against sinful behavior as he barnstormed across the country in his well-attended crusades during the 1950s and 1960s. He routinely urged his audiences to "create a culture with Christ at its center," but his message was consistent with the evangelical tradition of effecting change through personal persuasion, not political imposition. Graham delighted in rubbing shoulders with presidents and counseling them, but he offered no suggestions for altering the Constitution. By contrast, Rushdoony's concept of cleansing the land of sin by seizing the reins of government was genuinely revolutionary. In a political climate rife with Cold War hysteria, turmoil over the role of women, protest against the Vietnam War, campus unrest, countercultural contempt for established authority, and racial agitation, a growing number of evangelicals were receptive to hearing a new doctrine for the times from a new prophet.

In 1973, Rushdoony published his magnum opus, *The Institutes of Biblical Law*, an eight-hundred-page book deliberately invoking Calvin's Institutes of Christian Religion to suggest his traditionalism. Instead of appealing to a mass audience, the pedantic Rushdoony sought to influence an elite cadre in the expectation that they would distill his message for the grassroots. He labeled his philosophy "Christian Reconstructionism" and painstakingly outlined plans for the church to take over the federal government and "reconstruct" it along biblical lines. According to Frederick Clarkson, a pioneering researcher of the Christian right, "Reconstructionism seeks to replace democracy with a theocratic elite that would govern by imposing their interpretation of 'Biblical Law.' Reconstructionism would eliminate not only democracy but many of its manifestations, such as labor unions, civil rights laws, and public schools. Women would be generally relegated to hearth and home. Insufficiently Christian men would be denied citizenship, perhaps executed."

Calling for the literal application of all 613 laws described in the Book of Leviticus, Rushdoony paid special attention to punishments. Instead of serving prison sentences, criminals would be sentenced to indentured servitude, whipped, sold into slavery, or executed. "God's government prevails," Rushdoony wrote, "and His alternatives are clear-cut: either men and nations obey His laws, or God invokes the death penalty against them." Those eligible on Rushdoony's long list for execution included disobedient children, unchaste women, apostates, blasphemers, practitioners of witchcraft, astrologers, adulterers, and, of course, anyone who engaged in "sodomy or homosexuality."

Burning at the stake, death by "the sword," and hanging were some of Rushdoony's preferred modes of execution. However, his son-in-law Gary North, a self-styled Reconstructionist economist (who eventually fell out with his father-in-law) and former adviser to libertarian Republican Representative Ron Paul of Texas (a one-time outspoken admirer of the John Birch Society), advocated stoning evildoers to death. Rocks, North argued, are free and plentiful, making them ideal tools for the financially savvy executioner.

Although Rushdoony's *Institutes* and his other books are hard to find and remain obscure, his anti-government ideas attracted the interest of an emerging group of southern pastors rankled by the forced integration of public schools. Among them was Jerry Falwell, a firebrand reverend from Lynchburg, Virginia, who gained his early prominence as a local leader of massive resistance to civil rights.

When the Supreme Court handed down its *Brown v. Board of Education* decision in 1954, Falwell inveighed against the court from the pulpit. Like Rushdoony, Falwell posited segregation as a biblical mandate. "The facilities should be separate," the basso profondo preacher boomed from above his congregation during a 1958 sermon. "When God has drawn a line of distinction, we should not attempt to cross that line. The true Negro does not want integration." Falwell promptly enlisted with the FBI's director J. Edgar Hoover to distribute propaganda leaflets attacking Martin Luther King Jr. as a Communist subversive, and he publicly denounced King for daring to mix politics and religion. Finally, in 1966, with the pace of integration intensifying, Falwell founded the Lynchburg Christian Academy—"a private school for white students," as the *Lynchburg News* described it the week its doors opened. Falwell's school was one of the many "seg academies" christened across the South—the last redoubt for him and his brethren.

Some of those around Falwell felt uneasy about Rushdoony's underground influence. In 1986, two of Falwell's associates at Liberty University, Ed Dobson and Ed Hindson, wrote an article warning against Rushdoony's "scary vision." "Rushdoony distrusts democracy," they wrote. And they noted that he prescribed the death penalty for homosexuals and alcoholics. Rushdoony wrote in response that Dobson and Hindson had misrepresented his views. Never, he indignantly maintained, had he said he was in favor of executing drunkards.

For Falwell and the figures who would later constitute the leadership of the Christian right, race was the issue that galvanized their political activism. But as America grew increasingly weary of overt, ugly displays of Dixieland racism, their resentment transmuted into a more palatable moral crusade. The strategy to win that crusade—the one that would propel the Christian right tantalizingly close to Rush-doony's theocratic vision—was conceived an ocean away by an icono-clastic theologian named Francis Schaeffer.

CHAPTER 2

CREATING A MONSTER

With a puffy white goatee and a mane of gray hair, and sporting burlap knickers and suspenders, Francis Schaeffer was the picture of the Reformation-era Christian patriarchs he assumed as his models. Schaffer's aesthetic preferences were a perfect fit for the bucolic outskirts of Geneva, Switzerland, that he chose as the site for L'Abri, a Christian commune he founded in 1946. The setting evoked nostalgia for Calvin's own presence in the area four hundred years before, when he reigned over Geneva and outlawed cursing, mandated church services for all citizens, and burned dozens of heretics at the stake. But the community Schaeffer nurtured assumed a markedly more tolerant tone than Calvin's Geneva. "If [you] had come to L'Abri," Schaeffer's son Frank told me, "you would have eventually figured you were in a Jesus-oriented hippy commune, and nothing would have made you think you were in a right-wing environment."

L'Abri was deluged during the late 1960s by a diverse, international band of cultural refugees who had dropped out and tuned in—first to the counterculture and then to Jesus. Syvester Jacobs, an African American photographer from Oklahoma, took shelter at L'Abri in 1968 with his wife, a white woman from Britain. Condemned by his parents for his interracial marriage, Jacobs found a uniquely welcoming home in Schaeffer's commune. Upon his arrival, Schaeffer took the jittery young man aside and assured him, "I would have been happy to have you marry one of my daughters." Jacobs told his friends back home that Schaeffer was the first white man to treat him like a human being.

Young gay people also found sanctuary at L'Abri. During the mid-1950s, an open lesbian named Carla announced that she would work topless in the garden alongside the men, a defiant gesture intended to provoke Schaeffer's ire and opposition. "That's fine, Carla," Schaeffer coolly demurred.

In 1963, Schaffer's eleven-year-old son Frank discovered his father sobbing uncontrollably in his study. "Why are you crying?" Frank asked. Schaeffer said he had just received terrible news from the mother of one of his former acolytes, an openly gay French man who converted to Christianity under his wing. The young man had been found dead, beaten mercilessly by a band of homophobic thugs. Schaeffer, who was given to spontaneous fits of rage, stood before his son and slammed his fists furiously into a wall. "I wish I had been there!" he screamed. "They wouldn't have messed with him if I was there!"

Back in the States, Schaeffer's writings riveted the counterculture. Led Zeppelin guitarist Jimmy Page carried Schaeffer's book *Escape from Reason* in his back pocket when he met with the Christian philosopher. (Decades later, Bono pronounced himself a fan of Schaeffer's work.) Countercultural interest in Schaeffer's commune reached such a degree that Timothy Leary, the avatar of acid, made his own pilgrimage. For self-proclaimed "Jesus People," L'Abri seemed a more spiritual version of Haight-Ashbury. And Schaeffer, who once declared that "one of the greatest injustices we do to young people is ask them to be conservative," was their guru.

True to the free-wheeling spirit of the times, the fifty-something Schaeffer cast aside the Bible and focused his lessons instead on the modernist art and existentialist literature that captivated his young guests. He was convinced he could channel the restive energy of the "Jesus People" into a movement that would rejuvenate the dour, politically impotent church. "The hippies of the 1960s did understand something," he wrote. "They were right in fighting the plastic culture, and the church should have been fighting it too." (Schaeffer went on to quote approvingly from the "longshoreman philosopher" Eric Hoffer.)

But when the Supreme Court legalized abortion with its 1973 *Roe v. Wade* ruling, Schaeffer snapped. He transformed suddenly into a fiery herald of doom unrecognizable in the all-embracing counselor of

L'Abri's halcyon days. Schaeffer now cast the counterculture as a cancerous side effect of modernism, and the modern age as a giant sickness that imperiled the survival of civilization. In 1976, he published a best-selling polemic that inspired the Christian right's advance guard, *How Should We Then Live? The Rise and Decline of Western Civilization and Culture.* The book concluded by proclaiming legalized abortion—"infanticide," Schaeffer called it—the final leg in Western civilization's death march. To preserve Judeo-Christian society, Schaeffer implored evangelicals to organize a crusade to stop abortion by any means.

By this time, Schaeffer's twenty-four-year-old son had become a force in his own right. Having studied film and painting in Europe, Frank Schaeffer applied his talents to advance his father's mission, producing a three-part documentary film version of *How Should We Then Live?* In the film, the elder Schaeffer appeared beside a suburban sewage drain warning that the secular elite would soon begin infusing the public water supply with anti-aggression drugs and birth control pills. Frank Schaeffer and his father hoped that by showing their film to church audiences, they would cultivate a new generation of shock troops for the coming culture war. But impressing the value of opposing abortion on the new generation of politically assertive evangelicals would be a daunting task.

Paul Weyrich, a right-wing Washington operative and anti–Vatican II Catholic, had already tried to sell evangelicals such as Falwell on anti-abortion. The issue had riveted America's Catholic community and pushed elements of it deep into conservative politics. In his discussions with Falwell, however, Weyrich's pleas for pivoting resentment on a wedge issue other than race fell on deaf ears.

"I was trying to get those people interested in those issues and I utterly failed," Weyrich recalled in an interview in the early 1990s. "What changed their mind was Jimmy Carter's intervention against the Christian schools, trying to deny them tax-exempt status on the basis of so-called de facto segregation."

In this tumultuous atmosphere, Schaeffer became an evangelist in the truest sense of the word. He insinuated himself into Republican Washington and befriended then representative Jack Kemp, a former

professional football player elected to the Congress from suburban
Buffalo. Kemp was best known for his advocacy of supply-side economics and tax cuts, but he also became an ardently anti-abortion
evangelical. Kemp arranged a series of speeches for Schaeffer before
conservative lawmakers and movement luminaries. Kemp's wife
Joanne led a book club of congressional wives, including Elizabeth
Dole, who diligently read Schaeffer's works. One of Schaeffer's acolytes
at L'Abri was Michael Ford, son of Michigan congressman Gerald
Ford, who became president upon Richard Nixon's resignation in
1974. At Michael's urging, Schaeffer was invited to a private dinner
with President Ford at the White House.

In his spare time, Schaeffer lobbied Falwell on the strategic importance of joining the "pro-life" cause. Finally, he brought Falwell onto
the anti-abortion bandwagon and even sold the anti-papist Baptist on
the concept of "co-belligerency," or working with conservative Catholics and other non-evangelicals to assail the secular establishment.
Under Schaeffer's guidance, in 1979, Falwell founded the Christian
right's first lobbying front, the Moral Majority, and made certain to
place abortion at the top of the group's agenda. Whether or not Falwell shared Schaeffer's passion for banning abortion, the Moral Majority's swelling membership convinced him of the issue's popular
appeal.

As Schaeffer's crusade gradually expanded beyond his influence,
he grew disenchanted with his retrograde Southern Baptist allies. He
privately called Falwell a charlatan and mocked his followers as "the
low IQs." Schaeffer was particularly disgusted by the homophobic
passions of Falwell and his allies. Abortion was the issue that made
Schaeffer's blood boil, not the presenßce of gays at the head of public
school classrooms and Boy Scout troops. "My dad would have identified with the left if they had picked up on the issue of abortion,"
Frank Schaeffer told me.

Suffering from depression and sapped of strength after undergoing
several grueling rounds of cancer treatment, Schaeffer channeled his
final ounces of energy into pushing his movement in a truly radical
direction—into the streets and toward domestic terrorism. "There
does come a time when force, even physical force, is appropriate,"

Schaeffer wrote in his 1981 book *A Christian Manifesto*. "When all avenues of flight and protest have closed, force in the defensive posture is appropriate."

In *Manifesto*, Schaeffer described Christians as victims of persecution at the hands of a tyrannical secular elite not unlike the Romans who dragged Christians before teams of lions two thousand years before. So long as the "establishment elite" held sway, Schaeffer argued, Bible-believing Christians were powerless to stop the mass slaughter of innocent fetuses. To defend their supposedly threatened rights, Schaeffer suggested that Christians at least consider righteous violence as a last recourse.

In spite of the fact that Schaeffer repeatedly rebuffed R. J. Rushdoony's requests to meet, Rushdoony's son-in-law, Gary North, accused him of "the nearly verbatim lifting of certain material from Rushdoony's *The One and the Many*." Whether or not North's claim was true (he did not produce any evidence in his essay containing the allegation), Schaeffer and Rushdoony clearly influenced one another and mutually shaped the Christian right's philosophy as a result.

Even though *Manifesto*—and its call for literally attacking the foundations of liberal democracy—went unnoticed by mainstream America, it sold a whopping 250,000 copies in its first year after publication. "What's amazing about *Christian Manifesto*," Frank Schaeffer remarked to me, "was that my father was practically calling for the overthrow of the United States government. If his words had come out of the mouth of anyone other than a white American it would have been called sedition. Instead, we were invited to the White House and I went swimming in Michael Ford's pool."

■ ■ ■

As he lay dying at the Mayo Clinic in Rochester, Minnesota, Schaeffer agonized about the rise of the Christian right. He was convinced that he had created a monster. When former orange juice industry poster child and outspoken homophobe Anita Bryant appeared to beseech Schaeffer for his deathbed blessing for her anti-gay crusade, Schaeffer angrily rebuked her. "My dad simply told Anita off and told her he would have no part of what she was doing under any circumstances," Frank Schaeffer recalled. "He said if she had any concern for the well-being of homosexuals this was a hell of a way to demonstrate it."

When Schaeffer finally succumbed to cancer in 1984, his acolytes had assumed key positions within the Republican Party. The Republican National Convention plank that year not only reiterated the party's call for a constitutional amendment asserting legal rights for fetuses, it insisted for the first time that the Fourteenth Amendment's legal protections apply to them as well and called for the appointment of more anti-abortion judges. Four years later, the party plank invoked the civil rights anthem "We Shall Overcome" to demand that *Roe v. Wade* be overturned. With Schaeffer's inspiration, the movement that once mounted massive resistance against civil rights had regenerated itself by co-opting the very tactics used to defeat it.

Schaeffer had influenced not only Jack Kemp and Jerry Falwell. He had also had a lasting impact on Tim LaHaye, a Christian right leader he considered a huckstering extremist. After visiting Schaeffer at L'Abri, LaHaye went on to coauthor the best-selling apocalyptic pulp fiction *Left Behind* series. The Reverend Pat Robertson, whom Schaeffer believed to be pathologically insane, and who once boasted to Schaeffer of burning a Modigliani painting in his fireplace, praised his books. Late in Schaeffer's life, a popular child psychologist named James Dobson became a fixture at his lectures. Schaeffer resented Dobson's machinations, privately deriding him as a disingenuous power-monger concerned with politics above all else. But with Schaeffer dead, Dobson cast himself as torchbearer of his legacy. "Thank God for Francis Schaeffer," Dobson declared in a 2002 speech. "He saw everything that we're going through today . . . He said that there was a connection between abortion and infanticide and euthanasia."

Born-again Watergate felon Chuck Colson assumed a similar posture, styling himself as Schaeffer's intellectual heir. Colson marketed his 1999 polemic *How Should We Now Live?* as a twenty-first-century remix of Schaeffer's seminal tome *How Should We Then Live?* But the admiration was not mutual. "Dad absolutely couldn't stand Colson," Frank Schaeffer said.

Other less prominent but significant activists felt Schaeffer's impact. Two young Pentecostals, Randall Terry and Rob Schenck, studied Schaeffer at the Elim Bible Academy in upstate New York during the early 1980s. Upon their graduation, the two founded Operation Rescue, a militant anti-abortion group that organized blockades of Planned Parenthood clinics and spawned closely affiliated offshoots that engaged in acts of domestic terror and the assassination of abortion doctors. Terry, a self-described Christian Reconstructionist, credited Schaeffer as his inspiration: "You have to read Schaeffer's *Christian Manifesto* if you want to understand Operation Rescue," he said.

Schenck, who had converted from Reform Judaism to evangelical Christianity after attending a Pentecostal revival at age seventeen, became renowned for his outrageous anti-abortion stunts. He was arrested a dozen times during protests outside women's health clinics and abortion doctors' homes, and he made news when he dangled an aborted fetus in Bill Clinton's face outside the 1992 Democratic National Convention. When Clinton vetoed a partial-birth abortion ban in 1996, Schenck approached the president at a National Cathedral Christmas service and told him, "God will hold you to account, Mr. President." He was then removed from the chapel and interrogated by Secret Service agents.

One night in 1998, while cooking dinner for his wife and four children, Barnett Slepian—an abortion doctor in Buffalo, New York, whose home had been the site of protests by Schenck and his followers years before—was shot to death through his kitchen window by James Kopp. Kopp, a former resident of Schaeffer's L'Abri and a volunteer at Randall Terry's Binghamton, New York, office, was promptly placed on the FBI's Top Ten Most Wanted List. The National Memorial for the Prevention of Terrorism identified him as a terrorist.

Slepian's assassination became a public relations disaster for Operation Rescue, and even though Schenck denounced the killing, the organization's more extremist members, who had nicknamed Kopp "Atomic Dog," insisted that it was justified. When Schenck placed flowers at the doorstep of Slepian's office, they were returned abruptly by his infuriated wife, along with a letter—later made public—that read,

"It's your 'passive' following that incited the violence that killed Bart [Barnett Slepian] and took away both my and my children's future."

. . .

Once Schaeffer died, his son stood to inherit his throne. Dobson hosted Frank Schaeffer on his radio show in 1985 and then excitedly printed 150,000 copies of Schaeffer's book *A Time for Anger: The Myth of Neutrality*, a strident attack on cultural liberalism. He was a smashing success with a constituency that was larger and more fervent than anything his father knew. Having been raised in Europe in a cosmopolitan environment, however, Schaeffer was alienated by the backwardness and parochialism of the southern evangelical subculture. And unlike his father, he was still young enough to entertain doubts: "I realized that these are crazy people and as soon as they win, the first person they're going to put up against the wall and shoot is me," Schaeffer remarked. "I was not one of them. Once I made that break and looked at their politics, I really disagreed with what they stood for. I didn't see the world the way they did. If you started questioning anything it all came away in your hands. For me, it started out as a matter of taste and culture and it ended as a matter of ideology."

Reflecting on the movement he left, Schaeffer saw its greatest danger in the tendency of its leaders to celebrate cultural decline. "We thrived on bad news, we thanked God that education was falling apart and teen pregnancy was going up," he recalled. "We couldn't peddle solutions unless there was a crisis. We were in business the same way an oncologist was—if there was no cancer he'd be out of business. Quite simply, we were trying to manufacture crisis."

Having watched the movement take his father's post-Roe polemics to their logical conclusion—domestic terrorism—Frank Schaeffer believes his father would recant them if he had lived long enough. "My dad had become someone who unleashed something where people were being killed," Frank told me. "He would have come to a time where he basically said, 'I'm sorry I did this and I think I was wrong to do that.' And I base that on his earlier, much more compassionate work. He was such a friend and counselor to so many people. What happened is so insane. It is such a tragedy."

But Schaeffer never saw the growth of the seeds of destruction he had sown. In his wake, movement leaders proclaimed him their god-father, while Rushdoony's tracts remained tucked away on their bookshelves. Indeed, Rushdoony was still very much alive, operating out of Chalcedon, a Reconstructionist foundation in northern California that *Newsweek* dubbed "the think-tank of the Christian right." The radical cleric reaped the fruits of his budding friendship with Howard F. Ahmanson Jr., a reclusive trust fund baby who had spent the late 1960s in a mental institution and emerged as a devoted follower of Reconstructionism.

CHAPTER 3

WHAT GOD WANTS HIM TO DO

For more than three decades, Howard F. Ahmanson Jr. has been one of the major financial angels of the right. "Intelligent design," the schism in the Episcopal Church, state initiatives against gay marriage, George W. Bush's theme of "compassionate conservatism"—Ahmanson has been behind them all. Yet few Americans have heard of him, and that's the way he likes it. He donates cash either out of his own pocket or through his unincorporated corporate entity, Fieldstead and Co., to avoid having to report the names of his grantees to the IRS. His Tourette's syndrome only adds to his reclusive persona, because his fear of speaking leads him to shun the media. And while a Daddy Warbucks of the right like Richard Mellon Scaife travels the world in his own jet, Ahmanson shuns luxury for a lifestyle of down-to-earth humility. As his wife, Roberta Green Ahmanson, told me, he once gave up his seat on an airplane for a refund. And when he goes out for a spin in his neighborhood in Newport Beach, a posh coastal community forty-five minutes south of Los Angeles, he drives a Prius. It's a modest choice for a man who could afford an entire Hummer dealership, but nevertheless a considerable upgrade from his old Datsun pickup.

When Howard F. Ahmanson Jr. was born in 1950, his father, then forty-four years old, was entertaining visiting kings and queens and basking in the opulence of his mansion on Harbor Island, an exclusive address in southern California's Newport Harbor. Junior was tended by an army of servants and ferried to and from school in a limousine.

Watching the world glide by through darkened windows, he was gripped with a longing to cast off his wealth and disappear into anonymity. He burned with resentment toward his father, a remote, towering presence referred to by friends and foes alike as "Emperor" Ahmanson. While Ahmanson Sr. showered local institutions in the Los Angeles area with charitable gifts, his son was starved for attention.

"Emperor" Ahmanson had been born in Omaha, Nebraska, where he had founded an insurance and savings and loan association, H. F. Ahmanson & Company, during the Depression. He used that nest egg to make his fortune financing California's postwar housing boom. H. F. Ahmanson & Company became Home Savings & Loan and more recently was known as Washington Mutual until it was placed in receivership by the FDIC in late September 2008. In his later years, Ahmanson spent as much as 60 percent of his money on philanthropy. His name is emblazoned on a cardiology center at UCLA's Medical Center, on a wing of the Los Angeles County Museum of Art, and on one of Los Angeles's leading theaters. His son was raised to continue his philanthropic legacy.

But the Emperor's succession plans began to erode when the young prince turned ten and his beloved mother served his father with divorce papers. Howard Sr. remarried, choosing Caroline Leonetti, a close friend of President Richard Nixon and later Ronald Reagan, who was renowned for her cosmopolitan flair and support of the arts. Steve Clemons, the openly gay director of the New America Foundation, a left-leaning foreign policy think tank, recalled chauffeuring Leonetti from local galas to her swank Beverly Hills penthouses. Meanwhile, Howard Jr.'s mother died a few years after her divorce, in the late 1960s.

When Howard was eighteen his father died, too, sinking him into depths of despair. With his $300 million inheritance, he was now California's—and perhaps America's—richest teenager. But he was without direction, afraid, and utterly alone. The tics, twitches, and uncontrollable verbal spasms caused by his Tourette's syndrome worsened. He could not cope with his emotions, and during increasingly stressful episodes he would uncontrollably blurt out shocking statements. Unable to look people in the eye when he spoke to them, he became socially paralyzed. Diagnosed as schizophrenic, he spent two years at the Menninger Clinic, a Topeka, Kansas, psychiatric institution. "I resented my family background," he told the *Orange County Register* in 1985. "[My father] could never be a role model, whether by habits or his lifestyle, it was never anything I wanted."

Ahmanson's physical and psychological problems worsened upon his return. While backpacking through Europe and "being grungy," as he later explained, he developed a near-crippling case of arthritis, which forced him to return to Los Angeles for urgent medical care. Once he recovered, he imposed a strict $1,200-a-month allowance on himself, drove around town in a battered truck, and lived in cheap flophouses. Racked with guilt and self-loathing, he seemed destined for self-destruction.

Ahmanson enrolled at Occidental College in Los Angeles, majoring in economics and receiving poor grades. His downward spiral began to reverse, however, when he suddenly accepted the invitation of some college buddies to attend fundamentalist church services in Pasadena, California. Most of his fraternity brothers from Occidental had become evangelical Christians while he was away, and reconnecting with them also sparked a new interest for him. He joined a singles group organized by Mariners Church, an evangelical church in Newport Beach, which he credits with his spiritual and social salvation. It was there, he told the *Register*, that he was convinced to take full advantage of his inheritance and to stop "cheating God." His friends introduced him to a politicized brand of Christianity that was growing popular in evangelical circles. Soon Ahmanson discovered the writings of R. J. Rushdoony, which struck a deep chord, particularly *The Politics of Guilt and Pity*, in which the theologian mocked wealthy liberals. "The guilty rich will indulge in philanthropy, and the guilty white men will show 'love' and 'concern' for Negroes and other such persons who are in actuality repulsive and intolerable to them," Rushdoony wrote. Ahmanson read avidly, as though Rushdoony were describing his own life.

Still, Ahmanson did not yet convert to Reconstructionist theology, and he gave no indication that he shared Rushdoony's racism. But through Rushdoony's scathing critique of "the guilty rich," he began to release himself from the burden of responsibility to carry on his father's legacy. He promptly sold his stock in his father's company and invested it in lucrative real estate acquisitions, with the goal of earning returns of 20 to 25 percent per year. That ensured that his wealth would grow quickly, but it also made him vulnerable to people who manipulated his residual guilt complex to get a cut of his fortune. These exploiters were often those closest to him. One former college roommate asked Ahmanson to fund his surf shop, explaining that the shop could bring in potential Christian converts off the street. Ahmanson wasn't convinced. "If you don't do this, these kids will go to hell," his roommate threatened. Almost immediately (in that very hour, according to his wife), Ahmanson became a full-fledged Calvinist, embracing Calvin's doctrine of predestination, which holds that God "elects" individuals for salvation on the basis of factors beyond their control.

"If someone's eternal goal is dependent on him [Ahmanson] giving a grant, then we're all in trouble," Roberta Green Ahmanson explained. "So that made Calvin's approach that God is in charge of all of this quite appealing."

After his awakening, the sensitive scion discovered a new father figure: Rushdoony. Rushdoony reveled in his discovery of a financial angel willing to fund the growth of his think tank, Chalcedon, while expanding the influence of Reconstructionist philosophy. He rewarded Ahmanson's generosity by giving him a seat on Chalcedon's board of directors, a gesture of acceptance. Ahmanson was profoundly grateful. At last, in Rushdoony, he had found the attentive and approving father he had yearned for his whole life.

"Howard got to know Rushdoony and Rushdoony was very good to him when he was a young man and my husband was very grateful and supported him to his death," Roberta Green Ahmanson told me.

■ ■ ■

When Roberta Green Ahmanson joined the *Orange County Register* as its religion reporter, she was practically living in Ahmanson's shadow. But her path to Orange County's nascent Christian right contrasted sharply with his. As the daughter of fundamentalist Baptists from the hard-bitten railroad town of Perry, Iowa, she was raised on her parents' Depression era values. Austerity and piety were the orders of the day. During high school, Green was forbidden from partaking in the teen rituals of her classmates; dancing and movies were strictly off-limits. She later described herself as "big and ugly," "scared of people," and profoundly lonely. But Green found an outlet in the well-worn Bible she carried everywhere and, later, in journalism devoted to religious coverage.

After graduating from Calvin College, a conservative Christian school in Iowa, Green moved to Orange County, where she joined the *Register*. Working on an assignment about the Christian right, she became acquainted with Rushdoony. His plan for governing the country according to biblical law appealed to her, and she soon turned her attention to Rushdoony's silent, thirty-something financial backer. Upon learning that she and Howard shared many of the same friends, she inquired about his availability.

Their first date nearly ended in disaster. As Howard drove Roberta home in his convertible with the top down, his body began jerking around wildly. Warned that her date was eccentric, Roberta struggled to control what she thought was an epileptic seizure. But Howard wasn't epileptic. When his spasms finally subsided, he turned to Roberta and explained, "I believe a bird has just crapped on me." His odd joke provoked her laughter, dispelling the uncomfortable silence that had filled most of the evening.

The two spent their next date discussing the authors they both enjoyed, from Francis Schaeffer and Rushdoony to Christian novelists such as J. R. R. Tolkien and C. S. Lewis. When Howard poured out his painful personal history in a series of revelations that he worried might repel her, Roberta drew closer. They soon felt they were soulmates: cerebral but taciturn, image-conscious but socially hapless, in the world but not of it. Howard and Roberta married on January 25, 1986, the feast day of the conversion of St. Paul, and thus became one of America's new Reconstructionist power couples.

I first met the Ahmansons in 2004, when they agreed to an interview request I had recorded on the answering machine of Fieldstead and Co., Ahmanson's unincorporated, unlisted business entity. The Ahmansons' exchanges with me marked the first time since 1985 that Howard had agreed to make contact with a journalist, and the first time since 1992 for Roberta. Howard agreed to answer questions only by e-mail because, according to Roberta, his Tourette's syndrome made chatting on the phone with a stranger nearly impossible. He functions "like a slow modem," she said. Her dual role as her husband's spokesperson and nurse quickly became apparent.

For her part, Roberta was personable and even chatty during the course of three lengthy phone conversations. Although she attempted to deceive me on one occasion, telling me that Howard went to junior college in Kansas during the time when he had been committed to a mental institution, she was otherwise forthcoming. She disclosed that Howard maintained a vigil at Rushdoony's bedside when he died in 2002 and that her husband identifies with Frodo, the Hobbit protagonist of Tolkien's novels who must destroy a magical ring in order to save the world.

Roberta was not reticent about her political views. When I asked her whether she favored biblical law as a governing model for the United States, for example, she casually responded, "I'm not suggesting we have an amendment to the Constitution that says we now follow all 613 of the case laws of the Old Testament. . . . But if by biblical law you mean the last seven of the Ten Commandments, you know, yeah."

Her remark was a barely qualified reprise of her husband's stunning proclamation to the *Orange County Register* in 1985: "My goal is the total integration of biblical law into our lives." That statement highlighted Ahmanson's entrance into the political arena. By leveraging his financial muscle into political influence, Ahmanson's theocracy-based philanthropy has made possible some of the most pivotal right-wing campaigns in recent history. Yet Ahmanson has remained in the shadows, deploying surrogates and highly disciplined John Birch Society–style political cell groups to do his bidding and then wiping the scene clean of his fingerprints when their work is done.

CHAPTER 4

MARCHING THROUGH THE INSTITUTIONS

In 1992, Howard F. Ahmanson Jr. initiated a string of stealth political successes, banding together with four right-wing businessmen to back the campaigns of anti-gay, anti-abortion, pro-big-business candidates for the California Assembly. Two years later, the cabal of secret funders scored a major victory, propelling the Republican Party's takeover of the California Assembly. With $3 million funneled through seven right-wing political action fronts, Ahmanson and his cohorts captured a startling twenty-five of the GOP's thirty-nine legislative seats for their candidates. Their push ushered two important movement cadres into office: Tom McClintock, a veteran activist and former director of economic and regulatory affairs of the Ahmanson-funded libertarian think tank Claremont Institute, and Ray Haynes, an unknown lawyer from another Ahmanson-funded group, the Western Center for Law and Justice, which once filed a brief defending a local school district for banning Gabriel Garcia Márquez's novel *One Hundred Years of Solitude.*

Upon his election, McClintock sponsored a bill that restored the death penalty to California. In 2003, he and Haynes were instrumental in organizing the campaign to recall Democratic Governor Gray Davis. Haynes personally convinced a fellow archconservative, U.S. Representative Darrell Issa, to bankroll the recall ballot qualification. After the measure qualified with the help of $1.7 million from Issa, McClintock entered the recall campaign as a candidate for governor, ultimately finishing third. As in the 1992 campaigns he backed, Ahmanson provided the money and personnel for McClintock's campaign: John Stoos, an avowed Reconstructionist associated with Chalcedon, served as his deputy campaign manager, while Ahmanson hosted James Dobson, Phyllis Schlafly, and other key movement leaders for a Colorado fund-raiser in September that raised $100,000 for their handpicked candidate.

To complement his electoral efforts, Ahmanson has pumped enor-mous amounts of money into ballot measure committees, dramatically altering California's social landscape in the process. In 1999, Ahmanson helped to sharply restrict affirmative action in California through a $350,000 donation to Proposition 209. That same year he helped ban gay marriage with a donation of $210,000—35 percent of its total funds—to Proposition 22. Though the anti-gay initiative was later overturned by California's Supreme Court, the Ahmanson-supported cause became a national model for similar statewide initiatives put on the ballots of swing states as President Bush ran for reelection in 2004. It also created fodder for the movement's next crusade in California, a ballot measure to ban gay marriage once and for all in 2008.

Ahmanson has been especially generous with those who share his experience of coming to Jesus—and culture war politics—through the pain of personal crisis. Among his grant recipients is Donna Rice-Hughes, the woman who brought down Gary Hart's 1988 presidential campaign after tabloids published photographs of her perched on the candidate's lap while carousing on his yacht, "Monkey Business." In the wake of the sex scandal, Rice-Hughes (then known only by her birth name, Rice) became born-again, joining the anti-pornography group Enough Is Enough! as its vice president in 1994. "Through 'Enough Is Enough!' God is using what I've learned to impact others' lives and bring him glory," she told *Christianity Today* magazine in 1996. "He's brought purpose to my pain." Rice-Hughes's activism at-tracted Ahmanson's attention, and in 1997, he gave $160,000 to her group, helping it develop into one of the country's most muscular anti-porn lobbies. Seven years later, Rice-Hughes successfully pressed Congress to mandate Web filters in public library computers, an im-portant victory against civil libertarians and advocates of free speech.

One of Ahmanson's most significant political investments was in the career of Marvin Olasky, a man of multiple conversions, who was instrumental in creating George W. Bush's 2000 campaign theme of "compassionate conservatism." The Yale graduate joined the Communist Party USA in the early 1970s, a bizarre attachment at a time when the Communist Party was thoroughly discredited and had dwindled to a tiny gaggle. Then Olasky was suddenly drawn to evangelical Christianity, and he abandoned his Jewish background to join Rushdoony's ultraconservative Presbyterian Church in America. While toiling in obscurity during the 1980s as a journalism professor at the University of Texas at Austin, Olasky sparked a relationship with Ahmanson. (Afflicted with Tourette's syndrome, Ahmanson was studying for a master's degree in linguistics.) Olasky's first book, *Turning Point: A Christian Worldview Declaration*, was published by Ahmanson's privately held philanthropic entity, the Fieldstead Institute, and coauthored by Fieldstead's director, Herbert Schlossberg. Even though theological scholars and reviewers generally ignored the book, it helped promote Olasky within Washington's conservative circles, and in 1989 he was offered a well-paying Bradley Foundation stipend as a resident scholar at the Heritage Foundation.

In 1992, Olasky wrote *The Tragedy of American Compassion*, an argument for transferring government social welfare programs to the church, which he claimed was the traditional and most effective approach until the New Deal—the very policy Rushdoony and his acolytes had long advocated. In this work, Olasky cited his "conservative Christian" friend Howard Ahmanson as proof that faith can cure poverty, describing how Ahmanson "found that poverty around the world is a spiritual as well as a material problem—most poor people don't have faith that they and their situations can change." Eventually, Ahmanson funded four of Olasky's books.

In 1993, *The Tragedy of American Compassion* earned Olasky an invitation from Republican strategist Karl Rove to meet with an evangelical Christian running for governor of Texas—George W. Bush. The following year, after the Republicans gained control of the Congress, the new speaker of the House, Newt Gingrich, gave every Republican member a copy of Olasky's book. The political thinker whom the *Los Angeles Times* dubbed an "unlikely guru" became a key advisor to Governor Bush, packaging for him the politics of "compassionate conservatism." During the brutal Republican primaries of 2000, the ex-Jew Olasky slammed Jewish neoconservative supporters of Bush's chief competitor, Senator John McCain, smearing them as educated atheists who worshiped the "religion of Zeus." When the newly inaugurated President Bush signed an executive order to create a White House Office of Faith-Based and Community Initiatives in January 2001, Olasky was standing by his side, beaming with pride as the new president turned his brainchild into government policy.

Another figure on the religious right who owes his success to Ahmanson is Bruce Chapman, a former Reagan administration official and founder of the Seattle think tank Discovery Institute, a bastion for the intelligent design movement, which seeks to debunk Darwin's theory of evolution with scientific-sounding arguments. Americans United for Separation of Church and State calls Discovery "the most effective and politically savvy group pushing a religious agenda in America's public school science classes."

President Reagan appointed Chapman, a conservative Republican former secretary of state from Washington State, to a succession of posts: director of the Census Bureau, deputy assistant in the White House Office of Planning, and U.S. ambassador to the United Nations in Vienna, a post that included the highly sensitive job of representing the United States to the International Atomic Energy Agency. After the Reagan administration and a stint at the conservative Hudson Institute, Chapman founded the Discovery Institute in 1990. Ahmanson gave him $1.5 million in seed money to create its Center for the Renewal of Science and Culture, the institute's "intelligent design" wing, devoted to spreading a version of creationism that argues that only God could have fashioned the intricacy of life on earth. In 2003, Ahmanson granted $2.8 million to develop Discovery's "Wedge Strategy," which focused on attacking the theory of evolution through stealth political tactics and "cultural confrontation." Dozens of well-heeled research fellows, directors, and advisors, almost all boasting advanced

degrees from respectable universities, were hired. With these creden-
tialed cadres, Discovery has sought to burnish "intelligent design"
with the gloss of scientific legitimacy that scriptural literalist creationism never enjoyed. Chapman's Catholicism has also proved useful in
helping to evangelize for the cause.

The "Wedge Strategy" produced a string of victories, including a
2002 decision by the Ohio Board of Education to adopt science standards that allow students to examine criticisms of evolution, but then
it hit a wall. In 2005, the strategy received a stinging rebuke in a federal
court in Dover, Pennsylvania. There John Jones, a Republican judge
appointed by President George W. Bush, ruled in favor of parents who
sued the school board after it ordered teachers to read students a statement introducing intelligent design in ninth-grade biology class. In
his decision, Judge Jones accused the defendants of harboring ulterior
religious motives and of "breathtaking inanity" in their attempt to
push the teaching of what he called "creationism relabeled."

"It is ironic that several of these individuals," Judge Jones stated,
"who so staunchly and proudly touted their religious convictions in
public, would time and again lie to cover their tracks and disguise the
real purpose behind the I.D. [intelligent design] policy." Yet if Jones
had known the origins of intelligent design, he might not have seemed
so shocked by the schemes of its proponents. Under Reconstructionist
rules of engagement, lying, deception, and stealth are considered legitimate tactics and are even encouraged. There is no requirement for
Christians to be truthful "in acts of war," Rushdoony wrote. "Spying is
legitimate, as are deceptive tactics."

Indeed, deception has proved essential to the success of the Ahmansons' campaign to undermine mainline churches. The National
Council of Churches—the governing body of the mainline Episcopal,
Methodist, and Presbyterian churches—is one of America's most effective progressive institutions. During the past fifty years, the NCC
has advanced civil rights, environmentalism, and peace movements.
The NCC's symbolism as a liberal bulwark made it a natural target.
Progressive Methodist minister Andrew Weaver explained three years
before his death in 2008, "NCC church members' influence is dispro-
portionate to their numbers, and [they] include remarkably high

numbers of leaders in politics, business, and culture. . . . A hostile takeover of these churches would represent a massive shift in American culture, power and wealth for a relatively small investment."

In 1981, when the Reagan administration ratcheted up military support for anti-Communist juntas in Central America, a group of anti-Communist Democratic operatives and right-wing moneymen responded by organizing a Washington think tank called the Institute for Religion and Democracy (IRD) to mount an "inside-outside" attack on the mainline churches' social activism. In short order, the new outfit shopped material to the mainstream press alleging that the NCC was diverting collection plate donations to Communist guerrillas. In 1982, this propaganda and pressure translated into two devastating and false reports in *Reader's Digest* and on CBS's *60 Minutes* about NCC's purported Communist links. (Twenty years later, *60 Minutes* producer Don Hewitt described the broadcast on the NCC as the greatest regret of his long and illustrious career. "The next morning I got a congratulatory phone call from every redneck bishop in America and I thought, 'Oh my God, we must have done something wrong last night and I think we probably did,'" Hewitt told CNN's Larry King in 2002.)

In the wake of the Soviet Union's collapse, the IRD changed tactics, replacing Communism with homosexuality as its wedge issue. The group's shift of focus from the red menace to the lavender one was made possible by hundreds of thousands of dollars in donations from the Ahmansons throughout the 1990s and by a grant of over $1 million in 2000 and 2001—the same year Roberta Ahmanson told me she was "inveigled" into joining the IRD's board of directors.

The Ahmansons' money was promptly funneled into a smear campaign against the Rt. Rev. Eugene Robinson, the first openly gay man ever consecrated as a bishop by the Episcopal Church. The IRD cranked up its Mighty Wurlitzer to full blast in August 2004, generating a column by *Weekly Standard* editor Fred Barnes titled "The Gay Bishop's Links." Barnes, who neglected to mention his membership on the IRD's board of directors in his column for the neoconservative magazine, falsely alleged that the website of a gay youth group Robinson founded contained links to "a pornographic website," and he claimed without independent sourcing that Robinson "put his hands on" a Vermont man "inappropriately" during a church meeting "several years ago." The IRD circulated the column to various cable news networks, but only Fox News (which also employed Barnes as a regular pundit and host of a talk show) agreed to broadcast it.

Although a panel of bishops investigating the charges discredited Barnes's smear, it helped widen the rift within the Episcopal Church and divide it from its global affiliates. In May 2007, eleven ultraconservative congregations from Northern Virginia bolted from the Episcopal Church and joined forces with the Anglican Church of Nigeria, led by the demagogic Archbishop Peter Akinola. In a country where more than 50 percent of the population lives below the poverty line, Akinola has managed to grow his congregation while replacing traditional church concerns about social justice with hysteria about homosexuality. Akinola spent much of 2006 lobbying Nigeria's legislature to pass a bill meting out five-year prison terms to any gay people who dared to gather—or even touch one another—in public.

As the IRD pressed its exploitation of homosexuality to divide Episcopal congregations, it initiated a parallel campaign accusing the mainline Presbyterian Church of anti-Semitism for its protests against Israel's continued illegal occupation of Palestinian land. The IRD complemented this new tactic by mailing out 100,000 copies of Likudnik Israeli historian Ephraim Karsh's tract "Islamic Imperialism" to pastors. With this tactic, at an expense of $1.5 million, the Christian right raised Islamophobia as its new wedge for the post-9/11, post-Bush era.

For Ahmanson, the quest to transform the United States into Calvin's elitist "church of the elect," or what Rushdoony called a "spiritual aristocracy," is not solely a political endeavor. Before Ahmanson and his wife were galvanized into funding conservative advocacy groups, mainline church schisms, and far-right moral crusades, they had been paralyzed by their own social handicaps and unresolved psychological issues. Emotional fulfillment was unattainable for the Ahmansons until they embraced Rushdoony's inverted vision of free will: "The flight from freedom is always first of all the flight from God, who created man to be responsible and to exercise dominion over the earth under him. The choice is always God or slavery." By exchanging free will for Reconstructionist mandates—by "doing what God wants him to do," as Roberta Ahmanson told me her husband does—Ahmanson ironically experienced his first sense of liberation.

Ahmanson's identification with Tolkien's hero, Frodo, illuminates his sensibility. Both Frodo and Ahmanson were socially withdrawn boys who lost their parents at an early age. Just as Frodo found the childless Bilbo Baggins to nurture him, teach him Elvish, and pass along to him the One Ring that would ultimately have to be destroyed to save the world, Ahmanson found Rushdoony. Like Frodo, who gained a sense of camaraderie from the Fellowship of the Ring that was formed to protect him, Ahmanson gathered around himself a wife, a social network, and a community by throwing down the gauntlet against an evil secularism. Without the drama that flowed from their respective missions to save civilization, Frodo and Ahmanson would have never fulfilled many of their most basic needs.

In brief, written responses to questions I e-mailed to Howard Ahmanson, he attempted to show his independence and demonstrate his own reasoning by placing special emphasis on his disagreement with Rushdoony's opinion that homosexuals should be executed. "Due to my association with Rushdoony, reporters have often assumed that I agree with him in all applications of the penalties of the Old Testament Law, particularly the stoning of homosexuals," Ahmanson wrote. "My vision for homosexuals is life, not death, not death by stoning or any other form of execution, not a long, lingering, painful death from AIDS, not a violent death by assault, and not a tragic death by suicide. My understanding of Christianity is that we are all broken, in need of healing and restoration. So far as I can tell, the only hope for our healing is through faith in Jesus Christ and the power of his resurrection from the dead."

For crisis-wracked individuals such as Ahmanson, radical Christian conservatism is more than politics and more than a style. As Ahmanson readily admits, it makes possible his psychological survival in the whirlwind of an increasingly chaotic society. "We are all broken," as he told me.

Ahmanson confirms Erich Fromm's insight, stated in the introduction to this book, that authoritarian ideology and practice can be compared to the workings of neurotic symptoms and that "Such symptoms result from unbearable psychological conditions and at the same time offer a solution that makes life possible."

James Dobson is another psychologist who grasps this phenomenon, but he approaches it from a diametrically opposite angle. Through his mega-ministry, Focus on the Family, which has been handsomely funded by Ahmanson through its California front, the Capitol Resource Institute, Dobson has cultivated his movement's culture of personal crisis and exploited it to become far and away the Christian right's most influential leader. Through his unparalleled influence, Dobson and his minions gained the keys to the Republican kingdom in 2008. Although Dobson speaks of a return to traditional values, he is a new type of figure. His background as a trained child psychologist, rather than as a theologian or preacher, reflects the dominant character of the Christian right, and his rise reveals the little-understood transformation of the movement.

CHAPTER 5

THE PERSONAL CRISIS INDUSTRY

Constructed in the shadow of the snow-capped Rocky Mountains, and above the sprawling city of Colorado Springs, Colorado, the campus of Focus on the Family offers a breathtaking view. Inside the eighty-one-acre compound, cheery employees greet visitors to take them on the official tour, ambling across neatly trimmed grass lawns to one of many lavishly furnished, Mission-style office buildings.

Each weekday at the same time, James Dobson is escorted into his radio studio deep in the recesses of the campus's central building by a platoon of grim armed guards who accompany him everywhere he goes. Visitors are invited to watch from behind two thick panes of plate glass in an adjacent room as Dobson and his co-host, John Fuller, prepare the daily broadcast. Then Dobson's nasal voice is beamed out to one of the largest radio audiences in America and to tens of millions of people across the globe.

James Dobson moved Focus on the Family to Colorado Springs from Pomona, California, in 1991. Half of his original employees followed him to his new mountain kingdom in a caravan of seventy moving trucks, lured by the promise of affordable housing, good schools, and the chance to remain part of one of the evangelical movement's fastest-growing ministries. Dobson and his business-savvy lieutenants, meanwhile, were attracted by the city's low taxes and cheap land—a promised land in which to build a divinely inspired empire.

The fact that the population of Colorado Springs was nearly all white was an additional draw.

According to Dobson's one-time co-host and former senior vice president of Focus on the Family, Gil Alexander-Moegerle, Dobson was repelled by Pomona's flourishing racial diversity. "His complaint was that nonwhites brought with them cultural ideas and religious ideas foreign to the traditional American view of life which Jim [Dobson] defined as Western and Christian," Alexander-Moegerle wrote in his searing tell-all memoir, *James Dobson's War on America*. "He clearly wished for an America that was just like him."

Dobson recently resigned his position as chairman of Focus on the Family, turning the largely administrative role over to a former executive from defense contractor Nothrup Grumman, Air Force Lt. Gen. Patrick P. Caruana. The move was merely cosmetic, however, as Dobson remains in firm control of his organization, hosting Focus on the Family radio as he has since the mid-1970s. Since Dobson's arrival in Colorado Springs, the following of his radio shows has ballooned to 6 to 10 million weekly listeners, who donate over $150 million a year to Focus. Dobson's daily radio broadcast is now the third most popular show in the country, just behind those of Rush Limbaugh and Paul Harvey. Together with Dobson's newsletters, Focus media reach more than 200 million people worldwide, from the Americas to Africa. After the Republican victories in the 2004 campaign (top Republican political strategists credited Dobson with helping to reelect George W. Bush as president and keep far-right Republicans in control of the Congress), Dobson was given a direct political line to the White House; he was even invited to a personal meeting with the President on U.S.–Iran policy.

With an approval rating of 73 percent among evangelicals—more than 25 points higher than that of the gaffe-prone Reverend Pat Robertson—Dobson is today acknowledged within the highest echelons of the Republican Party as the most influential leader of the Christian right. And with large parts of the Republican Party, especially its nominating wing, in the grip of his movement, he is therefore one of the most powerful men in America.

"He has gained the stature of a pope in the Middle Ages, the ability to direct the masses politically one way or the other in the name of the Almighty," said Scott Fagerstrom, former religion reporter of the conservative *Orange County Register*, in 1997. "And, unfortunately, the masses don't question him." Dobson's authority over the movement, and the movement's somnambulistic veneration of him, have intensified so much since Fagerstrom's observation that it sometimes seems as though Dobson is leading a cult.

Yet to most of the 250,000 visitors who flock to Focus on the Family every year, and who have made it the second biggest tourist site in Colorado, Dobson is presented as he wishes to be seen: as a reluctant activist utterly uninterested in earthly power or influence. As soon as they are greeted at the gates of the Focus campus by one of several unflaggingly pleasant female tour guides, visitors are presented a portrait of Focus on the Family as a benign, albeit slightly conservative, Christian nonprofit organization that spreads the Gospel along with Dobson's self-help advice. Any hint of Dobson's radical-right activism is softened by the tour guides' programmatic recitation of code phrases about his struggle to save "The Family."

■ ■ ■

To those not initiated into the special language of the group, references to "The Family" might seem as anodyne as the root beer floats served in the mock-1950s malt shop in the basement of Focus on the Family's "Welcome Center." To Dobson's flock, however, the phrase is clearly understood as a reference to the mass movement of right-wing evangelicals that excludes from its ranks all homosexuals, members of minority religions, and liberal and moderate Christians.

Despite the Stepford-like smiles of the tour guides, members of Dobson's movement affect an insular, even paranoid worldview. They are a society within a society that peers at outsiders with a mixture of disgust and hostility, fixating on their sinfulness to the point of voyeuristic obsession. When outsiders, collectively referred to by Dobson as "the culture," dare to pull back the curtain, the Christian right's self-appointed father figure typically deploys a smokescreen of contrived piety and howls of persecution.

"What I said is being spun like a top by the ultraliberals who don't care about human life," Dobson complained in May 2005, after Jewish groups demanded that he apologize for his on-air comparison of stem cell research to Nazi experiments on live human beings. ("That's what Francis Schaeffer told us to say," he muttered in an aside.) Dobson's response, a fusion of indignation and denial, typified his loathing of scrutiny. What happens in "The Family" must stay in the family—the first of Dobson's unwritten commandments.

In the secretive empire of Dobson, the less appealing aspects of Focus on the Family's Welcome Center are kept hidden from outsiders. Visitors with small children are treated to a tour of the center's colorful "Adventures in Odyssey" playroom, modeled after Focus on the Family's popular children's cartoon of the same name. But they are never told of Dobson's 1990 memo to the creators of "Odyssey," ordering them to weave insidious right-wing themes into the show. Since Dobson's mandate, young viewers have been subjected to episodes warning against abortion ("Pamela Has a Problem"), evolution ("Choices"), and trial lawyers ("A Victim of Circumstance").

Visitors are invariably told that the Welcome Center was constructed thanks to donations from "a family in Michigan." They are not informed, however, that this particular family happens to be the Prince clan.

Edgar Prince, the family patriarch, was an auto parts magnate who became a born-again evangelical after a heart attack brought him face-to-face with death and aroused his concern with the afterlife. He soon befriended Dobson, who was searching for benefactors, and used his vast fortune to bankroll the expansion of Focus on the Family. Although Prince died in 1995—Dobson gave the eulogy at his funeral—his wife still serves on the board of Focus and vacations with Dobson's wife, Shirley. The Princes' son Erik, who served as an intern at Dobson's organization, is founder and CEO of the controversial international mercenary firm Blackwater, described by journalist Jeremy Scahill as "a politically connected private army that has become the Bush administration's Praetorian Guard."

Taking a cue from Blackwater, Dobson has implemented a vast security apparatus that monitors every move of Focus visitors. Well-concealed security cameras are strategically posted throughout the campus, and heavily armed security guards clad in bulletproof vests lurk around corners, ready to confront what Focus's website has called "difficult guests." According to a job application obtained by reporter Cara DeGette in 2006, Focus security guards have collected an arsenal of 2,000 weapons and take target practice at the nearby Air Force Academy.

On the wall by the campus's main entrance a bullet still remains lodged, the product of a hostage siege ten years ago, when a disgruntled former employee stormed the office, demanding worker's compensation that he had been denied. Focus tour guides make a point of explaining that God guided the bullet away from their fellow employees. The symbolism of the magic bullet has acquired almost religious significance as a sign of divine protection. Dobson has made more than his share of enemies in the wilderness of secular society, but so far, he has emerged unscathed.

■ ■ ■

At the heart of James Dobson's ministry is its correspondence department. When visitors are escorted there, however, they are presented with only the briefest description of its inner workings. They are informed that Focus receives so much correspondence it requires its own zip code and told that its streamlined system immediately diverts desperate pleas for help with personal problems to a special counseling section of the department. There, counselors administer twenty-minute "stabilizing" phone sessions before referring needy callers to one of hundreds of Focus-approved therapists across the country.

But who are these therapists? According to Alexander-Moegerle, before earning their stamp of approval from Dobson, therapists must first pass a litmus test of beliefs that includes the question "Do you, in your practice, condone abortion?" The most prominent of Dobson's house psychologists was Neil Clark Warren, the avuncular founder of the popular dating website eHarmony.com. Dobson single-handedly propelled Warren's success, driving business to his private practice while promoting Warren's books and website on his radio show. One of Dobson's on-air promotional plugs drove 90,000 new members to eHarmony in one day. "No one has been more helpful for my entire career," Warren said of Dobson.

In 2005, however, Warren concluded that Dobson's radical-right profile was hindering eHarmony's expansion, and he publicly severed his ties with the Focus founder. Since the split, Warren has nevertheless maintained a Focus-inspired strict policy of rejecting homosexual applicants to his site. In March 2005, a New Jersey man sued Warren under his state's anti-discrimination law for denying him the chance to seek a relationship with another man on Warren's site. Warren responded by claiming that matching same-sex couples "is just not a service we offer now based on the research we have conducted." Warren has never disclosed the findings of this "research." In November 2008, in order to sidestep the lawsuit, Warren created an independent website, "Compatible Partners," for gay and lesbian users.

Those troubled individuals who turn up at Focus on the Family for help with their personal problems fuel Dobson's industry in another way: The moment their personal data are entered into the computerized Focus database, they are targeted for aggressive fundraising solicitations, most of which are political in nature. Breathless letters are fired off each month to the homes of crisis-wracked Focus members, warning them of the latest threat to the movement, from "the homosexual agenda" to the Christian right's latest hobgoblin, "radical Islam." Members are urged to contribute to Focus on the Family Action (Dobson's political lobbying arm), to vote for anti-gay ballot measures and conservative candidates, and to flood Capitol Hill with calls whenever a piece of "anti-family" legislation hits the floor.

Dobson's closed relationship with the media enables him to keep both constituents and critics in the dark about his machinations. He has effectively stonewalled nearly every news organization that has sought to interview him. Only the reliably right-wing Fox News, where Dobson is guaranteed deferential treatment from the likes of self-proclaimed "culture warrior" Bill O'Reilly, is granted regular access to the Focus founder. On those infrequent occasions when an odd reporter from what Dobson likes to call "the secular media" is permitted to enter his inner sanctum, he has usually been able to cast himself in the light in which he wishes to be seen.

This was the case when *Newsweek*'s Howard Fineman interviewed Dobson in his office in Colorado Springs in May 2005. Fineman was mightily impressed by Dobson's manner. "It's that decency and civility that has made Dobson such a force in the country," he remarked. The grateful reporter continued on about his gracious host, invoking a theme that Dobson has cleverly encouraged throughout his career. Dobson, Fineman concluded, "is plunging headfirst [into politics] after a lifetime of staying away from it."

The real Dobson, however, is, as Alexander-Moegerle put it, "a master of clandestine politics." Unlike Jerry Falwell, Pat Robertson, and other lions of the early Christian right, Dobson has no theological credentials. He is a licensed child psychiatrist who has risen to the top of the Christian right through his ability to answer its members' most intimate concerns. Dobson rarely invokes the Gospel in any explicit fashion, especially when issuing a call to political action. Instead, he exploits the culture of personal crisis that has united his constituents into "The Family." He is their strict father, the one who helped them repair their marriage after an adulterous affair, treat their child's bedwetting problem, or "cure" their homosexual tendencies. On election day, Dobson's flock repays him with political fealty.

Dobson has carefully encouraged the perception that he is above politics. But in fact, he has been aggressively political since his public career began. The issues that he claims galvanized his activism—abortion and the gay rights movement—were practically irrelevant to Dobson when he first entered the political arena. In the beginning, Dobson was fixated on inducing the submission of unruly children to authority. His draconian methods for ending childhood rebellion form the essence of his philosophy and have helped cultivate the authoritarian sensibility of the radical right-wing movement he commands today.

CHAPTER 6

THE KING OF PAIN

James Dobson was born in 1936 in Shreveport, Louisiana. His father, James "Big Jim" Dobson Sr., was an itinerant preacher who spent much of his time on the road riling up tent revival crowds with fire-and-brimstone sermons. Dobson's mother, Myrtle, accompanied James Sr. wherever he went, often leaving young Dobson in the care of his great aunt. During her occasional stints at home, Myrtle routinely lashed out at her only son with the wrath of God, battering him for such offenses as spouting the phrase "Dad-ummit!"

Dobson later reflected on his mother's child-rearing techniques:

I learned very early that if I was going to launch a flippant attack on her, I had better be standing at least ten or twelve feet away. This distance was necessary to avoid being hit with whatever she could get in her hands. On one occasion she cracked me with a shoe; at other times she used a handy belt. The day I learned the importance of staying out of reach shines like a neon light in my mind. I made the costly mistake of "sassing" her when I was about four feet away. She wheeled around to grab something with which to hit me, and her hand landed on a girdle. She drew back and swung that abominable garment in my direction, and I can still hear it whistling through the air. The intended blow caught me across the chest, followed by a multitude of straps and buckles, wrapping themselves around my mid-section. She gave me an entire thrashing with one massive blow! From that day forward, I cautiously retreated a few steps before popping off.

As fearful as he was of his volatile mother, Dobson formed a close bond with his father and emulated his Nazarene Christian faith. Derived from the Calvinist-inspired teachings of John Wesley, the theology to which Nazarene Christians adhere is a doctrine of "Entire Sanctification." After undergoing a life-changing crisis, they walk the sawdust trail to the altar to become "born again," thus freeing themselves forever from the shackles of sin and embarking on a straight path to heaven. The strictures of their faith forbid their listening to music, watching movies, or participating in any way in popular culture. Women are not permitted to wear makeup, or even wedding bands, which Nazarenes consider "adornment."

Tent revivals serve as a release valve for the Nazarenes' pent-up passions. Open crying, glossolalia (speaking in tongues), and intensely personal confessions were strongly encouraged at James Sr.'s revivals. Dobson said that at one of his father's jubilees, he broke town in tears and became "born again." He was three years old at the time. As Dobson entered adulthood, he adapted the Nazarenes' emotionalism to his charismatic public speaking style, and although he largely ignored its restrictions against enjoying popular culture, the religion's concept of crisis and redemption through enforced austerity formed the basis of his hard-right ideology.

Instead of following his father into the ministry as he was expected to do, the ambitious Dobson enrolled at the graduate school of psychology at the University of Southern California in Los Angeles. From there, he entered the USC School of Medicine, where he spent much of the late 1960s and early 1970s as a professor of pediatrics. Although his work began to gain some professional notice, Dobson was preoccupied with the tumult outside his window. Sandwiched between Los Angeles's riot-charred inner city and a college campus roiled by antiwar protests, Dobson seethed and blamed the upheaval on the counterculture and radical politics.

Dobson flatly rejected the notion that the residual ravages of Jim Crow, the ever-escalating violence of the Vietnam War, or the resentful style of President Richard Nixon had provoked any of these problems. Instead, he homed in on a scapegoat: Dr. Benjamin Spock, a pediatrician whose perennially best-selling book *Baby and Child Care* advised parents to treat their children respectfully as individuals. To Dobson, the nurturing style of parenting that Spock advocated was dangerous and "off the wall." "Is it merely coincidental that the generation raised during the [postwar] era has grown up to challenge every form of authority that confronts it?" Dobson asked. "I think not . . . We have sacrificed this generation on the altar of overindulgence, permissiveness, and smother-love."

Before Spock, parents were often encouraged to control their children with threats of violent retribution and physical discipline. This mode of child-rearing was particularly prevalent among white Protestants. Prescott Sheldon Bush Jr., the brother of President George H. W. Bush and a patriarch of one of America's most prominent Republican families, neatly encapsulated the parenting style of his social milieu: "My father was a gentleman and he expected us to be gentlemen," Bush recalled. "If we acted disrespectfully, if we did not observe the niceties of etiquette, he took us over his knee and whopped us with his belt. He had a strong arm and boy did we feel it."

For many new parents of the burgeoning postwar middle class, Spock's methods seemed a more humane alternative to the stern methods of their own mothers and fathers. What's more, they worked. Spock's recommendation that parents pick their children up and comfort them when they cried might seem like conventional wisdom today, but when *Baby and Child Care* was first published in 1946, it was nothing short of revolutionary. Indeed, Spock's prescription for kindness incited critics from the start. And when Spock lent his voice to the anti–Vietnam War movement he became a hate figure for the conservative movement. Among the doctor's most vociferous attackers was Vice President Spiro Agnew, an early and forgotten icon of the New Right who sneered at Spock as "the father of permissiveness."

Dobson envisioned himself as Spock's foil. He pecked away at his typewriter, hoping to produce the definitive child-rearing manual for conservative Americans revolted by the "permissive" passion play of the 1960s. Dobson was convinced that if his teachings reached a wide enough audience, they would forge a new generation of loyal counterrevolutionaries that would return America to the golden days of the 1950s—where boys once again wore pants, girls wore skirts, and, as he wrote, "Farmer John could take his sassy son out to the back forty acres and get his mind straight."

■ ■ ■

Dobson's manual, *Dare to Discipline*, read like a manifesto for domestic violence when it finally appeared in 1970. He urged parents to beat their young children, preferably with a "neutral object" such as a belt or a rod, lest they turn into drug-addled longhairs. He also advised administering a healthy spanking every now and again. "A little bit of pain goes a long way for a young child," Dobson wrote. "However, the spanking should be of sufficient magnitude to cause the child to cry genuinely. After the emotional ventilation, the child will often want to crumple to the breast of his parent, and he should be welcomed with open, warm, loving arms."

For parents struggling with children who refused to cooperate in public, Dobson recommended a slightly less vigorous technique than spanking. "There is a muscle, lying snuggly against the base of the neck [and] when firmly squeezed, it sends little messengers to the brain saying, 'This hurts; avoid recurrence at all costs.'" Dobson instructed his readers to firmly pinch the necks not only of their own sons and daughters, but of the inadequately disciplined children of complete strangers as well. "It can be utilized in countless situations where face-to-face confrontations occur between child and adult," Dobson said of his technique. To reinforce his advice, Dobson offered an anecdote that read as though it were lifted from the script of *Dirty Harry*:

> I had come out of a drug store, and there at its entrance was a stooped, elderly man, approximately seventy-five or eighty years of age. Four boys, probably ninth graders, had cornered him and were running circles around him. As I came through the door, one of the boys had just knocked the man's hat down over his eyes and they were laughing about how silly he looked, leaning on his cane. I stepped in front of the

poor fellow and suggested that they find someone else to torment . . .
One of the little tormentors ran straight up to my face, and stared defiantly in my eye. He was about half my size, but he obviously felt safe
because he was a child. He said, "You just hit me! I'll sue you for everything you're worth." I have rather large hands, and it was obviously the
time to use them; I grasped his shoulder muscles on both sides,
squeezing firmly. He dropped to the ground, holding his neck. One
of his friends said, "I'll bet you're a school teacher, aren't you?" All four
of them ran.

When Dobson updated his child-rearing advice in his 1992 manual *The Strong-Willed Child*, he extended his advocacy of corporal
punishment to unruly household pets. Dobson described a confrontation between himself and his dog, Siggie (named for Sigmund
Freud), over the dog's reluctance to sleep in his designated area:

> The ONLY way to make Siggie obey is to threaten him with destruc-
> tion. Nothing else works. I turned and went to my closet and got a
> small belt to help me "reason" with Mr. Freud.
>
> What developed next is impossible to describe. That tiny dog and
> I had the most vicious fight ever staged between man and beast. I
> fought him up one wall and down the other, with both of us scratch-
> ing and clawing and growling and swinging the belt. I am embar-
> rassed by the memory of the entire scene. Inch by inch I moved him
> toward the family room and his bed. As a final desperate maneuver,
> Siggie backed into the corner for one last snarling stand. I eventually
> got him to bed, only because I outweighed him 200 to 12!

To Dobson, children were to be treated no differently than dogs.
Both were preternaturally prone to rebellion, so both should be
"crushed" with violent force. Rebellious adolescents, though impervi-
ous to spankings and neck pinches, deserved heavy-handed punishment according to Dobson's rules. The tumult on high school and
college campuses "paralleled the decline in authority in the home," he
insisted. Because student radicals were beyond the reach of parental

authority, Dobson outlined a ten-point plan that school administrators and law enforcement officers could use to induce their submission instead.

Dobson proposed sex-segregated dormitories, fining of student protesters, and the immediate termination of faculty members found guilty of "encouraging revolution." He went on to endorse FBI director J. Edgar Hoover's counter-subversion campaign against the campus left. "Juvenile justice must be designed . . . to sting the child who has challenged authority," Dobson proclaimed.

■ ■ ■

The timing of Dobson's manifesto was fortuitous for his career. On May 8, 1970, just as *Dare to Discipline* went to press, a thousand students gathered in front of New York's City Hall to protest the massacre, four days before, of students at Kent State University in Ohio by National Guard soldiers. In a show of solidarity with the dead students, liberal Republican New York City Mayor John Lindsay ordered that flags be flown at half-mast.

Across the street from the protest, a battle line of two hundred burly ironworkers clanged metal pipes against the girders of an unfinished building and chanted, "Lindsay is a queer!" Then, NYPD officers stood aside and watched as the workers savagely attacked the students, chasing them onto the campus of nearby Pace University. There, the hard-hats continued their assault, brutalizing dozens of innocent bystanders with metal bludgeons. "I didn't see Americans in action," said one ironworker disgusted by the violence of his coworkers. "I saw the black shirts and brown shirts of Hitler's Germany."

Organizers of the assault, which became known as the "hard-hat riot," were later revealed to have been instigated to violence by President Richard Nixon's special counsel, Charles Colson.

A White House tape of May 5, 1971, captured the riot's initial planning phase, revealing Colson's role. "Chuck is something else," says Nixon. H. R. Haldeman, Nixon's chief of staff, says, "He's gotten a lot done that he hasn't been caught at." He goes on: "And then they're going to stir up some of this Vietcong flag business, as Colson's going to do it through hard hats and legionnaires. What Colson's going to do on that, and what I suggested he do—and I think that they can get away with this—do it with the Teamsters. Just ask them to dig up their eight thugs." "They've got guys who'll go in and knock their heads off," Nixon gleefully replies. "Sure," says Haldeman. "Murderers. Guys that really, you know, that's what they really do . . . regular strikebuster-types . . . and just send them in and beat the shit out of some of these people. And hope they really hurt 'em, you know what I mean? Go in with some real—smash some noses."

Two weeks after the White House organized the attack, Colson arranged a ceremony at the White House to honor its field general, Peter Brennan, president of the Building and Construction Trades and later appointed secretary of labor.

By the summer of 1973, Colson was preparing for his trial for obstruction of justice. With the prosecution preparing its case against him and the press corps homing in on his role in the Watergate break-in, Colson knelt on the floor with his friend Raytheon CEO Tom Phillips. While Colson fought back tears in an embarrassed state of silence, Phillips prayed for his soul. Driving through Washington afterward, Colson suddenly began to cry "tears of release." "I repeated over and over the words, Take me . . . " Colson wrote in his best-selling memoir, *Born Again*. "Something inside me was urging me to surrender." Soon after, Colson sought out Dobson and Francis Schaeffer as prayer partners.

When Colson finally came to Jesus, he became America's best-known born-again Christian, lending exposure to a cultural phenomenon erupting below the radar of the mainstream press and secular America. In the *Washington Post*, columnist Nicholas Von Hoffman mocked his conversion as a cynical ploy, panning it as "a socially approved way of having a nervous breakdown." While Colson appeared to remove himself from politics, he quietly planned a strategy to regain his former influence.

After serving seven months in prison, Colson returned to convert the godless criminals he encountered there. In 1976, he founded Prison Fellowship, now a multimillion-dollar organization that operates with public funding in several states and 110 countries. The hundreds of thousands of inmates who have enrolled in Colson's InnerChange Freedom Initiative—motivated by coercive enticements such as extended visits with family members and access to musical instruments and better food—are promised by official program material that they will be transformed "through an instantaneous miracle."

Colson read R. J. Rushdoony with avid interest upon his release from prison, and he was among the first evangelical leaders to latch on to Schaeffer's anti-abortion crusade. His 1995 science fiction novel *Gideon's Torch* revealed his radical passions. The book follows a heroic band of Christian guerrillas who must stop the National Institutes of Health from harvesting brain tissue from aborted fetuses to cure AIDS, a plan funded by Hollywood liberals. To do so, they launch a righteous killing spree of abortion doctors, eventually firebombing the National Institutes of Health. Not surprisingly, *Gideon's Torch* became a recruiting tool for those wishing to realize its fictional narrative. It has been excerpted at length on the website of the Army of God, a radical anti-abortion group responsible for the killing and bombing of abortion providers.

■ ■ ■

When Dobson first entered public life, his understanding of politics was amateur at best. Colson became his counsel, providing him with high-level Republican contacts and help devising a strategy to transform his growing flock into an influential political bloc. Colson could never have fulfilled the strategy on his own. Indeed, no figure in the burgeoning evangelical movement shared Dobson's psychological understanding of his audience on an intimate level. Only Dobson recognized events such as the hard-hat riot as integral parts of a gathering backlash against liberalism. His advocacy of corporal punishment was carefully intended to channel the violent backlash in the streets into a coherent grassroots movement with himself as its guru.

Dobson's teachings resonated on a profound level with the backlashers. By 1976, *Dare to Discipline* had been reprinted eighteen times and sold over a million copies. His success propelled him into the rapidly expanding evangelical broadcast industry. Dobson's new radio show and ministry, Focus on the Family, became immensely popular as well. Now, the followers eager to implement his harsh methods had grown into a belt-wielding army of millions. Corporal punishment was back with a vengeance.

Philip Greven, a professor of history at Rutgers University and a leading expert on Protestant religious thought, is one of the few researchers of American conservatism who has recognized the impact of corporal punishment on the sensibility of movement members. In his incisive book *Spare the Child: The Religious Roots of Punishment and the Psychological Impact of Physical Abuse*, Greven analyzed *Dare to Discipline* in detail, concluding that Dobson's violent child-rearing methods served an underlying purpose, producing droves of activists embarked on an authoritarian mission.

"The persistent 'conservatism' of American politics and society is rooted in large part in the physical violence done to children," Greven wrote. "The roots of this persistent tilt towards hierarchy, enforced order, and absolute authority—so evident in Germany earlier in this century and in the radical right in America today—are always traceable to aggression against children's wills and bodies, to the pain and the suffering they experience long before they, as adults, confront the complex issues of the polity, the society, and the world."

But the infliction of pain on young children, social deviants, and other weaker beings is only one half of a binary solution Dobson has prescribed to his followers for curing America's social ills. As Dobson has consistently made clear to his flock, they must first purify their own souls of sin before striking out, literally, to purify the land.

Dobson's self-purification process, adapted from his father's Nazarene faith, compels his followers to confess their darkest transgressions before pleading for forgiveness. Finally, to attain what Dobson and others in the evangelical culture call "holiness," a permanent state of spiritual perfection, followers must submit their individual wills to the order of a higher power—either God, or men of God such as Dobson. Every sinner who submits must be convinced that, as Dobson has insisted, "Pain is a marvelous purifier."

Dobson's emphasis on pain, simultaneously inflicted on weaker beings and the self, reflects the sadomasochism at the core of his philosophy. As Greven noted, books such as *Dare to Discipline* that urge parents to beat their children are hardly distinguishable from S&M manuals such as Larry Townsend's "The Leatherman's Handbook," which advise men on erotic techniques of "discipline" and "punishment." The principal distinction between the two is that the methods Townsend advocates are applied to adults who have chosen to participate, whereas Dobson's techniques are wielded against the wills of small children.

"Wherever children suffer from painful physical punishments and humiliating submission to more powerful authorities, sadomasochism will be present," Greven wrote. "Sadomasochism is thus one of the most enduring consequences of coercive discipline in childhood."

Erich Fromm, in his book *Escape from Freedom*, insisted that sadomasochism was more than a sexual kink. It was, he claimed, a defining characteristic of the authoritarian personality, finding its most dangerous expression in the political sphere. "The essence of the authoritarian character," Fromm wrote, "has been described as the simultaneous presence of sadistic and masochistic drives. Sadism was understood as aiming at unrestricted power over another person more or less mixed with destructiveness; masochism as aiming at dissolving oneself in an overwhelmingly strong power and participating in its strength and glory."

Dare to Discipline and several of Dobson's subsequent tracts are little more than how-to guides for the cultivation of sadomasochists. As Dobson's own personal history shows, many of those raised on a steady diet of corporal punishment demonstrate a tendency later in life to reenact the painful experiences familiar to their childhoods, through either radical-right political activism or cruel interpersonal behavior, or both. The appeal of illicit, even macabre sexual behavior to some social conservatives—a trend that has produced no end of colorful scandals—further reflects their sadomasochistic tendencies.

The sadomasochism that is latent in so many figures of the new radical right is often activated by a traumatic personal crisis. As Fromm explained, "Both the sadistic and the masochistic trends are caused by the inability of the isolated individual to stand alone and his need for a symbiotic relationship that overcomes this aloneness."

Many of those who once crumpled to the breast of a parent after a thorough beating have found themselves prostrate at Dobson's feet later in life. Only through Dobson have they been able to fulfill the urge to simultaneously give and receive pain, an urge that they developed during infancy. Thus it is hardly a coincidence that some of the worst, most sadistic serial killers America has known have been granted redemption by the leader of Focus on the Family, who has time and again inserted himself as their father confessor and counselor. No matter how malignant their sins might have been, once they confessed them to Dobson and submitted to his rigid authority, they were welcomed with open arms into "The Family" and were assured of eternal salvation.

PART TWO

Pride goes before destruction, a haughty spirit before a fall.

PROVERBS 16:18

CHAPTER 7

SATAN IN A PORSCHE

The 1980s brought new opportunities—and new dragons to slay—for James Dobson. With the Reagan administration, Dobson was able to establish a foothold in Washington. His closest White House ally was Gary Bauer, the elfin undersecretary of education who used his post to limit funding for public schools, which he blamed for eroding the country's moral character. A born-again Baptist reared in Kentucky, Bauer became an informal liaison between Reagan and the Christian right, the first person to serve in a position that became a regular job in succeeding Republican administrations. He regarded Dobson and his "pro-family" image as a special asset to the White House, especially as it battled the perception that Reagan's economic policies favored the very wealthy against the interests of working families.

Dobson's Focus on the Family was in the midst of a rapid expansion fueled by the popularity of a new form of media technology: the VCR. Dobson was a natural on camera, and through the magic of home video he invited himself into millions of homes across the country. A short video Dobson produced in 1981 titled "Where's Dad?" urged career-obsessed fathers to spend more time at home with their children; it remains one of the most effective and profitable vehicles for his message. In the first three months after the video's release, Focus hired 200 new staffers to keep pace with the demand for literature related to its recommendations. Today Focus claims that more than 100 million people worldwide, including many on U.S. military installations, have seen "Where's Dad?"

But the VCR was a boon to the Dark Side, as well as to the children of light. Cheap home-recording technology enabled the adult film industry to reach an endlessly expanding mass audience. Porn patrons no longer needed to sneak away to seedy urban red-light districts to get their skin-flick fix; now they could watch their favorite Vanessa Del Rio epics or Long Dong Silver adventures from the comfort of their Craftsmatic adjustable beds instead. The prospect of porn playing well in Peoria piqued Dobson's indignation and imagination. In his book *Children at Risk*, he warned that the viewing of obscene material would inevitably lead to "sex between women and bulls, stallions or boars."

Few organizations kept statistics on pornography addiction rates during the 1980s. But a wealth of data collected since then suggests that porn has been a particularly pernicious problem within the evangelical community. ChristiaNet.com, an evangelical anti-porn group, found in a 2007 survey that 50 percent of evangelical men and 20 percent of evangelical women are addicted to pornography; 37 percent of evangelical pastors who responded to a 2001 survey by *Christianity Today* magazine called porn addiction a "current struggle." And since Focus on the Family opened a counseling hotline for troubled pastors, at least 25 percent of calls have come from clergymen struggling with porn addiction. "I tell [my clients], 'God does not make perverts, and God is your physician,'" said Simon Sheh, an evangelical counselor affiliated with Focus on the Family. "'He healed me. He can heal you, too.'"

Dobson recognized early on the extent to which his followers addictively consumed demon porn. In 1986, at Dobson's urging, the Reagan administration created a national commission on pornography chaired by Attorney General Edwin Meese, a member of Reagan's original California entourage and an ally of the religious right. Supported with $1.5 million in federal funds, the commission was headed by Alan Sears, a close friend of Dobson's who simultaneously chaired the Resolutions Committee of the Southern Baptist Convention, which was now under the control of its right wing. Wearing his SBC hat, Sears promoted a church resolution congratulating the Meese commission, while killing another that would have condemned apartheid in South

Africa. Sears was joined on the Meese commission by Dobson and nine fellow anti-porn crusaders, only two of whom were women. Together, they convened a marathon of public hearings in cities across America, hoping to build a compelling case against the scourge of smut and sin.

The public hearings of the puritan tribunal quickly turned into burlesque. The commissioners meted out indignant tongue-lashings to porn actors and producers, and they elicited plaintive testimonies from prominent opponents of pornography. But strange bedfellows vaulted onto the stage. Andrea Dworkin, a feminist radical with a shock of frizzy hair, highlighted one hearing in New York City. Once an abused wife, Dworkin proclaimed in one of her polemical books that, "men will have to give up their precious erections." Like Dobson's followers, she had projected her personal crises into the political sphere.

Dworkin testified before the commission about a sexual practice she described as "skull-fucking," a pornographic paraphilia "apparently brought back from Vietnam." "These are films in which a woman is killed and the orifices in her head are penetrated with a man's penis— her eyes, her mouth and so on," Dworkin went on. Rather than producing any evidence that such horrific films existed, Dworkin assured the panel that her "information comes from women who have seen the films and escaped." Dworkin's animadversions reduced one commissioner to tears.

The pornography commissioners soon revealed an ardent appetite for viewing and discussing porn (particularly of the violent and kinky variety) that could only have been matched by hardcore addicts. They pored over "evidence" seized by the government, such as the magazine *Here's the Beef*, paperback books including *Horny Holy Roller Family* and *Raped by Arab Terrorists*, and film classics such as *Romancing the Bone* and *Passionate Pissing*. The amateur material they publicly perused included "Personal Polaroids shot at home by swinging 'families,'" and an advertisement for "Women Who Fuck Anything Magazines" that featured "a drawing of a female bent over with a dog's snout near the crotch."

As they viewed the obscene material, the commissioners copiously took notes. The commission padded its "research" with a series of field trips into the heart of the sexual underworld. Under the protective gaze of a federal marshal, commissioners burst into a Times Square adult bookstore, chasing from a peep booth two men apparently engaged in a sex act. Immediately afterwards, Sears proclaimed that the commission had to do something about the "literature of enemas." He offered an example of this new genre: "One close-up photograph of a Caucasian female with a douche bag inserted in her nose, extending through her legs to her anus."

In their final report, the commissioners published (with taxpayer financing) an account of a pornographic scene so explicit, and yet so clinical, that it read like a *Penthouse Forum* letter from an avidly active lesbian reader:

> A white female (represented to be known porno star Marlene Willoughby) [is shown] inserting one finger in the vagina of another female (represented to be known porno star Vanessa Del Rio). Then Willoughby inserts two fingers in Del Rio's vagina. One finger has a large ring. A close-up is shown of the insertion. Then Willoughby uses her left hand and inserts one finger in Del Rio's vagina; then two fingers are inserted; then three fingers are inserted. Then she inserts her fist in Del Rio's vagina, twisting it around . . .

The fixation on the seedy and perverse rankled one of the commission's female members. Speaking on background to a reporter, she observed that Sears was particularly obsessed. "I couldn't figure out why he was so taken by that 42nd Street stuff," she said.

Unknown to most observers of the commission, or even to some of his fellow panelists, however, Sears had fallen for a woman much younger than his wife. In the heat of the commission's sex tribunals, Sears suddenly announced his divorce and married his new fling, according to Reverend Barry Lynn, a Baptist pastor who testified against the work of the commission. (The Southern Baptist Convention routinely defrocked pastors for divorce, but Sears retained his post.) Dobson, for his part, maintained silence about the divorce and subsequently appointed Sears president of Focus on the Family's legal arm, the Alliance Defense Fund.

Like Sears, commission member Father Bruce Ritter was captivated by the "42nd Street stuff." Founder of the faith-based charity Covenant House, Ritter claimed to help teen runaways "find a way out of the gutters and brothels and strip joints where their young bodies are in demand as objects of pleasure for lustful adults." From his post on the commission, Ritter called for the abolition of pornography and strip clubs from Times Square and insisted that homosexuality was an abnormal perversion. And unlike several commission members who opposed only violent pornography, Ritter opposed *any* publication of graphic sexual images. "Pornography's greatest harm," he declared, "is caused by its ability—and its intention—to attack the very dignity and sacredness of sex itself, reducing human sexual behavior to the level of its animal components."

Yet four years after the commission concluded, Ritter's own lustful ways exploded into the open when a gay porn actor and prostitute named Kevin Kite accused him of paying him $125,000 from Covenant House coffers for sexual favors. Three former residents leveled similar allegations against the priest soon thereafter. Although Ritter faced no charges after resigning from Covenant, a law firm's internal investigation found significant evidence of his transgressions with vulnerable young men.

These revelations could have fatally damaged the commission's credibility. So long as they remained suppressed, the movement embraced its goals, honoring its most prominent member, Dobson, with a keynote speech at the 1986 convention of the National Religious Broadcasters, the evangelical broadcast industry's lobbying arm. Before the rapturous audience, Dobson disclosed his relief upon returning home after a hard day of viewing scatology, fetishism, and barnyard carnality as part of his chores in the campaign against sin. "My children were safe from all that misery, molestation, death, in their bedrooms," he sighed. But Dobson reminded the evangelicals not to be complacent. The innocent were always in peril. He recounted how a black Porsche piloted by Satan had tried to run his two children over. The master of evil, Dobson said, had sought revenge on his family for battling to restore biblical moral standards to America. "I think the Lord said to me, 'Yes, these things are connected and I did do a miracle on behalf of your children.'" Then Dobson asked the assemblage to pray for him as he embarked on the holy work of preparing the commission's final report.

Yet after ten months of grueling work, and with its final report due in three weeks, the commission still had not resolved one of its central questions: Which types of porn are the most harmful? Although some commission members leaned toward urging a law enforcement crackdown on only the most violent strains, Dobson demanded that mainstream publications such as *Playboy* and *Penthouse* be censored as well.

In a breathless letter warning that America was drowning in a "river of smut," Dobson sought to frighten and intimidate his colleagues to back his position. In purple prose mimicking that of pornographers, he reveled in perverse detail. "Does it not insult every self-respecting female in the world to see a woman sip semen from a champagne glass after men have filled it with ejaculate? . . ." Dobson asked. "Is it degrading to women to publish magazines entitled *Oriental Snatch, Blond Fuckers, Cum Hungry Girls, Chocolate Pussy, Super Bitch, Cum Sucking Vipers, Hot Fucking She Male* and *Pussy Pumping Ass Fuckers*?"

In the end, however, the commission fell far short of Dobson's hopes. It concluded that only some porn—particularly of the violent variety—causes "harm," though not quite as much as Kung-Fu or (gasp!) horror movies. After issuing a vaguely worded call for a federal law enforcement crackdown on such material, the commissioners closed their rambling 2,000-page report with an earnest but forlorn plea: "We urge that many of the recommendations we suggest be taken seriously."

Unknown to Dobson, Ted Bundy, one of the most notorious serial killers in American history, was passing his time on death row poring over the Meese Commission report, carefully reading its federally funded bibliography of porn page by page. Soon he had an idea for one last publicity coup.

CHAPTER 8

THE KILLER AND THE SAINT

During the weeks leading up to his scheduled execution on January 29, 1989, Ted Bundy confessed to raping, bludgeoning, and strangling to death at least thirty women. Investigators suspected that he might have killed scores more. An admitted necrophiliac, Bundy sometimes visited the discarded corpses of his victims to have sex with them until they were rotted beyond recognition. As his execution date drew closer, Bundy insisted that his killings were fueled by his alleged addiction to pornography. Before facing the electric chair, Bundy demanded an opportunity to meet face to face with one man, whom he proclaimed a hero—James Dobson.

If Dobson ever harbored ethical concerns about giving a mass murderer the chance to blame his barbarity on outside forces, they were immediately assuaged when he learned that Bundy had announced he had become a born-again Christian in prison. Dobson also saw the interview as an opportunity to bask in the national spotlight without having to endure the media's critical scrutiny. Under guidelines that Bundy set, Dobson could control the light in which he wished to be seen. And so, on a hot, muggy evening in Starke, Florida, just hours before Bundy's execution, Dobson strode confidently past a cluster of reporters and into the prison's death row, where Bundy prepared for his grand confession in the last scene of his drama of death.

At the start of the interview, the child psychologist homed in on Bundy's professed porn addiction, ignoring elements in the killer's background that might have offered a more salient explanation of his

73

violent tendencies. Dobson, for instance, neglected to ask Bundy whether he was beaten during his childhood. Like many who demonstrate sadistic behavior as adults, including Dobson himself, Bundy was in fact a victim of child abuse.

Raised by his maternal grandfather, who was rumored in the neighborhood to be his biological father (his real father left his mother after impregnating her), Bundy suffered a childhood fraught with confusion and abuse. His grandfather was a fanatical racist, who routinely attacked his wife, amused himself by swinging cats over his head by their tails, and mercilessly beat the family dog. A deacon at his local church, the grandfather frequently disappeared into a greenhouse behind his house where he stashed a voluminous collection of pornography. Despite his violence, or because of its power, Bundy idolized the vicious old man.

Imbued with ambition and endowed with handsome looks, Bundy graduated from college with a degree in psychology and, like Dobson, devoted himself to resolving the private trauma of others. While studying at the University of Washington, Bundy volunteered at a Seattle suicide crisis center. Governor Dan Evans, a Republican nicknamed "Straight Arrow" for his lofty ethical standards, appointed Bundy assistant director of the Seattle Crime Prevention Advisory Commission. In that capacity, Bundy reviewed Washington state laws on hitchhiking and then authored a detailed and widely distributed rape prevention pamphlet for women.

Soon Bundy was elevated to a key position on Evans's 1972 reelection campaign. The young operative posed as a college student, sometimes wearing a fake moustache, to get close to Evans's Democratic adversary, former governor Albert Rosselini. "I just mingled with the crowds and nobody knew who I was," he said at the time. With a camera in hand, Bundy recorded Rosselini routinely altering his patrician speech inflections to appeal to the populist sensibilities of rural audiences. Bundy's novel research tactics enabled Evans to paint the more polished Rosselini as a phony limousine liberal. The charge stuck, and it helped propel Evans to an easy victory over his rival.

Evans rewarded Bundy again, installing him as assistant director of the Washington State Republican Party. Bundy became a frequent dinner guest of the governor's and even babysat his children on occasion. He seemed destined for a bright future in Republican politics. Yet beneath his attractive veneer, Bundy harbored horrifically destructive impulses. A year later, when Bundy's longtime girlfriend Stephanie Brooks ended their relationship with only a scant justification, the mask of sanity he had worn so convincingly suddenly fell, and his killing spree began.

Bundy's modes of savagery varied, but the profiles of his victims were nearly uniform. Each of his victims was white, middle-class, and educated, and each had dark hair parted in the middle. Bundy's ex-girlfriend also happened to possess these characteristics. Obviously, his targeting was hardly coincidental. Though he was also addicted to pornography, his murderous impulses were clearly triggered by Brooks's abrupt termination of their relationship. From 1974 until 1978, Bundy killed between nineteen and thirty-six young women in six states. During this period, Bundy repeatedly evaded suspicious law enforcement officers with cool denials and escaped prison twice after being sentenced to fifteen years for kidnapping one of his victims.

In 1986, as Bundy awaited his murder trial, John Tanner, a Republican Florida prosecutor who regularly ministered to local prison inmates, befriended him. Tanner and Bundy developed a close relationship, spending at least six hundred hours together before Bundy's execution. Tanner declared himself Bundy's "spiritual advisor" and claimed to have helped the killer become a born-again Christian. After several intense prayer sessions with Tanner, the killer convinced his new Christian brother that the spirit of Satan had in fact controlled him.

Tanner was no stranger to such paranormal concepts. An aggressive anti-porn crusader, Tanner was born again at the age of forty. According to a law partner, Tanner converted in the throes of a midlife crisis when he first claimed to hear the voice of God instructing him to teach his children "spiritual things." After hearing God's commandment again, this time ordering him to tell a handicapped stranger that God loved him, Tanner finally surrendered his will to the cause of Christ.

Tanner saw the newly saved Bundy as a fellow Christian soldier, and he firmly believed that the killer's execution could be prevented.

Although Tanner claimed to support Bundy's death sentence, he and Bundy conspired to postpone his date with the electric chair as long as possible by offering to assist investigators with detailed information on unsolved murders in Washington State. Reporters dubbed this plan the "bones-for-time scheme," and Bundy's own lawyer recoiled when he learned of the grim strategy. An outraged Governor Bob Martinez rumbled, "For [Bundy] to be negotiating with his life over the bodies of others is despicable."

As Bundy's execution date drew closer, Tanner introduced the killer to Dobson's books. Bundy declared himself to be blown away by Dobson's insights. He demanded a copy of the Meese Commission report and claimed to have studied every one of its 2,000 pages. Finally, at Bundy's request, Tanner approached Dobson, asking him to interview Bundy on camera. Dobson leapt at the opportunity. The Bundy interview materialized before him like a miracle. According to top Dobson aide Peb Jackson, Bundy was "a poster boy for exactly what Jim [Dobson] saw as the extreme end of what could happen if you get hooked on this stuff [pornography]."

But even as Bundy poured his heart out to Dobson, warning, "pornography can snatch a kid out of any house today," he remained a cunning operative. Ann Rule, a true-life crime writer who had worked alongside Bundy at the Seattle crisis hotline, believed the killer's last confession was little more than a disingenuous ploy calculated to generate one last burst of media exposure. "I knew," she wrote in her book *The Stranger Beside Me*, "that if the day ever came when Ted saw the shadow of the death chamber and knew his time had run out, he would want to go out in a glare of klieg lights and with his last words ringing in everyone's ears."

By the end of Dobson's hour-long encounter with Bundy, the Focus leader appeared convinced of the killer's tale of redemption. During a May 1989 radio interview with Tanner, Dobson called for Bundy to be forgiven: "To those who say that Ted Bundy should burn forever in eternity," Dobson proclaimed, "I would only say, 'So should I. So should all of us . . . it's not more difficult for God to forgive Ted Bundy than it is for me. It's simple repentance and believing on the name of Jesus Christ. That's what we teach. Do we believe it?'"

As soon as Dobson emerged from death row, his aides distributed footage of his interview with Bundy to the frenzied media gaggle waiting outside the prison. The tapes were free, but Focus applied one condition: Media outlets were required to air the footage in its entirety without editing or interruption. This guaranteed Dobson unprecedented exposure when his interview aired on news programs and talk shows for a week after Bundy's execution.

The interview became Dobson's cash cow. Selling the Bundy tapes reaped a windfall profit of nearly $1 million within the span of one year. The Focus leader initially pocketed the money for himself, but after a public outcry, he donated $600,000 of his profits to anti-pornography and anti-abortion groups, including some affiliated with his own ministry. And so, what began as a killing spree turned into a spending spree for the Christian right. But, even more significant, Ted Bundy had provided James Dobson with prolonged national media exposure. The two psychologists, the killer and the saint, had found common cause in the shadow of the valley of death.

CHAPTER 9

A DANGEROUS WOMAN

I n January 1992, John Tanner thrust himself into the spotlight of another serial killer's trial. This time he was not the killer's compassionate spiritual counselor but rather the prosecutor charged with securing a death sentence. Tanner's task was complicated by the fact that the killer was a woman, Aileen Wuornos, a prostitute who had preyed on men she claimed had initially preyed on her.

Falsely labeled America's first female serial killer by many in the media and widely portrayed as a man-hating lesbian (primarily because she was involved in a relationship with another woman at the time of her arrest), Wuornos was in fact a mentally disturbed prostitute who killed seven of her johns for dubious reasons. On the surface, this pathetic figure, whose story was dramatized in the 2004 film *Monster*, seemed to be the mirror opposite of the seductive Bundy. But Wuornos shared with Bundy two important characteristics omitted from the Hollywood version of her life: She was adopted, and she was severely abused as a child.

Wuornos's childhood was a living hell. The man reputed to be her father, Leo Dale Pittman, was a convicted child molester who hanged himself in jail. After being abandoned by her mother, Wuornos was adopted by her grandparents. Wuornos's grandfather, who sexually abused her and whipped her with a belt (a "neutral object," as Dobson recommended in *Dare to Discipline*), had actually fathered her himself by raping his daughter. Trapped in a cycle of brutality and deceit, Wuornos became a truck-stop prostitute by the time she reached adolescence.

Wuornos's first victim was Richard Mallory, a middle-aged electronics repair shop owner who spent his weekends binging on alcohol and sex. Wuornos claimed that Mallory, who was drunk and drugged up when he picked her up by the roadside in December 1989, drove her to a remote location and violently raped her. Then, she said, Mallory bound her and prepared to rape her again. When he returned, however, Wuornos said she pulled a .22 pistol from her purse and fired three bullets at his chest. Wuornos's tale of self-defense was at least plausible: Mallory had served ten years in prison for another brutal rape. A psychological evaluation of Mallory before his release from prison warned, "Because of his emotional disturbance and his poor control of his sexual impulses, he could present a potential danger to his environment in the future."

Tanner was too immersed in the drama of the trial to bother with mitigating circumstances. "That's his favorite time," Tanner's wife said of his cross-examinations. "That's like recreation for him." When he grilled Wuornos on the witness stand, Tanner focused on the inconsistencies between her police confession and her testimony in court. After twenty-five times invoking her right not to incriminate herself, Wuornos finally lost her composure, lashing out at Tanner in a series of furious outbursts. The prosecutor had undermined any credibility Wuornos might have had—at least in the eyes of the jury. In his closing statement, Tanner labeled Wuornos a "predatory prostitute" whose "lust and control had taken a lethal turn," and he claimed that she "had been exercising control for years over men." Wuornos was found guilty and sentenced to death.

Tanner insisted on witnessing Wuornos's execution. Even for a prosecutor in a capital case, this was an unusual request. But Tanner claimed he had a personal interest in seeing her victims avenged. "She liked to be in control," he said. "In fact, these killings, as much as anything, were acts of ultimate control, and we've seen that in serial killer patterns in the past. She killed these men to bring about the ultimate in control over their lives, which was to terminate it." Now seated in the witness gallery, Tanner was back in charge.

Strapped to a gurney, her senses dulled with sedatives, and lethal poisons beginning to course through her veins, Wuornos was pacified at last.

"I'd just like to say I'm sailing with the Rock and I'll be back like Independence Day with Jesus, June 6, like the movie, big mother ship and all," Wuornos babbled incoherently. "I'll be back," she added before her eyeballs rolled back into her head.

The discrepancy between Tanner's conduct during Bundy's trial, when he sought to delay his friend's execution as long as possible, and his behavior during his prosecution of Wuornos, when he pressed for the execution of the "predatory prostitute" and fought to bar evidence of mitigating circumstances from her trial, raised a serious question: Why did Tanner display an apparent double standard?

Phyllis Chesler, a well-known feminist and journalistic observer of Wuornos's trial who attempted unsuccessfully to advise her bungling lawyer, framed her story with a radical-feminist narrative. In her essay "A Woman's Right to Self-Defense," Chesler suggested that in contrast to Bundy, who was treated relatively fairly, even favorably, by the judicial system despite the perverse crimes he committed against women, Wuornos was hastily sentenced to death because she depicted her murders as acts of self-defense against male attackers. Wuornos's harsh treatment by the criminal justice system, Chesler argued, reflected the patriarchy's resentment of women who dare to defy their assigned gender roles.

"Judges, jurors, Senate Judiciary Committee members, and 'We, the People' still value men's lives more highly than women's and feel compassion for male—but not for female—sinners," Chesler wrote. "When a woman is accused of committing a crime (and even when the woman is the crime victim), her story is rarely believed by men or by other women, even less so if she is accusing a man of being the aggressor."

Chesler's portrayal of Wuornos as a feminist martyr was seriously flawed, however, not only because the author virtually ignored Wuornos's admission that six of her seven victims had never attempted to rape her, but also because she overlooked a simpler, and far more salient, explanation for the discrepancy between the justice system's treatment of Wuornos and its treatment of Bundy. Even though Tanner and his conservative movement allies displayed a misogynistic attitude, they ultimately favored Bundy because he was a born-again Christian, and scorned Wuornos because she was not.

Whereas Bundy immersed himself in the Meese Commission report and took communion with Tanner, Wuornos passed her time on
death row listening to a CD of fem-pop icon Natalie Merchant's "Carnival." Bundy, the one-time sadist, had become transformed under
Tanner's wing into the anti-porn poster boy, the masochist. Wuornos,
meanwhile, was an unrepentant, mentally unstable criminal who had
vowed, "I killed those men . . . And I'd do it again, too." She had no
value to anyone except her huckster lawyer, Steven Glazer, a wannabe
rock musician who lined his pockets with interview fees from Geraldo
Rivera. By contrast, Bundy earned a seat at the movement's table and,
by their lights, in paradise.

The discrepancy between Bundy's and Wuornos's treatment by the
Christian right fits a disturbing pattern. Throughout their careers,
Dobson, Tanner, and their cohorts have consistently advocated on behalf of criminals solely on the basis of their evangelical faith, while demanding draconian punishment for others guilty of the same crimes.
In 1998, for example, Pat Robertson unsuccessfully pressed then Texas
Governor George W. Bush to commute the execution of convicted ax
murderer Karla Faye Tucker on the grounds that she had been born
again in prison. Only two years earlier, however, Robertson railed
against President Clinton's nomination of Rosemary Barkett to the
federal judiciary. Barkett, Robertson argued, was disqualified by her reluctance to apply the death penalty in similar cases. "The Bible is very
clear about this," Robertson declared, "that when blood is shed, blood
cleanses the land." Tanner, meanwhile, used the prestige he had earned
from his prosecution of Wuornos to exonerate an evangelical minister
arrested for lewd behavior.

Tanner's friend, Robert Moorehead, was a ferociously anti-gay
pastor who led the largest mega-church in Washington State. In 1996,
Moorehead was arrested for masturbating openly in a Daytona Beach,
Florida, men's room. Just four months after rushing to the pastor's side
to defend him in court, Tanner was appointed chief prosecutor for four
counties in Central Florida—including the one in which Moorehead
was arrested. As one of his first acts in office, Tanner personally dismissed the charge against Moorehead, claiming, without citing any evidence, that the police had arrested the wrong man. Although Daytona

police adamantly rejected Tanner's contention, the pastor was released, returning to Seattle a free man.

When news of Moorehead's arrest filtered through the pews of his Overland Church, however, seventeen male parishioners came forward with allegations that the pastor had sexually molested them. One man claimed that Moorehead shoved his hands down the crotch of his tuxedo pants and fondled his genitals only moments before he presided over the man's wedding. Moorehead's accusers were immediately bombarded with menacing letters and anonymous death threats. Denouncing his accusers from his pulpit, Moorehead assured his flock of his raging heterosexuality. "If I was ever going to inappropriately touch somebody, it would never be a man. It would be a woman." As he spoke, his wife stood by his side.

After a hasty investigation, Overland's elders cleared Moorehead of all charges. According to the elders, none other than the Devil had concocted the accusations against their leader to punish the financially flush church for its success. "Satan likes none of this!" one elder proclaimed in a newsletter to parishioners. "He has always opposed a soul-winning church, and we're no exception."

But the cover-up Tanner orchestrated was exposed when the *Daytona News-Journal* sued to unseal Moorehead's court records. According to those records, Moorehead had signed a plea agreement that allowed him to maintain his innocence, while warning that he would be convicted if arrested again for lewd behavior. The gravity of this revelation at last forced Moorehead to resign his post as Overland's pastor, though he was allowed to remain a member of the congregation. Tanner, for his part, was unaffected by the scandal.

Having forgiven Bundy and profited handsomely from his dramatic confession, Dobson sought other serial killers to redeem. When David Berkowitz, known popularly as the "Son of Sam" killer, published a long series of memoirs describing his come-to-Jesus experience in prison, Dobson seized upon the serial killer as another Bundy. During a two-part Focus on the Family broadcast in 2004, Dobson encouraged the killer he now dubbed the "Son of Hope" to describe his miraculous conversion. Like Bundy, Berkowitz assured Dobson and his audience of millions that evil demons had programmed him to kill. Only by embracing the spirit of Christ, Berkowitz said, was he able to harness the darkness in his soul. With this plaintive confession, Berkowitz was welcomed into the movement with open arms.

"I was there when we interviewed Berkowitz," Focus associate producer Scott Welch told the *Rocky Mountain News*. "To me, he's like a brother . . . He's a gentle, humble, kind and loving person who is not out for personal gain at all."

Immediately after recording Dobson's interview with Berkowitz, Focus on the Family packaged the encounter into cassette tapes, marketing them to members for a "suggested donation" of $7. But Dobson's profiteering enraged law enforcement officials working to curb the booming memorabilia business that Berkowitz had been running from his prison cell in New York. "I'm just incredulous that a church group would try to make a buck on a serial killer," New York Department of Corrections spokesman James Flateau remarked. But even in the face of harsh criticism from police, Dobson refused to relent. Tapes of his Berkowitz interview are still available on Focus's website for a "suggested donation" of $9, $2 more than when they first went on the market. The publicity has been good for the product.

Members of the movement believe they are subject to a different set of laws than outsiders. No matter how horrendous their sins have been, sinners can be forgiven time and time again simply by absolving themselves through being born again and by absorbing the sado-masochistic culture of the Christian right. Thus the fallen ones pay fealty to Family men like Dobson and shower these leaders with veneration as they reveal themselves as murderers.

Having redeemed some of the worst killers in American history, and having enhanced his public profile in the process, Dobson, the child psychiatrist, moved on to new patients. He found them in Washington, in the leadership of the Republican Congress that had swept into power in 1994.

CHAPTER 10

CHEAP GRACE

When the Republicans swept into the House of Representatives in 1994 on a wave of resentment against President Bill Clinton, James Dobson swiftly maneuvered to assert his influence. Many of the party's rising stars were more than fervent conservatives; they were Focus on the Family devotees whose lives had been changed by his teachings. Republican representatives from Tom DeLay to Frank Wolf to Jim Talent credited Dobson with helping them overcome personal crises. They saw him as the spiritual godfather of the new Republican Congress.

Talent, then a lawyer in the St. Louis suburbs and adjunct professor at the Washington University Law School, according to his account of his born-again experience, heard Dobson like the voice of God over his car radio, pulled over on the roadside, and committed his life to Christ. "It is the single most important thing that has ever or will ever happen to me," he said of his Dobson-inspired conversion from Judaism to evangelical Christianity. Dobson also enjoyed a close relationship with rookie congressman Steve Largent, a Hall of Fame former National Football League wide receiver, who had accompanied him on hunting trips and had volunteered as a speaker for Focus on the Family for three years before his election to Congress.

But Dobson's team remained on the back bench when Congress opened its session in 1995. Speaker of the House Newt Gingrich and Majority Leader Dick Armey were in command. Gingrich, a former history professor at West Georgia College, was a fervent conservative, but he catered to Christian-right demands only when it served his personal ambition. Dick Armey, a gruff former economics professor at North Texas State, was also extremely conservative, but his interests lay in privatization schemes and deregulation, not in moral crusades. Dobson viewed the two Republican leaders as obstacles, if not as enemies, and quietly committed himself to their ouster, plotting with his followers in the House.

The ten-point "Contract for America" that Gingrich and Armey drafted upon entering Congress was a right-wing wish list, from term limits and denying welfare to teen mothers to drastically expanding the criteria for imposing the death penalty. But its authors pointedly omitted mention of Christian-right hobgoblins such as abortion and homosexuality. From his Colorado Springs mountain kingdom, Dobson looked on the scene of Republican triumph in the Congress, after forty years in the wilderness, with displeasure. "He'd made encouraging promises," Dobson grumbled in 1995, "but it became obvious to me Newt Gingrich wasn't going to follow through."

During the 1996 presidential campaign, Dobson began to strong-arm the Republican leadership. Leading up to the campaign, Colin Powell, chairman of the Pentagon's Joint Chiefs of Staff and a self-described moderate Republican, polled highest among potential Republican candidates. When some conservatives advanced the notion of Powell as the GOP's most viable presidential nominee, Dobson moved to intimidate and silence the general's boosters, fearing destruction of the party's anti-abortion faction. Among Powell's fans was the Francis Schaeffer acolyte Jack Kemp, who called him "Republican on almost every issue." Neoconservative former education secretary William Bennett repeatedly praised Powell on the pages of the *National Review*, and *Weekly Standard* editor William Kristol argued in an editorial that Powell was the only figure who could defeat the increasingly popular Bill Clinton. Already annoyed by the swell of movement support for the pro-choice Powell, Dobson was furious when Christian Coalition president Ralph Reed refused to condemn Powell's possible candidacy during his appearance on *This Week with David Brinkley*.

Immediately, Dobson faxed a five-page letter to Reed accusing him of unholy motives. "Is power the motivator of the great crusade?" Dobson asked the fresh-faced operator. "If so, it will sour and turn to bile in your mouth . . . This posture may elevate your influence in Washington, but it is unfaithful to the principles we are duty-bound as Christians to defend." Bauer copied the letter and blasted it out to other Powell-friendly conservatives, including Bennett, whom Dobson baselessly accused of being "pro-abortion." Shaken by Dobson's jeremiad, Reed hastily composed a letter suggesting that attacks from the Christian right would only provoke Powell into running. The situation "required a delicate balancing act," Reed insisted.

After halting Powell, Dobson moved to stifle the ambitions of Senator Bob Dole, a Republican moderate from Kansas who won the party's nomination. Summoned to a meeting with Dobson and his Washington lobbyist, Gary Bauer, Dole was forced to sit through a litany of Christian-right demands. Dobson and Bauer insisted that their constituents had delivered the Congress to the party in 1994 and would deliver Dole the presidency if he would give them a direct hand in crafting his domestic agenda. The meeting lasted three hours before Dole, who had been the Senate majority leader, his party vice presidential candidate, and chairman of the Republican National Committee, stormed out of the meeting. Unaccustomed to being lectured and threatened, Dole had had enough. Dobson, for his part, was indignant. He promptly transferred his support from Dole to his longtime friend Howard Phillips, a far-right stalwart running under the banner of the theocratic U.S. Taxpayers Party.

Even among obscure minority party candidates for president, Phillips was among the most extreme in recent history. Reflecting on his ideological formation in 2005, he told journalist Michelle Goldberg that R. J. "Rushdoony had a tremendous impact on [my] thinking." Phillip's newly formed U.S. Taxpayers Party endorsed Rushdoony's call for executing homosexuals and doctors who performed abortions, urged stripping AIDS patients of basic civil rights, and supported the panacea of returning the United States to the gold standard.

With its radical platform, Phillips's party became a natural vehicle for domestic terrorists, militiamen, and assorted others from the dregs of society. In 1995, only months before Dobson endorsed Phillips for president, the leader of a domestic terrorist group called Missionaries to the Preborn, Matthew Trewhella, addressed the U.S. Taxpayers Party's national convention: "This Christmas I want you to do the most loving thing and I want you to buy each of your children an SKS rifle and 500 rounds of ammunition."

Dobson's endorsement of Phillips had no noticeable impact on the outcome of the 1996 election. Phillips won 184,820 votes, or 0.2 percent of the total cast. Dole lost by nine percentage points to Clinton. Dobson's influence was felt only by its absence within the Republican base.

When Clinton returned to the White House for a second term, Dobson redoubled his efforts against the Republican leadership, particularly in undermining Newt Gingrich, whom conservatives within the House Republican Conference and outside it had come to regard as chronically unreliable because of deals he had made with Clinton, despite his shutting down the federal government twice. Dobson and DeLay agreed that Gingrich lacked not only the lust for confrontation that they sought in a party leader but also the moral qualities to be "a friend of The Family." Referring to the Speaker, DeLay later wrote, "Men with such secrets are not likely to sound a high moral tone at a moment of national crisis." Throughout his career in public life, Gingrich brushed off concerns about his moral fitness as mere distractions, reflecting to journalist Gail Sheehy, "I think you can write a psychological profile of me that says I found a way to immerse my insecurities in a cause large enough to justify whatever I wanted it to."

Newt Gingrich was born Newt McPherson to teenaged parents. Gingrich's mother divorced his father and married a Marine officer, who adopted him and throughout his childhood savagely beat him and his mother. (Gingrich's half-sister, Candace, became a lesbian activist. At the moment Newt became Speaker, she became the Human Rights Campaign's National Coming Out Project Spokesperson.) As a young man, Gingrich, fascinated with zoos and dinosaurs, longed for an illustrious career in academia. He wound up teaching history and environmental studies at West Georgia College.

Gingrich grew his hair long, emulating the style of the counterculture that he secretly yearned to join. In 1974, as the Vietnam War drew to a close, the ambitious draft dodger entered politics, attempting to win a congressional seat in a suburban Atlanta district populated by conservative whites who fled the city when its public institutions and neighborhoods were desegregated. Appealing to the backlash sensibility of these voters, Gingrich declared the "Great Society countercultural model" his nemesis and their enemy.

Initially, Gingrich proved a lackluster politician, losing his first bid for the House. His campaign scheduler offered a candid assessment of the candidate's failures: "We would have won if we could have kept him out of the office and screwing [a young campaign staffer] on his desk." Gingrich was married at the time to his former high school geometry teacher, Jackie Battley, seven years his senior, whom he married when he was nineteen years old. Soon after his first extramarital tryst, Gingrich became involved with another woman, Ann Manning, who was also married. Manning said of her encounters with Gingrich, "We had oral sex. He prefers that modus operandi because then he can say, 'I never slept with her.'"

In 1978, Gingrich was finally elected to the House of Representatives. A year earlier, he had divorced Battley, serving her papers while she lay in bed recovering from cancer surgery. "She wasn't pretty enough to be first lady," he later remarked of his ex-wife. Gingrich refused to pay alimony or offer child support for his two children, forcing Battley's church to take up a collection for her. In 1981, he married the mistress he had left her for, Marianne Ginther.

Within the Congress, Gingrich immediately fell under the influence of the Republican whip, Dick Cheney. Cheney, who had been President Gerald Ford's White House chief of staff and was granted deference among House Republicans, acted as the hidden hand promoting Gingrich's rise. Gingrich's staff soon ginned up a whisper campaign falsely accusing Speaker of the House Tom Foley, a Democrat, of being a closet homosexual. Gingrich stoked yet another manufactured scandal over some House members' supposed abuse of their credit union, and this attack inadvertently led to the resignation of several Republicans and also tainted the House as a whole as corrupt. Gingrich was willing to sacrifice even close allies in his own party to advance his cause and ambition. The bodies of others were rungs on his ladder.

When President George H. W. Bush appointed Cheney secretary of defense, Gingrich, his secret protégé, filled his job as the House whip. With Clinton's reelection, however, Speaker Gingrich's career reached its nadir. When his national approval rating plummeted to 28 percent, he devoted his last reserves of political capital to press for Clinton's impeachment. On cable news shows, he accused Clinton of felony perjury for his convoluted explanation of his affair with Monica Lewinsky. But Gingrich's leading role in the witch hunt compounded his private problems. Away from the klieg lights, Gingrich was embroiled in yet another affair, this time with Calista Bisek, a young blonde staffer twenty-three years his junior who he had arranged to be put on the House payroll. The wild mood swings that had always characterized Gingrich's behavior intensified. Staffers discovered the Speaker crying at his desk.

Unknown to Gingrich, a cabal of Republicans led by DeLay and Largent were conspiring to force his resignation. They had the blessing of Dobson, who envisioned his hunting buddy Largent as the next majority leader. During a meeting in Largent's office in the summer of 1997, the group of twenty congressional "rebels" hatched a plan to confront Gingrich with an offer they thought he could not refuse: Step aside or face certain defeat in a vote of no confidence in the House Republican Conference. At the last moment, however, the rebels lost the support of Armey as soon as he realized he was not their choice to succeed Gingrich. Armey dispatched his chief of staff to alert Gingrich to the plot against him, effectively halting the coup in its tracks. Gingrich emerged severely weakened, but for the moment his position appeared secure.

Dobson remained determined to dislodge Gingrich from his post. At a February 1998 meeting of the Council for National Policy (CNP), Dobson sought to mobilize the Christian right for another coup attempt. The CNP is a highly secretive group that brings together top right-wing activists with conservative moneymen to shape political strategy. Its membership lists are never disclosed, and its meetings are strictly off-the-record. But Dobson's speech to the CNP resounded beyond the walls of the Phoenix hotel where it was delivered. And although he did not address Gingrich by name, Dobson's audience clearly recognized his target.

After an introduction by Elsa Prince, the kindly mother of Black-water founder Erik and widow of Focus on the Family financial angel Edgar, whom Dobson had eulogized at his funeral three years before, Dobson appeared at the podium. He immediately launched into a jeremiad. The Republicans "are so intimidated. They are so pinned down," he moaned. Then he threatened to carry out the political equivalent of a suicide bombing:

> Does the Republican Party want our votes—no strings attached—to court us every two years, and then to say, "Don't call me. I'll call you?" Dobson asked. And not to care about the moral law of the universe? Is that what they want? Is that what the plan is? Is that the way the system works? And if so, is it going to stay that way? Is this the way it's going to be? If it is, I'm gone, and if I go—I'm not trying to threaten anybody because I don't influence the world—but if I go, I will do everything I can to take as many people with me as possible.

A month later, Dobson summoned twenty-five House Republicans for a meeting in the Capitol basement. There he restated his threats, pledging to bolt from the GOP unless Congress acceded to his far-reaching demands, from eliminating the National Endowment for the Arts to defunding Planned Parenthood. Dobson's tone was so severe that he reduced the wife of one congressman to tears. Armey confronted Dobson, accusing him of "whining and complaining" as well as knowing "nothing about the legislative process." Dobson retaliated by directing another failed coup attempt, this time pitting Largent against Armey. Focus on the Family mobilized its members by informing them falsely that Armey was a paid consultant to the ACLU. The majority leader later whimpered, "I was never so wrongfully and viciously attacked in all my eighteen years in Washington as I was by the Christian leaders."

As midterm elections approached, Gingrich advanced impeaching the president as his party's unifying campaign theme. Armey lent the Speaker his full-throated support. "If I were in the President's place I would not have gotten a chance to resign," Armey told a reporter at the time. "I would be lying in a pool of my own blood, hearing Mrs. Armey standing over me saying, 'How do I reload this damn thing?'" But the strategy backfired, resulting in the loss of five Republican House seats—the worst midterm-election defeat in sixty-four years for a party that did not control the White House. Gingrich promptly resigned from Congress. The intimate knowledge that other House Republican leaders had of his affair had sealed his fate.

Gingrich now turned to matters of the heart, dumping his second wife, Ginther, as soon as he quit Congress. He announced his intention to divorce her just as he had done with Battley—while she was lying in a hospital bed, immobilized after a major medical procedure. (Ginther's appendix had ruptured). He never bothered to tell his wife in person that he was leaving her for another woman. He simply called her on the phone, delivered the news, and hung up. Gingrich's curious predilection for recovery room breakups suggested that his fear of confrontation ran deeper than even DeLay suspected.

In the political wilderness, Gingrich bided his time, waiting for the right moment to reenter the fray. He cooled his heels at the neoconservative American Enterprise Institute, churning out op-ed articles and speeches battering away at the neocon punching bag, the State Department. He also found the time to author a trilogy of "alternative" historical novels in which the Confederacy won the Civil War. Then as DeLay's ethical transgressions made his decline seem inevitable, Gingrich stepped back into the political spotlight.

During a November 2006 speech in New Hampshire, a key presidential primary state and requisite stop for White House hopefuls, Gingrich warned that "before we actually lose a city" to a terrorist attack, the government should consider limiting free speech. He complemented his brave stand against terrorism with a book-length appeal to the sentiments of the Christian right. In this manifesto, entitled *Rediscovering God in America*, Gingrich asserted America's status as a Christian nation. "There is no attack on American culture more deadly and more historically dishonest than the secular effort to drive God out of America's public life," he insisted.

Gingrich's renewed activity generated questions about whether he would try to run for president in 2008. For some in the conservative movement, however, Gingrich could never live down his serial philandering. Jeffrey Kuhner, editor of the right-wing Web magazine

Insight, neatly summarized the movement's mood. "Mr. Gingrich," Kuhner wrote in March 2007, "views women as little more than sex objects who are discarded like an empty Coke bottle when they fail to satisfy his near-limitless appetite." Kuhner concluded, "He is yesterday's man."

But for all his flaws, Gingrich remained a clever operator. He had a strategy to refurbish his image, if not resurrect his political career. And so in March 2007, Gingrich picked up his phone and dialed in to Focus on the Family. A producer promptly transferred him to a studio line, and the radio broadcast that he and Dobson had planned a month earlier during a meeting in Washington began.

Dobson led into the broadcast by reading portions of Gingrich's New Hampshire speech calling for restricting the rights guaranteed by the First Amendment. After this glowing introduction, Gingrich launched into an extended polemic about the threat of Islamic extremism and introduced a vague plan for splitting the FBI into two agencies, only one of which would "respect every civil liberty." Everything between the former Speaker and the broadcaster seemed to be going swimmingly. Then Dobson turned to Gingrich's marital history.

"Let me ask you about your family life," Dobson said. "You've been married three times under some circumstances that have disappointed your supporters. There are some questions of that era that remain unanswered with regard to an affair and maybe more than one." Dobson then asked his subject about the affair he had with Bisek while leading impeachment proceedings against Clinton. With that, Gingrich's volatile temper flared. "This is one of the things the left tries to do," he snapped at his host.

"The challenge I was faced with wasn't about judging Bill Clinton as a person," Gingrich continued. "I wasn't going to cast the first stone because I can't cast the first stone. Because I have in fact as every member of every jury of America has had weaknesses. And if that was the standard our whole system would collapse."

Gingrich's argument noticeably irritated Dobson. Dobson was convinced that at least *he* had the right to cast the first stone. He was a Nazarene, after all, and had been spiritually perfect since he was a toddler. Further, Gingrich's assertion that "every member of every jury of

America has had weaknesses" ran counter to Dobson's Manichaean vision of a struggle between secular humanists and pure-hearted Christian possessors of absolute truth. The more Gingrich defended himself, the more the host's tone sharpened.

"You answered that question in regard to Bill Clinton instead of referring to yourself," Dobson reminded Gingrich. "May I ask you to address it personally? I believe you to be a confessing Christian and you and I have prayed together, but when I heard you talk about this dark side of your life when we were in Washington, you spoke about it with a great deal of pain and anguish, but you didn't speak about repentance. Do you understand the meaning of repentance?"

With Dobson's questioning of Gingrich's faith, the sinner suddenly turned reflective. "They say when you're younger you want justice and when you're older you want mercy," Gingrich said. "I also believe there are things in my own life that I have turned to God and got on my knees and prayed to God and asked for forgiveness. I don't know how you could live with yourself without breaking down and trying to find some way to deal with your own weaknesses and to go to God about them."

Dobson seemed pleased by Gingrich's confession, and especially by the image of the sorry politician on his knees before the Lord. The depth of Gingrich's sincerity was beside the point. What mattered most was that Gingrich, like a modern-day Lazarus, had given Dobson the power to lift him out of darkness and depravity. Having given his host ultimate satisfaction, Gingrich was worthy to receive the good graces of Dobson's empire.

From his office in Lynchburg, Virginia, Jerry Falwell listened intently to Gingrich's confessional interview. He was richly satisfied by what he heard. "I was pleased to hear Mr. Gingrich state, 'I've gotten on my knees and sought God's forgiveness,'" Falwell said. "He has admitted his moral shortcomings to me, as well, in private conversations. And he has also told me that he has, in recent years, come to grips with his personal failures and sought God's forgiveness." That day, Falwell invited Gingrich to speak at the graduation ceremony of his Liberty University's senior class, a prominent forum for conservative political figures.

Two months later, Falwell was found slumped over his desk, dead at the age of seventy-three. Funeral arrangements for the legendary pastor were complicated by the arrest of a Liberty University student, Mark David Uhl, who had disclosed to a family member his plot to commit mass murder. The family of notorious Kansas pastor Fred Phelps, known for picketing soldiers' funerals with signs reading "Fag Troops" ("Military funerals are pagan orgies of idolatrous blasphemy," Phelps reasoned) had scheduled a protest outside Falwell's funeral. Uhl had assembled several bombs he planned to deploy against the Phelpses.

The young would-be terrorist, whose personal computer was discovered by investigators loaded with images of young people giving Nazi salutes, had honed his destructive techniques by attacking his former high school on prom night with a homemade teargas bomb. Afterward, he claimed righteous motives, boasting to a friend that he had "saved a lot of people from losing their virginity that night."

The dreary atmosphere that had consumed Liberty University's campus began to brighten at the school's commencement ceremony four days later. There, Gingrich issued a rousing call for graduates to honor the spirit of Falwell by confronting "the growing culture of radical secularism." The students, assembled before him on the field of Liberty's football stadium, responded with thunderous chants: "Jerry! Jerry!" Gingrich's sins seemed to evaporate with the rising euphoria he had incited.

In October 2007, as the Republican presidential primary season commenced in earnest, Dobson invited Gingrich to appear alongside the rest of the GOP presidential contenders at the Family Research Council's annual Value Voters Summit in Washington. Gingrich was rewarded with the final speaking slot of the conference. When he strode on stage, the crowd of 1,500 evangelical activists rose to their feet to salute their prodigal son.

At the podium, Gingrich read the results of a poll he commissioned that supposedly provided conclusive evidence of how out of touch "secular elites" were from average Americans. The poll consisted of a series of tilted questions and hyped answers packaged as bombshell revelations, such as the news flash that 93 percent of respondents "believe Al Qaeda poses a very serious threat for the United States." Seated at tables in front of the stage, several middle-aged women diligently wrote down this statistic and other important numbers on paper napkins.

Afterward, a line for Gingrich's signing of his book *Rediscovering God in America* snaked around the convention's exhibition hall for almost fifty yards. Young evangelicals approached the former Speaker in droves, posing beside him while their doting parents snapped pictures. Gingrich's presidential aspirations would remain a distant fantasy, but with Dobson's help, yesterday's man had become a sought-after novelty act.

Gingrich's instant and relatively easy redemption was not unique. He followed a long line of sinners, including serial killers such as Ted Bundy and David Berkowitz, forgiven and redeemed by Dobson simply because they had confessed their evil deeds and professed a commitment to evangelical religion. The sincerity of their tales was never questioned, even if, like Gingrich and Bundy, they had displayed established patterns of deception and cynicism throughout their lives. These reconstructed sinners were too useful to be doubted—useful both as poster children for the ravages of secular society and as charismatic fundraisers for the movement.

Dietrich Bonhoeffer, a German clergyman executed by the Nazis for publicly opposing Hitler and denouncing church leaders who acquiesced to his rule, had a phrase for this phenomenon. He called it "cheap grace." "Cheap grace means grace sold on the market like a cheapjack's wares," Bonhoeffer wrote in 1943 in his book *The Cost of Discipleship*. "The sacraments, the forgiveness of sin, and the consolations of religion are thrown away at cut-rate prices . . . In such a Church the world finds a cheap covering for its sins; no contrition is required, still less any real desire to be delivered from sin."

Unlike Gingrich, who sought absolution from sin through Dobson after his fall from power, Tom DeLay covered his sins with Dobson's "cheap grace" as soon as he entered Congress. Behind the scenes, Dobson was a major force fueling DeLay's rise to power, directing his grassroots troops to support his legislative initiatives, and shielding him from critics. Even when evidence surfaced that DeLay may have engaged in a pattern of illegal activities and consorted with sleazy lobbyists who had exploited Dobson for their own financial gain, the Focus on the Family leader remained a stalwart at DeLay's side.

CHAPTER 11

THE ADDICT AND THE ENABLER

On the eve of the House of Representatives vote on the impeachment of President Clinton, upon Newt Gingrich's sudden resignation as Speaker, after the debacle of the 1998 midterm elections, Republicans chose Bob Livingston, a congressman from Louisiana, as acting Speaker. Although Livingston was a conservative, he was a competent deal maker who privately opposed Clinton's impeachment. One month after Gingrich's departure, on December 20, 1998, Livingston resigned when porn publisher Larry Flynt threatened to release audiotapes of an adulterous relationship. Speaking on the House floor, Livingston said, "We are all pawns on the chessboard and we're playing our parts in a drama that is neither fiction nor unimportant." DeLay quietly cheered Livingston's political death. That same day, the House Republicans, whipped into line by DeLay, voted for impeachment. DeLay now was the ultimate power in the House.

The job of Speaker fell to Representative Dennis Hastert, a dull and dutiful politician and former high school wrestling coach from Illinois. Hastert was in reality little more than an extension of DeLay, who gave him his daily marching orders. With Hastert as his vassal, DeLay turned Congress into his fiefdom. He locked Democrats out of committee hearings and blocked them from amending bills involving more than three-quarters of legislative votes. On the wall of his office next to his Ten Commandments plaque, he hung a bullwhip, and he delighted in being referred to as "The Hammer." DeLay disciplined his troops in a way Gingrich never did, transforming the Republican

Congress into a lockstep machine whose function was to perpetuate his dream of creating a one-party state. The Congress became a plaything of DeLay's coercive personality.

"But while Gingrich was autocratic (answering to no one else)," former Nixon counsel John Dean wrote in his book *Conservatives Without Conscience,* "he was not dictatorial (imposing his will on others). Dictatorship in the House would not occur until DeLay held full sway."

Like many authoritarian leaders, Tom DeLay was raised in a climate of abuse and addiction. DeLay's father, Charlie Ray, was an oil wildcat who toiled in the petroleum fields of Texas and Venezuela. A Baptist who became the first in his family to break a long tradition of sobriety, Charlie Ray liked to knock back an entire fifth of Chivas Regal scotch after a hard day of work. The abuse he inflicted on young DeLay and his two brothers when he was drunk left them with physical and psychic scars.

"I pretty much raised myself. My parents didn't participate in much of what I did . . . I think I've been an adult all my life," DeLay confessed to *Washington Post* reporter Peter Perl. His profile on DeLay for the *Washington Post Magazine* in 2001 provides one of the clearest windows into the politician's conflicted background.

According to Perl, DeLay was expelled from Baylor University for alcohol-fueled hijinks. Upon election to the Texas state legislature, DeLay, a married man, moved with several single male legislators into a condo that they called "Macho Manor." With a taste for bawdy liquor-sodden bashes and rowdy sex with women other than his wife, DeLay earned the nickname "Hot Tub Tommy." His hard drinking intensified when he was elected to Congress in 1984. "I would stay out all night drinking till the bars closed," DeLay said. "I just did it, and then I got up sober and went to work."

DeLay's signature mark in the Texas legislature was his one-man crusade to allow the use of an ant-killing pesticide the EPA had banned. "People would stand in the back [of the Texas legislature] and chant: 'De-Lay, De-Lay,'" veteran Texas journalist Lou Dubose recalled. "He was not a good speaker and there was only one topic: deregulation." DeLay was obsessed with removing restrictions imposed by the Environmental Protection Agency (which he labeled "the

Gestapo") on use of the pesticides that he claimed would be a boon to the extermination business he owned. His sheer hatred of government was his platform for his campaign for the Congress.

If DeLay had not met Republican Representative Frank Wolf during his first year in Congress, he might have remained just another pro-business Republican—perhaps a slightly crankier, more obscure version of Dick Armey. But Wolf, a born-again Christian, hounded DeLay in the hallways of the Capitol, urging him time and again to see the video he said had changed his life—"Where's Dad?" starring James Dobson. This short film, Wolf told DeLay, had transformed him from a workaholic into a responsible Christian father who opposed abortion and homosexuality almost as fervently as he loved his children. Wolf buttonholed fellow Republican members and urged them to see it. He himself watched it repeatedly. Finally, DeLay gave in to Wolf's beseeching and followed him into a darkened room in the Capitol basement, where Wolf showed him the film.

DeLay claimed to be forever altered by "Where's Dad?" When Dobson stared into the camera and sang Harry Chapin's schmaltzy folk ballad "Cat's in the Cradle," DeLay broke down in tears. "I started crying because I had missed my daughter's whole childhood," he said. "It was awful. My daughter in third grade asked her mother 'if somebody adopted Daddy, because he was never around.'" The guilt that consumed DeLay became the impetus for his redemption. "Hot Tub Tommy" became submerged in a baptismal pool of born-again righteousness.

"It wasn't just being raised in a dysfunctional family, though," DeLay reflected in an interview published in Focus on the Family's political newsletter. "It also led me to Christ, which I am eternally grateful for—and Dr. Dobson had a big part to play in that. For the last 20 years I've been walking with Christ, and I think as I look back over my life, the Lord has had a major part in developing who Tom DeLay is . . . I'm a different person now."

But DeLay's born-again experience had only transformed his alcoholism into another addiction. "The convert maintains the same addictive thinking as before," University of Kansas professor of religious studies Robert Minor wrote of alcoholics who trade liquor for evangelical religion. "There's a similar level of intensity in their dependence upon religion as [in] their dependence upon the previous addiction. And the substitution will remain successful as long as the religion continues to produce a more fulfilling high than the substance or process they abandoned."

With his conversion, DeLay gained the loyalty of the evangelical grassroots. Writing in 2001, when DeLay's influence was at its zenith, Peter Perl observed that "DeLay's faith has solidified his political base and fundraising with the Christian Coalition and other religious and socially conservative groups. They love him, because DeLay's America would stop gun control, outlaw abortion, limit the rights of homosexuals, curb contraception, end the constitutional separation of church and state, and adopt the Ten Commandments as guiding principles for public schools."

But the bond between DeLay and the Christian right went beyond politics. DeLay's evangelical supporters derived profound emotional satisfaction from his reign over the House. He embodied their sensibility, proudly representing the culture of personal crisis that kept the movement knit together. The visceral connection between DeLay and his base lent his leadership style a dynamic quality that few House figures could replicate. As DeLay headed into a sea of scandal, the Christian-right leaders who revered him became his enablers.

"If we do not see the unconscious suffering of the average automatized person," Erich Fromm wrote in *Escape from Freedom*, "then we fail to see the danger that threatens our culture from its human basis: the readiness to accept any ideology and any leader, if only he promises excitement and offers a political structure and symbols which allegedly give meaning and order to an individual's life."

With moralists like Dobson by his side, DeLay seemed to believe he was insulated from accountability. He proceeded to tap the miracle-working powers of corporate lobbyists for piles of campaign cash. Together with anti-tax zealot Grover Norquist, who notoriously compared the federal income tax to "date rape" and the estate tax to "the Holocaust," DeLay created what his aides dubbed the "K Street Project" to corral powerful lobbying firms into the Republican machine. DeLay demanded that firms hire Republican lobbyists or be denied access to members of Congress. His harsh mandates forced firms to hire dozens of his former aides, who were referred to along the glass canyons of Washington's K Street as "graduates of the DeLay school."

DeLay's system of shaking down corporate cronies for massive campaign donations helped make possible sweeping Republican electoral victories in 2002 and 2004. "As Republicans control more and more K Street jobs," journalist Nicholas Confessore presciently wrote in 2003, "they will reap more and more K Street money, which will help them win larger and larger majorities on the Hill."

DeLay's K Street Project provided the fuel for an illegal redistricting scheme he implemented in Texas to enhance his power. During the 2002 Texas elections, DeLay tapped corporate funders from Enron to Phillip Morris for donations to the Texas GOP and laundered the money through his own political action committee. With the Texas Republicans' campaign war chest flush with corporate donations forbidden by state law, they seized a majority in the statehouse. Then DeLay's plan to redraw the thirty-two Texas congressional district lines to create more Republican districts and destroy Democratic ones, giving DeLay a bigger majority in the House, went into effect.

Fifty-one Democratic legislators fled the state, holing up in a motel in Oklahoma, to try preventing a vote on DeLay's plot, but, illegally, DeLay ordered the Department of Homeland Security's Air and Marine Interdiction and Coordination Center, in Riverside, California (used to track terrorist threats) to locate them and force them back to Texas. Redistricting passed with a narrow majority. The following day, millions of black and Latino citizens were removed from integrated districts that elected Democrats and reassigned into racially concentrated voting zones. DeLay achieved a kind of electoral ethnic cleansing in Texas. Longtime Democratic members of Congress, including conservatives such as Charlie Stenholm, stood no chance of winning in the new, homogeneously white, conservative districts to which they had been assigned. DeLay's project enabled the House Republicans to increase their narrow majority by five seats in the 2004 elections. The "permanent Republican majority" seemed more permanent than ever.

But back in Washington, DeLay's elaborate schemes had finally attracted scrutiny. The nearly neutered, Republican-run House Ethics Committee rebuked the majority leader in 2004 for his hijacking of

Homeland Security in the Texas redistricting war. Later that year the committee found DeLay culpable for soliciting donations from an energy corporation just before a bill that the corporation had lobbied for came up for a vote. Again the committee slapped DeLay on the wrist for attempting to bribe Representative Nick Smith to change his vote on a hotly contested Medicare bill—in the middle of the night and on the floor of the House, no less. In February 2005, DeLay got his retribution. The chairman of the House Ethics Committee, Joel Hefley, was unceremoniously removed and replaced by a reliable DeLay flunky. Speaker Hastert, DeLay's agent, executed the purge, adding two new members to the committee, Lamar Smith and Tom Cole, whose political action committees had given thousands of dollars to DeLay's legal defense fund.

That legal defense was needed because a scrappy Texas district attorney named Ronnie Earle had convened a series of grand juries to investigate DeLay's shady campaign finance methods. Through his investigation, Earle uncovered evidence of one of the largest influence-peddling scandals in American history. Jack Abramoff, a lobbyist and Republican activist whom DeLay had called "one of my closest and dearest friends," and his business partner, former DeLay aide Michael Scanlon, registered on the prosecutor's radar when one of their clients, a tribe called the Mississippi Choctaws, anxious about control of its casino, inexplicably donated $1,000 to DeLay's Texas redistricting scheme. The revelation of this donation led to a trail of e-mails disclosing a far-flung criminal syndicate that operated with impunity at the highest levels of the Republican Party's apparatus.

But the e-mail trail also led in a more unexpected direction: to the heart of the Christian right. Movement leaders from James Dobson to Pat Robertson had been enlisted, perhaps unwittingly, by Abramoff to help him lobby against casinos that infringed on his clients' territory. When the scheme came to light, Dobson and his wrathful minions directed their ire not at Abramoff's "dear friend" DeLay, but at the investigative journalists who helped expose it.

CHAPTER 12

CASINO JACK, THE FACE PAINTER, AND THE SAUSAGE KING

By 2007, Jack Abramoff was living in a prison cell, serving a sentence of five years and ten months at a minimum-security prison camp in Cumberland, Maryland. He had pled guilty to a host of crimes, including defrauding Indian tribes of millions of dollars, corrupting public officials, and using wire fraud in an attempt to take over SunCruz, a cruise business operated by the very late Konstantinos "Gus" Boulis. Twelve people, including a congressman, Representative Bob Ney, were convicted of crimes related to their collusion in Abramoff's scams. From prison, Abramoff was cooperating with federal investigators in their wide-ranging probe, fingering others.

Two months after quarreling with Abramoff over the terms of selling SunCruz for $23 million, Boulis was found shot dead in his car in Fort Lauderdale, Florida. He was murdered execution style, with a single gunshot wound to the head that suggested a professional hand in his killing. Abramoff's business partner, Adam Kidan, a Republican fundraiser, whom Boulis had stabbed with a pen during their dispute, was alleged to have paid $95,000 to one of three Mafia wiseguys arrested for killing Boulis—Anthony "Little Tony" Ferrari, James "Pudgy" Fiorillo, and Anthony "Big Tony" Moscatiello. The fee paid was marked for unspecified "security services." Abramoff was not implicated in the killing, although his prison term was reduced to the minimum under sentencing guidelines because he agreed cooperate in a federal investigation of it.

While hovering on the fringes of the criminal underworld, sometimes clad in a trademark black overcoat and black fedora, Abramoff maintained an inside track on Republican Washington. He was, for example, a glad-handing Bush "Pioneer" who raised more than $100,000 for George W. Bush's presidential election bids, and he visited the White House hundreds of times, where he conferred more than eighty times with Bush's chief political strategist and White House deputy chief of staff Karl Rove. (The Bush White House sought to keep Abramoff's visits secret and even went to court to prevent the records from being made public.)

Typically, after long days trolling the hallways of Republican power, Abramoff's lobbying continued into the night. He frequently wined and dined DeLay and other Republican congressmen and power brokers at his downtown Washington restaurant, Signatures, where he picked up the tab. He also entertained DeLay and others in one of the sports arena skyboxes he rented. And he generously took DeLay and three other congressmen on a golfing trip to Scotland. Their good times rolled with the tens of millions in casino cash that Abramoff received from Indian tribes and channeled through DeLay's U.S. Family Network, a conservative shell organization that described its mission as defending "moral fitness" in the public sphere.

Abramoff, like DeLay, had a strange penchant for bullying, apparent since his youth. Indeed, as long as Abramoff's acquaintances could remember, he had enjoyed hurting those he perceived as weaker than himself. Journalist and self-described former "nerdy soft kid" Jonathan Gold, a high school classmate of Abramoff's at Beverly Hills High, described him as an inveterate bully. "In my most notable instance, I was walking down the hall to history class, and he hip-checked me. . . . I went sailing down the stairs with my cello," Gold recalled. "He was laughing about it with his friends. I suspect he forgot about it five minutes later. I didn't."

Abramoff's business partner, Michael Scanlon, also exhibited the same sort of sadistic tendencies. Scanlon, self-described as a "graduate of the DeLay school," served as the majority leader's communications director for several years. At the height of impeachment proceedings against Bill Clinton, Scanlon emailed his colleagues to describe his fantasy of a Mafia-style execution of the president. "This whole thing about not kicking someone when they are down is BS," Scanlon wrote. "Not only do you kick him—you kick him until he passes out—then beat him over the head with a baseball bat—then roll him up in an old rug—and throw him off a cliff into the pounding surf below!!!!!"

Abramoff hired Scanlon from DeLay's staff, and together the dynamic duo courted Indian casino tribes, promising to lobby aggressively for relaxed gambling restrictions in exchange for whopping fees. While they ripped off the tribes for a total of $85 million, Abramoff and Scanlon gleefully mocked them as "mofos," "troglodytes," and "monkeys." Whenever a new payment rolled in, Abramoff and Scanlon celebrated like frat boys. "You iz da man!" Abramoff wrote to his business partner. "Do you hear me?! You da man!! How much $$ coming tomorrow? Did we get some more $$ in?"

But to the duo's dismay, other casino tribes had hired high-powered lobbyists of their own, such as Republican super-lawyer and current Mississippi Governor Haley Barbour. These tribes planned to build new casinos near those of the clients of Abramoff and Scanlon. So the duo concocted a daring scheme to exploit the grassroots power of the Christian right to push for new anti-gambling laws that would stifle competing casinos. "The wackos get their information through the Christian right, Christian radio, mail, the internet and telephone trees," Scanlon wrote Abramoff. "Simply put, we want to bring out the wackos to vote against something and make sure the rest of the public lets the whole thing slip past them."

To implement their scheme of manipulating "the wackos," Abramoff and Scanlon turned to evangelical super-operative Ralph Reed. Reed and Abramoff had a long and complicated history. When Abramoff chaired the College Republican National Committee in the early 1980s, Reed served as the organization's executive director. His mild manner and baby face masked his vicious streak. In the University of Georgia student newspaper, Reed boldly asserted his conservative values by attacking Mahatma Gandhi as the "Ninny of the 20th Century." His article cost him his job at the paper, not because of its controversial content, but because its infantile name-calling was entirely plagiarized from other sources.

Reed moved to Washington after school to join the Reagan Revolution, where he found Jesus in a phone booth. While hunched over the bar at an upscale pub in Washington, Reed suddenly felt the Holy Spirit beckoning him. That Holy Spirit "simply demanded that I come to Jesus," he recalled. He stumbled into the street in a drunken haze, searching for the closest phone. Finally finding one, he flipped through the Yellow Pages until he found the "churches" listings and signed up as a born-again Christian the following day. Or so his story goes.

In 1985, Reed helped organize mobs that shouted epithets at staff and women entering the Fleming Center for reproductive health in Raleigh, North Carolina, which dispensed birth control and performed abortions. He was arrested after rushing into the waiting room and avoided prosecution by signing a court statement promising not to harass people at the clinic again.

At a dinner for George H. W. Bush in 1989, Reed met the man who would become his political benefactor, the Reverend Pat Robertson. The son of Senator Willis Robertson, a Southern Democrat and patriarch of Virginia aristocracy, the young Robertson was once on the fast track to a brilliant political career. His father secured him a post in a champagne unit during the Korean conflict, sent him to the finest schools, and arranged a job for him on the Senate Appropriations Committee. But Robertson grew alienated from his imperious father, turning instead to his evangelical mother, who taught him to speak in tongues. He impregnated a Catholic woman from a working-class background, married her just weeks before their child was born, and then moved her to a black neighborhood in Brooklyn. But visions of Jesus Christ riveted Roberston's imagination, compelling him to leave his wife while she was eight months pregnant with their second child. As he departed to the Canadian woods to be closer to God, his wife excoriated him. "I'm a nurse," she said to him. "I recognize schizoid tendencies when I see them, and I think you're sick."

In Reed, Robertson recognized a kindred spirit. Once his campaign for the Republican presidential nomination sputtered out in failure, he hired Reed as executive director of the Christian Coalition, which became the largest political arm of the religious right. Reed conjured up the Christian Coalition with the advice of his old pal, Jack Abramoff, an Orthodox Jew. (In 2000, Abramoff wrote to Rabbi Daniel Lapin, who had long been on his payroll for lobbying duties, about his application to join the Cosmos Club in Washington, a distinguished private club. "Problem for me is that most prospective members have received awards and I have received none," Abramoff said in a September 15, 2000, e-mail. "I was wondering if you thought it possible that I could put that I have received an award from Toward Tradition with a sufficiently academic title, perhaps something like Scholar of Talmudic Studies?" It would "be even better if it were possible that I received these in years past, if you know what I mean." Lapin responded: "Let's organize your many prestigious awards so they're ready to 'hang on the wall.'")

Reed flourished as a political boss, using the Christian Coalition as a new kind of Tammany Hall. He described his methods as stealth and assassination. "I want to be invisible," he said in 1991. "I do guerilla warfare. I paint my face and travel at night. You don't know it's over until you're in a body bag."

By 1995, after the stunning Republican capture of the Congress, Reed's signal role in the Republican victories earned him a reputation as one of America's top political consultants. His boyish face was splashed on the cover of *Time* magazine that year, above a caption hailing him as "The Right Hand of God." But two years later, with the Christian Coalition under IRS investigation and Reed facing accusations of cronyism from the group's chief financial officer, he left under a cloud to start his own consulting firm, Century Strategies. The Christian Coalition never recovered from his financial mismanagement and collapsed as a national organization. Reed contacted Abramoff right away. "I need to start humping in corporate accounts," Reed told him the following year. "I'm counting on you to help me with some contacts."

Even though Abramoff apparently was never fond of Reed, he always viewed him as a useful tool. "I know you (we!) hate him [Reed], but it does give us good cover and patter to have him doing stuff," he wrote in a February 2002 e-mail to Scanlon. "Let's give him a list of things we want . . . and give him some chump change to get it done." Reed, who once called Indian casinos "a cancer on the American body politic" and who had organized protests against gambling, thus became Abramoff and Scanlon's liaison to the Christian right, enlisting evangelicals into a web of shadowy casino hustles that filled his bank account with nearly $4 million in "chump change."

Reed's first sleight of hand involved enticing religious-right leaders Tony Perkins, Jerry Falwell, and Pat Robertson to try blocking a 2001 bill in the Louisiana legislature loosening restrictions on riverboat casinos, which would have posed a competitive threat to Abramoff's clients, the Coushattas. At the time, Perkins was a right-wing Republican state representative hailed by Reed as the legislature's "anti-gambling leader." As Perkins lobbied his colleagues against the riverboat bill, he pushed Reed to pour money into an aggressive phone-banking campaign to rally conservative Christian voters.

Abramoff dumped a heap of "chump change" into Reed's war chest for PR efforts against his clients' rivals, the Jena Choctaws. The money supplemented the $10,000 in tribal gambling money that Abramoff funneled into Reed's 2001 campaign to become chairman of the Georgia Republican Party and the millions he deposited into Reed's personal account. Reed recruited Falwell to record a phone message against the bill and solicited the help of his former boss at the Christian Coalition, Pat Robertson, thanking him for his "leadership for our values." Like the answering of a prayer, tens of thousands of Louisiana Republicans suddenly were bombarded with the voice of God against vice, intoned by Robertson and Falwell.

On March 22, 2001, the bill was resoundingly defeated in the legislature. "You are the greatest!!!" an ecstatic Abramoff wrote Reed.

Miracle accomplished, Abramoff tapped Reed's services once again in January 2002, when his clients learned that then Louisiana governor Republican Mike Foster had approved a casino site for the Jena Choctaws. Following a battle plan devised by Scanlon (who inexplicably signed a memo outlining the plan "Mike 'The Sausage King' Scanlon"), Reed reenlisted his evangelical allies to rev up grassroots pressure on Gail Norton, then Bush's interior secretary, who had the final say on the Jena deal.

Reed first prompted Dobson to attack the Jenas' lobbyist, Haley Barbour, during a Focus on the Family broadcast. (Months later, in his 2002 campaign for governor, Barbour touted himself as "a five-point Calvinist" on Dobson's American Family Radio.)

"Let me know when Dobson hits him," Abramoff wrote Reed on February 6, 2002. "I want to savor it." That same day, he e-mailed Scanlon, "He [Dobson] is going to hit Haley by name! He is going to encourage people to call Norton and the WH [White House]. This is going to get fun."

Abramoff transferred more cash to Reed to blast Dobson's tirade against the Jena casino across Louisiana airwaves. Abramoff was confident that his Bush administration contacts would make sure all the right people heard Dobson's hit. "Dobson goes up on the radio next week!" he told Scanlon on February 20. "We'll play it in WH [the White House] and Interior." Abramoff's gamble paid off when word of the ad filtered through the tension-filled halls of the Interior Department. "[White House liaison] Doug [Domenech] came to me and said, 'Dobson's going to shut down our phone system,'" an unnamed former Interior Department official recounted to the *Washington Post*. "'He's going to go on the air and tell everyone who listens to Focus on the Family to call Interior to oppose the Jena compact.'"

But Abramoff's fun didn't stop there. Reed urged a Who's Who of the Christian right to lobby Norton against the Jena compact with a stream of breathless and threatening letters. On February 19, Perkins warned Norton that gambling leads to "crime, divorce, child abuse." American Family Association chairman Don Wildmon sent a lengthy missive to Norton filled with statistics on gambling's adverse social impact. Veteran anti-feminist leader Phyllis Schlafly sent another. Gary Bauer, Dobson's former protégé, now heading his own advocacy outfit, declared in a letter to Norton that the compact ran "contrary to President Bush's pro-family vision." Focus on the Family vice president Tom Minnery wrote Norton and White House Chief of Staff Andy Card to demand that they stop the deal. Dobson capped the mail blitz with his own letter against gambling expansion.

Despite the best efforts of Abramoff and the Christian soldiers Reed had recruited, Norton approved the Jena compact. Haley Barbour's clout proved to be greater. Soon, Louisiana's new governor, Democrat Kathleen Blanco, reversed the deal on the basis of her opposition to casino growth. Abramoff's mission accomplished thus became mission impossible. And his machinations were beginning to take an emotional toll. "I hate all the shit I'm into," he moaned to Scanlon in a February 2003 e-mail. "I need to be on the Caribbean with you!"

But Abramoff's ordeal turned out to be a blessing for most of its Christian-right players. Perkins had had a chance to prove his mettle in a national campaign, prompting his appointment the following year by Dobson as president of the Family Research Council. Dobson, for his part, had demonstrated his grassroots pull to the Bush White House, raising his visibility to Karl Rove and helping him increase his influence over the Bush administration's social agenda as the presidential election approached.

Of the Christian-right activists involved in the Abramoff scandal, only Reed was tainted. When the Senate Indian Affairs Committee released Abramoff's, Scanlon's and Reed's e-mails in late 2004, Reed was preparing the groundwork for a campaign to become lieutenant governor of Georgia, a stepping-stone on his planned path to higher office—governor, senator, and then even higher. But Reed was dogged with questions on the campaign trail about his business dealings with Abramoff. Reed went from denying that he had accepted gambling money to claiming unconvincingly that Abramoff had lied to him about the source of his fees.

In order to generate a strong turnout for a stump speech at a Georgia Christian Coalition meeting, Reed was reduced to paying off his dwindling band of "supporters" with cash and free hotel rooms. In the end, Reed's contorted answers were not enough to mollify Georgia's Republican voters. On election night, his dreams of political grandeur ended in a landslide defeat; he lost the primary by twelve points. His face once having appeared on the cover of *Time*, his fall from grace was steep. At the Georgia Republican Party convention in 2007, presidential candidate Mitt Romney greeted Reed, "Why, it's good to see Gary Bauer here."

When the full scope of the Abramoff casino scandal came to light, Jamie Dean, a young writer for Marvin Olasky's conservative evangelical news magazine *World*, published a devastating exposé of Reed's involvement. Olasky added his editorial voice to Dean's reporting, proclaiming on his blog that Reed "has shamed the evangelical community by providing evidence for the generally untrue stereotype that evangelicals are easily manipulated and that evangelical leaders are using moral issues to line their own pockets."

Whereas Reed's collusion with Abramoff was confirmed by documents subpoenaed by the Senate, Dobson's involvement remained murky. Senate documents showed a clear link between Reed and Dobson, but the connection between Dobson and Abramoff, if there was one, remained unknown. Acknowledging collusion with a disgraced casino lobbyist would have been suicidal among Dobson's followers. But there were also risks in Dobson's casting himself as a useful idiot in Abramoff's game. That would reveal the "pro-family" movement as just another gear in a sordid Republican political operation. Instead, Dobson denied any involvement at all, even claiming he had never been in contact with Reed, despite several Senate-subpoenaed e-mails that suggested he had.

"Now, as it happens," top Dobson flak Tom Minnery claimed on the February 17 edition of Focus on the Family, "we, Focus on the Family, were fighting this new Indian casino in Louisiana at the very same time. Not because Ralph Reed asked us. Not because Jack Abramoff asked us."

When Dean called Focus on the Family, hoping to clarify the nature of Dobson's involvement in the scandal, and reported that Focus had essentially stonewalled her, she incurred Dobson's wrath. In an angry letter to his supporters in April 2005, the Focus leader declared that Dean "added fuel to the fire of those on the left who welcomed any hint, however contrived, of impropriety at Focus on the Family." Warren Smith, an editor for *World*, told me that in response to Dean's factual reporting, Focus on the Family ordered its members to cancel their subscriptions, leading to the loss of thousands of readers. Within the authoritarian movement Dobson cultivated, dissent was forbidden and swiftly punished.

When I reported on Dobson's role in the Abramoff casino scandal for *The Nation*, Media Matters for America, and the *Huffington Post*, an ad hoc group called the Campaign to Defend the Constitution (Defcon) ran ads in Colorado Springs and Washington newspapers depicting Dobson, Reed, and Sheldon seated at a blackjack table across from

Abramoff. I joined Defcon at a press conference with members of the Colorado media who were drawing attention to Dobson's involvement in the scandal. Although I never accused Dobson of receiving money from Abramoff or having foreknowledge of his schemes, I raised the very same question *World* had asked: What did Dobson know and when did he know it?

Focus on the Family responded to Defcon's campaign by firing off a mass e-mail to its members that sounded a call to arms. "While this ad reads like an indictment against Dr. Dobson," the e-mail said of Defcon's commercial, "it is in reality a declaration of war against the entire pro-family movement." The letter went on to identify various evildoers behind Defcon: the former president of a "pro-abortion" group, "'religious left' leaders," "a homosexual pastor," and of course George Soros. All the enemies of the Family were finally gathered in one convenient place.

Within hours, my e-mail box was flooded with vitriolic messages from Focus on the Family followers. Two weeks later, the tide of angry e-mails rose to a total of nearly 7,000. These e-mails opened a window into the mentality of Dobson's followers. I read as many as I could, searching for signs of dissent within the movement or, at least, some degree of variety among the opinions of its members. I found none. Those who wrote to express their outrage at me often claimed to owe their entire lives—their very existence—to Dobson. He was the magic father who had ushered them through the wilderness to a sanctuary of order, certainty, and meaning. Any criticism of Dobson, even criticism with a factual basis, threatened the paper-thin shell of protection that kept his supporters' inner demons at bay.

Highlighting the view of Dobson as a deity, Albert Tremaine of Carpinteria, California, e-mailed me with the subject line "Your lies about St. Jim Dobson." "His focus is on helping families," Tremaine reminded me. "Why are you so determined to destroy America?"

Robert Ragle from Milford, Ohio, was so infuriated by Defcon's activities that he challenged me to a duel. "Please, come to Ohio and introduce yourself to me and I'll deal with you myself," Ragle wrote. "You 'people,' and I use that term loosely, should be sued, arrested, and shipped out of the country."

Yolanda Glatfelter of Stockton, California, warned me that unless Ragle got to me first, the sin of criticizing Dobson would be punished during the Second Coming. "Sometimes I am thinking if these ACLU or these liberal Democrats still beleive in God," Glatfelter mused in halting English. "Pres. Bush won the re-election bec. of the conservatives I wished they should opened up their eyes & their mind that there are signs that these world is about to end."

"The reasons why a person is bound to a magic helper are, in principle, the same that we have found at the root of the symbiotic [sadomasochistic] drives: an inability to stand alone and to fully express his own individual potentialities," Erich Fromm wrote in *Escape from Freedom*. The e-mails I received from Dobson's flock were perfect documents of the symbiosis of sadism (punishing evildoers and subversives who deserve no mercy) and masochism (bowing before a higher force) that authoritarian followers so often display.

Dobson weathered the Abramoff casino scandal, but not by establishing his innocence through documented evidence. Instead, he cast himself as the victim hero in an apocalyptic battle between good and evil. His followers reveled in the drama he had created for them, rushing to the trenches at his orders to defend him against the enemies of the movement. Although increased awareness of Dobson's machinations might have harmed him in the eyes of outsiders, his position at the helm of the Christian right was only strengthened.

Having survived the slings and arrows of critics, Dobson now mobilized his troops to defend Tom DeLay from calls for his resignation and criminal charges. But under DeLay's direction, the battle to save his career morphed into a grim passion play revolving around the fate of a clinically brain-dead woman in Florida.

CHAPTER 13

TALK TO HER

Terri Schiavo, a forty-one-year-old Florida woman, had been in a persistent vegetative state since 1990 when she suddenly lost consciousness as the result of an eating disorder. When Florida circuit court judge George Greer, a Republican, approved a petition in 2000 by her husband and legal guardian, Michael Schiavo, to have Terri's feeding tube removed, her case became a flashpoint of righteous rage for the Christian right.

Terri Schiavo's parents, the Schindlers, opposed their daughter's euthanasia and launched a public crusade. They first hired militant anti-abortion activist Randall Terry as their spokesman. Terry, a self-proclaimed Christian Reconstructionist and acolyte of Dominionist godfather Francis Schaeffer, helped marshal Christian militants to join the struggle to prolong Schiavo's life. This spokesman was soon joined by an order of maroon-robed Franciscan monks who kept a constant vigil outside Schiavo's hospice. "We pray that this modern-day crucifixion will not happen," one of the monks declared during a press conference.

When Judge Greer denied a final petition from the Schindlers in March 2005, DeLay thrust himself into the conflict. His speech at an emergency meeting of the Family Research Council, Dobson's lobbying arm, revealed his motives. "It is more than just Terri Schiavo," DeLay told his rapt audience. "I tell you, ladies and gentlemen, one thing God has brought to us is Terri Schiavo to elevate the visibility of what's going on in America."

DeLay then linked his struggle to save his own political life with the crusade to preserve the life of Schiavo. "This is exactly the kind of issue that's going on in America, that attacks against the conservative movement, against me and against many others." Attacking liberal financier George Soros and the "do-gooder organizations" he has funded, DeLay proclaimed, "That whole syndicate that they have going on right now is for one purpose and one purpose only, and that is to destroy the conservative movement. It is to destroy conservative leaders . . ."

In DeLay's version of the Schiavo passion play, the Republican Judge Greer and the liberal George Soros doubled as Pontius Pilate. DeLay, in the ultimate martyr's pose, cast himself as Christ-like: the real victim of a "modern-day crucifixion." Terri Schiavo's inert body became a political stage prop.

When DeLay and Senate Majority Leader Bill Frist (R-TN) summoned Congress back from its spring recess to vote on a special bill to save Schiavo's life, a revealing memo by an aide to Florida Republican Senator Mel Martinez who used to work for a DeLay-linked lobbying firm—a "graduate of the DeLay school"—was circulated among Republican senators. It read, "This is an important moral issue and the pro-life base will be excited that the Senate will be debating this important issue."

On March 21, 2005, more than two-thirds of the House voted for a special bill that would take the case out of the Florida court and transfer it to a U.S. district court. The Senate overwhelmingly approved in a voice vote. President Bush rushed back from his Crawford, Texas, ranch to the White House in order to sign it. "I tell you I won't feel good until that tube is put back in," said DeLay. But the special bill, unconstitutional as it was, was nullified by Judge Greer's final ruling.

DeLay's handling of end-of-life issues in his own family contrasted starkly with his obsession with preserving Schiavo's life. In 1988, DeLay's 65-year-old father, Charlie Ray, was left brain-dead by a tram accident in his backyard. DeLay and his mother promptly ordered doctors to remove Charlie Ray from the respirator that was keeping him alive. The chart by his hospital bed read, "Do not resuscitate." "Tom knew, we all knew, his father wouldn't have wanted to live that way," DeLay's mother told the *Los Angeles Times*.

DeLay, who had spent much of his tenure in Congress railing against trial lawyers who slap big business with "frivolous, parasitic lawsuits," joined his family in filing a wrongful-death suit against the distributor and maker of a part they blamed for the accident that killed Charlie Ray. The DeLays were eventually awarded $250,000 in an out-of-court settlement. Once the incident was over, DeLay withdrew himself from his family. According to Perl, he had not spoken to his mother or brothers since his father's death. A flack from DeLay's Capitol Hill office, Dan Allen, rejected accusations of his boss's contradictory behavior. "The situation faced by the congressman's family was entirely different than Terri Schiavo's," Allen said. "The only thing keeping her alive is the food and water we all need to survive. His father was on a ventilator and other machines to sustain him."

DeLay's Christian-right enablers also rushed to his defense, echoing the official line almost word-for-word. "Two different situations," Family Research Council President Tony Perkins insisted about DeLay's conflicted position on euthanasia. "With Terri Schiavo, there was no plug pulled, there was no respirator taken away from her."

Schiavo was removed from her feeding tube on March 15, 2005. When she died two weeks later, CT scans taken of her brain during an autopsy confirmed that she was totally brain-dead. The public, meanwhile, recoiled at the spectacle of the Republican Party's exploitation of Schiavo's pathetic predicament for dramatic effect. They increasingly saw the Republican Party and the Christian right as a single, merged entity.

Congress's public approval rating sank to 34 percent, lower than at any time since shortly after Republicans impeached President Bill Clinton. Meanwhile, 66 percent of respondents to a March 23 CBS News poll approved the removal of Schiavo's feeding tube. Only months after massive GOP victories in the 2004 elections, which Jerry Falwell had cheered as "a slam dunk," the right had set itself on an irreversible downward trajectory.

Fearing their marginalization by the Christian conservatives who increasingly dominated the GOP, libertarian conservatives such as Dick Armey voiced revulsion at the Schiavo spectacle. "Where in the hell did this Terri Schiavo thing come from? There's not a conservative, Constitution loving, separation-of-powers guy alive in the world that could have wanted that bill on the floor. That was pure, blatant pandering to James Dobson," Armey told reporter Ryan Sager.

He continued, "Dobson and his gang of thugs are real nasty bullies. I pray devoutly every day, but being a Christian is no excuse for being stupid."

DeLay and his Christian-right allies, however, appeared oblivious to the consequences of their exploitation of Terri Schiavo's death. They reasoned away the public's rejection of their crusade as further evidence of liberal media bias, the hidden hand of Soros, and the supposed hostility to Christianity in "the culture." The notion that the majority of good-hearted Middle Americans were not united with the far right in an ironclad bond would have complicated the pseudo-populist tone of the retaliatory campaign it planned against the federal judiciary. The persecution drama instantly morphed into an ugly plot for blood revenge.

■ ■ ■

In the immediate wake of Schiavo's death, Republican senators Sam Brownback and Richard Shelby introduced a bill called the Constitution Restoration Act. A version was promptly brought to the House floor by one of DeLay's closest allies, Representative James Sensenbrenner. One of the most radical pieces of legislation ever offered in modern times, it authorized Congress to impeach judges who failed to abide by "the standard of good behavior" supposedly required by the Constitution. Refusal to acknowledge "God as the sovereign source of law, liberty, or government," or reliance in any way on international law in their rulings, would also trigger impeachment. In effect, the bill would have turned judges' gavels into mere instruments of "The Hammer" and his Christian-right cadres.

"The judges need to be intimidated," DeLay declared.

The Constitution Restoration Act championed by the Republican leadership was authored during a 2004 gathering of leading theocrats. Its principal author, former Alabama Supreme Court Chief Justice Roy Moore, who was ousted for refusing a court order to remove a Ten Commandments monument from courthouse grounds, had been a star speaker at Christian Reconstructionist rallies. Coauthor Herb Titus, the founding dean of Pat Robertson's Regent University Law School, was fired when he refused to stop teaching R. J. Rushdoony alongside constitutional law. (Robertson correctly saw Titus as the key obstacle to Regent's American Bar Association accreditation). And Howard Phillips, who added his rhetorical flourishes to the bill, was an avowed acolyte of Rushdoony and a Dobson ally.

All three men appeared at the "Judicial War on Faith" conference, an April 2005 gathering in Washington where the Christian right and its Republican surrogates rallied support for the Constitution Restoration Act. Organized by Pastor Rick Scarborough, author of a book titled *In Defense of Mixing Church and State*, the conference brought to Washington the sort of ornery theocrats the Republican Party normally tried to keep in the closet. Congressional surrogates of the Christian right such as Senator Brownback politely—and perhaps wisely—refused invitations to speak. DeLay was only one of two sitting members of Congress to show his face at the conference, although he did so by satellite link-up from the Vatican, where he had junketed to attend the Pope's funeral.

With the movement's righteous rage at a fever pitch, the conference quickly degenerated into an orgy of violence-laden rhetoric. The 2004 presidential candidate of the Constitution Party (a theocratic offshoot of the U.S. Taxpayers Party), Michael Peroutka, called removal of Terri Schiavo's feeding tube "an act of terror in broad daylight aided and abetted by the police under the authority of the governor." Red-faced and sweating profusely, Peroutka shouted, "This was the very definition of state-sponsored terror!"

Edwin Vieira, a lawyer and author of *How to Dethrone the Imperial Judiciary*, went a step further, suggesting during a panel discussion that Soviet dictator Joseph Stalin offered the best method for reining in the Supreme Court. "He had a slogan," Vieira said, "and it worked very

well for him whenever he ran into difficulty: 'No man, no problem.'"
The complete Stalin quote is "Death solves all problems: no man, no
problem."

I attended this conference as a journalist. After listening to hours of
jeremiads against "judicial activism," I stepped outside the downtown
hotel, where I encountered a middle-aged man in a rumpled suit
whom I recognized as Michael Schwartz. Schwartz, a founder of the
Washington, DC chapter of Operation Rescue, had become the chief
of staff to Oklahoma Republican Senator Tom Coburn, a longtime
anti-condom activist elected to the Senate in 2004, despite (or perhaps
because of) his stated belief that abortion doctors should be executed.

Before I could introduce myself as a reporter, Schwartz turned to
me and another observer and announced with a crooked smile, "I'm
a radical! I'm a real extremist. I don't want to impeach judges. I want
to impale them!"

David Gibbs, a soft-spoken, pudgy-faced evangelical lawyer who
had filed appeal after appeal to keep the brain-dead Schiavo alive,
headlined a dinner banquet capping the conference's last day. With the
Washington press corps apparently gone for the day, conference goers
exuded a sense of liberation. Now they really let loose. As they ate dinner, many festooned themselves with "Hooray for DeLay" stickers on
their lapels and listened to Gibbs's lurid suggestion that Schiavo fell
into a persistent vegetative state as the result of "some form of strangulation or abuse at the hands of her husband, possibly."

As the audience let out a collective gasp, Gibbs proceeded to paint a
fantastic portrait of Schiavo in her hospital bed. "Terri Schiavo was as
alive as anyone you see sitting here," he said. "She liked my voice. It was
loud and deep and she would roll over and try to talk back." But after
Judge Greer "literally ordered her barbaric death," everything changed.

Gibbs described his visit to Schiavo's hospital room after her feeding tube had been removed. Schiavo lay in bed "with her eyes sunken
deep in her head . . . she was skeletal," Gibbs recounted. "Then she
turned to her mother suddenly, like she wanted to speak, and she just
started sobbing." By now, members of the audience were weeping.

With their passionate interest in Schiavo, Gibbs and his allies recalled Benino, the socially timid, emotionally stunted character from

Pedro Almodóvar's Oscar-winning 2002 film *Talk to Her*. A nurse at a hospital for the comatose, Benino became transfixed by Alicia, a beautiful young woman mentally incapacitated by a terrible accident. At home, Benino tended continuously to his sick mother and her constant demands, forfeiting any opportunity for social contact with the opposite sex. While alone with Alicia at the hospital, cooing words into her ear or bathing her naked, still body with a sponge, Benino experienced his first sense of intimacy with a woman. Of course, it was a fraudulent sensation—Alicia could not talk back to Benino or respond to his touch—but Benino convinced himself he was in love. Overwhelmed with passion, he penetrated the comatose woman and impregnated her, an act that resulted in his imprisonment. When Benino was released from prison, he learned that Alicia had emerged from her coma. Stalking her from a distance as she went through her daily routine, Benino was seized with fear of the living, breathing woman. From his terror grew an intense, all-consuming sense of loathing.

Like Alicia, Terri Schiavo was useful to the movement only as an inanimate prop. Only in her devivified state could they exploit her to embody their perceived persecution at the hands of secular-humanist tyrants. Although she could not respond to their greetings or receive their bedside prayers, Gibbs and his allies discussed Schiavo as they would have a sister, mother, or wife, referring to her simply as "Terri." As their grim passion play approached its conclusion, they seemed to believe their own fantasy: "Terri" was alive, but only they could hear her desperate pleas. Meanwhile, the movement heaped jealousy-tinged scorn on the only man who had shared real intimacy with her— her ex-husband, Michael, accusing him without evidence of beating her into a coma. In its exploitive, one-sided love affair with Schiavo, the movement displayed all the traits of what Erich Fromm called the "necrophilious character."

In his 1973 book *The Anatomy of Human Destructiveness*, Fromm analyzed the phenomenon of necrophilia, concluding that it extended beyond the traditional concept of erotic attraction to rotting flesh and also manifested itself in "malignant aggression . . . unalloyed from sex, in acts of the pure passion to destroy." The necrophilious character,

Fromm wrote, is passionately attracted "to all that is dead, decayed, putrid sickly . . . It is the passion to tear apart living structures."

Together with his research partner, Michael Maccoby, Fromm surveyed a diverse group of research subjects for necrophilious, "anti-life" tendencies. Across the board, Fromm detected a profound link between necrophilious character traits and right-wing ideology. "The study asked the respondents a number of questions that permitted correlating their political opinions to their character . . . " Fromm wrote. "In all of the samples, we found that anti-life tendencies were significantly correlated to political positions that supported increased military power and favored repression against dissenters."

Fromm identified necrophilious characters as among the most dangerous members of any society. "They are the haters, the racists, those in favor of war, bloodshed and destruction," he wrote. "They are dangerous not only if they are political leaders, but also as the potential cohorts for a dictatorial leader. They become the executioners, terrorists, torturers; without them no terror system could be set up. But the less intense necrophiles are also politically important; while they may not be among its first adherents, they are necessary for the existence of a terror regime because they form a solid basis, although not necessarily a majority, for it to gain power."

The link that Fromm detected between necrophilious destructiveness and radical right-wing ideology was particularly pronounced at the conclusion of the "Judicial War on Faith" conference, when participants launched spontaneously into imprecatory prayer, a disturbing ritual in which worshippers call upon God to murder the satanic enemy. Replacing Gibbs at the podium, a pastor asked all the men in the room to get down on the floor and pray. With no other choice, I moved my plastic upholstered chair aside, took to my hands and knees, and listened as plaintive voices rose all around me with vengeful maledictions against judicial evildoers.

One preacher piped up: "Father, we echo the words of the apostle Paul, because we know Judge Greer claims to be a Christian. So as the apostle Paul said in First Corinthians 5, in the name of our Lord Jesus Christ, when you are gathered together, with the power of our Lord

Jesus Christ, deliver such a one to Satan for the destruction of the flesh, that his spirit may be saved in the day of our Lord Jesus."

While the supine dinner guests prayed, a saccharine version of Pachelbel's "Canon" emanating from the player piano in the hotel lobby seeped through the banquet hall's open doors, suffusing the ceremony with a weird, dream-like atmosphere. When I finally dared to look up from the ground, I realized that my head was only inches from the posterior of William Dannemeyer, the former congressman who once issued a letter to his colleagues listing twenty-four people with some tangential connection to Bill Clinton who supposedly died "under other than natural circumstances."

As the conference attendees filed out of the banquet hall and into the humid, rain-flecked night, mostly silent except for the few who were still sobbing, they seemed prepared to do anything—absolutely anything—against judges. "I want to impale them!" as Michael Schwartz told me.

For weeks afterward, Judge Greer lived under police protection until the climate of violence cultivated by DeLay and the radical right dissipated. "This isn't Colombia. This isn't drug lords terrorizing the judiciary," Greer remarked with befuddlement. "It's America."

While Schiavo was interred, DeLay still hung on for his political life. In May 2005, with the Schiavo affair not even a distant memory, the American Conservative Union, the Family Research Council, and other conservative groups organized a massive "salute" to DeLay. A *Houston Chronicle* poll had just shown that the voters in DeLay's Sugar Land, Texas, congressional district had turned against their congressman. The majority leader's declining fortunes suggested that this "salute" was, in fact, a farewell party.

■ ■ ■

Nine hundred right-wingers appeared for the gala on May 12 at the Capitol Hilton, including most Republican members of Congress. Missing the event would have earned them the still-potent wrath of the "The Hammer" and his henchmen. At the event, DeLay was visibly moved by the show of support. As the ceremony got under way, he wiped a single tear from his eye. Then Brent Bozell, a bearded old conservative warhorse who, as president of the Media Research Council, lived off the notion of "liberal media bias," brought the crowd to its feet by pledging to defend DeLay from "this whole sorry inquisition."

By the time attendees of the "salute" to DeLay polished off their hammer-shaped desserts, however, hushed conversations about the majority leader's chances of evading prison time had begun. The tribute was more like a funeral with the departed able to hear his eulogies. Five months later, Earle indicted DeLay for criminal conspiracy and money laundering. DeLay was forced to resign his leadership post; his resignation from Congress was inevitable. The Christian right sought to arouse defiance, unleashing a blizzard of attack lines recycled from its crusade against Judge Greer. DeLay set the tone, designating the prosecutor "an unabashed partisan zealot."

Dobson emerged to accentuate the outrage. "Today's indictment of Majority Leader Tom DeLay bears all the signs of a trumped-up, political witch-hunt," he stated in a lengthy press release. "The extreme left has seized this chance to take a swipe at one of America's leading advocates of family values." The irony of conservatives attacking a prosecutor as a "zealot" and a member of the "extreme left" was lost on Dobson and his cadre. They were like Richard Nixon's last defenders in the Watergate scandal, blaming the law for the lawbreaker's plight.

DeLay's trial date was not set by the time this book was completed. But the looming encounter with justice weighed heavily on him. I met DeLay in July 2007, in a cavernous hallway inside Washington, DC's convention center, after he had just left Christians United for Israel's (CUFI) "Washington-Israel Summit," a massive gathering of evangelical Armageddon enthusiasts who had converged on Washington to lobby against a two-state solution to the Israel–Palestine crisis and the peace process. Earlier in the evening, when DeLay's smiling face flashed on a giant screen above the stage, the crowd of 4,000 erupted in boisterous cheers. DeLay was still wearing a broad smile when we crossed paths. "The second coming of Christ is everything that I'm living for," he told me. "And I hope the Rapture comes tomorrow."

When I asked DeLay about his legal troubles, he cast his struggle in apocalyptic terms. "Satan" is behind his prosecution, DeLay said, adding, "Satan is behind the left." His explanation was eerily similar to that offered by two others who turned to James Dobson for eternal absolution: the born-again mass murderers Bundy and Berkowitz. The key difference was that Bundy and Berkowitz, as a kind of born-again insanity defense, claimed Satan had wired them to kill. DeLay, by contrast, maintained his total innocence while accusing his prosecutor of satanic motives. DeLay's enablers, especially Dobson, supported his blameless attitude, encouraging him to view himself as a spiritually perfected being unfairly limited by the rules of secular devils. "Enabling thereby helps the addict remain in denial," as Robert Minor, the expert on religious addiction, wrote.

In the end the addict burned out, as addicts so often do. DeLay's enablers, meanwhile, had used him to grow stronger. Tony Perkins, appointed head of the Family Research Council after a failed and tumultuous political career, had managed to squeeze himself into the national spotlight through his close alliance with DeLay. With DeLay gone, Perkins, who was far more youthful and energetic than Dobson or most other leaders in the Christian right's pantheon, went searching for a new leader to tout, a new addict to enable.

CHAPTER 14

THE BAD COP

Tony Perkins seems like the very model of an evangelical Republican operative—what Ralph Reed might have been had he never fallen in with Jack Abramoff. In naming Perkins to its list of America's one hundred most influential conservatives in 2007, the British *Daily Telegraph* highlighted his personal qualities as critical assets: "Clean-cut, telegenic and highly articulate, he has a calm, unthreatening manner that makes charges of extremism difficult to level." Perkins puts his family values forward as his best credential to lead. When his wife, Lu-anda, gave birth to their sixth child, Perkins introduced the baby to his supporters in a mass e-mail as "Louisiana's newest pro-lifer."

As the president of the Family Research Council, the Washington lobbying arm of Focus on the Family and the most powerful of the movement's bastions inside the Beltway, Perkins finds his opinions routinely sought by major cable networks such as CNN and Fox News, and for the editorial pages of the country's most influential news-papers. His radio show, broadcast from a studio inside the Family Research Council's expansive offices in downtown Washington, is beamed to hundreds of Christian-themed radio stations across the country. Perhaps most important, Republican presidential hopefuls beseeched him for his support during the 2008 primaries.

A little-known former Louisiana state legislator named Woody Jenkins, publicly obscure but highly influential within the right wing, served as Perkins's mentor and carefully crafted his early career. "To Jenkins, Perkins was like a son, and the feeling was and is mutual," wrote his former staffer Christopher Tidmore. Jenkins, who lost a special election in 2008 to Democrat Don Cazayoux in a heavily Republican district, earned his influence in the conservative movement as the first executive director of the secretive Council for National Policy. The group later served as a vehicle for moving Perkins up through the right-wing ranks and into the nerve center of the Christian right's political apparatus.

"Ronald Reagan, both George Bushes, senators and cabinet members—you name it, almost anyone of consequence has been to speak before the Council," Jerry Falwell told journalist Craig Unger. "It is a group of four or five hundred of the biggest conservative guns in the country. It is the group that draws the battle lines. It is on the right what the Council on Foreign Relations is for the left."

■ ■ ■

The CNP had its roots in the sordid saga of T. Cullen Davis, a Texas oil billionaire who inspired the character of J. R. Ewing, the diabolical and swaggering anti-hero of the hit 1980s TV mini-series *Dallas*. Davis's name exploded into national headlines when he was first accused of hiring a hitman to kill his ex-wife and her family and then of personally attempting the job himself, murdering his step-daughter and his ex-wife's boyfriend, while paralyzing an innocent bystander and badly wounding his ex-wife in the process, according to his prosecutors. Two trials later, and after burning through three million dollars in legal fees to convince jurors that his former wife, a glitzy Dallas socialite, was a harlot and pathological liar, Davis emerged a free man.

Exhausted and anguished, Davis was impelled by his narrow escape from prison to his "escape from freedom." His savior was a local televangelist named James Robison, who was known as "God's angry man." Born to a rape victim who had tried and failed to abort him, Robison grew into a dark-visaged, draconian Pentecostal preacher who railed against gays and liberals with a degree of vitriol that even contemporaries such as Jerry Falwell could not match. When his anti-gay rhetoric provoked the cancellation of his television show in 1979, Robison submitted to an exorcism procedure that he credited with delivering him from the dark demons dragging his career downward. He claimed afterward to have gained the power to deliver others from the hosts of darkness. (His personal assistant was a young evangelical minister from Arkansas named Mike Huckabee.)

Bringing Davis to evangelical Christianity in 1980 was the preacher's first act of spiritual beneficence. Grateful for his deliverance, the born-again billionaire offered to donate to Robison's ministry the million-dollar collection of ivory, gold, and jade Asian religious artifacts that he and his ex-wife had purchased. Instead, Robison demanded that Davis destroy the objects in obedience to Biblical restrictions against idolatry. As Robison looked on ecstatically, Davis smashed his treasures and then threw the shards in a nearby lake. With several strokes of a sledge-hammer, Davis's sins (which almost certainly included the murder of a little girl and an innocent man), were expiated once and for all. Now, through the grace of the Reverend James Robison, he was anointed a member of the Family.

"My goal," Davis told reporters David Gates and Nikke Finke-Greenberg in 1983, "is to make it to heaven. I'll do anything that it takes to get there, and I'm not going to let anything stand in my way."

To pave his stairway to heaven, Davis devoted himself to right-wing causes. His money bankrolled some of the first major Christian-right rallies, including one where Republican presidential candidate Ronald Reagan famously told the crowd, "I know you can't endorse me, but I endorse you." But Davis's most significant contribution was the hundreds of thousands of dollars in seed money he plowed into the Council for National Policy, sewing a cash crop that enabled the incipient conservative movement to grow for many seasons.

Upon the Council for National Policy's founding in 1981, Woody Jenkins made a bold prediction to a *Newsweek* reporter: "One day before the end of this century, the Council will be so influential that no president, regardless of party or philosophy, will be able to ignore us or our concerns or shut us out of the highest levels of government." Jenkins's dream came true eighteen years later when Texas Governor George W. Bush appeared before the Council for National Policy to promise the appointment of exclusively anti-abortion judges to the high courts if he were elected. By this time, however, Jenkins had fallen from the national stage, having suffered a crushing loss in his bid for the Senate. It was up to his protégé, Tony Perkins, to fill his shoes. During Bush's second term, Perkins proved his mettle, ably mobilizing the evangelical grassroots in support of Bush's contentious appointments to the federal bench and Supreme Court.

In one of his most strident editorials written during this momentous period, published by the *Washington Post* in May 2005, on the eve of the Senate debate on President Bush's far-right judicial selections, Perkins laid out his vision of the coming apocalyptic battle over Bush's nominees between people of faith and Democrats determined to wage a "campaign against orthodox religious views." Only if the Senate voted for Bush's appointments, Perkins argued, would the judiciary eventually come to respect the law. "In their zeal to preserve an imperial judiciary," he wrote, "liberals have taken abuse of the confirmation process to a new low."

Time and again during his campaign to confirm Bush's judges, Perkins hit on the theme that the Democrats were out of step with the law. He played up his former career as a policeman to emphasize his authority. "A former police officer," his Family Research Council biography stated, "Mr. Perkins brings a unique perspective to the public policy process." But an incident from Perkins's past revealed his relativistic interpretation of the law—an episode that Perkins conspicuously omitted from his biography.

■ ■ ■

The long, hot summer of 1992 marked the climax of anti-abortion protests in Baton Rouge. Declaring a "Summer of Purpose," organizers from the militant Operation Rescue came to town with the intent of shutting down the city's Delta Women's Clinic—a longtime target of anti-abortion terrorists, who firebombed it in 1985. Inspired by the "direct-action" tactics advocated by Francis Schaeffer, Operation Rescue leader Randall Terry shepherded hundreds of shock troops from local fundamentalist churches onto clinic property, where they staged daily protest vigils, confronted patients in the clinic parking lot, and attempted on several occasions to attack the clinic.

At the time, Woody Jenkins operated a local television station called Woody Vision that served as a low-budget predecessor of the Fox News Channel. When the abortion wars of the 1990s spread to Louisiana, Jenkins's network became a de facto propaganda arm of the movement, determined to stop abortion by any means necessary. Jenkins dispatched Perkins as a reporter to cover the ongoing conflict outside Delta Women's Clinic.

Serving as Jenkins's top correspondent was part of Perkins's grooming as his political protégé. But for Perkins, who simultaneously worked as a reserve officer for the Baton Rouge Police Department, there was a stark conflict between his loyalty to his mentor and his sworn oath to uphold the law. As the protests outside Delta Women's Clinic intensified, so did the clash between Perkins's interests.

In the end, Perkins chose his conscience—and political career— over the law. According to Victor Sachse, owner of a classical record label in Baton Rouge who volunteered as a patient escort for Delta Women's Clinic during the protests, Perkins positioned himself and a camera crew from Woody Vision among the Operation Rescue demonstrators and focused on the supposed injustices visited on them by the Baton Rouge Police Force—his employer. Perkins's reporting was so consistently slanted and inflammatory, Sachse said, that the clinic demanded his removal from its grounds.

"Perkins never dealt with the fact that people were illegally trying to bar access to the clinic," Sachse told me. "He never talked about the fact that the protesters who were there, even when they weren't breaking the law by going onto the property, would yell at women entering the clinic. They would walk right in front of [these women] to intimidate them and do things like imitating the baby screaming out to the mom, 'Please don't murder me.' Perkins wasn't even trying to be objective, and we didn't see any reason to let him stay on clinic property."

The protest might have caused far worse damage to the clinic and the city's reputation were it not for the actions of Baton Rouge's newly appointed police chief, Greg Phares. On the advice of an officer he had dispatched to observe Operation Rescue protests in Buffalo, New York, Phares ordered the erection of a chain-link fence to separate anti-abortion forces from pro-choice counter-protesters who had also gathered outside the clinic. Phares called in sheriff's deputies and prison guards to shore up his ranks. Although anti-abortion activists bitterly attacked him in the media, some confessed grudging respect for his levelheaded handling of the situation. "Greg has done a yeoman's job with what he's had to work with," Richmond Odom, a lawyer for the anti-abortion protesters, told the *Baton Rouge Advocate* on April 10, 1994.

Perkins, however, was outspoken in his criticism, even violating departmental policy to write a commentary for a right-wing Christian publication denouncing the police department's tactics, according to the *Advocate*. When Perkins learned of plans for anti-abortion protesters to break violently through police lines and send waves of protesters onto clinic grounds, he kept silent rather than informing his superiors on the force. Instead, Perkins waited outside the clinic with his camera crew, poised to report on the action as it unfolded. Scores of anti-abortion protesters were arrested that day.

Perkins's actions infuriated the police department. He was immediately suspended, and Phares asked Perkins to surrender his reserve commission for six months. The disgraced lawman-turned-anti-abortion activist rushed to the media to blame Phares for his suspension. "I think he was green for the position," Perkins complained to the *Baton Rouge Advocate* in 1994. When his suspension ended, Perkins resigned.

Shed of his badge and uniform, Perkins jumped into the rough-and-tumble of Bayou country politics. His first experience came as the campaign manager of Jenkins's quixotic 1996 campaign for the U.S. Senate. Before facing off against a daughter of the Democratic Landrieu dynasty of New Orleans, Mary Landrieu, Jenkins had to vanquish several foes in the state's notorious "jungle primary." Notable among these rivals was David Duke, the former Ku Klux Klan leader who had nearly won election to the Louisiana governorship in 1990 and still maintained a substantial base of loyal supporters.

When Jenkins defeated Duke and moved on to the general election, he and Perkins hatched a plan to consolidate his conservative support. Under the table, Perkins paid Duke $82,500 for his phone banking list, which the candidate used to target voters with robo-calls on election day. In one of the closest elections in Louisiana history, Jenkins lost to Landrieu by two percentage points. When Jenkins contested the election, Perkins's surreptitious payment to Duke was exposed through an investigation conducted by the Federal Elections Commission, which fined the Jenkins campaign for attempting to cover it up. The FEC disclosed Perkins's signature on the check to Duke as Exhibit A in its case against the Jenkins campaign.

Even after the Duke imbroglio, Perkins continued to mingle on the fringes of the racist right, headlining a 2002 fundraiser for the Louisiana chapter of America's largest white-supremacist organization, the Council of Conservative Citizens (CofCC). Descended from the White Citizens' Councils that battled integration in the Jim Crow South, the CofCC is designated a "hate group" by the Southern Poverty Law Center. In its "Statement of Principles," the CofCC declares, "We also oppose all efforts to mix the races of mankind, to promote non-white races over the European-American people through so-called 'affirmative action' and similar measures, to destroy or denigrate the European-American heritage, including the heritage of the Southern people, and to force the integration of the races."

The CofCC had hosted several conservative Republican legislators at its conferences, including former representative Bob Barr of Georgia and ex-senator Trent Lott of Mississippi. Lott, who spoke to the Council five times during his career in Congress, told its members during one appearance that they "stand for the right principles and the right philosophy."

In 2003, former Republican National Committee chairman and Mississippi Governor Haley Barbour took a photograph with revelers at the CofCC's "Blackhawk Rally," a fundraising event for whites-only "private academies" not unlike those that Jerry Falwell and other fundamentalist ministers founded decades earlier. In the subsequent hailstorm of media criticism after reporters discovered that the CofCC had posted photos of Barbour on its website, Barbour pointedly refused to demand that the group remove them. Although Barbour came from an influential old-line Mississippi family in Yazoo, his long lobbying career in Washington complicated his attempts to appear authentic. "In Mississippi, one of the biggest problems he had was they thought Barbour was a scalawag. So [the photos] didn't hurt him in Mississippi," CofCC national president Gordon Baum told me. "Nobody said, 'Oh my golly!'" Despite the CofCC photos becoming a campaign issue, or perhaps partly because of it, Barbour handily won reelection in 2003.

But mostly the Council has been a source of embarrassment to Republicans hoping to move their party beyond a race-baiting image. Former Reagan speechwriter and conservative pundit Peggy Noonan pithily declared that anyone involved with the CofCC "does not deserve to be in a leadership position in America."

When I asked Perkins at the Family Research Council's 2006 Value Voters Summit what he had said when he spoke to the CofCC, his discomfort was apparent. He cringed and quickly backpedaled until he disappeared into a mob of waiting reporters eager for his opinions on the upcoming midterm congressional elections. After I reported in 2005 on Perkins's purchase of David Duke's mailing list, the Family Research Council issued a statement that flatly dismissed my reporting as "false," claiming the "connection [to Duke] was not known to Mr. Perkins until 1999. Mr. Perkins," the statement added, "profoundly opposes the racial views of Mr. Duke and was profoundly grieved to learn that Duke was a party to the company that had done work for the 1996 campaign." Yet Perkins remained unable to explain how his signature wound up on the check to Duke, and he refuses to acknowledge that the FEC fined his former boss for attempting to cover up the Duke connection he brokered.

Yet Perkins's dealings with Duke became an issue when he declared his candidacy for the U.S. Senate in 2002. Though Perkins flatly denied that he had ever had anything to do with Duke, and denounced the ex-Klansman for good measure, his signature was on the document authorizing the purchase of Duke's list.

Despite endorsements from James Dobson and a host of nationally known conservative leaders, most of them CNP members, Perkins did not even finish as the top Republican in his state's Senate campaign. With his defeat among Republicans, Perkins had seemingly reached the end of his political lifeline, and under ordinary circumstances he would have faded into obscurity. But instead, his relationship with Dobson would enable him to wield even more influence over the Republican congressional leadership than he might have enjoyed had he been elected Louisiana's junior senator.

■ ■ ■

Just as Perkins conceded the election, Gary Bauer, the Family Research Council's longtime president, was forced out of his post. Members of the Council's board of directors were rankled by Bauer's hapless bid for the presidency in 2000, a crusade that he mounted against their advice, and one that was remembered better for the image of the candidate falling over backward off a stage while flipping pancakes than for any measurable benefits it brought to the Christian right. Meanwhile, rumors that Bauer engaged in an extramarital affair with his twenty-seven-year-old deputy campaign manager prompted two top staffers to quit his campaign in protest of his "inappropriate behavior." Dobson, who (according to reporters Thomas Edsall and Hanna Rosin) had joined the Family Research Council board members in ordering Bauer to stop meeting behind closed doors with the young staffer, was livid.

At a press conference in September 2000, Bauer denied the affair as a "rumor" and insisted that despite his "pro-family" campaign theme, he should not be held to a higher standard than any other politician. "I am not a minister," he lectured reporters. "I am not a pastor." Soon after, Bauer withdrew from the race and inexplicably endorsed Senator John McCain, a figure loathed by the conservative movement. Dobson was so infuriated by Bauer's move that he broke off all contact with his former friend. According to Dobson's official biographer Dale Buss, the two did not restore their working relationship until 2004.

With Bauer momentarily cast into the political wilderness, Dobson anointed Perkins the new Family Research Council president in 2002. Perkins's appointment to the influential role arrived at a fortuitous moment. He came to Washington in the immediate wake of 9/11, when the president enjoyed record approval ratings, when the Republicans controlled both House and Senate, and when everything seemed possible. The "war on terror" electrified the radical right's domestic agenda, enabling movement activists such as Perkins to press for ambitious initiatives to roll back abortion and civil rights for gays and minorities.

Born-again Watergate felon Charles Colson highlighted the radical right's attempt to intertwine the war on terror with the culture war. "Let's acknowledge that America's increasing decadence is giving aid and comfort to the enemy," Colson wrote in a 2002 editorial for the evangelical magazine *Christianity Today.* "When we tolerate trash on television, permit pornography to invade our homes via the internet, and allow babies to be killed at the point of birth, we are inflaming radical Islam." Colson's suggestion, as difficult as it was to accept at face value, was crystal clear: The United States needed to bring its laws governing morality in line with those of Islamic theocracies. Bin Laden's minions needed to be appeased.

When Bush ordered the invasion of Iraq in 2003, the White House deployed Colson to market the war to fellow evangelicals in the context of St. Augustine's Just War doctrine—a dubious exercise, considering Augustine's explicit rejection of preemptive, unilateral warfare. Meanwhile, the popular televangelist and former Southern Baptist Convention president Charles Stanley warned, in a February 2003 sermon, that those who opposed or disobeyed the U.S. government in its drive to war "will receive condemnation upon themselves" from God.

Even though the Christian right conducted its campaign to mobilize the conservative grassroots almost entirely within the insular realm of mega-churches, online journals, and radio airwaves, it affected public opinion dramatically. Evangelicals rallied to Bush's side with unmatched fervor, supporting the invasion and its eventually discredited justifications in a greater percentage than any other demographic group. The Christian-right leaders who orchestrated this PR push waited patiently for their reward, hoping that the appointment of far-right nominees to the federal bench and Supreme Court was not far off.

In a grudging show of respect for their Republican hosts, Christian-right leaders shrank into the shadows during the 2004 Republican National Convention. Instead of culture war cant, the halls of New York City's Madison Square Garden resounded with fervid chants of "Whatever it takes! Whatever it takes!" each time a speaker invoked the war. And that slogan could have applied equally to the parade of moderate Republicans—and the absence of conservatives—on the podium. Primetime speeches by figures such as New York mayor Rudy Giuliani, Senator John McCain, and California governor Arnold Schwarzenegger lent the convention a relatively moderate tone, while Christian-right figures were practically quarantined by party elites afraid of alienating independent voters.

Mormon publishing executive Sheri Dew was one of the meager sops the GOP tossed the Christian right during the convention. Dew, an unmarried forty-six-year-old woman who delivered the convention's opening invocation, had earned renown among evangelicals for her anti-gay invective, particularly her declaration that proponents of gay marriage were "lining up with Hitler."

Meanwhile, at the Plaza Hotel across the street from the convention, the Council for National Policy quietly plotted its second-term strategy. Inside the secret meeting, the movement's leading lights united behind a strategy to seize the reins of the judicial branch once and for all after the 2004 election. Perkins, who presided over the meeting, demonstrated his clout by arranging for the new Senate majority leader, Bill Frist, to speak.

Frist, a former brain surgeon and wealthy heir to a hospital chain fortune, emerged from the white-gloved, patrician tradition of Tennessee Republicanism, but he took a turn to the hard right in order to rise through the Republican ranks in Congress. Now, he represented the key to the radical right's court-packing plan. At the Plaza Hotel, Perkins and his fellow Council for National Policy members presented the grateful Frist with its "Thomas Jefferson Award." The only reporter able to gain access to the meeting, David Kirkpatrick of the *New York Times*, reported that Frist told his glowing hosts, "The destiny of the nation is on the shoulders of the conservative movement."

Then, in December 2004, one month after Bush won reelection, Frist donated $5,000 through his political action committee to Perkins's failed Senate campaign. Considering that the donation was made two years after Perkins's campaign had sputtered to a halt, and that Frist had endorsed Perkins's rival in the race, thus contributing to his defeat, the donation appeared as a tribute by which the majority leader ingratiated himself with the Christian right's point man on Capitol Hill. Perkins gladly accepted the money, recognizing that Frist would shepherd the president's most radical judicial nominees through the Senate.

Senate Democrats had confirmed nearly two hundred of Bush's nominees to the federal bench by the time Bush was reelected—more than in Reagan's first term, Bush's father's term, or Clinton's second term. Yet the Democrats refused a handful of especially radical nominees who reached the Senate floor for a vote. The filibuster, which requires a two-thirds majority of senators to override, enabled the Democrats to stop the confirmation of some judicial picks for years and also forced the withdrawal of other nominations.

The White House, however, devised a clever strategy to place the Democrats on the defensive: deliberately nominating a handful of black archconservatives to the federal bench. Expecting the Democrats to filibuster, the White House enlisted Perkins and a phalanx of right-wing movement surrogates to present these nominees to their followers as victims of "liberal racism." Perkins and his allies, whose history of racial politics had been something of an embarrassment, leapt at the opportunity.

BOLDLY AFFIRMING
UNCLE TOM

When James Dobson, Tony Perkins, and their movement allies mobilized for the coming battle over court appointments, they reminisced fondly about President George H. W. Bush's nomination of Clarence Thomas. By accusing his Democratic opponents of staging "the high tech lynching of an uppity black man," Thomas applied an effective racial patina to the right's persecution complex. After enduring damaging accusations of sexual harassment and pornography use, Thomas developed a vengeful anti-liberal streak that colored his draconian opinions on the Supreme Court. Having closely observed Thomas's career and recognized his utility, the movement s legal activists urged George W. Bush to nominate more conservative minorities to the federal bench. If and when Democrats opposed the nominees' confirmation, the movement planned to accuse them of every form of discrimination, from anti-Christian bigotry to elitism to simple racism. In doing so, they could once again obscure the Republican Party's agenda of bigotry.

An African American sharecropper's daughter named Janice Rogers-Brown, nominated to the 11th circuit federal court of appeals, became a spearhead of Bush's strategy. Appointed to California's Supreme Court by Republican governor Pete Wilson despite the state bar's warning that her "judicial opinions were insensitive to established precedents and improperly reflected [her] philosophical and personal views," Rogers-Brown had distinguished herself with frenzied anti-government tirades. "[W]e no longer find slavery abhorrent. We embrace it," she opined.

"We demand more. Big government is not just the opiate of the masses. It is the opiate—the drug of choice for multinational corporations and single moms; for regulated industries and rugged Midwestern farmers and militant senior citizens."

When Democrats filibustered Janice Rogers-Brown, responding to calls from the NAACP and the Black Congressional Caucus to block her confirmation, the movement spewed forth a flood of manufactured outrage. In an editorial for the *San Francisco Chronicle*, Deborah Saunders, a conservative columnist, attacked the Congressional Black Caucus. "Caucus members will hound any black person who escapes the liberal plantation," she wrote. An op-ed by the *Wall Street Journal* editorial board accused the Democrats of filibustering Rogers-Brown for being "too qualified—and black." And the executive director of the right-wing Committee on Justice, Sean Rushton, claimed that Democrats construed Brown as a "race-traitor, Uncle Tom sellout . . . because she is a conservative black woman."

Rogers-Brown's radicalism was matched, if not exceeded, by another of Bush's African American judicial picks, Claude Allen. Raised in inner-city Washington, DC, Allen was warned by his mother that he would ruin his career by becoming a Republican. He proved her wrong when, immediately after graduating from college, he joined the staff of Republican Senator Jesse Helms of North Carolina, a demagogue who had devoted his career to race-baiting, gay bashing, and various other moral crusades.

While toiling for the Helms machine as a press aide, Allen smeared his boss's Democratic opponent in his 1984 reelection campaign, former governor Jim Hunt, as a tool of "the queers," but he remained silent when Helms voted against making Martin Luther King Jr. Day a federal holiday. (He later claimed he had left work early in protest.) Allen befriended Clarence Thomas in 1991 and soon became the judge's protégé. "He would always say to make sure I conducted myself appropriately," Allen recalled. After a stint clerking for federal justice David Sentelle, another product of the Helms machine, Allen was pipelined into the administration of Virginia's right-wing Republican governor, Jim Gilmore. There, he collaborated with Christian-right allies to undermine abortion rights and sex education.

When Bush nominated Allen in 2003 to the 4th circuit federal court of appeals, covering the southeastern states, the most conservative jurisdiction in the country and a possible springboard to the Supreme Court, Senate Republicans pressed aggressively for his confirmation. Senator Orrin Hatch, the Utah Republican who helped shepherd Clarence Thomas through the confirmation process, asked Allen toward the end of his hearing what his grandfather, the first member of his family born out of slavery, would say about his nomination. Allen, stirred with emotion, sought to summon a response. Finally, he declared, "He would say, 'Keep serving our nation and giving back to those you have received from.'" Like Allen's past patrons, Helms and Gilmore, Bush was assured of his grateful nominee's loyalty.

Yet Senate Democrats filibustered Allen, forcing Bush to withdraw his nomination. When his second term began, Bush appointed Allen his chief domestic policy advisor, a plum post that paid as much as any other in the White House. Allen, acting in his role as government agent for the Christian right, immediately ordered the removal of information about condoms from the Centers for Disease Control's website. He then prohibited federal grant recipients from even discussing contraceptives unless they specifically described them as "not effective."

"I love you and appreciate you," James Dobson told Allen, a guest on his radio show in August 2005, "and it comes directly from my heart."

For all of Bush's talk of "compassionate conservatism," he nominated Charles Pickering Sr. to the federal bench. Pickering, who switched from the Democratic Party to the GOP to protest the Civil Rights Act of 1964, had collaborated during the late 1960s with the Mississippi Sovereignty Commission—his home state's anti-civil-rights secret police—in a plot against integration. (In 2002, Pickering's son, Charles Jr., dispatched campaign staffers to plumb for votes at a Council of Conservative Citizens meeting during his successful bid for Congress.) Pickering's history of racial animus made his nomination too contentious to pursue, and he was forced to withdraw.

To advance the right's campaign to confirm other filibustered nominees, Tony Perkins pointed to Pickering, who happened to be an evangelical Christian, as a victim of liberal religious bigotry. "It's almost as if there's a radical minority in the U.S. Senate that's saying this: 'You have to choose between your faith and public service,'" Perkins complained to Pickering during an April 2005 broadcast of his Family Research Council radio show. "Tony, that's exactly right," the former nominee responded. By Perkins and Pickering's logic, the burden of oppression had passed from racial minorities to pure-hearted evangelicals opposed to abortion and "the homosexual agenda."

The following week, Perkins initiated a campaign to pressure Senator Frist and the Republican leadership to obliterate opposition to Bush's judicial nominees by deploying the so-called "nuclear option," an arcane parliamentary maneuver that would have eliminated the two-hundred-year-old practice of the filibuster. Perkins made his case at a massive, nationally telecast rally dubbed "Justice Sunday" that he convened at a Kentucky mega-church. Besides Dobson, Colson, and the usual warriors of the Christian right, Perkins corralled Frist into appearing. A flier for Justice Sunday leveled the time-tested accusation of anti-Christian persecution against the liberal evildoers. "The filibuster was once abused to protect racial bias," the flier read, "and now it is being used against people of faith." This theme would dominate the rally, as Bush's blocked nominees were portrayed as helpless Christians thrown to ravenous liberal lions while a coliseum full of pointy-headed secular elites howled for their blood.

With Perkins emceeing in his typically dour style, the role of rabble-rouser fell to Dobson, who exclaimed, "The biggest Holocaust in world history came out of the Supreme Court" with the *Roe v. Wade* decision. Dobson seemed oblivious to the fact that he was speaking on the second night of the Jewish holiday Passover. On his radio show nearly two weeks earlier, Dobson offered a new variation on the theme of liberal anti-Christian bigotry, comparing the "black robed men" on the Supreme Court to "the men in white robes, the Ku Klux Klan."

Justice Sunday also featured a token Catholic, the gruff New York warhorse William Donohue, head of the nation's only "Catholic civil rights organization," the Catholic League. In the battle to confirm William Pryor, a far-right nominee who happened to be Catholic, Donohue was deployed to argue that the Democratic senators who filibustered him were motivated by nothing more than base anti-

Catholicism. "There isn't de jure discrimination against Catholics in the Senate," Donohue complained at the top of his lungs. "There is de facto discrimination. They've set the bar so high with the abortion issue, we can't get any real Catholics over it."

But for all his concern with anti-Catholicism, Donohue had no qualms about sharing the stage with Southern Baptist Theological Seminary president Dr. Albert Mohler. "As an evangelical, I believe that the Roman Catholic Church is a false church," Mohler declared during a 2000 TV interview. "It teaches a false gospel. And the Pope himself holds a false and unbiblical office." Donohue, who had raised feverish cries of protest against Democrats who made no such comments about Catholics, was silent about Mohler. In fact, the site of Justice Sunday, Highview Baptist Church, was Mohler's home church.

"We're fed up and we're on the same side," Donohue explained. "And if the secular left is worried, they should be worried."

The evening culminated with Frist's appearance on a giant screen hovering above the audience. Introduced as a "friend of The Family" by Perkins, Frist boldly endorsed the nuclear option. "I don't think it's radical to ask senators to vote," Frist opined. "Only in the United States Senate could it be considered a devastating option to allow a vote." His face then disappeared as Perkins rushed onstage to urge viewers to call their senators.

While Frist and the Republican leadership fell in line behind the Christian right, a coalition of moderate Republicans and centrist Democrats converged almost spontaneously against the nuclear option. Led by Republican John McCain and Democrat Joe Lieberman, who has since abandoned his party over its opposition to the war on Iraq, the so-called "Gang of 14" brokered a compromise that allowed Rogers-Brown, Pryor, and another of Bush's filibustered nominees, Priscilla Owen, to go to the floor for a vote. Two other nominees, William Owen and Henry Saad, were withdrawn. The deal represented a tactical victory for conservatives, allowing three of the most extreme judges ever nominated to the federal bench—those supposedly victimized most by liberal bigotry—to be confirmed. But when Dobson awoke from his dream of a euphoric total victory, he grew despondent.

"This one hit me personally harder than anything has coming out of Washington," he moaned during a May 2005 broadcast in the wake of the deal. "I literally went home and hugged Shirley [his wife] and pulled over the covers and went to bed."

Perkins, who joined Dobson by phone, chimed in with his own plaintive confession. "I'll tell you what—I wanted to cry," he admitted.

Then Dobson's expressions of sorrow gave way to his outsized persecution complex, as he claimed suddenly and without evidence that a liberal radio network wanted him assassinated. "Air America said they wish I would die and my son—and that they're praying I would die," he stammered. "And I would appreciate the prayers of God's people out there because I'm not Superman." Finally, the wounded Dobson summoned his army for one last charge into the teeth of the secular artillery. "The culture war's been going on for 25 years and this is the climax," he said. "This is the decisive battle. That's why we're all being hit."

The Gang of 14's compromise was followed by the confirmation as chief justice of the Supreme Court of John Roberts, a former Reagan functionary with a thin but doctrinaire conservative record—a stealth nominee—aided by a second, slightly less passionate Justice Sunday rally. Then Supreme Court Justice Sandra Day O'Connor suddenly resigned. With the court's moderate Republican swing vote gone and Bush poised to nominate a radical, Dobson thrust himself into what he believed was the "decisive battle" for civilization.

■ ■ ■

In October 2005, the White House gathered together Dobson and fifteen other members of the Arlington Group, an informal Christian-right outfit operating under the umbrella of the Council for National Policy, in a conference call about Bush's next nominee to the Supreme Court: Harriet Miers, Bush's White House counsel. Bush nominated Miers for two reasons: first, because Bush was urged to nominate a woman to replace O'Connor, just as his father was urged to replace Thurgood Marshall with a black man; and second, because Miers was an integral part of his personal Texas machine that followed him to

Washington, a crony who flattered the president by publicly proclaiming him "the most brilliant man" she had ever met.

But in the eyes of the Christian right, all that mattered was the nominee's culture war credentials. And Miers did not have any. Tony Perkins, one of the activists who took part in the Arlington Group conference call, avoided openly condemning Miers. However, he pointedly refused to hold a Justice Sunday III on her behalf. "To support Roberts was a step of faith," Perkins said at the time. "Miers is more a leap of faith."

Bush and his inner circle were convinced they could sway Dobson. They knew he had sympathized with serial killers such as Ted Bundy and David Berkowitz simply because they were born-again Christians. And they recognized that his steadfast support for the embattled House Majority Leader Tom DeLay stemmed from his faith-based affinity for the fellow evangelical. To win Dobson to Miers's side, Bush's political handlers believed they simply had to paint her as a true-blooded Christian conservative—"a friend of The Family."

And so the White House dispatched former Texas Supreme Court Justice Nathan Hecht, a fifty-five-year-old bachelor and Miers's erstwhile cocktail party date, to make the case to Dobson. Hecht assured Dobson that Miers had undergone a born-again experience that dramatically changed her worldview and that she would undoubtedly vote to overturn *Roe v. Wade*. Bush consigliere Karl Rove reportedly uttered the same magic words to Dobson in a follow-up call. The strategy worked like a charm.

Two days after Miers's nomination, Dobson hyped her to his radio audience as a "deeply committed Christian." Then he claimed to hold secret information about her background that he could not reveal but that justified his total confidence. "When you know some of the things I know," he assured his followers, "that I probably shouldn't know, that take me in this direction, you'll know why I've said with fear and trepidation I believe Harriet Miers will be a good justice . . . You will have to trust me on this one."

As other Christian-right leaders joined secular conservatives in fervent opposition to Miers, and late-night talk show hosts made light of the sixty-year-old nominee's lifelong unmarried status, entertaining

lurid rumors circulating on blogs that she was a lesbian, Miers withdrew her nomination. Then the previously steadfast Dobson underwent another magical conversion, suggesting that he had in fact
endorsed Miers through gritted teeth. "In recent days I have grown increasingly concerned about her conservative credentials," he claimed
to his listening audience on the day of the nominee's withdrawal.
"Based on what we now know about Miss Miers, it appears that we
would not have been able to support her candidacy."

Despite his efforts at damage control, Dobson's inexplicable shilling
for the White House threatened to undermine the dominant position
he occupied within the Christian right. He had always stressed independence as the most vital asset of his leadership, and on repeated occasions he insisted to his radio audience that "Focus on the Family is not a
political organization"—an incredible assertion but one Dobson's flock
accepted nonetheless. Now, some of his allies questioned his fitness to
lead. "Dobson didn't call here asking for any advice," one Family Research Council staffer told journalist Dan Gilgoff. "He just relied on the
word of Karl Rove. The only comment I have is complete puzzlement."

With the movement at odds with the White House and Dobson
on the defensive, Bush nominated Samuel Alito as Miers's replacement. Like John Roberts, Alito was a little-known and minor former
Reagan staffer and an undistinguished federal judge—another stealth
nominee—who seemed to hold conservative positions on the social
issues that mattered to the Christian right. He had made a few anti-
abortion statements throughout his career, but nothing inflammatory enough to excite the passions of the conservative base. Yet when
an element of racial animus surfaced from far back in Alito's past,
prompting Democratic members of the Senate Judiciary Committee
to question his integrity, the conservative movement—including
every faction under the umbrella of the Council for National Policy—
immediately reunited after the Miers debacle.

■ ■ ■

When Alito's alma mater, Princeton University, lifted its quota on black
students in the late 1960s and then began admitting women in 1969, a

group of disgruntled right-wing graduates formed the Concerned Alumni of Princeton to fight back. In 1983, the Concerned Alumni, which organized on campus as a whites-only "eating society," published in its journal, *Prospect*, an essay that exemplified the bigotry at the group's core. Titled "In Defense of Elitism," the essay fumed, "People nowadays just don't seem to know their place. Everywhere one turns blacks and hispanics [sic] are demanding jobs simply because they're black and hispanic, the physically handicapped are trying to gain equal representation in professional sports, and homosexuals are demanding that government vouchsafe them the right to bear children."

Alito, who graduated from Princeton in 1972, was a member of the Concerned Alumni, and he cited that fact on a 1985 job application to burnish his credentials. When his membership was revealed during the opening days of his confirmation hearing, Senator Edward M. Kennedy immediately demanded a subpoena for Concerned Alumni's records. Washington, DC, Delegate Eleanor Holmes Norton, a member of the Congressional Black Caucus, then denounced the nominee as "a special danger to people of color and women." With race thrust to the forefront of the debate, the right reverted again to its Clarence Thomas strategy, deploying a phalanx of African American conservatives to protect Alito behind the shield of blackness.

Project 21, a conservative front group that calls itself "a leading voice in the black community," spearheaded the counterattack. Although Project 21's black spokespeople lip-synched the right's talking points for cable news audiences, the group was masterminded by a white Republican operative named David Almasi from the office of the National Center for Public Policy Research, a think-tank that Jack Abramoff had used to illegally launder $1 million in Indian casino lobbying fees and bankroll a golfing trip for Tom DeLay. Almasi blew his cover in July 2004 when he decided to fill in for a Project 21 member who got a flat tire on his way to an appearance on C-SPAN. While introducing Almasi, the show's bemused host turned to him and stuttered, "Um . . . Project 21 . . . a program for conservative African Americans . . . you're not African American."

One month before Alito's confirmation hearing commenced, Project 21 sprung into action, issuing a press release announcing that the Congressional Black Caucus had "clearly aligned itself with the extreme liberals who share their contempt for those who would uphold the Constitution as it was envisioned by our Founding Fathers." Project 21 dispatched one of its members, Peter Kirsanow, a union-busting lawyer who also served on the U.S. Commission on Civil Rights, to testify in Alito's confirmation hearing to the judge's racial sensitivity. According to Kirsanow, in a column for the *National Review* published just before his testimony, there was "no factual or logical bases" for the Democrats' criticisms of Alito's record on civil rights.

But Kirsanow's defense of Alito conflicted with the negative view of Constitutional protections for minorities that he himself had displayed in the past. In the wake of 9/11, for instance, Kirsanow had shocked an audience of Arab Americans by warning them that if there is another terrorist attack in America "and they come from the same ethnic group that attacked the World Trade Center, you can forget about civil rights."

Charles Colson joined the chorus of Alito defenders with an unusual revision of civil rights history. Colson, who once burned a cross on the lawn of a black law partner in what he later described as a "prank," and who exploited resentment of forced school desegregation to win ethnic white votes for Richard Nixon, declared in a January 2006 radio commentary that Martin Luther King was "a great conservative. Were he alive today, I believe he would be in the vanguard of the pro-life movement and would be supporting Judge Alito." Colson's logic, remarkable as it was, was actually part of a premeditated Christian-right effort to link Alito to the legacy of King. This campaign culminated when Tony Perkins convened Justice Sunday III at a black church in inner-city Philadelphia.

The event featured a strange cast, beginning with Bishop Wellington Boone, an African American church leader and spokesman for the evangelical men's group known as the Promise Keepers. Perkins had recruited Boone to lend his rally a bold splash of color; however, the bishop had lost any credibility he might have enjoyed in the black community years before when he wrote, in his book *Breaking Through*, "We need to boldly affirm Uncle Tom. The black community needs to stop criticizing Uncle Tom. Uncle Tom is a role model." In the same tract, Boone declared, "I believe that slavery, and the understanding of it when you see it God's way, was redemptive."

Herb Lusk, another conservative black clergyman close to Perkins, joined Boone on stage to shout down the liberal hosts of darkness who opposed Alito. "Don't fool with the church because the church has buried many critics," Lusk thundered from his podium. "All the critics we have not buried, we're making funeral arrangements for!" Lusk, whose Greater Exodus Baptist Church played host to Justice Sunday III, was a former NFL tailback and lifelong Democrat who suddenly shifted his party allegiance to the GOP in 2002 when Republican Senator Rick Santorum guaranteed him $900,000 in faith-based federal grants.

Neither Boone nor Lusk expressed any qualms about appearing alongside Perkins, an associate of Bayou country white supremacists, or Jerry Falwell, the former segregationist who had once branded Martin Luther King Jr. as a Communist puppet. Although the 1954 *Brown v. Board of Education* decision striking down public school segregation prompted Falwell to join the conservative campaign to impeach Supreme Court Chief Justice Earl Warren, he now claimed that the *Roe v. Wade* decision sparked his activism—yet another historical revisionist.

"We were able to hold off Michael Moore, most of Hollywood, most of the national media, George Soros, and the Kennedys and other crowds who fought so fiercely against the reelection of George Bush," Falwell boomed before Justice Sunday III's mostly black audience. "And now, now we're looking at what we really started on 30 years ago—a reconstruction of a court system gone awry."

Behind Falwell, in a throne-like chair, sat Martin Luther King Jr.'s niece, Alveda King. Her appearance at Justice Sunday III represented a major publicity coup for Perkins and his allies, providing them the royal link they so desperately sought. Perkins played up King's participation for maximum dramatic effect, identifying her in a Family Research Council press release as "the daughter of slain civil rights leader A. D. King." As compelling as this biographical detail was, it was false: A. D. King drowned in a swimming pool.

Although Alveda King admired her father's fight for racial justice, her own crusade, kindled by the traumatic personal crises she endured, represented a rupture in her family's tradition of social justice. A self-described "post-abortive mother," King claimed to have undergone an "involuntary abortion" in the immediate wake of the *Roe v. Wade* decision, and then another one prompted by violent threats from the baby's father. Afterward, she became consumed by nightmares, eating disorders, and sexual dysfunctions. "I felt angry about both abortions, and very guilty about the abortion I chose to have," King recounted. "The guilt made me very ill."

King assuaged her searing sense of regret by embracing evangelical Christianity and its anti-abortion politics. Her ability to weave her father and uncle's lilting rhetoric into the Christian right's reactionary narrative earned her the recognition of movement leaders. "Oh, God, what would Martin Luther King Jr., who dreamed of having his children judged by the content of their characters [sic], do if he'd lived to see the contents of thousands of children's skulls emptied into the bottomless caverns of the abortionists pits?" King pleaded in a speech. By 1992, King had earned a sinecure at the Alexis de Tocqueville Institute, a right-wing think-tank funded by business interests and the tobacco industry, and was being ferried around the country as a paid speaker at Christian-right confabs. Like so many others belonging to the conservative culture of personal crisis, King traded in the moral glamour of her family's reputation for the lucre and emotional euphoria of culture war activism, medicating her anxiety along the way.

King's sermon at Justice Sunday III provided an emotional crescendo to the evening, which concluded with a heartfelt rendition of the civil rights anthem "We Shall Overcome." When the crowd rose from the pews to sing along with King, Falwell haltingly lifted himself from his chair and began to mouth the words. A look of discomfort washed across his face. Dobson and Perkins, who sat beside him throughout the rally, joined in with a similar lack of enthusiasm, as though they were reading a kidnapper's ransom letter against their will.

One of the reporters in attendance, Michelle Goldberg, reflected afterward, "The entire evening had a surreal, upside-down quality, as if history had been caught in a whirlpool and come back all jumbled." But by conferring the moral authority of the black church on a reactionary judicial nominee, while conveying the optical illusion of a link between the civil rights movement and the Christian right, Justice Sunday III fulfilled its aim.

The Senate confirmed Alito on January 31, 2006, on a narrow party-line vote. A month later, Alito personally thanked Dobson for mobilizing Focus on the Family's shock troops on his behalf. "My entire family and I hope that you and the Focus on the Family staff know how much we appreciate all that you have done," Alito wrote to Dobson. Dobson immediately took to the airwaves with news of Alito's gratitude, reading the letter aloud to his supporters as evidence of his own influence and the new justice's loyalty to the Christian right. In concluding his broadcast, Dobson asked his listeners to "please be in prayer that by the time that prohibition on abortion reaches the Supreme Court, there will be one more conservative justice sitting there."

Seated beside archconservatives Thomas, Scalia, and new Chief Justice John Roberts—the so-called Roberts Court—Alito formed the anchor of a radical judicial bloc that quickly and dramatically reversed decades of civil rights legislation. The court, in a 5–4 decision in June 2007, ruled that public schools could no longer integrate on the basis of race, essentially eviscerating the landmark *Brown v. Board of Education* decision. Clarence Thomas remarked bluntly in his majority opinion, "It is unclear whether increased interracial contact improves racial attitudes and relations."

Writing on behalf of the court's four dissenting members, Justice Stephen Breyer lashed out for seventy-seven pages at what he called a "radical" decision "that the court and the nation will come to regret." In a voice trembling with emotion, the normally dispassionate Breyer held forth for twenty minutes before a packed courtroom. "It is not often in the law that so few have so quickly changed so much," he said.

By the middle of Bush's second term, the president and the Republican Congress had managed to seat one of the most radical Supreme Courts in history and to confirm scores of right-wing ideologues to lifetime positions on the federal bench. This accomplishment will

probably be the most enduring legacy of the Republican majority that
dominated government between 2002 and 2006. However, as the Republican Congress sank deeper into bizarre personal scandals, the
euphoric mood that sprang from Alito's confirmation rapidly degenerated into bitter acrimony and outright embarrassment.

■ ■ ■

The saga of strange scandals that engulfed the Republican Party in
Bush's second term began to grow stranger in January 2006 when
Claude Allen informed Miers, who was back in her old post as White
House legal counsel, that he had been charged with a misdemeanor
in a credit card misunderstanding. The White House took him at his
word and even rewarded him with a seat next to First Lady Laura
Bush for Bush's State of the Union address. The following month,
however, Allen suddenly resigned, claiming he needed to spend time
with his family—a canned explanation that few believed. Finally, in
March, when Allen appeared in court, the reason why he had resigned was revealed.

After a grinding day of anti-condom activities, Allen liked to go
shopping. Typically, he would visit a department store such as Target
and purchase hundreds of dollars worth of electronic goods. After
loading those goods into his car, he would return to the store with his
receipts, fill a shopping cart with the same exact items he had just purchased, and return them, getting the refunded money back on his
credit card. Allen had repeated this scheme at least twenty-five times,
according to the police who arrested him after he was detained by
store security guards. Facing eighteen months in prison, Allen pleaded
guilty and was sentenced to two years' criminal probation, forty hours
of community service, and a $1,350 fine.

With tears streaming down his face, Allen claimed to his sentencing judge that his kleptomania was sparked by the stress of the "tumultuous time" after Hurricane Katrina. During the hurricane, as
impoverished, black residents of New Orleans died by the hundreds,
drowning and starving while the Bush administration stood by im-
potently, the White House delegated Allen to speak to the president's

sensitive side. "Just the mere fact you have pictures of the president on TV embracing grieving mothers, embracing pastors of churches that have been destroyed," Allen said on the tenth anniversary of the Million Man March, "that speaks about the personal character of our president, who is truly concerned about healing our nation." Now, as he groped for excuses for his stealing spree, the disgraced aide presented himself as a victim of the tragedy that engulfed New Orleans.

"Something did go very wrong," Allen wept to the judge. "I failed to restrain myself."

Presumably, most people who make $161,000 a year, as Allen did, do not battle the urge to steal items they could easily afford. But Allen was, by his own admission, afflicted by inner demons that he had tried to "restrain" for perhaps his entire adult life. During moments of stress, the temptation to sin gathered inside him until it finally exploded in ways he may have been unable to control. Only through the strict dictates of evangelical religion and the rigid control of his conservative overseers could Allen contain his urges. The masochistic tendency demonstrated by Allen suggested that more complex psychological factors than blind ambition fueled his attraction to right-wing moral crusades.

But like so many other social conservatives who turned to masochism as a form of self-medication, Allen discovered that he had merely transmuted his problems, not solved them. As Fromm wrote in *Escape from Freedom*, "The masochistic 'solution' is no more of a solution than neurotic manifestations ever are: the individual succeeds in eliminating the conspicuous suffering but not in removing the underlying conflict and the silent unhappiness . . . It springs from an unbearable situation, tends to overcome it, and leaves the individual caught in a new suffering."

■ ■ ■

Just as black movement figures such as Allen advanced their ambitions by endearing themselves to race-baiting white politicians, conservative women secured a special status within the movement by inveighing against the feminist legacy that made their careers possible. Seemingly

unaware of the irony of their cause, they blamed the smashing of traditional gender roles for inflicting the sexual traumas that led them to
seek out the fatherly protection of Jesus. Through Bush and the Republican Congress, the personal became political as the women of the
movement designed federally funded abstinence education programs
for a new generation of vulnerable young women.

CHAPTER 16

FEEDING BABY MONSTERS

For two days in October 2007, the entire field of Republican primary candidates paraded on stage before James Dobson, Tony Perkins, and thousands of their followers at the Family Research Council's annual Value Voters Summit. Mitt Romney, a one-time liberal Republican governor of Massachusetts, hailed the good works of Dobson on behalf of "The Family"; former Arkansas governor Mike Huckabee declared America has to import so many workers because "for the last 35 years we have aborted more than a million people who would have been in our workforce"; and Senator John McCain, still reviled by the movement, touted his crusading to help persecuted Christians around the globe.

Even John Cox, an unknown California businessman running for the GOP nomination, parachuted into the conference to flash his culture war credentials. Cox made certain to recount to every "value voter" he met that his father had conceived him by raping his mother. "She had no choice [but] to have me," he told me, "and so I am pro-life to the core of my being." By channeling the culture of personal crisis undergirding the Christian right, the long-shot Cox desperately hoped to somehow distinguish himself from his better-funded, well-established rivals.

On the summit's final evening, silver-haired couples clad in tuxedoes and sequined evening dresses shuffled into a hotel ballroom for "A Night to Honor James Dobson." In spite of the fact that the Dobson tribute was an annual affair, speakers behaved as though they

were sending their Dear Leader off into the sweet hereafter, bestow-
ing on him gushing tributes that sounded like eulogies. Dobson reveled in their panegyrics, smiling wistfully and guffawing at every
corny anecdote, while the crowd cheered his beneficent acts, reflecting their sense of privilege at being present at a gathering of America's most pro-family Family.

The tribute was made to seem like an intimate affair, as though the
entire audience had been invited to Christmas Eve at the Dobsons'
house. Dobson's wife, Shirley (or "Shirl-sey," as he affectionately called
her), boasted that she had married the "biggest catch" in her high
school, then exuberantly gushed before hundreds of strangers, "I love
you, James Dobson!" Dobson's son, self-styled evangelical "youth
speaker" Ryan, revealed through a prepared video address that even
though he once spurned his father's pro-corporal-punishment child-
rearing manuals, they now guide him as he raises his own strong-
willed infant son.

Next, one of Dobson's closest friends, Elsa Prince-Broekhuisen, the
septuagenarian mother of Blackwater Worldwide founder Erik Prince,
and wife of the late Focus on the Family financial angel Edgar Prince,
recounted in painstaking detail a trip to France she took with the
Dobsons—not the stuff of National Lampoon vacations. Finally,
Dobson strode triumphantly to the stage to accept a "lifetime achievement award" from his own Washington lobbyist, a man he hired and
whose salary he oversees: Tony Perkins. The crowd rose from their
seats with a roaring ovation for Dobson's manufactured milestone.

Only one speaker captured my waning attention. She was Danae
Dobson, the perky, blonde, thirty-something daughter of James Dobson. Danae began working for Focus on the Family in high school. "I
was in the correspondence department, and I would read the letters
that came in about, for instance, women whose husbands were hooked
on pornography," she told her father's official biographer, Dale Buss.
"My eyes were kind of opened at a tender age to all of the things that
could go wrong in a marriage."

When she ascended into her father's media empire, Danae cultivated an eager audience of teenage girls. Focus on the Family has published over a dozen of Danae's books, including her 2003 opus *Let's*

Talk! Good Stuff for Girlfriends About God, Guys, and Growing Up.
Danae's advice columns are featured regularly in her father's magazine for adolescent girls, *Brio!*, where she has informed aspiring evangelical hipsterettes that "God is cool! In fact, he's so cool there are no
words to describe him!" ("I use the word cool to describe everything
from cars to movies," Danae explained. "It's a reliable way to reveal
how much we like something.") But God is not only cool; he's creative.
"Snow is created by God, too," Danae wrote. "Who else could have
thought of something you can ski on one day and drink the next?"

In 2004, Mel Gibson selected Danae Dobson to help him quell the
controversy surrounding his film *The Passion of the Christ*. After a private screening with Gibson, Danae composed a letter extolling his
film as "a realistic depiction of what Christ did." Her widely distributed missive caused damaging blowback, however, when conservative
commentator Cal Thomas, an erstwhile friend of James Dobson,
revealed that her letter was plagiarized almost word-for-word from
one of his columns. (The rest of it appeared to have been lifted from
The Passion's promotional material.)

Despite her prominent role in her father's "pro-family" empire,
Danae remains unmarried. According to Dobson's official biographer,
Dale Buss, "Danae has been involved in a number of serious relationships. But she acknowledges the difficulty of any potential husband
measuring up to the standards she sees in her father—or passing his
muster." Then again, Danae might have better things to do than tend
to children and perform the wifely duties that her father mandates for
his female followers. As Danae's mother, Shirley, told Buss, although
Danae would "love to be married and have a family, she wants to go
on with her life." And so she does, publishing books, touring the
country on speaking junkets, living the life of a modern, independent
woman while attacking the feminist ideals that have made it possible
for her to do so.

In choosing work over family, Danae joined a long tradition of
women activists who propel the conservative movement's anti-feminist
agenda. As the sociologists Margaret Power and Paolo Baccheta noted
in their book *Right-Wing Women: From Conservatives to Extremists*, the
most comprehensive analysis ever conducted of conservative women

around the world, "One striking feature of a great many right-wing women leaders and full-time activists is their system of double standards. There is a huge gap between how right-wing women . . . live out their lives as individuals on the one hand, and the subjectivities they propose for other women on the other."

Danae Dobson may dally around with boyfriends in her private time, but she is required to play daddy's little girl when speaking before Christian-right audiences. At the Value Voters Summit, Danae offered tender childhood memories of "cuddling up in front of the TV watching movies" with her father; of making sand castles, going out for ice cream cones, and doing the things that daddies and daughters do. But then Danae's tribute took a strange and sudden detour when she invoked the scandal of Pastor Ted Haggard, a former friend and political ally of her father who had been defrocked for having sex with a male escort and abusing methamphetamines:

> Last year there was a prominent Christian leader who was involved in a very unthinkable scandal and he was asked to step down from his role as pastor which the board decided to do because it was the right thing to do. And I just was so deeply saddened by that, and I saw a photo of this gentleman's wife and she had such an expression of sadness on her face. And I heard from someone who knew his children that his children were traumatized. . . . It caused me to really step back and consider my dad and what a prominent leader he was in the Christian world. And I was just overwhelmed with a sense of peace because I knew that I was never gonna have to go through and suffer that type of pain. I knew that my dad would never cause me to endure and go through what this man's family is going through. And on Father's Day this year I wrote on my dad's card these words: 'Thank you for never causing me to have to lie in bed wondering what you were up to and how it was going to affect us and how it was going to affect our ministry. Thank you for being a man of character and integrity. A man who I can trust.'

Many women have spent anxious nights wondering where their wayward husbands were and what they were doing, but few women of

Danae's age suffer similar anxieties about their fathers. In the subculture of the Christian right, however, Danae's expression of total dependence on her dad is idealized as "agape love," a self-destroying, masochistic love that women are supposed to harbor for authoritarian male archetypes. By dissolving themselves into the movement's authoritarian structure, women like Danae gain the protection and encouragement of omnipotent father figures, extra-magic helpers who release them from the terror of going it alone in an exploitive society.

Focus on the Family has cultivated this masochistic sensibility by sponsoring "purity balls" across the country. At these mock cotillions, evangelical fathers dance and dine with their adolescent daughters as though they are their husbands. When the gala reaches full swing, the fathers rise and read a pledge "to cover my daughter as her protection and authority in the area of purity." Then, the daughters stand and drop white roses at the foot of a cross, symbols of the chastity they will attempt to maintain until marriage.

But more often than not, girls who drop flowers at purity balls are deflowered soon after. Over half of them wind up having sex before marriage, and with a man other than their future husband, according to sociologists Peter Bearman and Hannah Bruckner. Bearman and Bruckner also note that communities with the highest populations of purity ball attendees also have some of the country's highest rates of sexually transmitted diseases (STDs). In Lubbock, Texas, where abstinence-only education has been mandated since 1995, the rate of gonorrhea has risen to double the national rate, while teen pregnancy has spiked to the highest level in the state. A congressionally funded study of adolescent behavior, Add Health—the most comprehensive of its kind in history—revealed another dirty secret of the Christian right: White evangelical women lose their virginity on average at age sixteen, younger than any group besides black Protestants.

These statistics should have discredited the movement's morality machine once and for all. Instead, the exploding rate of sexually related disasters in evangelical communities has sustained the Christian right, enabling its activists to exploit personal crises for fundraising and recruitment drives. For every crisis pregnancy there is a crisis pregnancy center where anti-abortion activists propagandize vulnerable teenage girls. Because many of these centers are funded by Focus on the Family, the teens passing through their sterile back rooms may be presented with a copy of *Brio!* or given the popular tract by former Focus on the Family counselor Steve Arterburn, *Every Young Woman's Battle*, a book that posits masturbation as a dangerous gateway drug, while unintentionally revealing its appeal. "Once you begin feeding baby monsters," Arteburn warned, "their appetites grow bigger and they want MORE! It's better not to feed such a monster in the first place."

The women who oversee the Christian right's personal crisis industry are very often products of the same trauma-wracked culture that they mine for recruits. When they advocate for abstinence-only education or against abortion, they stir their audiences with lurid confessions about their own horrific experiences in secular society—their demeaning sexual encounters, their abortions, their shame. Redemption from a life of sexual sin is the right-wing woman's business card; it is all the expertise she needs. "I've been that woman," said Leslee Unruh, a leading female culture warrior who boasts of her "common sense background" in the field of sexual health. "There is no freedom after an abortion. You carry an empty crib in your heart forever. There is no freedom."

Unruh had an abortion when she was in her early twenties. It was her fourth pregnancy with her first husband, whom she divorced soon thereafter. Unruh converted into a hardcore Dominionist after meeting her second husband, Allen Unruh, a chiropractor and anti-abortion activist. In 1984, Leslee Unruh founded her own "Christian counseling" business, The Alpha Center, in her hometown of Sioux Falls, South Dakota. There she hosted purity balls and evangelized young pregnant women against abortion, even, on a number of occasions, offering them illegal bribes to carry their babies to term and then give them up for adoption. In 2006, Unruh pleaded guilty to several misdemeanor charges of adopting babies without their mothers' permission. In exchange, the state dropped four felony charges it had planned to bring against her.

"There were so many allegations about improper adoptions being made [against her] and how teenage girls were being pressured to give up their children," Tim Wilka, one of the state's attorneys at the time, said. Like Serena Joy, the barren female televangelist of Margaret Atwood's fictional portrait of the United States as a Dominionist dystopia, *The Handmaid's Tale*, the childless Unruh apparently believed the movement's future was contingent on forcibly indoctrinated children pried from "unfit" but very fertile parents.

Unruh's crusading reached a crescendo the same year she battled criminal charges. South Dakota's legislature had passed a bill she authored banning abortion even in cases of rape and incest, or when the mother's life was in danger. Unruh's husband, Allen, served on a state task force a year earlier that recommended a total restriction on abortion to the state's Republican Governor Mike Rounds. In the wake of her apparent victory in the statehouse, Unruh still found time to wage a futile parallel campaign to ban a new over-the-counter pill—"a pesticide," she called it—that enables women to shorten their periods. "I'm giving women freedom," Unruh proclaimed. "We are giving back to the women what they really want. This is true feminism."

Even though Unruh's abortion ban was overturned by popular fiat, her influence continued to grow. Her Abstinence Clearinghouse, a nonprofit that designs programs for public schools across the country, reaped millions of dollars in grants from Bush's Health and Human Services Department. Unruh leveraged her financial infusion to pump propaganda-laden textbooks into public school classrooms, informing impressionable students that AIDS could be transmitted through sweat and tears and that heavy petting causes pregnancy. One Unruh-reviewed textbook informed teens, "Women gauge their happiness and judge their success on their relationships. Men's happiness and success hinge on their accomplishments." Researchers for Representative Henry Waxman who reviewed material created by Unruh and her allies concluded that 80 percent of their data on reproductive health was false or misleading.

Abstinence education propaganda is valuable perhaps only as a document of the philosophy of right-wing women like Unruh. To Unruh, sex for the purpose of pleasure is a satanic act that ultimately harms women. By coercing girls to deny their essential urges, she and her cohorts believe they can protect them from demonic male aggressors on sexual hit-and-run missions. It is no wonder right-wing women insist they are the "true" feminists. And it is no coincidence that Unruh's portrait of the ideal male partner is exactly what the radical feminist and former domestic abuse victim Andrea Dworkin might have conjured up had she not foresworn men for lesbianism—both women despise male sexual virility. "I just met with a woman whose husband was paralyzed from the waist down—he was in a wheelchair," Unruh told me during a 2004 interview. "And the love she has for him has only grown. That to me is so beautiful, that is what it's really all about."

• • •

Unruh's apocalyptic battle against sexual evil was influenced as much by her *kulturkampf* as it was by a former Yiddish socialist and Captain Kangaroo songsmith named Judith Reisman. "Judith Reisman has affected my life personally through the enormous amount of scientific research she's done," Unruh told me. "And without Judith's impact on my life, I don't believe the abstinence community would have been impacted."

Who is Reisman? She is responsible for volumes of polemical articles and federally funded studies conjuring up a dark world in which *Playboy* magazine insidiously pushes kiddie-porn, sex-crazed homosexuals lure America's youth into leather dungeons, and "erotoxins" as powerful as crack cocaine fill the somatosensory cortexes of porn watchers. Like Unruh, Reisman's radical politics were formed in the crucible of a terrible sexual trauma.

Reisman was raised far from most of her Christian-right compatriots, in prewar Newark, New Jersey, a haven for Jewish immigrants that also served as the setting for Phillip Roth's best-selling novel about a covert Nazi conspiracy to seize control of the United States, *The Plot Against America*. Like Roth, Reisman has portrayed Newark as a garden of innocence, a refuge from the storm of cultural tumult gathering around her. Her mother was a Yiddish theater actress and her father a folk singer; both passed their musical talents on to her. "I lived at a wonderful time," Reisman recalled in a short memoir she published. "I felt safe with neighbors, uncles or cousins as was the custom of that time." It was morning in America.

By the dawning of the Age of Aquarius, Reisman claimed she was still a naïf. "I married, and the hedge of protection about my life was not breached until 1966 when my 10-year-old daughter was molested by a 13-year-old adored and trusted family friend," she wrote. "He knew she would like it, he said, he knew from his father's magazines." According to Reisman, the boy slipped out of the country with his family while her daughter slipped into a deep depression that may have contributed to her death from a brain aneurysm fifteen years later.

Thrust into a state of all-consuming anxiety by the incident, Reisman sought solace from a college friend living in the countercultural mecca of Berkeley. She claims her friend told her that "children are sexual from birth." "I did not know it then," Reisman recounted, "but as a young mother, I had entered the world according to Kinsey." She referred, of course, to Dr. Alfred Kinsey, the controversial postwar biologist whose best-selling studies destroyed archaic sexual mores by revealing that, for example, Middle Americans have engaged in homosexuality at the same rate as cosmopolitan city dwellers, masturbation is practiced universally, and sex does not begin or end at marriage.

But before Reisman set her sights on Kinsey, her career as a songwriter would have to collapse under the weight of the liberal media. In 1973, after earning acclaim as a music video creator for various local children's shows, the producer of *Captain Kangaroo* recognized her gift for catchy, kid-friendly compositions. Soon after he hired her, however, the producer informed Reisman that she would need to adapt her songwriting style to the changing tastes of American kids, who were tuning in to cartoons at increasing rates. "I would have to speed up my tempo to compete with the fast-action and the increasing violence of the cartoons on other stations. . . . I found myself unwilling or unable to write for children that way," Reisman recalled.

Reisman spent her royalties from *Kangaroo* to put herself through graduate school at Case Western Reserve in Cleveland, where she says she studied the mass media's effects on the minds of children. She emerged from her studies convinced that images of Winnie the Pooh,

Mickey Mouse, and other cuddly characters that appeared "in *Playboy/ Penthouse* would cause sexual acting out on children." After she delivered a lecture on the *Playboy*/kiddie-porn conspiracy at a conference on Love and Attraction at Swansea University in Wales in 1977, Reisman said she was taken aside by an unidentified "Canadian professor" who informed her that only one man was responsible for the "global child sex abuse epidemic": Kinsey.

"Now I finally knew there was a source authority for children increasingly being viewed sexually," Reisman wrote. "[M]y friend Carole had . . . gotten the idea that 'children were sexual from birth' from Kinsey." Suddenly, the boy who molested Reisman's daughter became a mere extension of Kinsey. And although the boy had disappeared, Reisman saw Kinsey living on in the mounting women's liberation and gay rights movements.

The onset of the Reagan Revolution presented Reisman with a wealth of opportunities. In 1984, Justice Department official Alfred Regnery, now a prominent conservative publisher, provided Reisman $734,371 to analyze thirty years' worth of *Playboy* back issues. When she turned in her findings at American University, where she was based, the university refused to publish them. Even Regnery confessed that the grant was a mistake. "This is not science, it's vigilantism: paranoid, pseudoscientific hyperbole with a thinly veiled, hidden agenda. This kind of thing doesn't help children at all," Dr. Loretta Haroian, a leading expert on childhood sexuality, said of Reisman's findings. Reisman's report nevertheless formed the centerpiece of presentations by Dobson and his allies at the Meese Pornography Commission hearings.

Reisman's paper prompted the coup de grâce for Regnery's collapsing career. When it arrived on his desk, the hard-charging lawyer was struggling to suppress an embarrassing story from his past that had resurfaced. In 1976, during the last weeks of Regnery's flagging campaign for district attorney in Madison, Wisconsin, his wife Christina reported to the police that two men had warned her husband to drop out of the race and then had slashed her seventy-six times with an embroidery knife before forcing her to perform oral sex on them. The police recorded her tale:

Both men got up, and the [Negro male] grabbed her by the hair and pulled her towards the bathroom. He dragged her to the edge of the tub while he got into the tub behind her. She explained again that the bathroom is extremely small, and that the man had to get into the tub to be anywhere behind her. The [white male] dropped his pants to his knees and raised the lid of the seat of the toilet. She stated that he had an erection, and he leaned towards her. The [Negro male] directed her head motions by jerking on her hair and head, and the [Negro male] forced her head a little forward so that she had to take the [white male's] penis into her mouth.

The police swiftly determined that Christina Regnery had fabricated the attack—the lurid story was a fantasy—possibly with the assistance of her husband. During a subsequent search of the Regnerys' home, police discovered a large cache of pornography, including "several catalogues for various prophylactic devices and erotica." When this sordid tale circulated through the Washington press corps, Regnery resigned, citing (what else?) a desire to spend more time with his family.

While Regnery retreated into his conservative publishing empire, Reisman found a newly receptive audience for her discredited ideas. At a May 1994 conference sponsored by Focus on the Family in Colorado Springs, described by the *Washington Times* as "top secret," Reisman introduced her theory of a proselytizing homosexual movement. "I would suggest to you," she told the conference, "that while the homosexual population may right now be 1 to 2 percent, hold your breath, people, because the recruitment is loud; it is clear; it is everywhere. You'll be seeing, I would say, 20 percent or more, probably 30 percent, or even more than that, of the young population will be moving into homosexual activity." By the meeting's conclusion, representatives of the forty organizations in attendance agreed to move anti-gay politicking to the forefront of the movement's long-term agenda.

While winning friends among the Christian right, Reisman was also seeking to influence people on Capitol Hill in her push for an investigation into whether Kinsey had sexually abused children during his research. Reisman's lobbying piqued the interest of Texas Republican Representative Steve Stockman, a former drifter with well-established ties to anti-government militia leaders. In 1995, Stockman introduced HR 2749, "The Child Protection and Ethics in Education Act," a bill Reisman helped author that proposed "to determine if Alfred Kinsey's [books] *Sexual Behavior in the Human Male* and/ or *Sexual Behavior in the Human Female* are the result of any fraud or criminal wrongdoing." Even in the House's right-wing atmosphere, the bill went nowhere. A year later, Stockman lost his reelection campaign, depriving Reisman of terra firma on Capitol Hill.

But when George W. Bush entered the White House, Reisman's anti-porn crusade gained steam again. In February 2003, Bush appointed her longtime friend Bruce Taylor as senior counsel to the assistant attorney general. Taylor has prosecuted over seven hundred obscenity cases in his career, including the famed 1981 *Ohio v. Larry Flynt* trial (Flynt was paralyzed outside the trial by a bullet fired by serial killer Joseph Paul Franklin, an American Nazi Party member incensed by an interracial *Hustler* photo spread.) With a $5 million annual budget, Taylor oversaw a beefed-up FBI task force responsible for jailing pornographers such as Paul Little, who was sentenced in October 2008 to over three years in federal prison for the monstrous crime of distributing pornography "over the internet and through the mail."

"We should probably call her Detective Reisman for finding the hidden clue to Kinsey's crimes against children and families," Taylor said in a quotation Reisman published on her personal website. "'Kinsey: Crimes and Consequences' is a blueprint for justice for victims of sexual exploitation and abuse."

In November 2004, Reisman spent a week on Capitol Hill at the invitation of Republican Senator Sam Brownback, a Catholic traditionalist from Kansas who waged a hapless campaign for president in 2008. Reisman testified before the Senate Subcommittee on Science, Technology and Space on "The Science Behind Pornography Addiction," declaring that "Pornography triggers myriad kinds of internal, natural drugs that mimic the 'high' from a street drug. Addiction to pornography is addiction to what I dub 'erotoxins'—mind-altering drugs produced by the viewer's own brain." She added, "A basic science research team employing a cautiously protective methodology should study 'erotoxins' and the brain/body." Although Reisman's tacit plea for government funds to study "erotoxins" was never answered, she managed to ingratiate herself with the federally funded Abstinence Clearinghouse.

Reisman met Unruh through a mutual friend, Eunice Ray. Ray is the founder and director of Camp American, a summer camp where kids can play volleyball, go canoeing, and attend workshops led by theocrats such as Gary DeMar, an acolyte of R. J. Rushdoony who openly advocates the death penalty for gays, abortion doctors, and adulterers. Other options for campers have included shooting seminars with Larry Pratt, the Gun Owners of America president who once argued that right-wing "citizen defense patrols" modeled after Guatemalan death squads should assume law enforcement responsibilities in American cities. Ray's promotional material assures parents, "Students will discover the deception of evolution, the importance of purity and morals in a free society, and the pagan connection to the radical environmental movement." But she admonishes them: "NO 'Speedo' style swimwear for young men. Shorts style swimwear only."

Reisman was the guest of honor at the Abstinence Clearinghouse's 2004 leadership conference. After being greeted by White House public liaison Tim Goeglein, she took the stage alongside Eunice Ray to warn, "Pornography is training all your sex educators." (Goeglein resigned his White House post in 2007 after admitting to plagiarizing over thirty of the columns he wrote for a local newspaper; he is now the Washington lobbyist for Focus on the Family.) Unruh told me that Reisman received several standing ovations and "everyone just loved her." Later in the evening, President Bush addressed the conference by video link-up, promising to double federal funding for abstinence-only programs. Finally, Reisman received an "Abstie Lifetime Achievement Award," her crowning achievement.

When the Democrats seized control of Congress in 2006, the abstinence education movement's fortunes shifted dramatically. Although the Democrats failed to defund abstinence-only education, they made it easier for states to opt out of Title V funding that mandated the discredited programs. Unruh and her panicked allies responded by forming a trade association, the National Abstinence Education Association, to pressure legislators for a slice of federal largesse. But with congressional committee chairs occupied by Democrats, their machinations were futile; by June 2008, at least twenty-two states had opted out of abstinence education. The social wreckage wrought by youth deprived of medically correct sex education by abstinence activists had become too much of a burden for local governments to bear.

But all was not lost for the movement's female vanguard. Amid the rubble of the GOP after its 2006 midterm decimation was a newly elected woman from the Last Frontier who would become an unlikely symbol of the movement's future. A former beauty pageant runner-up and self-described "feminist for life," Alaska's new governor, Sarah Palin, was an archetype of right-wing womanhood. Adored by Dobson and his allies, Palin would soon play a pivotal role in consolidating the Republican Party's radical image.

■ ■ ■

Back in Washington, the movement had mobilized to defend its fallen ones, especially David Vitter, a staunchly conservative Louisiana senator the Christian right had helped elect. Vitter, who had been dogged for years by rumors that he had had an affair with a prostitute, was finally exposed as a serial customer of high-priced hookers, New Orleans bordellos, and possibly even S&M dungeons. Not content to let a reliable ally lose his seat, his family values cadre committed itself to saving his career.

CHAPTER 17

HUMAN TOOLS

The 2004 election turned on fear—fear of enemies at the gates and fear of enemies within. In eleven states, the Christian right placed ballot measures that successfully banned same-sex marriage. James Dobson and his close allies, Tony Perkins and Gary Bauer, mounted a ferocious effort to pass these measures, packing stadiums for rallies to "Stand for Marriage." Dobson incited crowds by reciting from his new polemic, "Marriage Under Fire," which warned that the legalization of same sex marriage would lead to "group marriage," "marriage between daddies and little girls," and "marriage between a man and his donkey." Same-sex marriage, he railed, threatened to "destroy civilization."

The "Stand for Marriage" rallies were also furtive campaign events for right-wing Republican senatorial candidates. Jim DeMint from South Carolina, who boldly opposed allowing homosexuals *and* single mothers to teach in public schools, was among Dobson's beneficiaries. DeMint's absurdities, which helped get him elected, were exceeded only by those of another gay-baiting Senate hopeful, Oklahoma pediatrician and longtime anti-condom activist Tom Coburn. Another Dobson acolyte, John Thune, a fresh-faced South Dakotan and graduate of Biola University (founded as the Bible Institute of Los Angeles), defeated Senate Minority Leader Tom Daschle with campaign ads proclaiming himself a "servant leader" for Jesus.

But no candidate gained more from Dobson's blessing than David Vitter, a conservative Louisiana congressman running to become the first Republican U.S. senator from his state since Reconstruction. In 2002, he had withdrawn from the governor's race amid a storm of lurid rumors. Although he claimed that mere marital troubles forced him to drop his bid, a week after his withdrawal New Orleans papers reported allegations that he had repeatedly patronized a notorious Canal Street whorehouse. When Vitter announced his candidacy for the Senate, he was alleged to have arranged a meeting with several leading evangelical activists, including Perkins, Dobson, and Gene Mills, executive director of the Louisiana Family Forum, a group founded by Perkins that functioned as a local Focus on the Family policy council. Appearing before this synod of virtue, Vitter proclaimed, "There are no skeletons in my closet." Heartened by Vitter's pledge of purity, the Christian right's college of cardinals directed their forces to get behind his campaign, lifting him to decisive victory.

The anti-gay fervor that catapulted candidates such as Vitter into national office during the fall of 2004 underscored a deep-seated anxiety about the crises that riveted evangelical families. If marriage was "under fire," as Dobson had claimed, the casualties could be quantified. A 1999 study by conservative evangelical pollster George Barna found the born-again Christian divorce rate to be significantly higher than that of the general public. Barna reported his findings with surprising stoicism. "While it may be alarming to discover that born-again Christians are more likely than others to experience a divorce, that pattern has been in place for quite some time," he remarked. "Even more disturbing, perhaps, is that when those individuals experience a divorce many of them feel their community of faith provides rejection rather than support and healing." According to Barna, Baptists had the highest rate of the major denominations: 29 percent. Born-again Christians' rate was 27 percent. But perhaps the worst news for born-again Christians was Barna's revelation that atheists and nonbelievers had the lowest divorce rate: 21 percent.

Tony Perkins, when he was a Louisiana state representative, was one of the first evangelical politicians to offer a remedy for the divorce explosion in his community; in 1997, he introduced a bill in the legislature to ratify the concept of "covenant marriage." Perkins's bill, which was eventually signed into law, offered couples the option of entering a biblically inspired marital contract that could not be broken unless one spouse could show proof of adultery, abandonment, physical abuse, or "habitual drunkenness for one year." When Perkins assumed the helm of the Family Research Council, his crusade went national, as he began lobbying unsuccessfully for the repeal of no-fault divorce laws in every state.

Mike Huckabee, an evangelical minister elected Arkansas governor in 1996, pushed Perkins's covenant marriage law as a panacea to his state's skyrocketing divorce rate, the nation's third highest by the time he left the governor's mansion in 2006, almost the same as when he entered. In selling covenant marriage to the masses, Huckabee and his wife Janet, who had married at age 18, converted their own marriage to covenant status along with 1,000 other couples on Valentine's Day in 2004, in a North Little Rock arena. The ceremony culminated with Janet Huckabee's vow to "gracefully submit" to her husband. With that, the thousand other wives stood en masse, lifted the wedding veils they had worn for the occasion and made their own pledges of submission to the will of their husbands.

Despite ceremonies of obedience and faithfulness, the families of Christian-right leaders often presented a stark contrast to the image of spiritual harmony projected to their flocks. James Dobson's thirty-something son, Ryan, exemplified this trend even as he became a rising star on the evangelical youth scene promoting the wonders of covenant marriage. A self-styled bad boy for Jesus, Ryan sports a handlebar moustache and hipster garb. When he is not cruising the mean streets of Colorado Springs on his Harley, according to the biography he has posted on his website, he likes to skate dangerous half pipes and surf the "top breaks" in Orange County, California, his former stomping ground. While preaching before packed youth revivals, at crisis pregnancy center benefit concerts, and in his ghostwritten book, *Be Intolerant: Because Some Things Are Just Stupid*, Ryan hits on many of the same political themes—gays, abortion—as his father. But he gears his message to the struggles of young evangelicals approaching marriage

age. Indeed, one of his favorite topics is the moral rot perpetuated by divorce-on-demand.

Ryan sermonized dramatically against this spreading social evil during an April 18, 2005, Web radio broadcast (one of the weekly shows he hosts through his website, KorMinistries.com) in the wake of the Terri Schiavo affair. "We have an over 50 percent divorce rate," he declared in a voice brimming with outrage. "That's not healthy either. We've stopped believing in till death do us part. People say 'Terri Schiavo's husband . . . all this stuff . . . blah, blah, blah . . . what do you think?' I say *until death do us part!* For sickness or for health [sic]. For better or for worse."

Ryan's father sat beside him in the studio throughout the broadcast, offering encouragement. "For rich or for poor," James Dobson seconded.

"For rich or for poor!" the son echoed.

With rising intensity, Ryan trundled on: "It's a commitment. It says something to a person. I'm committed to you no matter what happens . . . We have things that happen to us and I want to tell you I'm gonna be *committed* to you because . . . why am I passionate about this? Because I'm getting married in a couple months. And I'm thinking about it. I think about it a lot."

Often when members of the movement seem preoccupied with one particular form of sinful behavior—when they "think about it a lot," as Ryan Dobson said—they may be compensating for having committed the same sin, or knowing its temptation.

Adopted when he was six months old by America's foremost child-rearing authority, who prescribed harsh forms of corporal punishment, Ryan, whose real name is James Ryan Dobson III, suffered a difficult childhood. His father routinely warned him and his older sister, Danae, that if they did not follow his strict mandates they would not join him in heaven. According to Dobson's official biographer, Dale Buss, the children called their father's instructions on how to get to heaven the "Be There" talk.

Ryan struggled in school, failing at Illinois-based Olivet Nazarene University. Separated from his parents' financial support, Ryan worked odd jobs in Colorado until he convinced his parents to send him to

Biola University, an evangelical school in suburban Los Angeles that creates "servant leaders" for Jesus, such as Senator John Thune. But Ryan's problems worsened at Biola. His father's unrelenting pressure produced a constant state of anxiety. As stress mounted, Ryan sought therapy from one of his father's protégés, Christian psychologist Clyde Narramore. Narramore promptly diagnosed him with attention deficit disorder, prescribed a heavy dose of Ritalin, and warned the father against applying more pressure on his son. Ryan's stress suddenly but only momentarily lifted. He graduated from Biola in 1995 and moved back to Orange County with his new wife, Cezanne Williams, whom he had met at Biola. He had no income of his own. They lived in an expensive condominium purchased by his father.

Like many young couples who rush into marriage, Ryan and Cezanne's relationship rapidly deteriorated after their honeymoon. Ryan's marital troubles were compounded by his struggle to find a career. Even though he had just married, he was aimless, jobless, and depressed. He had failed to capitalize on his immediate opportunity—an internship at the Family Research Council and a job in the youth ministry of Rick Warren's Saddleback Community Church. "I had quit my job and at the time I just didn't care if I got another one," Ryan told Dale Buss. "My weight dropped down to 130. I lost my pride, some friends, and was quickly losing every cent I'd ever hoped to earn."

In September 2001, Ryan divorced Cezanne, citing "irreconcilable differences." Because Ryan initiated the proceedings, he was ordered to pay Cezanne $80,000 and transfer the deed of his condominium to her. Given the fact that Ryan was unemployed and penniless at the time, it is difficult to imagine how he was able to cover his costs without the assistance of his father—a man who has called no-fault divorce "a disaster for the family." James Dobson's financial compensation of the costs of Ryan's separation has not been confirmed. But during the year of the divorce, Dobson diverted $34,000 from Focus on the Family's coffers to his son's bank account for unspecified reasons that have never been explained.

Several months after Ryan's messy divorce, James Dobson demanded the resignation of his radio sidekick, Mike Trout, for having an extramarital affair. Besides introducing Dobson to his audience of millions each day, Trout oversaw Focus's National Bike Ride for the Family, an annual fundraising event. Now, to lead the twenty-fifth anniversary bike ride in Trout's place, James Dobson anointed his son. The job gave Ryan a newfound sense of direction, connecting him to the culture of personal crisis that undergirded his father's ministry. "It got me meeting people whose lives had been changed by Focus on the Family, who were on the brink of suicide, whose marriages had failed, who were out of control—but they turned on the radio and my dad's voice gave them hope and help and ideas," Ryan said. "All the anger got washed away doing those bike rides, meeting people who said, 'I just couldn't have done it without your dad.'"

Ryan Dobson became one of the minions who felt they owed salvation to his father's inspiration. But his redemption included additional benefits. The job also put Ryan on the trajectory for a lucrative public speaking career. In 2007 Ryan published his second book, *2Die4: The Dangerous Truth About Following Christ*, the ghostwritten sequel to *Be Intolerant: Because Some Things Are Just Stupid*. *2Die4* urged a violent crusade against "Satan"—"murderous war because our enemy is deadly." At the 2005 National Religious Broadcaster's convention, his father hosted an event to promote his forthcoming polemic. I joined those packing the small conference room to see the Dobsons speak. We were first required to take part in a ping-pong tournament. Focus staffers dressed in referee uniforms and rushed around the room keeping score of the matches going on all around, chalking up winners and losers, and finally choosing a couple of short, balding, middle-aged men to play against Ryan and James Dobson in an apocalyptic battle for ping-pong domination.

Before the championship match began, however, Ryan and his father sat on stools beside one of the referees for an informal discussion of some favorite topics: family, culture, and the homosexual agenda. James Dobson was uncharacteristically reticent, hunched over and speaking only when spoken to. He did not appear anything like the stern taskmaster who had answered a postelection thank you call from the White House by demanding that Bush get "more aggressive" or "pay a price in four years."

One of few times James Dobson spoke was to clarify a statement he had apparently wanted to issue for some time. "I did not say Sponge-Bob was gay," he told the crowd, responding to media ridicule of his attack a month before on the popular children's TV cartoon character. "All I said was he was part of a video produced by a group with strong linkages to the homosexual community that's teaching things like tolerance and diversity. And you can see where they're going with that. They're teaching kids to think different about homosexuality."

But the event belonged to Ryan, who took the floor to explain the thesis of *2Die4*. "Kids today are looking for something to die for, they're looking for a cause," Ryan said. "If you give them something to die for, they'll go to the edge of the earth for you. Kids like that give me hope for revolution in America."

During a brief Q&A session, I asked Ryan whether he would identify specific causes kids should die for. Without hesitation he replied, "People keep saying we need to change the discussion on abortion before we can ban it. We don't need to change the discussion. Like 80 percent of the country is against abortion," he stated, citing highly disputable polling data. "What kind of country fines people $25,000 for killing a bald eagle but doesn't do anything when unborn babies get thrown in the trash?" But before he could complete his apparent endorsement of a violent struggle to stop abortion, Ryan quickly shifted the discussion to his fiancée, who was seated in the front row. He pointed to his prospective second wife and proudly declared that he had kept himself "pure" for their wedding night.

Then the balding ping-pong challengers were summoned to a table in the center of the room to face off against the Dobsons. The father and son team spanked them like a disobedient child, dispatching the competition in short order. Ryan slammed the ball so hard across the table that it ricocheted into an unsuspecting female audience member's face. While the startled woman tried to collect herself, Ryan pumped his fist in celebration.

The Dobsons have never publicly acknowledged Ryan's divorce, and with good reason. Not only would any acknowledgement of this episode erode his credibility in the eyes of the impressionable evangelical youths who soak up his jeremiads, it would also damage his father's reputation. As Buss wrote in his hagiography of James Dobson, *Family Man*, "As the preeminent family-relationship guru of our time, Dobson is judged by how good a husband and father he is . . . Is he as advertised as a husband and father?"

Dobson may be at least as flawed as any other father whose children encounter troubles. But in order to remain elevated on a pedestal where he can denounce social deviants while shepherding his serried ranks from crisis to conservatism, he advertises himself as spiritually perfected—"St. Jim Dobson," in the words of one of his followers. The title of the biography Dobson commissioned about himself, *Family Man*, further illustrates his obsession with an image of purity. Concealing Ryan Dobson's true marital history, and by extension, James Dobson's claim as Holy Father, is essential to the marketability of the family brand.

With his past effectively hidden, Ryan leapt into the campaign against gay marriage with unbridled passion. "The studies show that countries that legalize same-sex unions and legalize gay marriage don't have a giant influx in gay marriage," he declared in a 2004 interview, mistakenly substituting the word *influx* for *increase*. "They have a huge decline in heterosexual marriage. Why get married if it doesn't mean anything?"

According to Ryan Dobson, then, gays are to be blamed for divorce. But the gay-bashing divorcé never explained what the existence or influence of gays might have to do with his own experience. Certainly, according to this rationale, he could not be held responsible for his own divorce. His logic, twisted as it is, has proved effective not only for Ryan Dobson but also for other right-wing figures struggling to divert attention from their own failed marriages and to advance their careers as crusading conservatives.

David Vitter, who admitted marital troubles but denied charges that he solicited prostitution, borrowed the Dobsons' feverish anti-gay invective to electrify his senatorial campaign. As the Christian right bristled with indignation at a 2004 Massachusetts Supreme Judicial Court decision that sanctioned same-sex marriage, Vitter released a statement breathlessly proclaiming, "The Hollywood left is redefining the most basic institution in human history, and our two

U.S. Senators won't do anything about it. We need a U.S. Senator who will stand up for Louisiana values, not Massachusetts's values. I am the only Senate Candidate to coauthor the Federal Marriage Amendment; the only one fighting for its passage."

Although Vitter's culture war cant propelled him to victory, the lurid rumors about his prostitution problem continued to haunt him. In 2002, New Orleans newspapers reported allegations that Vitter had paid $300 an hour for services at a bordello on the city's notorious Canal Street. Operated by Jeannette Maier, the brothel specialized in satisfying the fetishes of the Big Easy's power elite.

Maier made certain that chains, whips, cuffs, and leather accoutrements were always available, particularly when a prominent Republican client had booked time with one of her girls. After all, she explained, Republicans were her kinkiest clients. "They wanted to be spanked and tortured and wear stockings—Republicans have impeccable taste in silk stockings—and these are the people who run our country," Maier said.

Vitter was repeatedly confronted with these allegations during his 2004 campaign, once while appearing on popular Louisiana radio personality Jeff Crouere's local talk show. As the broadcast drew to a close, Crouere answered a call from David Bellinger, a legally blind political gadfly known as the "Flaming Liberal." Bellinger, who boasted of connections in City Hall and friends on Canal Street, had heard through the grapevine that Vitter regularly visited a high-priced prostitute named Wendy Cortez who occasionally worked with Maier. His confrontation with Vitter raised the still-unresolved rumors.

"Congressman, since spokesperson for the Republican Party William Bennett has said character counts," Bellinger said to Vitter, "I would like to put the same challenge to you that I put to [former] Representative [Tony] Perkins and he accepted. Would you be willing to sign under the penalty of perjury an affidavit saying you have never had an extramarital affair and you have never known, met or been in the company of one Wendy Cortez?"

Vitter unleashed an angry rant against his accuser. "'Flaming Liberal,'" he growled, "thank you for repeating all these vicious rumors that my political enemies are trying to bandy about and those rumors are absolutely [not] true and they really don't belong in any political campaign and I've stated very clearly that they're lies, but I'm not going to start jumping through hoops and taking orders from my political enemies who have absolutely no credibility."

As soon as he was elected to the Senate, Vitter devoted himself to repairing his tattered reputation. One of his first stops was the Family Research Council, where, just weeks after being sworn in, he came to a radio studio for an interview with Perkins, his old friend and ally in the Louisiana state legislature. Perkins, who had lost in his own bid for the Senate but now occupied the nexus of power between the party and the movement, told Vitter in no uncertain terms that he expected his total support for the Family Research Council's legislative initiatives. Vitter, the new standard bearer of the Louisiana Republican Party, in large part because of the support of Perkins and his cadre, pledged total loyalty to his host.

Dutifully, Vitter manned the trenches against the onslaught of gay marriage. In June 2006, as the Republican Party sought to energize its Christian-right base for the upcoming midterm elections, Vitter co-authored a bill to ban gay marriage. Even as his constituents reeled from the damage of Hurricane Katrina, Vitter preached on the Senate floor, "I don't believe there's any issue as important as this one. I think this debate is very healthy and we're winning hearts and minds." Yet many members of Vitter's party, including Senator John McCain, disagreed, sending the bill to easy defeat.

Just as Vitter seemed to have emerged as one of the Christian right's bright new senators, and to have outlasted his critics, his career suddenly took a turn for the worse. In the spring of 2007, a woman named Deborah Palfrey, also known as the "DC Madam," for operating a high-end prostitution ring in Washington, was indicted for racketeering. Unlike Maier, who never delivered on her promise to author a tell-all memoir, Palfrey immediately auctioned off her client list to compensate for the loss of her multi-million-dollar business.

ABC News investigative reporter Brian Ross was the first reporter to view the DC Madam's list. He quickly revealed that U.S. Aid and International Development director Randall Tobias was one of her high-profile clients. Tobias, a darling of the Christian right, had implemented a policy that forced any group accepting government anti-AIDS funds to take an anti-prostitution "loyalty oath" and had cut $40 million in aid to Brazil in retaliation for that country's successful policy of providing condoms to sex workers. Tobias had called the DC Madam on several occasions, specifically requesting that Central American escorts come to his home for "massages." With the revelation of his secret life, Tobias resigned his position and sank into obscurity.

But the DC Madam's trail soon grew cold, forcing ABC News reporter Brian Ross to end his investigation. Then Dan Moldea, a veteran true-crime reporter employed by *Hustler* magazine's publisher Larry Flynt, purchased the DC Madam's list, and the investigation gathered steam again. For weeks, Moldea pored over the Madam's records, cross-referencing name after name with political affiliations. Exhausted and increasingly frustrated with the dearth of high-profile figures on the list, Moldea planned to give up on his birthday. That day, however, he discovered a record of a call from David Vitter to the DC Madam's agency. When Moldea reported his discovery on the pages of *Hustler*, Vitter was finally forced to acknowledge that the rumors that had dogged him for so many years were true.

"I didn't have a crapload of clients," Wendy Cortez, Vitter's favorite escort, disclosed in an interview with *Hustler*. Cortez, whose real name is Wendy Yow Ellis, said that Vitter visited her twice a week for several years at a French Quarter apartment. He instructed her not to wear any perfume or lotion, and even forbade her to shower, for fear that the scent of another woman would pique his wife's suspicions. She described him as "a clean old man." When he finished, Vitter took his used condoms along with him, thus ensuring that the evidence would be destroyed. According to Ellis, Vitter told her, "This is my time with you. I don't want to spend my time anywhere else because I trust you. I know that I can come here because it's quiet and secluded."

"He was very quiet, very gentle. To me, he felt like a person who needed somebody just to be there," Ellis said. The escort explained that her motive in revealing his identity was that he had lied about seeing her. He lacked "cojones," she said. She added, cruelly, "His penis was very small."

Now Vitter publicly confessed to employing the DC Madam at a press conference on July 16, 2007. When Vitter made his grand confession, however, he stage-managed it to appeal to the sensibility of the Christian right, emphasizing his redemption from crisis through the wonder-working power of God.

"This was a very serious sin in my past for which I am, of course, completely responsible," Vitter, a Catholic, read in a prepared statement. "Several years ago, I asked for and received forgiveness from God and my wife in confession and marriage counseling. Out of respect for my family, I will keep my discussion of the matter there—with God and them. But I certainly offer my deep and sincere apologies to all I have disappointed and let down in any way." His wife, wearing a leopard print dress, sat next to him silently. He took no questions from reporters.

The following April, after being found guilty in federal court of running a prostitution ring, Palfrey, the DC Madam herself, composed a statement of her own. Overwhelmed by the notoriety she gained through her association with Vitter, and horrified by the prospect of a lengthy jail sentence, Palfrey wrote in a note to her mother, "I cannot live the next 6–8 years behind bars for what you and I have come to regard as this 'modern day lynching, only to come out of prison in my late 50s a broken, penniless and very much alone woman," She tied a nylon rope around her neck and hanged herself from the ceiling, dying from asphyxiation. While blogs exploded with rumors that Palfrey was killed to prevent her from revealing more high-profile clients, a medical coroner ruled her death a suicide.

■ ■ ■

Perhaps under other circumstances, Vitter's morality-obsessed allies might have called for his resignation. And perhaps a Republican leadership concerned about adhering to congressional ethics before the crucial 2008 elections might have joined their call. Indeed, this pressure sealed the fate of Vitter's predecessor Bob Livingston, the acting Speaker of the House (also from Louisiana), when his philandering came to light on the eve of the House vote on President Clinton's impeachment. But fortunately for Vitter, his old comrade, Perkins, held the key to his fate.

Perkins rushed to Vitter's defense. "The American people have shown themselves to be very forgiving toward a public official who admits their failures and takes redemptive steps," Perkins said in a press release distributed to evangelical news outlets immediately after Vitter's press conference. "I hope to see David back on his feet again."

Vitter also found a defender in Gene Mills, head of the local Focus on the Family policy council that Perkins had founded. "Vitter has repented of the allegations," Mills insisted. "He sought forgiveness, reconciliation and counseling."

The Reverend Billy McCormack, the leader of the Louisiana Christian Coalition who blocked moderate-Republican efforts to rebuke David Duke during his rise in the state political machine, and who pointedly refused to investigate charges that Duke was selling copies of Adolph Hitler's *Mein Kampf* from his legislative office, also joined the chorus of Vitter's evangelical protectors. "Senator Vitter may well be much more able as a senator now than before because people tend to learn from their mistakes when they are responsible," McCormack said, invoking the familiar Christian right theme of crisis and redemption. "I will continue to support him fervently."

Vitter returned to the Senate confident that the expired statute of limitations on his crimes prevented his prosecution. In a meeting of the Senate Republican Conference, he was welcomed with raucous applause from fellow Republicans. Mac Johnson, a writer for the conservative magazine *Human Events*, channeled the Republican id in a remarkable bit of unintentional humor. "David, embrace your rampant and unabashed heterosexuality and become a shining example of heterosexual identity," Johnson wrote. "Too long have heterosexual males been persecuted and criticized for who they are. . . . There is just one word for the dark motivation behind Vitter's outing and that is HETEROPHOBIA!"

Johnson concluded his defiant apologia with a paean to cognitive dissonance. "I'm a huge fan of hypocrisy," Johnson declared, "since the alternative is apparently a world without standards for anyone, lest someone risk being called a hypocrite. Here is the difference between the average hypocrite and the average liberal: the hypocrite has the common courtesy to be embarrassed about what he does. The liberal thinks what he does should be taught to your children at school." Suddenly, post-Vitter, moral relativism was all the rage on the right.

Why did Vitter's allies so casually forgive his sins? Certainly political expediency factored into their motives. Vitter was a fervent culture warrior from a state led at the time by a Democratic governor. If he resigned, his defenders reasoned, a Democrat would fill his seat, and the balance of power in the Senate would tilt even more against the Republicans. But there was more method to their madness than was apparent on the surface. Just two months after Perkins, Mills, and other Christian-right figures leapt to Vitter's defense, Vitter earmarked $100,000 in federal money to the Louisiana Family Forum, the policy council that Perkins founded and Mills directed. Whether or not the earmark was a financial reward to his two most ardent defenders, it represented at the very least a troubling conflict of interest.

Vitter claimed the earmark would help the Family Forum "to develop a plan to teach better science education." But in fact, the Family Forum was determined to introduce "origin science," or the notion that divine forces created the universe, into public school biology curricula. The group's blueprint, which it posted on its website, was entitled "A Battle Plan—Practical Steps to Combat Evolution," a paper written by a supposed expert, Kent E. Hovind, originator of what he called "Creation Science Evangelism."

Who was Hovind? The founder of Dinosaur Adventure Land, a creationist theme park based in Florida, and of the "Dr. Dino" website, Hovind was the designer of an exhibit demonstrating that humans and dinosaurs have coexisted for thousands of years and that small dinosaurs still walk the earth. Hovind was also a conspiracy-obsessed 9/11 denialist who has said that AIDS, Crohn's disease, Gulf War syndrome, and arthritis were creations of "the money masters and the governments of the world." In January 2007, Hovind was sentenced to ten years in federal prison for tax evasion and obstruction of justice.

Even though Vitter eventually succumbed to public protests and withdrew his earmark, his gesture had consolidated his position as a friend of The Family. Just as the Reverend Billy McCormack predicted, Vitter's redemption made him more determined than ever to demonstrate his fealty to the Christian right. In October 2007, Vitter introduced a bill the Family Research Council had long advocated that banned federal grants to women's health centers for STD testing, contraceptives, and pap smears. His argument that these services helped provide the overhead for abortion services fell on deaf ears in the new Democratic Congress, however, and his bill failed. But Vitter's bill was purely symbolic, another token of his gratitude to his masters in the movement.

"The higher one stands in the Party hierarchy, the more attentively is one's private life supervised," Czeslaw Milosz wrote in 1951 in his searing denunciation of Stalinism, *The Captive Mind.* "Love of money, drunkenness, or a confused love-life disqualify a Party member from holding important offices. Hence the upper brackets of the Party are filled by ascetics devoted to the single cause of the Revolution. As for certain human tools, deprived of real influence but useful because of their names, even if they belong to the Party one tolerates or sometimes encourages their weaknesses, for they constitute a guarantee of obedience."

Like the puritanical Communist Party bosses of Milosz's native Poland, James Dobson and Tony Perkins have exploited the secret transgressions of figures such as Vitter to ensure their servility. Dobson has even sent his son, Ryan, into the trenches of the culture war, knowing that Ryan's earnest desire to transcend the sins of his youth guaranteed his conformity to the movement's mandates. Only through passionate declarations of faith and frenetic political activity can the fallen ones be welcomed back into the movement. Thus they become "human tools," the most loyal soldiers of the Christian right's cultural revolution.

Then there are those, such as Idaho Republican Senator Larry Craig, whose sins may never be forgiven. Craig, who was arrested soon after the Vitter scandal broke for soliciting sex from an undercover police officer in a men's bathroom stall, had committed no worse offense than Vitter. But the object of his affection was a member of the same sex. Perkins and numerous other conservatives who had defended Vitter unanimously called for Craig's resignation. Was it just homophobia?

Craig occupied a safe seat that would certainly be filled by another conservative Republican. He was as dispensable as one of Newt Gingrich's wives. Also, Craig, who famously declared, "I am not gay!" at a press conference after his arrest, refused to submit to the evangelical process of confession and redemption, and was therefore perceived as insufficiently obedient and pliable. Finally, figures such as Perkins have been more comfortable in demonizing homosexuals, whom they view as hostile subversives, than in condemning the straight sinners among them. Morality mattered only to the extent that it was convenient.

But the Christian right's attempts to cast the gay demons from its sanctuary only exposed its contradictions further. The movement's closet had flown open for all to see, and it could not be nailed shut again.

THE CONFORMISTS

In the mind of James Dobson, a titanic battle is constantly being waged. This conflict is the central front in "a Second Civil War," an apocalyptic struggle pitting God-fearing straights against libertine gays, manly men against girly men, biblical absolutes against secular evil. Behind Dobson's Manichaean rhetoric, the reality of the culture war has been shrouded in shades of gray since its inception. Indeed, the anti-gay crusade mixed traditional homophobia with the self-loathing of the many closeted gays embedded within the movement's political nerve center.

When the Republican Revolution set up shop in Washington, it sold more than draconian anti-gay policies. Droves of closeted homosexuals were placed in key positions in Republican congressional offices, appointed to think-tanks, and honeycombed throughout the conservative media. Inside Washington, they formed an underground within the underground, a semisecret network that mingled on the fringes of Washington's gay community, working by day to undermine that community's movement for civil rights. While enabling the Republicans' social agenda, closeted conservatives earned the respect of America's most vicious gay-bashers, gaining protection and privilege. Girly men in private paraded in public as manly men among manly men. But at the same time, the danger of exposure loomed as an ever-present threat and made them vulnerable to damning accusations of hypocrisy. That fundamental hypocrisy highlights the radical right's most essential contradiction.

In 1996, Henry Adams, Lester Wright, and Bethany Lohr, psychiatrists and researchers at the University of Georgia, investigated the link between homophobia and repressed homosexuality, surveying over fifty self-declared heterosexual males on their opinions of gays. The subjects were then separated into two groups: homophobic and nonhomophobic. Both groups were shown gay male pornography and were monitored for signs of sexual arousal. (The results appeared in the *Journal of Abnormal Psychology*, published by the American Psychological Association.) The study revealed that by an overwhelming margin, the subjects who registered the largest increase in penis circumference—those most aroused by gay pornography—also held the most homophobic opinions. The remarkable findings of this experiment suggest a clue to why the modern radical right, the most homophobic political movement in American history, has become a sanctuary for repressed gay men.

The closeted homosexuality of the radical right has been present since the movement's earliest days. One of the key organizers behind the Council for National Policy, Terry Dolan, was a flamboyant conservative fundraiser who once distributed a flier warning, "Our nation's moral fiber is being weakened by the growing homosexual movement." Dolan notoriously said, "The shriller you are, the easier it is to raise money." He was still in the closet when he died of AIDS in 1987. Dolan's longtime associate, Marvin Liebman, who helped him organize some of the New Right's most successful fundraising drives, was also gay. But he rejected the tragic path his friend had taken.

When Liebman, propelled as a conservative for decades by anti-Communist convictions, became convinced that homophobia was becoming the enduring basis for right-wing grassroots organizing, he revealed the secret he had kept hidden for decades. In his 1992 memoir *Coming Out Conservative*, Liebman said that his work on behalf of the Republican Party made him "feel like a Jew in Germany in 1934 who had chosen to remain silent, hoping to be able to stay invisible as he watched the beginning of the Holocaust." Upon the publication of his *cri de coeur*, Liebman renounced the conservative movement once and for all and vowed to devote the remainder of his life to defending gay rights. Two years later, Newt Gingrich and Tom DeLay, the leaders of the new Republican-led Congress, fulfilled Liebman's ominous warning, aggressively integrating the Christian right's homophobic politics into their sweeping social agenda. Ironically, while the Christian right worked to ratify the congressional GOP's policies, the most industrious cadres were gay conservatives operating within the Republican apparatus.

David Brock, a gay political writer who moved to Washington in 1986 to work for the conservative *Washington Times*, was far and away the most influential journalist of the Republican Revolution. During the early 1990s, Brock's exposés of President Bill Clinton's sexual improprieties and his best-selling book-length assault on Clarence Thomas's accuser Anita Hill (whom he dubbed "a little bit nutty and a little bit slutty") earned him conservative rock star status. He became a favorite guest of radio rightists from Rush Limbaugh to James Dobson, and he brought conservative audiences to their feet with his stinging denunciations of Clinton as a chronic philanderer unfit to govern. When the Council for National Policy honored Brock in 1994 with its Winston Churchill Award, however, the searing doubt he had long suppressed began to surface.

"I knew I didn't belong behind that podium at the CNP, gazing out at Phyllis Schlafly's beehive hairdo," Brock wrote in his devastating 2002 tell-all memoir *Blinded by the Right*. "What no one in the room that night at CNP knew was that had I spent my Saturday night in Washington, I would have been prowling through the dark corridors of gay dance clubs . . . I was now, as Marvin Liebman had referred to himself earlier, a Jew in Hitler's army. Knee deep in this profound moral conflict, I wouldn't recognize it, for recognizing it would have forced me to question my own beliefs and discover my own self-loathing. I was only interested in self-promotion."

Brock's ambition was fatally damaged days later, when an anonymous letter describing his patronizing of Badlands, a DC gay bar, was circulated to gossip magazines. As rumors spread through Beltway political circles, and gay newspapers threatened to out Brock, he decided to come out. At that point, his motives were wholly cynical. "Overnight," Brock wrote, "I became the only openly gay conservative in the country. I prepared myself to use my presence in the movement to help the movement deflect legitimate criticism that it was anti-gay." Brock remained aligned with the conservative movement, drawing a paycheck from *The American Spectator*, for three more years, until he realized that the "friends" who stood behind him made exceptions to their anti-gay philosophies only because they saw him as a useful tool. Brock learned, for example, that the neoconservative pundit Bill Kristol, who privately encouraged him after he came out, had spoken at a conference promoting "ex-gay" therapy.

Brock's final rift with the movement came in 1996 when he wrote a biography of Hillary Clinton that challenged the right's cartoon-like stereotype of the First Lady as a megalomaniacal criminal. Under withering fire from his erstwhile friends, who condemned him as a traitor to their cause, he responded with a dramatic article for *Esquire* titled, "David Brock, the Road Warrior of the Right, Is Dead." Completing what he described as his "spiritual and moral conversion," Brock wrote letters of apology to people he believed he had unjustly hurt, from Anita Hill to Bill Clinton.

The anger of his former conservative friends rose to a fever pitch. Anti-feminist pundit Barbara Ledeen vowed to "firebomb" his home, a half-serious threat that typified the response of conservatives to Brock's break from their ranks. Meanwhile, many on the left doubted the sincerity of his conversion and were reluctant to welcome him after the havoc his writings had visited on them. Even though he had risked everything to regain his personal integrity, Brock's future was uncertain.

In 2004, Brock founded Media Matters for America, now one of the progressive movement's flagship organizations. The group, where I have worked as a researcher, is the realization of his tireless effort to create a counterweight to the conservative movement's efforts to influence the media. In the four years since its foundation, Media Matters has extensively reported on the distortions and hate speech spouted by conservative and other media figures. Top-rated radio jock Don Imus's defaming of the Rutgers University women's basketball team as "nappy-headed ho's," a comment that ignited a firestorm of controversy and temporarily cost him his job, might have gone unnoticed had Media Matters not recorded and reported his remark as soon as he made it.

Bill O'Reilly of Fox News has reacted with predictable displeasure to the unprecedented level of scrutiny he has received from Brock's researchers, describing Media Matters as "the most vicious element in our society today," a group staffed by "assassins." In March 2008, O'Reilly fumed about the organization's reporting of racially charged remarks he had made after visiting a restaurant in Harlem, when he confessed surprise that black patrons of the restaurant acted civilly, like people in "an all-white suburb," and did not shout, "M-f'er, I want more iced tea!" "I want Media Matters deported," O'Reilly barked. "And if anybody can work that—if Barack Obama can work that—I'm voting for him. OK?"

For many of those on the right beset by private trauma, it is far easier to seek shelter in an authoritarian movement than to do what Brock did—that is, to stand alone against extreme cultural and political pressures, and without any promise of finding a community for psychological support. This is especially true for gay men, who risk social castigation and even physical violence for leading an open lifestyle. It is no wonder that authoritarian personalities such as Jeff Gannon are so much more common than those who, like David Brock, follow a path to authenticity.

■ ■ ■

The contrast between the journeys of David Brock and Jeff Gannon is instructive on the byways of the right—and the confrontation between them became one of the critical episodes of conservative media in the

Bush era. Who is Gannon? For one brief shining moment, during President George W. Bush's second term, he was the most well-known reporter that nobody knew. Without any journalistic credentials or track record in politics, Gannon suddenly surfaced with the title of Washington bureau chief for Talon News, a mysterious website operated by the conservative public relations group GOPUSA. Despite his utter lack of professional qualifications, and despite the fact that the Senate and House press galleries had rejected his requests for credentials, Gannon breezed through a White House security check, scoring a front-row seat in the press briefing room. When President Bush called on him at a January 26, 2005, press conference, Gannon delighted the embattled president by ripping into the congressional Democrats. "How are you going to work with people [like the Democratic leadership] who are so divorced from reality?" Gannon asked. "Continue to speak to the American people," Bush replied.

With that question, Gannon gained instant celebrity. Reporters in the pressroom noticed that he had a pattern for lobbing softball questions to the White House press secretaries and briefers. While they gossiped among themselves, Brock deployed his Media Matters researchers to investigate. In February 2005, Media Matters revealed that Gannon's real name was James Dale Guckert and that he had literally cut and pasted entire White House press releases into several of his own articles. Guckert was an obvious fraud. But, then, who was Gannon really? And how did he make a living before his short career as a fake reporter?

On his own website, conservativeguy.com, Gannon presented himself as just another earnest and aspiring Republican activist. In his headshot, he appeared in a suit and tie, seated at an office desk before a stack of books. He wore a serious, even intense, look on his face. But his actual biography told a different story—that of a drifter who had endlessly and effortlessly changed jobs and identities to suit the constantly shifting demands of what appeared to be a very unstable life. "I've been a preppie, a yuppie, blue-collar, green-collar and white-collar," Gannon wrote. "I've served in the military, graduated from college, taught in the public school system, was a union truck driver, a management consultant, a fitness instructor and an entrepreneur. I'm a two-holiday Christian and I usually vote Republican because they most often support conservative positions."

For those trying to clarify Gannon's murky personal history, it seemed apparent that he was much more than a "two-holiday Christian." Lurid rumors filtered through Washington, DC's gay community that several tenacious gay bloggers soon confirmed: Gannon had worked for years as a high-priced male prostitute, advertising himself as a hypermasculine ex-Marine on the website militarystud.com, where he hawked the use of his "weapon," which he described as "8 inches cut," for $200 an hour. Gannon, who had never served in the Marines but only played one as a prostitute, lashed out at the bloggers with harsh anti-gay rhetoric, denouncing them as "radical gay activists" guilty of "hyper-hysterical homosexual hypocrisy."

As the press began to scrutinize the content of Gannon's articles, the *Washington Post* reported that somehow he had mysteriously gained access to highly sensitive CIA documents. In an October 2003 interview with Joseph Wilson, the former U.S. Ambassador to Iraq, Gannon referred to a confidential memo that identified Wilson's wife, Valerie Plame, as a covert CIA agent. Bush's deputy chief of staff and senior political adviser Karl Rove, Vice President Cheney's chief of staff I. Lewis "Scooter" Libby, and other members of the Bush administration circulated this document to a few chosen reporters days later, hoping to punish Wilson for his accurate and damaging claim, which he had reported to the CIA before the invasion of Iraq, that Saddam Hussein possessed no weapons of mass destruction. But for some reason, Gannon had that document in his possession first. In February 2005, Democratic Representatives Louise Slaughter and John Conyers wrote to independent prosecutor Patrick Fitzgerald, who had been appointed to investigate the leak of Plame's identity, demanding to know how Gannon procured the CIA memo. After the conviction of Libby for perjury and obstruction of justice, Fitzgerald's investigation effectively ended without providing an answer to their query, and Gannon has not cleared up the mystery.

The Washington press corps besieged Gannon with questions about his relationship to the White House and his suspect journalistic methods. How had he gained constant access to the White House pressroom without a proper credential? Who in the White House had waved him through the Secret Service's gates? In an attempt to fend off reporters' suspicions, Gannon pointed to a rousing defense of his ethics by the hysterically homophobic columnist Ann Coulter. "Gannon has appeared on television and given a series of creditable interviews in his own defense, proving our gays are more macho than their straights," Coulter opined. But her declaration of support only added to Gannon's infamy. Talon News disappeared from the Web almost as quickly as it appeared, and Gannon faded away, too, toiling on the far fringes as a blogger.

After his outing, Gannon made an appearance before a panel of gay rights activists, where he conceded that he was "absolutely" gay. But he remained conflicted about his identity. "If I talk to Jeff about a lot of gay issues, he freaks—he can't go there," a friend of Gannon's told *Vanity Fair*. "Jeff never stood in front of the mirror, he doesn't think he's part of the gay community, and he doesn't think what he's done affects the gay community. The guy at the end of 'American Beauty'—that's Jeff. He can't come to terms with who he is."

Gannon's hypocrisy on gay issues persisted. He filled his blog posts with anti-gay vitriol, decrying "the major media's pro-gay slant," and sniping at "judicial activists" seeking to undermine "traditional marriage." At the same time, he continued his desperate attempt to morph into a Middle American Everyman, blaming his downward career spiral on anti-Christian bias. "I'm everything people on the Left seem to despise," he claimed. "I'm a man who is white, politically conservative, a gun-owner, an SUV driver and I've voted for Republicans . . . Most importantly, I'm a Christian. Not only by birth, but by rebirth through the blood of Jesus Christ."

Cable news networks, newspapers, and major bloggers had broadcast the details of his double life to millions of Americans, yet Gannon reacted as though they were reporting on a complete stranger. In his mind—and perhaps only in his mind—he was just another "conservative guy." Like Luigi Pirandello, the Italian author who won an international audience through the beneficence of fascist dictator Benito Mussolini (a figure he privately detested even as he donated his Nobel

Prize medal to be melted into scrap metal to support Italy's invasion of Abyssinia), Gannon had become a tragic example of personal disassociation. "There is somebody who's living my life," Pirandello lamented in a diary entry before his death in 1936. "And I know nothing about him." Could not James Guckert have said the same thing about Jeff Gannon?

In the aftermath of the Gannon incident, another mysterious figure, Matt Sanchez, materialized instantly as an icon of the conservative movement. He too seemed to be the product of an immaculate political conception. And like Gannon, who had never been a soldier but played one on the Internet, Sanchez presented himself as the ideal of the hyper-male culture of the U.S. Marines. An inactive reservist trained in refrigeration mechanics, the thirty-six-year-old high school dropout described his military service in terms of personal transcendence. "Joining the Marines was a bit like a religious experience," Sanchez said. "You're constantly placed under enormous pressure and often your only way of being 'saved' is turning toward the Marine method. Honor, Courage, and Commitment are the 3 commandments."

By 2007, Sanchez was attending Columbia University as a commuter student—an anonymous figure on campus distinguished only by his hulking physique and gray, tight Marines t-shirts. Suddenly, after a fracas at the school broke out between anti-war protesters and campus military recruiters, Sanchez rocketed to conservative star status. In an article for the Columbia student newspaper, he alleged that while he was promoting the Marines on campus, a group called the International Socialist Organization shouted epithets labeling him a "baby-killer" and "stupid minority" (Sanchez is Puerto Rican). Although the incident was thoroughly investigated by Columbia and never confirmed, Sanchez was shuttled to the Fox News sets of *Hannity & Colmes* and *The O'Reilly Factor* to recount his horror story. Right-wing bloggers amplified his tale with righteous indignation, and the *New York Post* solicited him for hot exposés on the anti-Americanism of Columbia's latte liberals.

In honor of his courage in the face of liberal bigotry, Sanchez was presented with the Jeane Kirkpatrick Academic Freedom Award at the 2007 Conservative Political Action Conference, a massive annual gathering of right-wing activists that included appearances by Vice President Dick Cheney and White House Press Secretary Tony Snow. Basking in his fifteen minutes of fame, Sanchez had his photo snapped with Newt Gingrich and posed for a beaming portrait with Ann Coulter, who had called Democratic presidential candidate John Edwards "a faggot" minutes earlier. Sanchez even brushed shoulders for a moment with Jeff Gannon. When he posted photos of himself with these conservative idols on his personal blog that same evening, a light went on. A popular gay blogger named Andy Towle recognized Sanchez from a date he said they went on in 1999.

The following morning, photos spread like poison ivy across the Web depicting the muscle-bound Sanchez in action during his prior career as a gay porn actor. His screen names alternated between Rod Majors and Pierre LaBranche. Most of the photos showed Sanchez acting in one or another of the forty-five classics he starred in, including *Beat Off Frenzy*, *Touched by an Anal*, and *Tijuana Toilet Tramps*. Towle and other gay bloggers pointed to a still-active Web page, ExcellentTop.com, where Sanchez had apparently advertised himself as a $200-an-hour male escort. Sanchez attempted to block public access to this site but failed when bloggers dredged up a cached version.

Finally Sanchez came out, in a sense, in a confessional piece for the popular liberal Web magazine Salon.com. In it, he claimed his porn career made him feel "disgusted" with himself, stuck on a constant "emotional low," and convinced that "the people who surrounded [him] were like drug dealers." Sanchez's disillusionment stoked his attraction to backlash conservatism. "I didn't like porn's liberalism," Sanchez said. "In porn, everything taboo is trivialized and everything trivial is magnified." Repelled by "liberalism," Sanchez explained that he was transformed into "a 100 percent flag-waving red-blooded Reagan Republican."

Now that he was a "conservative guy," Sanchez claimed to have instantly exorcised his homosexual tendencies. "I don't consider myself gay or a member of the gay community," he told an interviewer from *Radar* magazine. "Have I ever been gay? No," Sanchez added for emphasis. "Have I had sex with men? Obviously." On his personal website, Sanchez claimed to have two girlfriends, then said he was married, and then retracted that claim after bloggers challenged him to produce a marriage license.

Then, just like Gannon, Sanchez projected his self-loathing onto homosexuals. "Gay men are like fundamentalist Muslims. If you leave their religion they have to send out a *fatwa* and demand your execution," Sanchez complained. Conservative gay-bashers were delighted by the Marine's impassioned denunciations and denials. "Cpl. Sanchez, it was an honor to meet you and a privilege to know you," wrote Michelle Malkin, a nationally syndicated right-wing commentator who posed for a photo with Sanchez at CPAC, in a lengthy defense of the "corporal" on her blog.

I, too, had the honor of meeting Sanchez at CPAC, and I described the encounter in an article for the *Huffington Post*. I noted that he was introduced to me by David Horowitz, a veteran conservative operative and former Communist agitator of the New Left, as the best and brightest in his campaign against college anti-war groups, or, as he called them, "campus fascists." The next day, I appeared on MSNBC's *Countdown with Keith Olbermann* to discuss Sanchez's outing in the context of the right's anti-gay politicking. When I returned home that night, I discovered an e-mail in my inbox. It was from Cpl. Matt Sanchez and consisted of a single sentence: "So do you have a crush on me or what?" Days later I learned that Sanchez had created a Wikipedia page about me, falsely identifying me as a homosexual. Then I understood why I had been suddenly deluged with e-mails from gay political junkies inquiring about my relationship status.

Even though I didn't respond to Sanchez, he took the liberty of adding me to his mailing list. I was now able to track his journey. I learned that he had been discharged from the Marines and embedded as a blogger with troops in Iraq with the express mission of providing pro-war coverage. In his dispatches he accused nonembedded reporters of harboring secret terrorist sympathies, claiming, in an article for the *National Review* in July 2007, that the press had waged "a very cunning strategy to win an asymmetrical war" against the United States. Sanchez's war cheerleading also appeared routinely in *WorldNetDaily*, a far-right Web magazine that had published an exhaustive four-part series headlined "Soy is making kids 'gay.'"

In an interview with Randy Thomas, a "former" homosexual serving as vice president of a self-described "ex-gay" ministry, Exodus International, Sanchez vehemently insisted that he had never been gay. He lashed out at the "gay fundamentalists" who outed him, likening them to pedophiles. "The bulk of the gay fundamentalists," he fumed, "the anti-religious, the pro-abortionist constituents—these are the people who feel you're 'born that way.' By that token, child molesters are just born that way and should be 'forgiven' for just doing what comes natural."

These projections inspired him to proclaim that he was writing a book, *Gay Jihad: What the Radical Homosexual Movement Has in Store for You and Your Family*, to be coauthored with Jeremy Duboff, an unknown right-winger. In "A Letter to Matt Sanchez" posted on Duboff's website, the coauthor explained his attraction to Sanchez: "You see, 15 or more years ago, when I was a very young adult, I too attempted to live 'the gay lifestyle.' This took place at UC Berkeley and in the San Francisco Bay Area, where the gay agenda figures especially prominently. Unlike you my prime motivation was not immoral and illicit sex but immoral and illicit politics—a clear commitment to a vague concept of Marxist–Leninist revolution. Yet like you I 'wasn't very good at being gay' either." So far, the promised book has not been published.

Personalities like Gannon, Sanchez, and Duboff—there are so many of them among the radical right that they are difficult to keep track of—recall Marcello Clerici, the protagonist of Italian writer Alberto Moravia's novel *The Conformist* and Bernardo Bertolucci's faithful cinematic adaptation of the same title. As a boy, Marcello was a social outcast, a weakling with a syphilitic, institutionalized father. His troubled youth culminated when he murdered a chauffeur who had coaxed him into sex. When he reached adulthood, Marcello resolved to subdue his inner demons by joining Italy's incipient fascist movement. He enlisted in Mussolini's bureaucracy as a counter-subversive spy and became engaged to an empty-headed lower-middle-class woman whom he secretly regarded with disdain. "I intend to construct my normality," he coldly vowed to a priest, promising to marry his fiancée. But because Marcello's normality hinged entirely on forces outside of himself, especially the endurance of the fascist bureaucracy, his relapse into loneliness was imminent. When Mussolini was forced from power in 1943, throwing Italy into chaos, Marcello stumbled upon the chauffeur he thought he had killed long ago, and the thin mask of normality he had constructed peeled back suddenly and irrevocably.

Like Clerici, many self-loathing homosexuals have confused authoritarianism with normality and have sought to transcend their tortured pasts by donning the cartoon-like costume of the Republican male social dominator—the political analogue of an "excellent top." But although they avoid the seedy lifestyles they once led, the conformist solution that Gannon, Sanchez, and countless other conflicted conservatives in crisis have chosen is always evanescent. The culture of the radical right may promise a resolution to unbiblical desires, but in the end, repressed homosexuals can only cover their supposed sins, not wash them away.

In some ways, Mark Foley's experience contrasted with that of figures such as Gannon and Sanchez who dissolved into the conservative apparatus as a method of escape. Foley, a gay Republican congressman, was open about his identity within his private political inner circle, but he kept it secret from the general public. As his party lurched to the far right, however, targeting gays as a scapegoat for America's social deterioration, Foley remained a loyal soldier. Meanwhile, he preyed on young male pages milling about the halls of Congress, placing his career and those of the many other gay Republicans who staffed his office in jeopardy. When Foley's conflicted personality unraveled, he created a political scandal of catastrophic proportions, one that drove a nail in the coffin of the Republican Revolution and became the symbol of the party's cultural crack-up.

LIVES UNLIVED

Although places such as Stonewall and Castro are more commonly associated with the rise of gay pride, South Florida also witnessed the birth of one of America's first viable gay rights movements. In 1977, Dade County gay rights activists orchestrated a successful push for an "affectional and sexual preference" ordinance that banned discrimination on the basis of sexual orientation. This groundbreaking measure inspired the passage of gay rights legislation in cities across the country. Its cultural impact, though difficult to measure, lifted the morale of a nascent movement still struggling for the credibility that the civil rights and women's liberation movements had attained.

Mark Foley grew up nearby in Lake Worth, but he existed a world away from South Florida's progressive cultural groundswell. During the mid-1960s, Foley served as an altar boy at Sacred Heart Church, a Roman Catholic congregation in his hometown. At age thirteen, Foley met Father Anthony Mercieca, an affable, energetic clergyman then in his late twenties. The two became fast friends, taking regular sojourns to the beach, the arcade, and local rodeos. They even traveled together to New York and Washington, DC to tour museums. The two were so inseparable that they seemed like brothers. But the friendship between Foley and Mercieca soon crossed over into the sexual realm when they began skinny-dipping and sleeping together in the nude. Mercieca claimed that his sexual encounters with the young Foley were consensual and entailed nothing more than fondling. "Once maybe I touched him or so, but didn't, it wasn't—because it's not something you call, I mean, rape or penetration or anything like that you know," the priest said. "He seemed to like it, you know? So it was sort of more like a spontaneous thing."

While Foley was coming of age, the Christian right targeted his native South Florida as a laboratory for the cultural holy war it hoped to ignite on a national level. Anita Bryant, the Miss America runner-up, singer, and national spokeswoman for the Florida Citrus Commission, emerged as the face of the Christian right's mounting anti-gay crusade. Under the stern watch of her husband, Bob Green, a draconian fundamentalist accused of emotionally damaging behavior by his live-in babysitter, Kathie Lee Gifford (who later became a famed daytime TV host), Bryant was transformed from a cheery commercial voice who compared a breakfast without orange juice to "a day without sunshine" into an anti-gay La Pasionara who compared homosexuals to "people who sleep with St. Bernards." Just months after Miami-Dade's anti-discrimination ordinance passed, Bryant summoned local right-wing forces for holy war under the sign of the cross, leading a crusade that swiftly repealed the law by a decisive margin. The Miami Archdiocese of the Roman Catholic Church—Father Mercieca's employer—played an instrumental role in Bryant's victory, securing 64,000 signatures for her ballot measure in one month.

Bryant pressed her case against the gay menace further, successfully lobbying for legislation banning homosexuals from adopting children in Florida—a law upheld by the 11th Circuit of the U.S. Court of Appeals in 2004. Her organization, Save Our Children, elevated her anti-gay politics to the national level by mass-distributing a flier titled "Why Certain Sexual Deviations Are Punishable by Death." Besides homosexuality, the damnable sins enumerated by Bryant included "racial mixing of human seed." Bryant's campaign inspired Christian-right elements in the California state legislature to propose a law that would have banned public school teachers from making any statement that could be interpreted as pro-gay. (The bill was voted down by a slim margin amid furious lobbying by gay rights forces under the leadership of San Francisco community activist Harvey Milk.)

South Florida's culture war was a microcosm of the one that would soon take hold on a national level, but it also encapsulated the personal conflict that Foley faced as he embarked on his first bid for Congress in 1994. Foley was a dyed-in-the-wool Republican—anti-tax, anti-environment, and anti-immigrant—but he was also gay. And though his homosexuality was an open secret in local political circles, Foley seemed to view it as an obstacle to his ambition. But by trumpeting his firm convictions on conservative core Republican issues, Foley calculated he could ensure that voters in Florida's Republican gerrymandered 16th district would not bother to question his sexual orientation. That assumption proved correct. In 1994, he coasted to victory, and he joined the drove of exuberant freshmen as shock troops of Newt Gingrich's revolution.

Although Foley had staked out a moderate reputation on social issues, he eagerly joined party zealots during the impeachment trial of President Bill Clinton. "It's vile," he said of Clinton's affair with Monica Lewinsky. "It's more sad than anything else, to see someone with such potential throw it all down the drain because of a sexual addiction." After the Senate rejected the House Republicans' coup-by-impeachment against Clinton, Foley assisted Tom DeLay's coup against Newt Gingrich. Foley became a central cog in DeLay's machine, a deputy whip, and earned the protection that the ruthless leader—"The Hammer"—extended to his vassals.

Under DeLay and his puppet, the hulking and phlegmatic Speaker of the House Dennis Hastert, Foley was rewarded with his dream assignment: chairman of the House Caucus on Missing and Exploited Children. Protecting children was Foley's lifelong passion, he declared, inspiring him to introduce legislation establishing strict guidelines for targeting online sexual predators. Away from the klieg lights of the Washington press corps, however, Foley's interest in boys took on a prurient quality. Foley was seen fondling male pages on several occasions by fellow Republican lawmakers, who said nothing. One page, Matthew Loraditch, warned fellow pages in 2001 to "watch out for Congressman Mark Foley." That same year, the parents of another page preyed upon by Foley contacted their son's sponsor, Republican Representative Rodney Alexander, to complain. Alexander went to National Republican Congressional Committee Chairman Tom Reynolds, but the complaint was buried as soon as Foley donated $100,000 to Reynolds's committee.

With the 2004 elections approaching, James Dobson, Tony Perkins, and a constellation of Christian right para-church leaders pressured the Republican leadership to introduce a constitutional ban on same sex-marriage. "What's at stake here," said Perkins, "is the very foundation of our society, not only of America but all Western civilization." The Reverend Jimmy Swaggart, the televangelist who had fallen from grace with his 1988 confession of soliciting prostitutes, now saw gay-bashing as his path back to moral respectability. "I've never seen a man in my life I wanted to marry," Swaggart proclaimed in 2003, prompting a chorus of "amens" from his audience. "And I'm gonna be blunt and plain: if one ever looks at me like that," the red-faced preacher growled, "I'm gonna kill him and tell God he died." As anti-gay fervor approached a boiling point, House Republicans introduced the same-sex marriage ban the Christian right had demanded.

Foley voted against the Republican bill but avoided making any public statement, apparently trying to maintain his personal integrity while hiding his identity. Meanwhile, as his predatory behavior grew increasingly brazen, the Republican leadership feared that exposing him would repel the conservative base at a time when their support was pivotal to the party's future. Thus a cover-up was set in motion, involving Kirk Fordham, a veteran Republican congressional staffer who had served as Foley's chief of staff by day and his chaperone by night, escorting him to parties to prevent him from making inappropriate advances on young men. Like Foley, Fordham was a semicloseted homosexual who feared that his outing would doom his career. When a leading gay reporter, Chris Crain, informed Fordham of his plans to report Fordham's sexual orientation in 2003, he begged him not to do so, explaining that he was "out in the community but not in the press." Crain, a Republican himself, complied. In turn, Fordham guarded Foley from public exposure.

Other gay Republican staffers were familiar with Foley's secret life, but none went public. These included Jeff Trandahl, an openly gay man who headed the House page program. Trandahl said he told a Hastert aide named Ted Van Der Meid that Foley posed a clear and present danger to the pages, but Van Der Meid avoided going public. (Republicans on the Hill widely believed that he was gay.) Trandahl also complained to Fordham that in 2003 Foley had stumbled into the pages' dormitory in a drunken haze seeking sex and had to be turned. away. Yet instead of going public, Fordham simply told Hastert's chief of staff, Scott Palmer, about the incident. Palmer, the subject of pointed gay rumors, warned Foley that he could expose himself if he repeated his behavior. (Palmer would later deny having discussions with Fordham, further complicating a doomed investigation by Florida law enforcement.) "From Foley's perspective," wrote Crain, "these slaps on the wrist from the fellow limp-wristed didn't carry any real sting because, in the end, he expected them to protect him, just as he protected their closets, however deeply in them each lived." So the scandal remained top secret.

In 2003, Foley made preparations for a campaign to succeed retiring Democratic Senator Bob Graham of Florida. In June, as his fundraising efforts began, Foley declared war on the American Association for Nude Recreation (AANR), a group that operated a nudist camp

for young people near Tampa. Foley fired off a breathless letter to
Governor Jeb Bush accusing the camp of "exploiting nudity among
minor children to make money." Demanding that the governor investigate the legality of the camp, Foley warned, "men have made their
way to the camp pool to get a 'glimpse' of these naked children . . . The
next time, these children may not be so fortunate: the trespasser may
have more on his mind than just peeping." John Cloud, a writer for
Time magazine who covered the controversy, wrote, "Foley has a
point . . . they have to keep an eye on creepy men."

While campaigning in Pensacola, the day before he planned to
formally announce his bid for the Senate, Foley withdrew to a hotel
room and signed on to an instant messaging service under his screen
name, Maf54. Then, the forty-eight-year-old congressman invited a
sixteen-year-old male page, Jordan Edmunds, to chat with him. Almost as soon as their chat began, Foley introduced a line of conversa-
tion heavily laced with graphic sexual innuendo:

Maf54 (7:37:27 PM): how my favorite young stud doing
[redacted screenname] (7:37:46 PM): tired and sore
[. . .]
Maf54 (7:48:00 PM): did you spank it this weekend yourself
[redacted screenname] (7:48:04 PM): no
[redacted screenname] (7:48:16 PM): been too tired and too busy
Maf54 (7:48:33 PM): wow . . .
Maf54 (7:48:34 PM): i am never to busy haha
[. . .]
Maf54 (7:53:54 PM): do you really do it face down
[redacted screenname] (7:54:03 PM): ya
Maf54 (7:54:13 PM): kneeling
[redacted screenname] (7:54:31 PM): well i dont use my hand . . . i
    use the bed itself
Maf54 (7:54:31 PM): where do you unload it
[redacted screenname] (7:54:36 PM): towel
Maf54 (7:54:43 PM): really
Maf54 (7:55:02 PM): completely naked?
[redacted screenname] (7:55:12 PM): well ya

Maf54 (7:55:21 PM): very nice
[redacted screenname] (7:55:24 PM): lol
Maf54 (7:55:51 PM): cute butt bouncing in the air
[...]
Maf54 (7:57:05 PM): i always use lotion and the hand
[...]
Maf54 (7:58:16 PM): just kinda slow rubbing
Maf54 (7:59:48 PM): is your little guy limp ... or growing
[redacted screenname] (7:59:54 PM): eh growing
[...]
Maf54 (8:08:31 PM): get a ruler and measure it for me
[redacted screenname] (8:08:38 PM): ive already told you that
[...]
Maf54 (8:10:40 PM): take it out
[redacted screenname] (8:10:54 PM): brb ... my mom is yelling

Although Foley's online predation was still secret when he declared his run for the Senate, his candidacy was dead on arrival. As
soon as Foley announced, several local newspapers rehashed a 1996
story from the gay-themed magazine *The Advocate* outing Foley as
gay. Foley hurriedly called a news conference to condemn the stories,
which he called "revolting and unforgivable." But he could not
muster a denial of his homosexuality. "Elected officials," Foley declared, "even those who run for the United States Senate, must have
some level of privacy. My mother and father raised me and the rest of
my family to believe that there are certain things we shouldn't discuss
in public. Some of you may believe that it's old-fashioned, but I believe those are good ideals to live by." Foley withdrew from the race
immediately, claiming that he wanted to support his cancer stricken
father. But he had already raised $3 million dollars, far more than his
Republican primary rival.

When he returned to his safe seat in the House, the "old-fashioned"
Foley continued courting pages through suggestive e-mail entreaties.
One page grew uncomfortable with Foley's come-ons—"sick," he called
them—and forwarded his e-mails to staffers of Representative Alexander. The e-mails leaked out of Alexander's office and circulated through

congressional e-mail inboxes until they found their way into the possession of ABC News investigative reporter Brian Ross in August 2006.
When Fordham learned that Ross planned to report on Foley's digital
dalliances, he rushed to the reporter to offer a deal: Withhold the
e-mails in exchange for an exclusive on Foley's resignation, which he
promised to secure. Ross refused the deal but was forced to hold his
story because of an already pending investigative project.

But one month later, Foley's lurid instant messages fell into the
hands of Lane Hudson, a gay rights activist, who said Foley had once
hit on him at a Washington-area gay bar. Hudson immediately published Foley's IMs on an ad hoc website he had created called "Stop
Sexual Predators." As bloggers disseminated the instant messages, the
story gathered momentum and exploded into the mainstream press.
Now Ross published his story on Foley's e-mails, adding damning
detail to the brewing scandal. Hudson, for his part, was fired from his
job at the Human Rights Campaign, a leading gay rights organization
in Washington, for supposedly misusing its resources. One of the
board members who voted to oust him happened to be Jeff Trandahl.

Another semicloseted gay conservative, the professional Internet
rumor-monger Matt Drudge (who once appeared unsolicited at David
Brock's doorstep with a bouquet of flowers), joined the cover-up of
Foley's crimes. Citing an unnamed source, Drudge reported that the
young page exchanging lurid instant messages with Foley, Jordan Edmunds, had actually goaded him into typing revealing statements and
had then distributed them to Democratic operatives as part of a prank.
Edmunds's lawyer dismissed Drudge's uncorroborated, unsourced
story as "a piece of fiction," and soon enough, it disappeared from his
website.

On September 29, House Majority Leader Nancy Pelosi demanded
on the House floor an investigation of Foley's behavior. Republican
Minority Leader John Boehner, who had known of Foley's actions
months before but appeared to do nothing, headed off Pelosi's investigation by referring Foley's case to the House Ethics Committee.

That same day, Foley tendered his resignation. Claiming his sexually
inappropriate behavior had been fueled by alcoholism, he shut himself
away in a rehabilitation clinic. Through his lawyer, Foley disclosed that

Father Mercieca had molested him when he had been a teenager, suggesting that the experience had conditioned him to act the same way with young, vulnerable boys. According to the Reverend Pamela Cooper White, an ordained pastor who has counseled victims of clergy abuse for over twenty years, many priests, like Mercieca, were sexually molested during their own childhoods. When they assume positions of power, White wrote, these priests often exhibit "poor impulse control; a sense of entitlement, or being above the law, or other narcissistic traits. . . ." The vicious cycle often continues through their victims, especially when they become powerful figures like Foley.

Foley's tragic confession failed to inspire sympathy among the Republicans who had previously protected him. His former leader in Congress, Tom DeLay, was also a child of abuse who fell into alcoholism and promiscuity during the first half of his adult life. But DeLay confessed his sins and bared his soul early in his career, earning the good graces of James Dobson and the Christian right. Foley's confession, on the other hand, seemed more like a clumsy attempt at damage control than an earnest plea for Christian forgiveness. His behavior mirrored that of many priests accused of abuse. "Sometimes— as when threatened with suspension by their denomination—they admit that they are in need of treatment to 'build up their fortitude against being seduced,'" White wrote. "What they generally fail to see is their own responsibility."

The political fallout from the Foley scandal shattered the Republicans' already shaky chance of holding Congress in the 2006 midterms. By law, even though Foley had resigned, his name remained on the ballot in his home district, compelling the Republican slated as his successor, Joe Negron, to campaign under the slogan "Punch Foley for Joe," a thinly disguised double entendre. But disgruntled voters, including many Republicans, instead elected Democrat Tim Mahoney, the first Democrat ever to represent the overwhelmingly Republican district since it was created in 1973.

In the wake of the Foley scandal, Hastert, who had become a symbol of his party's moral decay, ignored calls from voices of the conservative movement, from direct-mail dean Richard Viguerie to Michael Reagan, the son of Ronald Reagan, for his own resignation. Instead, he blamed his troubles on, "ABC News and a lot of Democratic operatives, people funded by [liberal billionaire philanthropist] George Soros." The Democrats exploited the image of Hastert with devastating effect, rolling out an ad blitz connecting five Republican incumbents to Hastert's cover-up of Foleygate. On election night, the GOP lost six Senate seats and thirty-one seats in the House. In a special election in March 2008, even the retiring Hastert's seat, which he had held for decades, fell to a Democrat. The political tide had shifted, in no small part because of the Republicans' Foley cover-up.

The impact of the Foley scandal was especially damaging for the Christian right, which had depended on the congressional Republicans to pipeline a steady stream of anti-abortion and anti-gay bills to the President's desk. Tony Perkins vented the movement's rage in a tirade against gay Republicans. "Has the social agenda of the GOP been stalled by homosexual members and or staffers? When we look over events of this Congress, we have to wonder," Perkins fumed in a mass e-mail to his supporters. He continued: "Does the [Republican] party want to represent values voters or Mark Foley and friends?" A photo of a smiling Trandahl appeared beside Perkins's angry missive.

The Reverend Don Wildmon, the churlish founder of the American Family Association, a Christian-right group based in Tupelo, Mississippi, went a step further. In early October, a group of gay rights activists had compiled a list of gay Republicans working on Capitol Hill and distributed it to Wildmon and other Christian-right leaders. Now the old reverend was furious and wanted a purge of "the homosexual clique" that he accused of boring from within the Republican infrastructure. "They oughta fire every one of 'em," Wildmon told me in his guttural Southern drawl. "I don't care if they're heterosexual or homosexual or whatever they are. If you've got that going on, that subverts the will of the people; that subverts the voters. That is subversive activity. There should be no organization among staffers in Washington of that nature, and if they find out that they're there and they're a member, they oughtta be dismissed el pronto."

Wildmon's demand for a gay purge recalled the real one carried out during the 1950s at the behest of Republican Senator Joseph McCarthy. Influenced by the wildly popular 1951 screed *Washington*

Confidential, which reported that "at least 6,000 homosexuals on the government payroll" were turning the nation's capitol into "a garden of pansies," McCarthy claimed the Roosevelt and Truman administrations had been infiltrated by a "hominterm" dead-set on undermining national security. His charges led to a massive inquisition of suspected homosexual bureaucrats, subjecting thousands to interrogations about their private lives. Many, if not most, were summarily fired. Some committed suicide after losing their livelihoods.

Then, as now, the far right's anti-gay crusade was orchestrated not only by bigots but also by self-loathing homosexuals. Chief among them was McCarthy's grand inquisitor, the ruthless Roy Cohn. Cohn, a deeply closeted homosexual, continued to terrorize gays well after the liquor-sodden McCarthy drank himself to death. Cohn opposed New York City's first gay rights law in the 1970s, declaring that homosexuals would threaten the safety of children if they were allowed to work as schoolteachers. Then, in the weeks leading up to his death from AIDS in 1986, Cohn, who falsely claimed he had liver cancer, launched another lobbying blitz against a New York City gay rights ordinance. This time, he justified his activism on the grounds that the proposed law "defended fags."

"Roy [Cohn] was not gay," Republican operative Roger Stone remarked to legal commentator Jeffrey Toobin. "He was a man who liked having sex with men. Gays were weak, effeminate. He always seemed to have these young blond boys around. It just wasn't discussed. He was interested in power and access." Cohn became a mentor to Stone, teaching him the hardball tactics he used to help Ronald Reagan sabotage George H. W. Bush in the 1980 Republican primary. Cohn and Stone's friendship extended beyond politics and into their mutual affinity for the sexual underworld. Stone resigned from Bob Dole's 1996 presidential campaign when tabloids connected him and his wife to an ad in a magazine called *Local Swing Fever*. "Hot, insatiable lady and her handsome body builder husband, experienced swingers, seek similar couples or exceptional muscular . . . single men," the ad stated. Stone, who freely admits he is a regular at Miami-area swinger clubs, boasted in 2007 of using his sex industry contacts to implicate then New York Democratic Governor Eliot Spitzer to the FBI in patronizing a high-priced hooker. "I'm not guilty of hypocrisy," Stone told Toobin. "I'm a libertarian and a libertine."

■ ■ ■

The Republican infrastructure is so honeycombed with closeted homosexuals that any attempt by homophobes such as Wildmon to ferret them out would be impossible. During my interview with the reverend, I rattled off names of gay conservatives that I thought were well known and might be on the list he had been provided: Lee La-Haye, the chief operating officer for the far-right Concerned Women for America and son of Tim LaHaye, author of the anti-gay tract *The Unhappy Gays*; John Schlafly, son of conservative movement doyenne Phyllis Schalfly (who has called gays "vicious") and director of the Illinois branch of his mother's Eagle Forum; and Robert Traynham, at the time the gay, African American spokesman for the hysterically homophobic Republican Senator Rick Santorum, who had infamously compared homosexuality to "man-on-dog" sex.

Wildmon interrupted me mid-sentence, and backpedaled on his earlier cry for a purge. "Well, if a senator's got a homosexual member of his staff," Wildmon said, "and if he's doing his job and he's working for the good of the senator, then I don't have a problem with that."

In the end, Wildmon's blustery threats did little more than put gay Republican staffers on notice. If they did not remain useful tools for the Christian right, he seemed to be saying, they would invite fire and brimstone from the movement. One gay Republican staffer told the *New York Times* that the right's hysterical reaction to Foleygate had brought him nothing but "siege and suspicion." While Wildmon and his fellow culture warriors lashed out at the lavender menace on Capitol Hill, they seemed blithely unaware of the extent to which their attacks contributed to an atmosphere that would further damage Republicans. Just as Foleygate seemed to wane, a new wave of right-wing sex scandals hit. Among those swept up in these scandals was one of the movement's most stalwart allies, Idaho Senator Larry Craig.

For years, the virulently right-wing Craig had batted away pointed rumors that he was gay and had sexual encounters with men in public bathroom stalls. In October 2006, gay rights activist Michael Rogers publicized interviews with four men who said they had had sex with Craig in the bathroom at Washington's Union Station. Craig denied these rumors, as he had done in the past, but his behavior did not change. Like Foley, even as suspicion of Craig's secret life mounted, the senator's behavior grew ever bolder, as though he harbored some sort of political death wish.

CHAPTER 18

THE WIDE STANCE

L arry Craig fostered an all-American reputation during his years at Midvale High, in rural Idaho, in the early 1960s, starring at center for the football team and helping the cash-strapped school band to find used uniforms so they could march in the Boise Christmas parade. A born leader, he went on to become student body president and president of its Delta Chi fraternity. But while he was leading Delta Chi, allegations about his homosexual tendencies first spread; one young pledge said Craig brought him into a room in the frat house and suggested they have sex. After graduation, Craig enlisted for a six-year tour in the Idaho National Guard but was honorably discharged in 1972 after six months, prompting rumors that homosexual indiscretions led to his dismissal. Craig insisted that foot problems were the reason for his discharge.

Four years later, Craig won a seat in the state legislature, and then he was elected to the U.S. House of Representatives. Once in Washington, a cosmopolitan city with a burgeoning gay subculture, Craig was exposed to temptations he hadn't encountered in the rigid climate of his native Idaho. In 1982, a CBS News story alleging widespread sex between congressmen and male congressional pages put Craig's political ascent into momentary peril. Craig was never implicated in the scandal, but when a reporter stopped by his office to ask his opinion on it, Craig felt compelled to deny his involvement, an unusual adamancy that left suspicion. The following year, Craig married Suzanne Scott, a divorcée with three children from her previous marriage. But still the rumors wouldn't go away. In 1990, when Craig declared his candidacy for the Senate, his opponent openly referred to Craig as gay. When a reporter asked him whether he was homosexual, Craig snapped, "Just ask my wife."

Despite the continuing allegations, Craig was elected to the Senate. There, he remained a reliable "yea" vote on any piece of social policy legislation the Christian right managed to get to the floor. He was also, like Foley, among the most vigorous proponents of impeaching Bill Clinton for lying about his affair with Monica Lewinsky. During an appearance on *Meet the Press* in 1999, Craig sneeringly vowed that he would "speak out for the citizens of [his] state who think like the majority that Bill Clinton is even a nasty, bad, naughty boy."

In 2004, Craig joined his conservative colleagues in voting to amend the Constitution to ban same-sex marriage, imploring the Senate to "stand up now and protect traditional marriage, which is under attack by a few unelected judges and litigious activists." Two years later, Craig endorsed a proposed ban on gay marriage and civil unions in Idaho. But in political circles from Washington, DC, to Boise, allegations about Craig's homosexuality intensified.

"I don't agree with the [gay] lifestyle," Craig told Matt Lauer, the host of NBC's *Today Show*, in September 2007. "And I've said so by my votes over the years and by my expressions. Have I viewed it as awful? I viewed it as a lifestyle I don't agree with."

In 2006, the *Statesman* launched a full-time investigation into Craig's alleged homosexual life, dispatching columnist Dan Popke to dig deep into the senator's past for evidence about the rumors that had dogged him for so long. Over the course of a year, Popke compiled testimony from five men who claimed they either were propositioned by Craig or had sex with him. One man, David Phillips, said he met Craig at a gay strip club in Washington, DC, in 1987. After having sex at a nearby house, Phillips said Craig handed him a $20 bill and warned ominously, "I can buy and sell your ass a thousand times over. You were never here." But before the *Statesman*'s editors were ready to go to press with their story, Craig was arrested.

On June 11, 2007, Craig ducked into a bathroom at Minneapolis Airport notorious for illicit gay encounters. "This place is THE most cruisy public place I have ever been," one person wrote about the restroom on the Internet chat room Squirt.org. Another remarked, "This is the best place for anonymous action I've ever seen." The "action" had become such a public nuisance that the Minneapolis police set up a sting to catch perpetrators in the act. Given the dubious honor of leading this dragnet, Sergeant Dave Karsnia sat for hours in a stall while dozens of men relieved themselves nearby, waiting patiently until one of them propositioned him.

Suddenly, a man hovered before the door of Karsnia's stall. Through the crack, Karsnia could see that the man, an older, bespectacled fellow with a shock of silver hair, was twiddling his fingers in odd motions and attempting to peer inside. Then the man settled in the stall next door, slid his foot under the stall divider, and bumped Karsnia's. Next, the man waved his hand under the divider, a coded request for sex. Karsnia flashed his badge under the divider and pointed to the exit. "No!" the man yelped. He met Karsnia outside the stalls and handed him a business card showing that he was a U.S. senator, an important lawmaker named Larry Craig. "What do you think of that?" Craig asked. Karsnia apparently did not think much of it; Craig was arrested and booked for lewd conduct.

At the police station, Karsnia subjected Craig to a withering interrogation. Craig was lawyerly to the point of self-parody, insisting that his bumping of Karsnia's foot resulted accidentally from his "wide stance" on the toilet. But he eventually pleaded guilty to misdemeanor disorderly conduct when he was assured that felony lewdness charges would be dropped. He then returned to Capitol Hill as though nothing had happened, keeping his arrest secret from his staff, wife, and family for two months. But when the *Statesman* obtained court records showing Craig's guilty plea, the scandal exploded. Craig's infamous phrase "wide stance" instantly became the universal code phrase for Republican sexual hypocrisy.

On August 21, 2007, Craig appeared before a mob of reporters in front of the Idaho Statehouse in downtown Boise. With Suzanne, his wife of twenty-five years, standing beside him, her hand on the small of his back, he indignantly declared, "I am not gay. I have never been gay!" Craig claimed his guilty plea had simply been "a mistake," as though he had admitted to committing such an embarrassing act out of confusion. "While I was not involved in any inappropriate conduct at the Minneapolis airport or anywhere else," Craig said, "I chose to plead guilty to a lesser charge in the hope of making it go away." The reason why he pleaded guilty and kept the arrest secret, he insisted, was that he was the victim of a "witch-hunt" conducted by the *Statesman*. "I should not have kept this arrest to myself . . . because *I am not gay!*" he said, visibly shaking with anger.

Whereas Senator David Vitter received a standing ovation from his fellow Republicans upon returning to the Senate after confessing to engaging in sex with female prostitutes, Craig's transgression invited the wrath of his peers. Republican Senate Minority Leader Mitch McConnell called his conduct "unforgivable," hinting at severe retaliation. Senator John McCain called for his resignation. And Mitt Romney, the former Massachusetts governor and Republican presidential candidate, dropped Craig as his Idaho campaign chairman.

Tony Perkins, who had been one of Vitter's most unabashed apologists, demanded Craig's ouster as well. During an August 28, 2007, broadcast of the MSNBC political talk show *Hardball*, Perkins called Craig's bathroom stall behavior "a part of a growing problem within the Republican Party, where value voters expect those that trumpet their issues to live by those same values . . . And I think it's going to be a real hurdle for the Republicans in the upcoming elections."

But Perkins's moralistic rationale for Craig's resignation concealed a political calculation. If Craig left the Senate, Perkins reckoned, he was certain to be succeeded by a Republican. Idaho was so conservative that one man running to succeed Craig in 2008, a strawberry farmer named Marvin Richardson, attempted to boost his chances by legally changing his name to "Pro-Life." If Vitter resigned at the moment his transgressions were revealed, however, a Democrat was likely to fill his seat. In its will to power, the movement forgave Vitter for his sins but crucified Craig for committing a hypocritical but legally insignificant crime.

Craig's lone Republican defender was Armstrong Williams, a conservative African American talk show host and former aide to Clarence Thomas who had gained renown in 1998, when, during an

interview, he provoked Republican Senator Trent Lott to compare
gays to alcoholics and kleptomaniacs. Although Williams stopped
short of calling for Craig to keep his Senate seat, he implored fellow
conservatives to reserve judgment on the senator's bathroom stall an-
tics. "We are often quick to judge people for their actions, when we
don't know the whole story," Williams wrote in a column for *Townhall*, a conservative Web magazine, after Craig's infamous press conference. "Lewd conduct is wrong, period, but it is impossible for us to
know Senator Craig's character based on this snapshot of his life."

But behind Williams's plea for compassion were transgressions, financial and sexual, of his own. The commentator is best known for accepting a $240,000 bribe from the Bush administration to promote its
No Child Left Behind policy in his columns, a sin that he acknowledged as a motivating factor in his empathy for Craig. Less well known,
yet more relevant in light of Williams's frequent public denunciations
of homosexuality, was his own documented gay past. In 1998, Williams, a single man, was accused of sexual harassment by a male ath-
letic trainer he had hired to produce his radio show. The trainer,
Stephen Gregory, had reported over fifty unwanted sexual advances by
Williams, including attempts to grope his penis and buttocks while on
business trips. Williams initially denounced Gregory's charges as "false,
baseless, and completely without merit," but he finally doled out a
$200,000 settlement.

"See, we all make mistakes," Williams opined in his apologia for
Craig. "We all sin, error, and fall short of expectations. To judge and
condemn others—even elected officials who should be held to the highest standard—usually just narrows our own heart and achieves nothing." For Williams, holding public officials accountable for illicit and
utterly hypocritical behavior was tantamount to casting the first stone.

Taking a cue from Armstrong Williams, Craig battled the pressure
to acknowledge that he was guilty of behavior he had repeatedly condemned. When the Senate Ethics Committee launched an investigation into Craig's peccadilloes, he hired star Washington lawyer (and
Democrat) Stanley Brand to argue that his arrest was "wholly unrelated" to his official duties and therefore was not worth investigating.
In the end, Craig received no more punishment than a letter from the

Ethics Committee lightly chiding him for attempting to evade his guilty plea.

Craig had weathered the storm of scandal, but he had tarnished his party's image as well as his own. In a ceremony planned before his arrest was made public, he was inducted into the Idaho Hall of Fame, immortalized beside figures from Sacajawea to Senate legend Frank Church. "It's a sad day to be a Republican," an Idaho precinct committeeman muttered when he heard of the ceremony. But even if Craig had heeded the call of Republican leaders to resign, his sacrifice would have had no impact on the endemic problem of sexual hypocrisy within the party's ranks. With or without Craig, the Republican Party had, through its descent into paranoid homophobia, transformed itself into the country's biggest walk-in closet.

■ ■ ■

One month after Craig's arrest in June 2007, Bob Allen, a socially conservative Florida legislator and co-chair of John McCain's 2008 presidential campaign, was nabbed outside a men's bathroom for attempting to pay an undercover cop to allow him to perform oral sex on him. Allen claimed, after being arrested, that he was "intimidated by [a] stocky black guy" in the restroom and offered to fellate the undercover cop so he wouldn't "become a statistic." Days later, Glenn Murphy Jr., the national chair of the Young Republicans conservative youth group, a rising star in Indiana Republican circles who advised candidates to use gay marriage as a wedge issue, was arrested for performing oral sex on a sleeping man during a Young Republicans convention.

In October, Republican Washington State Representative Richard Curtis, a stalwart gay rights opponent, was arrested after calling the police on a gay escort who had robbed him of $1,000 after Curtis refused to pay him for having anal sex with him. When a detective arrived at the scene of the crime, a cheap motel room, he discovered a plastic sack that Curtis had been reluctant to open. Inside, according to the detective, was "a light grey length of nylon rope, a plastic doctor's stethoscope, and other items I could not immediately identify." For days, Curtis, married with three children, pointed to his family as proof that he was not gay. But finally, after his escort's testimony was made public, bringing to light allegations that he was a "freak" who sneaked out to adult bookshops dressed in women's lingerie, he resigned.

This bizarre imbroglio occurred in Spokane, Washington, a conservative bastion just across the border from the Idaho panhandle—Larry Craig's political base. One of eastern Washington's most influential Republicans, Jim West, had a draconian record during his twenty years in the state legislature, including introducing bills to outlaw gays from teaching in public schools and teenagers from having consensual sexual contact. In 2003, West leveraged his popularity among local right-wing elements to win election as mayor of Spokane.

But West's tenure collapsed two years later when he was accused of molesting Boy Scouts and admitted to offering internships to young men in exchange for sex. Tipped off that West had solicited sex from young men by the gay chat website Gay.com, editors of the *Spokane Spokesman-Review* assigned a forensic expert to investigate the rumors. Posing as a sexually conflicted high school student, the expert engaged West (who registered online as "RightBi-Guy") in probing conversations until he finally confirmed his identity.

"I could never be into the gay scene with its politics and all," West revealed during one online chat with the Spokane *Spokesman-Review*'s undercover reporter. "I've just seen too many guys decide once they come out that it becomes everyone else's problem to deal with. I'm not into femmy guys." In December 2005, just months after messages like these appeared on the pages of the *Spokesman-Review*, disgusted Spokane voters ousted West in a special recall election. The following year, he died from colon cancer.

There are few documents more illuminating about the mentality of closeted conservatives than West's online chats. For West and so many other closeted conservatives, coming out was a fad exclusive among self-indulgent, excessively self-reflective semi-men—or, as he called them, "femmy guys." Despite his privately acknowledged bisexuality, West had apparently decided that gaining acceptance as he truly was, amid the retrograde culture in which he was raised, was an impossible fantasy. West kept his deviant lifestyle shrouded in secrecy while exploiting his public platform to denounce that lifestyle. That was the way it had to be, after all. "If someone hires you to paint their house red, then you paint it red," West said, explaining his anti-gay voting record. "Even if you think it would look better green." In the conservative closet, those who imagined the way things might be different were "femmy." Those who accepted the way things were were still real men. In their own minds they were not even gay.

"The authoritarian character worships the past," wrote Erich Fromm in *Escape from Freedom*. "What has been, will eternally be. To wish or to work for something that has not yet been before is crime or madness. The miracle of creation—and creation is always a miracle—is outside of his range of emotional experience."

Having submitted to the limitations of the past and internalized the nostalgia that has become so intrinsic to modern Republicanism, closeted conservatives carefully modeled their public identity after images of the rugged Middle American Everyman: a pastiche of icons from John Wayne to Rambo, from the Marlboro Man to Rock Hudson. Only by inhabiting alter egos (Maf54, RightBi-Guy) or as the anonymous, silver-haired man trolling airport bathrooms and patronizing male prostitutes with false identities (such as "Jeff Gannon" and "Rod Majors") have closeted conservatives been able to fulfill the essential urges they have denied themselves. But these secret identities, modeled after the hypersexual, leather-bound homosexual deviant of the right-wing imagination, are false, too. In the vast gulf between the public persona and the private life of the closeted conservative, there is no moral core. There is no conscience, no self; there is only a void.

The closeted conservative, sapped as he is of his real identity, may never experience actual intimacy through sexual fulfillment. Sex becomes like a drug, a fleeting rush of pornographic lust that can produce titillation, but never emotional connectedness to another person. Thus he is deprived of the sensation of true love, the most life-affirming experience there is. Self-destruction, then, is the leitmotif of the closeted conservative.

"The more the drive toward life is thwarted," Fromm wrote, "the stronger is the drive toward destruction; the more life is realized, the less is the strength of destructiveness. Destructiveness is the outcome of unlived life."

None of the radical right's myriad sex scandals generated a greater spectacle of self-destructiveness than the downfall of Ted Haggard. Haggard, a right-wing Colorado Springs–based mega-church pastor, confidant to James Dobson, and outside advisor to the White House, was one of the brightest stars of the Christian right's next generation— and one of its most effective crusaders against gay rights. Haggard's alter ego, Art, however, was a patron of gay prostitutes, a purchaser of methamphetamines, and an avid viewer of hardcore porn. The exposure of Haggard's hypocrisy, and the campaign by Dobson's minions to restore his image, paved a trail of carnage that culminated in a paroxysm of mass murder in the parking lot of the church he had founded.

CHAPTER 19

PASTOR TED'S EXCELLENT ADVENTURE

With a mane of sandy hair and a perpetual toothy grin painted across his face, Ted Haggard looked exceptionally youthful even as he settled into late middle age. He was approachable and unfailingly ebullient about sharing the Gospel, a refreshing contrast to mercurial figures such as James Dobson. Haggard even seemed progressive, popularizing the concept of "creation care," a Christianized environmental awareness initiative that asserted a biblical imperative for reducing global warming. As Dobson marshaled his ornery allies to denounce the notion of global warming, Haggard lapped up attention from secular pundits eager to tout the birth of a new generation of cosmopolitan evangelicals.

In the wake of September 11, when many evangelical ministers, such as Billy Graham's son Franklin, lashed out at Muslims—Graham called Islam an "evil and wicked religion"—Haggard was restrained, even criticizing Graham for placing the lives of missionaries in the Middle East at risk. *New York Times* columnist Nicholas Kristof praised Haggard for "moving toward religious civility." "Haggard and other evangelical leaders don't seem to disagree fundamentally with the loudmouths," Kristof said, "they just think that insults make bad public relations and put missionaries at risk."

Haggard's base for his mounting influence was the 11,000 members of his New Life Church, located just down the road from Focus on the Family headquarters in Colorado Springs. Every Sunday, Haggard whipped up his flock to let inhibitions go, urging worshippers to dance wildly to the top-flight Christian pop ensembles he brought to town, to run up and down the aisles, speak in tongues, and shower complete strangers with hugs and Jesus-loves-you's so that they might end up submerged in the church's digitally temperature-controlled, cross-shaped baptismal pool at afternoon's end. With over 7,000 seats, a Starbucks-style coffee shop, and a cavernous cafeteria, New Life was more than a place of worship. It was a prefabricated community offering an instant sense of solidarity to uprooted residents of the exurban landscape of faceless strip malls and subdivision housing that had sprung up to accommodate their mass migration from places not as spiritually afire as Colorado Springs.

Upholding a doctrine of "spiritual warfare" at the heart of his social gospel, Haggard established his church as a sacred bastion against the headshops, kebab spots, and gay bars that dotted downtown Colorado Springs—remnants of the Age of Aquarius before the city became what Haggard called "a Vatican for evangelical Christians." "When I arrived here Christians were discouraged and passive," Haggard told a reporter in 1995. "There was a very active but behind-the-scenes satanic community here, covens, thousands of Satanists, sixties leftovers into really bloody Satanism. But we either won them over to Christ or they felt the shift in energy and just left town. What we have here is a miracle."

Haggard told another reporter the following year, "People would try to escape from covens and tell us about the struggle to get out. I have an interest in satanic meetings. If people are going to covens, I have more of an interest."

■ ■ ■

Haggard's miraculous makeover began with a hallucination when he was in high school. His father was a veterinarian in Delphi, Indiana, who was born again during a convalescence watching a Billy Graham revival on television. At the age of seventeen, the newly born-again Haggard was seized by a vision of demons hovering over newborn

infants, infecting them with the urge to abuse narcotics and mastur-
bate. Haggard attended evangelical Oral Roberts University in Oklahoma (and was rewarded for going there by his father with a new
Chevrolet). At Oral Roberts he learned to speak in tongues; a course
called "Evangelicals in Communist Countries" inspired his mission to
spread the gospel. He married another student, Gayle Alcorn, whose
father was an Air Force colonel. Eventually they had five children.

In 1984, while on a four-day fast on a mountain 14,000 feet above
Colorado Springs, visiting his wife's retired father, another vision appeared to him. In his nutrition-deprived delirium, he beheld a stadium throbbing with men—all were men—engaged in charismatic
worship. "I saw thousands of people going into the world as missionaries," he said. Within a year, his vision began to be realized, though
not exactly before the throngs he had imagined.

A year afterward, in a Colorado Springs basement church, Haggard
was hollering sermons from a stack of five-gallon buckets while two-
dozen people, his congregation, sat in lawn chairs clapping, singing,
and speaking in tongues. His flock prayed outside gay bars for the
damned souls inside, they prayed over the names of randomly selected people in the phone book, and Haggard dispatched his "prayer
teams" into the pagan-infested streets to anoint major intersections
with a garden sprayer and cooking oil. New Life expanded practically
overnight, filling its pews with squares and misfits alike, all eager to be
saved through Haggard's unique charisma.

By the mid-1990s, New Life was not only the largest church in
town but also one of the biggest evangelical churches in the country.
Haggard moved rapidly to leverage his popularity to finance the construction of the World Prayer Center, a 55,000-square-foot structure
designed as a "spiritual NORAD"—the equivalent of the Colorado-
based North American Aerospace Defense Command—that would
project divine energy to rogue nations around the world. "The World
Prayer Center is the final push to make sure the Gospel is available to
everyone," Haggard said in 1993, the year the center was founded.
"God chose a time 2,000 years ago, when Rome was the only superpower, to send his son, Jesus. Now, America is the only superpower.
That means things are being set up for the end to come." Four times a

year Haggard retreated to the center's Praise Mountain to listen for the voice of God and receive new visions.

One of those visions apparently involved Haggard orchestrating the Republican takeover of his adopted city. In 1992, as soon as Focus on the Family relocated to Colorado Springs from California, Haggard organized a grassroots push for Amendment 2, a sweeping initiative that wiped anti-discrimination laws protecting homosexuals off the books. (The Supreme Court overturned the law in 1996). With the backing of Dobson as well as the region's evangelical pantheon, in 2003 Haggard was elected president of the National Association of Evangelicals, a 35-million-member umbrella organization comprising all of the country's major evangelical denominations. He became an informal advisor to President George W. Bush, using his weekly conference calls with the president and his advisors to push for a constitutional amendment banning gay marriage, a proposal that galvanized the Christian right behind Bush's reelection campaign in 2004. By 2005, Haggard himself was contemplating a run for Congress. Although holding elective political office was his lifelong ambition, he ultimately decided against the idea, fearing that a hard-fought campaign would somehow stain his sterling image as a man of God.

When the judicial battles of Bush's second term began, Haggard was on the front lines, assailing liberal "judicial activists" at the Family Research Council's "Justice Sunday II" rally and mobilizing the NAE's member pastors in support of Supreme Court nominee John Roberts. In his spare time, Haggard indulged his personal passion for healthy living, writing a weight loss handbook called *The Jerusalem Diet* that offered supposedly biblical methods for maintaining an ideal weight. Haggard formulated his diet after a terrible epiphany. "I'm a fat guy," he shrieked to himself during a 1998 vacation. "I'm getting ugly. My body is changing. I look better in clothes than I do naked! I'm in trouble." Because he admittedly had little self-discipline—"If interrogators threatened to withhold chocolate from me, I fear I might give up state secrets that would bring the end of freedom as we know it"—Haggard incorporated junk food into his weight-loss plan. After lengthy diet discipline (including the junk food), he claimed he was able to return to his "target weight" and stay there.

Haggard's weight loss book was not notable in itself; it was little more than a slapdash compilation of common-sense prescriptions laced with evangelical uplift. The book was remarkable, however, as a document of Haggard's unusual image within the culture of the Christian right. He was as socially conservative as any of his peers, yet he was unabashedly conscious of his body image. This trait was exceptional, considering Haggard's role in spawning the evangelical men's movement, a right-wing cultural phenomenon united by its followers' desire to maintain a supposedly traditional Christian brand of masculinity. Body consciousness, to the extent that it reflected any hint of assimilation to the values of "the culture," was anathema to such a men's movement. Worse, it displayed feminine tendencies, and women, especially those of the single, non-Christian variety, as Haggard taught, were vessels for demonic possession.

ULTIMATE FIGHTING JESUS V. BETTY JO "B. J." BLOWERS

Haggard's mega-church provided him with a constantly expanding platform, but it was the Promise Keepers that fulfilled his original dream. At its height in the late 1990s, just as he had envisioned, the Promise Keepers drew hundreds of thousands of men to raucous rallies where they pledged themselves to the "Seven Promises of a Promise Keeper." Chief among the group's strictures was sexual purity, compelling its members to have hotel room movies turned off to avoid the temptation of the adult porn pay-for-view. Promise Keepers were also furnished with advice on finessing domestic disasters, such as a son returning from college with an earring. The "feminization of men," said Promise Keeper founding member Tony Evans, was leading to the decline of civilization. Explaining his own attraction to the group, Haggard offered a motive that directly contradicted Evans and his coterie of manly men. To Haggard, the Promise Keepers gave men a private space where they could reveal their essential, unmanly selves. "When there are no women and children present the men feel uninhibited and free to worship because they're not concerned about having to be masculine," Haggard said.

The Promise Keepers was founded in 1990 by former Colorado University football coach Bill McCartney, an outspoken Christian firebrand, who turned his historically abysmal team into a championship team, even as twenty-four of his players were arrested within a three-year period for crimes including serial rape, and the team's star quarterback, Sal Aunese (arrested for assault) impregnated McCartney's twenty-year-old daughter Kristyn. They never married. Aunese died six months after the birth of their son, Timothy. Five years later, Kristyn had another son with another Colorado football player.

McCartney called Aunese's diagnosis of terminal stomach cancer in 1989 the "will of God." He also expressed his relief that the diagnosis was revealed on an off day. When the alternative weekly *Westwords* exposed Kristyn McCartney's affair with Aunese the following year, McCartney concocted a plan to assassinate the piece's author, Bryan Abas. He said he changed his mind only at the last moment when an elderly stranger handed him a stack of Bible verses inscribed on index cards and urging forgiveness.

"I wish I hadn't been so focused on winning football games that I didn't spend more time with my daughter," McCartney told the *New York Times*. "But now I see an opportunity to build a godly content into those two boys that can make a difference in their lives. So on the one hand, maybe I could have prevented some promiscuity. But on the other hand, wow, I love those two little guys."

McCartney preached that homosexuality was "an abomination before God" and warned Jews that they are "toast" unless they convert to Christianity. "A man's man, a real man, is a godly man," he said.

He launched Promise Keepers with the benediction of James Dobson, who featured him on his radio program. By 1997, the group had revenues of $85 million a year, charged $60 for attendance at its stadium rallies, and had drawn 2.5 million participants.

As the men's movement that McCartney and Haggard helped to popularize evolved, it spawned a new generation of leaders who cloaked the Christian right's *kulturkampf* behind an aesthetic of secular cool. One of these gen-next manliness marketers, Mark Driscoll, leveraged his ownership of one of Seattle's most popular indie music venues, Club Paradox, to style himself as the "hipster pastor." With a carefully calibrated edginess—the Disciples were "punch-you-in-the-nose dudes," he once proclaimed—Driscoll claimed to make church fun again for disaffected young men. His constituents were a "lost generation" that preferred all-night sessions of Grand Theft Auto to Galatians, and responded better to heavy metal and heavy-handed sarcasm than to soft moralizing. Driscoll assured his mostly single guy parishioners that the Jesus they worshipped was not some "Richard Simmons, hippie, queer Christ" or "a long-haired . . . effeminate-looking dude." He was "Ultimate Fighting Jesus," a Terminator of machismo with "callused hands and big biceps."

Brad Stine, a shaggy-haired Christian comedian promoted as "the Messiah of stand-up," took his unique act to the Christian men's industry, a whole new market, founding his own group, GodMen, a no-girls-allowed road show where, he said, "men can be men; raw and uninhibited; completely free to express themselves in the uniquely male way that only men understand." Inside his frat-boy-style revivals (think *Girls Gone Wild!* without the girls), Stine treated his chest-thumping crowd to vulgar comedic rants *against* casual sex and serenaded them with an anthem he composed called *Grow a Pair!*

> *We've been beaten down*
> *Feminized by the culture crowd*
> *No more nice guy, timid and ashamed . . .*
> *Grab a sword, don't be scared*
> *Be a man, grow a pair!*

While Driscoll and Stine amped up evangelical liturgy to appeal to twenty-something sensibilities, Haggard's friend John Eldredge introduced a compelling new archetype for movement followers to emulate. A reformed druggie who discovered Francis Schaeffer in his twenties and later went to work as a counselor for Focus on the Family, Eldredge wrote the men's movement's seminal tract, *Wild at Heart*. This book, which has sold over 2 million copies since it was published in 2002, called for men to model themselves after a hybrid of "Ultimate Fighting Jesus" and William Wallace, the virile Scottish separatist leader romanticized in Mel Gibson's movie *Braveheart*. Eldredge's superman was the very antithesis of the prince of peace. "He works with wood, commands the loyalty of dockworkers," Eldredge wrote. "He is the Lord of hosts, the captain of angel armies. And when Christ returns, he will be at the head of a dreadful company, mounted on a white horse, with a double-edged sword, his robe dipped in blood. Now that sounds a lot more like William Wallace than it does Mother Teresa. No question about it, there is something fierce in the heart of God." (This warrior Jesus resembled no other religious figure so much as Mohammed.)

White supremacists across the globe shared Eldredge's reverence for Wallace. William Pierce, the deceased, Idaho-based neo-Nazi leader known as the "Farm Belt Fuhrer," upheld Wallace as a model of personal sacrifice. "That, I think, is one of the strongest things in our people and is something we need to call on and recognize," Pierce said, "and for more people to be willing to do whatever is necessary, as William Wallace was." The Italian neo-fascist Umberto Bossi, who, while serving as reform minister to Silvio Berlusconi, proposed torpedoing boatloads of African migrant workers before they reached Italian shores, proudly adorned a wall of his office with a poster of Wallace. Meanwhile, back in Wallace's homeland, the *Scottish Sunday Mail* reported, "Hate-filled Nazis are using *Braveheart* fever to recruit Scots. They urge people who want to do something about the 'browning of our country' to watch Mel Gibson's movie about Scots patriot Sir William Wallace."

But the William Wallace who captivated members of Christian cell groups and would-be klansmen was nothing like the real-life knight; he was a fictitious action figure fabricated by actor/director Mel Gibson. Gibson, a pre–Vatican II Catholic traditionalist raised by a vociferous Holocaust denier who, like his son, had a penchant for anti-Semitic rants, channeled the sensibility of his far-right fan base. ("Fucking Jews!" Gibson growled during an arrest for drunk driving in 2006. "The Jews are responsible for all the wars in the world.") Gibson's films incited angry feelings of revenge through depiction of vivid atrocities, whether the scene took place in thirteenth-century Scotland, the American colonies during the Revolution, ancient Jerusalem, or even Mayan Mesoamerica—*Braveheart, The Patriot, The Passion of the Christ, Apocalypto*. Gibson's work appealed to sadistic yearnings, glorifying hideous acts of violence through graphic close-ups. By presenting scenes of hearts exploded by arrows, skulls split by maces, and entire torsos bisected by broadswords, along with innocents burned, slashed, and crucified, Gibson redefined the aesthetic of authoritarian right-wing movements across the globe.

The storyline of Gibson's *Braveheart* was custom-tailored to modern right-wing sensibilities. According to Gibson, Wallace's archenemy, the hapless English prince Edward II, was a girly homosexual who spent his days modeling ornate outfits and carousing with his lute-strumming male lover, while his soldiers fell before Wallace's swift sword. The film suggests that only after receiving a stern beating from his father did Edward take the Scottish rebellion seriously, dramatizing through sado-masochism that gays are unfit for leadership.

The rugged Wallace, meanwhile, stole away with Edward's sex-starved wife, Isabella (who in real life was an infant when Wallace led the Scots) to a verdant hillside where he brought her to an earth-shattering sexual climax. Gibson's contrasting of Wallace, the virile manly man, with Edward II, the effete girly man, was a deliberate appeal to the mentality of the Christian men's movement follower. Thus Wallace's triumphs over Edward's lavender legions were more than military victories. Through Gibson's lens, they represented the defeat of the liberal "culture crowd." It turns out that the culture war has been going on for seven hundred years!

No Gibson film is complete without a grotesque scene of extended torture. In *Braveheart*'s final scene, the defeated Wallace was martyred through an old-fashioned English quartering. With his legs and arms separating from his torso, Wallace bellowed his last rebel yell before a crowd of startled onlookers: "*Freeee-dom!*" In Gibson's telling, Wallace's greatest contribution to history was not the way he lived his life but the way he died: by sacrificing his body for the greater nationalist cause—for freedom. In this way Gibson balanced Wallace's sadistic side with deeply pronounced masochistic tendencies, completing his carefully executed makeover of the medieval historical person into a thoroughly modern right-wing authoritarian dominator.

In 2004, Gibson repackaged the brutal conclusion of *Braveheart* into an entire film about Jesus's crucifixion, *The Passion of the Christ*. Basing his script on the anti-Semitic passion play performed for centuries in Bavaria, Gibson presented a cabal of venal Jewish priests as engineers of Christ's death. For over two hours, Gibson bombarded viewers with excruciatingly graphic images of the nearly nude Jesus (played by burly actor Jim Caveziel) flayed by bullwhips, gored with myriad instruments of torture, and ultimately ground into chunks of bloody sinew during one of the most grisly scenes in modern film history.

The Jews, themselves controlled by a female Satan character, thirst after the blood of Jesus with a fervor that far exceeds that of the Romans. With the torture of Jesus approaching a pornographic crescendo of violence, and the Jews clamoring for more, Gibson's Christ whispers, "I make all things new." Here, Gibson asserted the theme that unified his films and most influenced his fans among the Christian masculinity movement: masochistic suffering as the ultimate form of redemption, pain as godliness.

"I can honestly say, without hyperbole, that *The Passion* ranks with the most moving artistic experiences I have ever had," Haggard remarked after Gibson personally previewed the film for him at his New Life Church. "It is a brilliant film—a compelling vision of Jesus's ministry, a challenging depiction of the violence of Roman crucifixion, and most important, a heart-rending portrayal of sacrificial love."

Although Haggard's quirkiness often set him apart, his assessment of *The Passion* reflected the masochistic mentality of the Christian right with perfect clarity. To Haggard, the suffering that Gibson's protagonists endured at the exquisite moment of death was not suffering at all, but "sacrificial love" for a higher cause. Both Wallace and Jesus were keenly aware of the horrible fate that awaited them, yet they soldiered ahead, convinced that they would make more powerful symbols for their movement as martyrs than as living leaders. To these true believers, Wallace's quartering and Jesus's crucifixion symbolized more than selflessness—they represented the triumph each man hoped to achieve over his own body. Only through a metaphorical torture did movement members believe they could achieve their liberation from sin.

Denial of the body is a universal theme in the movement's literature. According to *Every Man's Battle*, a best-selling manifesto on sexual purity, even the most fleeting glance at a woman's uncovered thigh or a moment's glimpse at a pair of bouncing breasts will inevitably lead to porn addiction, chronic masturbation, and serial adultery. A trip straight to the lower rings of hell is next. It is therefore best to avoid admiring the beauty of unmarried women, especially lascivious femme fatales such as the fictional Betty Jo "B. J." Blowers, an estrogen-infused evildoer who darkens the pages of the sequel, *Every Young Man's Battle*. If a Christian man has the terrible luck to set his eyes upon the body of any woman other than that of his wife, he should immediately "bounce" toward something decidedly unsexy, such as an episode of *Monday Night Football*. Naughty thoughts about women must be "taken captive" in order for a man to "fully function as a Christian," the book insists.

With the help of James Dobson, an enthusiastic promoter of the book's "battle" methods, its authors, Steve Arterburn and Fred Stoeker, have become leading Christian-right self-help gurus. Their expertise stems not from any academic training but from their ability to describe their own redemption from sexual addiction in accessible, evangelical language. Arterburn's come-to-Jesus moment arrived in college, when an extramarital affair he had led to an unwanted pregnancy, then an abortion—an act that weighed so heavily on his conscience that he believed he was guilty of murder. Stoeker's problems began with his discovery of an eight-inch ceramic dildo among his father's girly mags when he was in first grade. The find prompted a twenty-year porn obsession that ended only when, as Stoeker wrote, "Daily Bible study allowed the word of God to wash him clean and to begin to transform his mind." Born again, Arterburn and Stoeker counseled other prisoners of sexual sin, charging them well over $1,000 for three-day seminars that promised to free them from their shackles.

But Arterburn and Stoeker's disturbing impulses still roiled beneath the surface. The opening scene of *Every Man's Battle* finds Arterburn driving along a California byway in his 1973 Mercedes 450SL, enjoying the view from "the car of [his] dreams," on his way to a place that could have been named by any mischief-making adolescent: Oxnard. Suddenly he catches sight of a "goddesslike blonde," with "rivulets of sweat cascading down her tanned body" and dressed in "a skimpy bikini." Just "two tiny triangles of tie-dyed fabric struggled to contain her ample bosom." While ogling the "banquet of flesh" he had "feasted" his eyes on, "craning [his] neck to capture every image for [his] mental video camera," the distracted Arterburn crashes his luxurious ride into the back of a muscle car, badly crumpling his bumper. (Arterburn's tawdry opening scene unwittingly echoed the theme of *Crash*, a dystopian 1973 sci-fi novel by J. G. Ballard about a "TV scientist" whose erotic obsession with violent car accidents drives him to commit insane atrocities. While Ballard's novel is widely recognized as one of the most penetrating literary commentaries on modern man's alienation from himself, Arterburn and Stoker's revealing psychosexual journals also deserve consideration for this honor.)

In an online video that Arterburn produced to promote his purity seminars, he illuminated the Christian manhood movement's fixation on high-tech incarnations of eroticism. A cast of middle-aged, middle-class, middle-of-the-road men struggle to resist mammoth sexual temptations, without it ever occurring to them to seek the company of actual women. One character, seated in his sterile office, crinkles his face, expressing inner turmoil as he alternates his gaze between a laptop computer screen and the portrait on his desk of his smiling family. Should he go home to his wife and children, or stay late and pleasure himself with online surfing?

Viewers of Arterburn's video are insidiously warned that the anonymous cyber-sirens catering to·any fetish from behind the member's-only walls of Internet porn sites represent an even more irresistible temptation than living, breathing women. The wife in every man's desktop picture frame is dowdy, dull, and frozen. She is the Christian man's only permissible outlet for his sexual frustration—and therefore no outlet at all. If she does sleep with her husband, it is only to prevent his descent into total depravity, not to fulfill her own sexual needs. And if she fails to realize the fantasies brewing in what Arterburn and Stoeker call man's "mustang mind," her husband will inevitably stray outside his corral, riding into the dark wilderness of cyberspace, or beyond.

Every Man's Battle is not so much a struggle against temptation as it is a war against the temptress. As images of comely lasses flash by, Arterburn intones, "Those who won hated their impurity, they hated their sickness. They were going to war and they were going to win, or they were gonna die trying. And every resource was leveled upon the foe." Who were these enemies of purity promoting "sickness" everywhere they went? Against whom should Christian men declare spiritual warfare? Through a series of unsubtle cues, Arterburn left little doubt that single, sexually independent women—young ladies like the infamous Betty "B. J." Blowers—were the Enemy.

But then who was God? Who should Bible-believing Christian men love, and what does he look like? Men's movement literature made no secret about this. God is a man's man with "callused hands and big biceps," clad in a revealing loincloth, rippling with muscle, and invariably armed with a glistening broadsword. He is Fabio of Nazareth. With a sensibility shot through with homoeroticism, it should not have been any wonder that some of the movement's most ardent adherents turned out to live their fantasies.

COMPLETELY HETEROSEXUAL

As the 2006 midterm elections approached, Haggard basked in his media close-up. Among those beseeching him for face time were the producers of *Jesus Camp*, a documentary about the religious indoctrination of preadolescent evangelicals. Haggard cheerfully invited the filmmakers to his church to capture him in action. With cameras positioned at the foot of his pulpit, he performed with gusto. "We don't need to have a general assembly about what we believe," Haggard boomed. "It's written in the Bible! All right, so we don't have to debate about what we think about homosexual activity. It's written in the Bible!"

Haggard strutted toward the camera, growing closer until he was staring down its lens. He had a message for the liberal media. "I think I know what you did last night!" he exclaimed. Gales of laughter rippled through the pews. Haggard was on a roll. "If you send me a thousand dollars, I *won't* tell your wife." More laughter. Finally, as he paced back and forth on the stage, Haggard flashed his trademark toothy grin, punched his index finger at the camera, and warned half-jokingly, "If you use any of this, I'll sue you!" Pastor Ted's audience rolled in the aisles.

Haggard's rhetoric was classically anti-gay, but to have described his histrionics as hateful would be off the mark. His resentment of homosexuals was rooted more in envy than in loathing. Jeff Sharlet, a chronicler of the Christian right, noted that Haggard and many other leaders of the evangelical men's movement viewed what they call the "homosexual lifestyle" not as a dark dungeon of sin but as "an endless succession of orgasms, interrupted only by jocular episodes of male bonhomie." Homosexuality was dangerous because it was so tempting. "The gay man promises a guilt-free existence, the garden before Eve," Sharlet wrote. "He is thought [by movement members] to exist in the purest state of 'manhood,' which is boyhood, before there were girls." It was through his private admiration, and then emulation, of the stereotypical gay male that Haggard became the spitting image he had painted of the Antichrist.

Every month or so, starting in 2003, Haggard stole away on motorcycle trips to Denver, traveling as "Art from Kansas City," an anonymous, average white guy who just happened to be seeking impersonal gay sex. His excursions to the Mile High City began when he discovered explicit Internet advertisements placed by a bodybuilder and veteran male escort named Mike Jones on a website called rentboy.com. Over the course of three years, Haggard's sessions with Jones progressed from mildly erotic massage to kinky sex involving an increasing variety of adult toys. Jones described Haggard's favorite erotic instruments as "cock rings made of leather, rubber, or metal; jockstraps; tit clamps; and porn that he wanted to watch."

Eventually, Haggard asked Jones to procure methamphetamines for him, claiming he liked snorting it before having sex with his wife. In reality, Haggard snorted it during visits to Jones. Becoming more adventurous, he asked Jones to arrange an orgy with "6 to 8 college age guys from age 18 to 22." Because Jones could not organize Haggard's fantasy orgy, "Art from Kansas City" settled on voyeurism, watching Jones and a bodybuilder friend have sex—a spectacle he paid double to behold.

"You know all the surveys say that evangelicals have the best sex life of any other group," Haggard boasted in 2006 to Alexandra Pelosi, one of the documentarians who flocked to his exurban cathedral to spend some time with the Christian right's golden boy. Mugging for the camera, Haggard grabbed a random male parishioner from his church and asked him how often he brings his wife to sexual climax. "Every time," the man responded with an embarrassed grin. Haggard grinned. "Twice a day," the man said. Haggard laughed.

Despite Haggard's apparent enthusiasm for gay sex, both as participant and as voyeur, Jones said he detected a pronounced sense of shame from the preacher each time he visited. In his tell-all memoir *I Had to Say Something*, Jones compared himself to a "combat nurse" tending to "wounded men . . . showing the emotional battle scars of trying live a life other than the one they want to live." Jones said that once, after Haggard ejaculated, he noticed "tears form[ing] in his eyes, but I didn't say anything." Jones concluded, "When a man cries in front of another man, especially one he does not know well, there is some deep-seated pain there. I felt bad for him. I would have loved to ask him what was going on, but he didn't want to go there."

Jones resisted prying. He was a professional sex worker, after all, and anonymity assured him more business. It was not until Jones sat down before his television, flipping from channel to channel, that he realized "Art" was Ted Haggard. As Jones leisurely channel-surfed one evening, a bizarre History Channel special about the Antichrist flashed on the screen. "Every generation has thought they were the last generation," a man identified onscreen as Ted Haggard commented. A spooky soundtrack underscored Haggard's narrative, while images flashed across the screen of a handsome man—presumably Satan, the notorious Man of Sin—strutting through an adoring crowd of photographers and reporters.

The following day, Jones googled "Ted Haggard." He was shocked by what he found. "Bouncing around the World Wide Web," he recalled, "it became clear to me that gays, lesbians, and anyone else who was different would not fare well in one nation under Ted Haggard's

God. I had to do something, or at least, I had to say something." But Jones kept silent for several more months, enduring an agonizing series of visits from Haggard during which he said he had to resist urges to physically attack the preacher. Only when Haggard announced his support for Amendment 43, a Colorado ballot measure that would have banned same-sex marriage, did Jones snap, delivering to local news outlets several voice messages and letters Haggard had sent him requesting meth. Soon a local news crew intercepted Haggard in his driveway.

"I called him to buy some meth, but I threw it away," Haggard told a reporter from the driver's seat of his car. "I was buying it for me, but I never used it." Flashing a forced, weirdly incongruous grin, Haggard denied ever having had sex with Jones.

Haggard's peers were stunned by the allegations. James Dobson initially rejected the charges against his friend as a fabrication of the Enemy. "It is unconscionable that the legitimate news media would report a rumor like this based on nothing but one man's accusation," Dobson fumed in a prepared statement. Haggard's associate pastor, Rob Brendle, was dismissive as well. "This is clearly a political stunt," he said. "Ted is the farthest thing from a homosexual as you can get. Trust me."

On the afternoon that Jones's story surfaced, New Life Church organized a rally in downtown Colorado Springs to condemn the "politically motivated allegations" against Haggard. The faithful knew in their hearts that Haggard was not gay. He was one of them, after all. As Arterburn said of his first meeting with Haggard, "I had this overriding feeling he was so normal."

But just two days before congressional midterm elections, Haggard confessed. In a letter read aloud to New Life Church, Haggard wrote, "For extended periods of time, I would enjoy victory and rejoice in freedom. Then, from time to time, the dirt that I thought was gone would resurface, and I would find myself thinking thoughts and experiencing desires that were contrary to everything I believe and teach."

Haggard's teary confession prompted a rare outbreak of candor among the Christian right's PR-obsessed kingpins. During a Focus on the Family broadcast recorded hours after Haggard released his letter, Dobson and his leading allies conceded that their fallen friend's homosexuality was not an aberration but, rather, the latest incarnation of an epidemic rapidly engulfing their flock. "Though we're talking about Ted Haggard today, I guarantee you there are 50 or 100 cases like this breaking across the nation today," said Dobson's first cousin, H. B. London, whose own father—Dobson's uncle—was stripped of his ministerial credentials after he was caught boffing his secretary. London, who operated a Focus on the Family hotline for sexually transgressive pastors, added that four clergymen had called in to confess their affairs that week.

Even the saintly Billy Graham was drawn to sin, said Ravi Zacharias, an international evangelical radio personality who frequently appeared on Dobson's show. During a trip to Paris in the 1950s, Graham became so overwhelmed by his desire to experience "all this nightlife available to him," Zacharias remarked, that he locked himself inside his hotel room and tossed his key outside. "I think one of the biggest dangers here is solitude," the Reverend Albert Mohler interjected. "Someone has to be there to interrogate and investigate every aspect of our lives."

In the eyes of Dobson and his allies, Haggard was not a closeted gay man acting out his repressed desires; he was just a regular guy seduced by the queer "siren within" that tempts us all. Haggard conceded, "There is a part of my life that is so repulsive and dark that I've been warring against it all of my adult life." If Pastor Ted ever seemed virtuous, it was because, he admitted, he was "a deceiver and a liar."

Some of Dobson's disciples blamed Haggard's behavior on the seed of sin that they believed was implanted in all men. But the charismatic Calvinist minister Mark Driscoll, of the Mars Hill Church of Seattle, Washington, an incorrigible hipster, offered a more novel theory: Haggard's wife had become too fat. "It is not uncommon to meet pastors' wives who really let themselves go," Driscoll wrote on his blog the day Haggard admitted his sins. "They sometimes feel that because their husband is a pastor, he is therefore trapped into fidelity, which gives them cause for laziness. A wife who lets herself go and is not sexually available to her husband in the ways that the Song of Songs is so frank about is not responsible for her husband's sin, but she may not be helping him either." According to Driscoll, if Haggard's wife had only followed his "Jerusalem Diet" more rigorously, he would never have wound up in the arms of a studly male escort. And if the wives of other star pastors did not hit the elliptical machine for an hour each day, their husbands might surrender to their latent gay urges, too.

Contrary to Driscoll's flippant hypothesis, however, Haggard's wife, Gayle, was pretty and relatively fit. What's more, she was loyal to a fault. Had she been anything less than unswervingly devoted to her husband, she would not have accompanied him all the way to Tucson, Arizona, into an intensive "spiritual restoration" program that promised to purge him of his homosexual demons.

Under the watchful eye of Dobson's cousin, London, Pastor Ted was monitored for progress. Everything appeared to go swimmingly. Although Haggard's "overseers" publicly predicted his restoration would take as long as five years, after only three weeks they pronounced him "completely heterosexual."

Miracle accomplished, Haggard announced plans to follow in the footsteps of the movement guru Dobson and study for his master's degree in psychology. He accepted a payout of $130,000 from New Life under the condition that he never disclose details of his scandal (the church would also cover his living expenses for nearly a year) and left town, presumably to prepare for his return as the Christian right's prodigal son. New Life immediately convened a "Day of Hope" on February 18, 2007, a cathartic ceremony to christen the dawning of a new era. The House That Haggard Built would be born again—again.

But that day did not materialize as church leaders had hoped. Instead of ringing in the return of moral values to the evangelical Vatican on the slopes of the Rockies, New Life's already dejected flock was treated to the reading of yet another grim letter, this one revealing that several staffers were under investigation for "sin issues." Then parishioners were informed that the director of the church's youth group had been fired for "sexual misconduct with an adult." A month later, New Life sacked at least thirty more employees whom it could not afford to pay because the church had doled out Haggard's hush money and begun bankrolling his rehabilitation.

As Haggard's former congregation suffered shock after shock, Mike Jones, the male prostitute, stepped into the limelight, granting numerous interviews and earning national headlines by placing the well-worn massage table "where it all happened" for sale on the online auction site eBay. Pledging to donate his profits to an AIDS awareness group, Jones raked in bids that topped $1,000. His gesture outraged Christian-right groups, which pressured eBay into removing Jones's item.

Haggard and his family, meanwhile, had departed to the Phoenix Dream Center, a "deliverance ministry" where what Haggard called "broken people" such as prostitutes and drug addicts were treated and "restored." "I identify," Haggard said. Seeking therapy for his demons, Haggard studied new techniques to purge evil spirits out of others. According to Rick Ross, a noted cult expert and deprogramming specialist, "A deliverance ministry [like the Dream Center] basically tells their members that any type of negative feelings they may have—negative things that are occurring in their day-to-day lives—can be ascribed to demons or the devil, or that they are demon-possessed, and that they need to be 'delivered.' They go to someone in the group who's a self-styled exorcist who then joins together with others and they cast demons out of that individual. This can traumatize a person and cause almost irreparable psychological and emotional damage."

Haggard's fall from grace gave him another vision. The lost souls at the Dream Center could become potential recruits for the new army of Christian soldiers he planned to lead. Preparing to lay the foundation for his next religious empire, Haggard sent out a thinly veiled fundraising letter, pleading, "We are looking for people who will help us monthly for two years . . . Any help we get will . . . be rewarded in heaven." He urged heaven-bound financial angels to funnel their checks through an obscure outfit called Families with a Mission (FWAM). But Haggard avoided mentioning that FWAM had been essentially defunct for six months, and he omitted the fact that the group's president, Paul Huberty, was a registered sex offender who had been convicted of coaxing a seventeen-year-old girl to have intercourse with him. The exposure of Haggard's scheme by *Colorado Con-*

fidential, a Denver-based independent Web magazine, infuriated the preacher's "overseers," prompting them to administer the most severe punishment possible. Haggard was officially excommunicated, forbade from ever working in Christian ministry again.

The camera-hungry media darling known as Pastor Ted was defrocked. A spiritually neutered shell of a man—a "broken" person—stood in his stead. While Haggard planned a last desperate media blitz to restore the attention he craved, putting out feelers to Oprah Winfrey, Larry King, and filmmaker Alexandra Pelosi, the destruction that his hypocrisy and destructive behavior had fostered had only begun to spread. As it is said, the evil that men do lives after them.

CHAPTER 20

THE NIGHTMARE OF CHRISTIANITY

A few miles down the road from Colorado Springs, in the quiet
bedroom community of Eldredge, a deeply disturbed young
man named Matthew Murray followed the unfolding debacle at
New Life Church with an interest that bordered on obsession. Murray, a sallow-faced, bespectacled twenty-four-year-old, had been in-
delibly scarred by a lifetime of psychological abuse at the hands of his
charismatic Pentecostal parents. Murray's mind became crowded
with thoughts of death, destruction, and the killings he would soon
carry out in the name of avenging what he called his "nightmare of
Christianity."

On an online chat room for former Pentecostals, Murray heaped
contempt on his mother, Loretta, a physical therapist who home-
schooled him to ensure that his contact with the outside world was
severely limited. "My 'mother,'" Murray wrote, "is just a brainswashed
[sic] church agent cun,t [sic]. The only reason she had me was because she wanted a body/soul she could train into being the next Billy
Graham . . ."

He went on:

> . . . my mother was into all the charismatic "fanatical evangelical" in-
> sanity. Her and her church believed that Satan and demons were
> everywhere in everything. The rules were VERY strict all the time. We
> couldn't have ANY christian or non-christian music at all except for

a few charismatic worship CDs. There was physical abuse in my home. My mother although used psychotropic drugs because she somehow thought it would make it easier to control me (I've never been diagnosed with any mental illness either). Pastors would always come and interrogate me over video games or TV watching or other things. There were NO FRIENDS outside the church and family and even then only family members who were in the church. You could not trust anyone at all because anyone might be a spy.

An authoritarian Christian-right self-help guru named Bill Goth-ard created the home-schooling regimen implemented by Murray's parents. Like his ally James Dobson, Gothard first grew popular during the 1960s by marketing his program to worried evangelical parents as anti-hippie insurance for adolescent children. Based on the theocratic teachings of R. J. Rushdoony, who devised Christian schools and home-schooling as the foundation of his Dominionist empire, Gothard's *Basic Life Principles* outlined an all-consuming environment that followers could embrace for the whole of their lives. According to Ron Henzel, a one-time Gothard follower who coauthored a devastating exposé about his former guru called *A Matter of Basic Principles*, under the rules, "large homeschooling families abstain from television, midwives are more important than doctors, traditional dating is forbidden, unmarried adults are 'under the authority of their parents' and live with them, divorced people can't remarry under any circumstance, and music has hardly changed at all since the late nineteenth century."

At the Charter School for Excellence, a school in South Florida inspired by Gothard's draconian principles that receives $800,000 in state funds each year, children are indoctrinated into a culture of absolute submission to authority almost as soon as they learn to speak. A song that the school's first-graders are required to recite goes as follows:

> *Obedience is listening attentively,*
> *Obedience will take instructions joyfully,*
> *Obedience heeds wishes of authorities,*

Obedience will follow orders instantly.
For when I am busy at my work or play,
And someone calls my name, I'll answer right away!
I'll be ready with a smile to go the extra mile
As soon as I can say "Yes, sir!" "Yes ma am!"
Hup, two, three!

Former Arkansas governor and Republican presidential candidate Mike Huckabee is among the 2.5 million Americans who have attended Gothard's Basic Seminar. According to Huckabee, who once earmarked state funds to distribute Gothard's literature in Arkansas prisons, Gothard was responsible for "some of the best programs for instilling character into people." But to the deeply alienated Murray, Gothard was the original source of his pathology. "I believe that the truth needs to be exposed," Murray wrote in a September 2006 discussion forum of recovering Gothard followers. "People need to see through errornious [sic] and destructive doctrines and teachings including Bill Gothard's."

After graduating from Gothard's home-schooling seminars, which constituted the bulk of his education (Colorado has no educational records for Murray after third grade), he was presented by his parents with two options for higher education. The first choice was Haggard's alma mater, Oral Roberts University. ORU at the time was beginning to unravel under the weight of scandalous revelations that its new president, Richard Roberts—the scion of its beloved founder—had allegedly looted university coffers to pay for his daughter's junkets to the Bahamas and bankroll his wife's shopping sprees. (Oral Roberts's other son, Ronnie, was a cocaine-addicted closet homosexual who committed suicide in 1982). Murray's second option was the "Discipleship Training School" of Youth with a Mission (YWAM), a Christian Reconstructionist–inspired missionary group that trained bright-eyed youngsters to spread the gospel of Colorado Springs to under-evangelized Third World nations. Desperate to escape his parents' rigid order, Murray joined YWAM.

But as soon as Murray enrolled at YWAM's training center in nearby Arvada in 2002, he found himself trapped in an authoritarian culture even·more restrictive than home. He realized that, as another student of YWAM bluntly put it, the school's training methods resembled "cult mind-controlling techniques." Murray became paranoid, speaking aloud to voices only he could hear, according to a former roommate. He complained that six of his male peers had made a gay sex video and that others routinely abused drugs. Hypocrisy seemed to be all around him, or at least dark mirages of it. A week before Murray was scheduled to embark on his first mission, YWAM dismissed him from the program for unspecified "health reasons." "They admitted that I hadn't done anything wrong, just that they had prayed and felt I wasn't popular/'connected' and talkative enough," he recalled.

Two years later, Murray raged at two YWAM administrators during a Pentecostal conference his mother had dragged him to attend. The shocked staffers promptly warned Loretta Murray that her son "wasn't walking with the Lord and could be planning violence." Within days, an ornery local pastor was allowed to burst into the young Murray's room, rifle through his belongings, and leave with a satchel full of secular DVDs and CDs—apparent evidence of his depravity. Murray's mother searched his room for satanic material every day afterward for three months, stripping him of his privacy and whatever was left of his love for her. After the trauma-inducing raids, in which Murray estimated his mother and her friends destroyed $900 worth of his property, he concluded, "Christianity is one big lie."

Murray lurched to the polar opposite edge of his parents' fanatical faith, replacing their Bible as his inspiration with the writings of Aleister Crowley, a flamboyant, self-proclaimed Satanist. The *fin de siècle* British sensationalist declared himself the "Great Beast of Revelation" and claimed his birth was foretold in the Apocalypse of St. John. For two years Murray attended ceremonies of Crowley's mock-religious order, Ordo Templi Orientis, following in the footsteps of famous Crowley followers such as Scientology cult founder L. Ron Hubbard and Jack Parsons, the eccentric rocket fuel inventor who prayed to the Greek god Pan after each successful launch. "This man is like the antidote to what I was raised in," Murray wrote of his new hero Crowley. Murray was especially compelled by the fact that Crowley, like him, was raised by fundamentalist Christian parents he loathed.

Murray had been indoctrinated so thoroughly into charismatic Pentecostal culture, however, that even while he railed against his religious upbringing, he could not abandon his ingrained attraction to religiosity. So instead of fleeing hardcore Christian culture for secular humanism, a natural position for jaded skeptics like him, he traded his former faith for Crowley's occultism. Crowley's philosophy of sex "magick," narcotic hallucination, and self-degradation (he allegedly ordered his followers to have oral sex with goats and drink the blood of cats) was forged in reaction to his parents' Puritanism and, in fact, was first practiced in English boarding schools, where homosexual experimentation was practically de rigueur. Crowley became Murray's new lodestar. Like Jesus, who was so impressed by the ardor of a pagan Roman centurion whom he met that he remarked, "I have not found such great faith, even in Israel," Murray yearned for spiritual practice in its purest form.

Now he practiced Crowley's faux faith as fervently as his parents wished he had worshipped their neo-evangelical macho Christ. But the occult only led Murray into a confusing new world of cheap thrills. By his own account, he engaged in "every sort of sexual pervrsion [sic] . . . that's legal," from anonymous gay sex to bestiality. He boasted of his proclivity for binge drinking, his love for death metal bands, and his penchant for spewing "blasphemy." He envisioned his new experiences as positively transcendent. "In a way it's like I'm just about completely rebelling against christianity [sic] in any way that I can," the enragée mused, "but this is a little different of a rebellion."

But as Murray's detachment from his family and community intensified, so did his yearning for the interpersonal solidarity increasingly denied to him. In May 2007, Dr. Marlene Winell, a leading expert on treating ex-fundamentalists traumatized by the experience of leaving their faith, was notified about Murray's tortured online postings. Winell immediately posted a response to Murray. "I can see that you are in a great deal of pain and I'd like to invite you to contact me," she wrote on a website where he frequently posted. "I'd like to be helpful if I can. People do care about you and there is hope."

Murray recoiled. "It's so funny how many people want to help you and love you and counsel you when there is money involved," he replied.

Having refused one of the last means of human contact available to him, Murray plunged into a sinkhole of loneliness. His online postings now read like death wishes. In one of his final screeds, dated July 7, 2007, Murray offered a garbled attempt at death metal lyrics that captured his sense of complete despondency:

> ... *I am crying here in a buried kennel*
> *I have never felt so final*
> *Someone help me please, losing all reserve*
> *I am f***ing gone, I think I am fu**ing dying*
> *HANDSONMYFACEOVERBEARINGICAN'TGETOUT!*
>   *You all stare, but you ll never see*
> *There is something inside me ...*
> *Cut me! beat me! molest me! abuse me! @#%$ me! hate me!*
>   *break me! Rape me! kill me! show me!*
> *Here is my purity ... ...*
> *Enter this nightmare. ...*

Murray's desire to realize his emotional and intellectual aspirations had become completely blocked. His self-esteem and sense of spontaneity evaporated into a heavy cloud of hopelessness. At the same time, his destructive impulses grew. The self-described "rejected sheltered Christian boy" openly contemplated suicide, cutting his arms with sharp objects when his anxiety seemed unbearable. He burrowed himself into the mass-marketed aesthetic of goth culture, from Satanist screeds to plastic pagan chum to the calculated gloom of commercial death metal, still finding time to download literally thousands of fetishistic porn images on his computer. Murray had become what Erich Fromm called the "necrophilious character," a personality whose fixation on death leads them to acts of malignant destructiveness.

As Murray nourished his death obsession, his behavior grew increasingly aggressive. On July 22, he posted a diary entry boasting about haranguing his mother and mocking her "favorite pastor," Ted Haggard, or, as he called him, "Ted Faggard." "Hey, bit,ch [sic]," Murray said he barked in his mother's face, "using drugs, alcohol and having gay sex, I'm just trying to do what any Christian pastor would do, at least I'm not doing meth like Ted Haggard . . . but maybe I will try it and maybe I'll just OD on stuff just so I don't have to deal with you anymore . . . "

The violent rage roiling inside Murray overwhelmed his sense of self-pity. He was intent on suicide, but first Murray wanted to kill as many tongue-talking Pentecostal zealots as he could. Those who constantly invoked the wiles of Satan to frighten him into submission, or impelled him to wage "spiritual warfare" against the secular Enemy were the true spawn of the Devil. "You Christians brought this on yourselves," Murray proclaimed. "All I want to do is kill and injure as many of you . . . as I can especially Christians who are to blame for most of the problems in the world."

As winter approached, Murray acquired a fearsome arsenal of assault rifles, including a Bushmaster XM-15 ("Beltway Sniper" John Lee Malvo's weapon of choice) and an AK-47. At a local UPS store where Murray maintained a mailbox, employees observed that he was ordering "boxes and boxes" of ammunition. Murray's bogus tales of preparing to deploy with the Marines quelled whatever suspicions burned-out UPS employees might have had. Meanwhile, Murray's parents, who were adept at ferreting secular media material from his desk drawers, had no idea his stockpile even existed.

Late in the evening on December 8 (the same day that a psychotic young man named Mark David Chapman killed John Lennon in 1980), Murray suited up in black military fatigues, gathered two automatic rifles, three semiautomatic pistols, and 1,000 rounds of ammo, then jumped in his car. Besides his weapons, Murray carried in his pants pocket Aleister Crowley's *The Book of the Law*, a tract the author claimed to have transcribed from messages dictated to him by ancient Egyptian gods, and which he summarized in one phrase: "Do as thou wilt shall be the whole of the law."

In the back seat of Murray's car was another of his favorite books. It was *I Had to Say Something*, by Mike Jones.

Murray sped toward Arvada, where the Youth with a Mission complex stood. The time for spiritual warfare had come. Upon arriving at the complex, he stomped to the front desk and demanded to stay overnight. A receptionist calmly refused his demand. Without hesitation, Murray whipped out a .40 caliber semiautomatic Berretta pistol and opened fire on a group of staffers chatting away as they wandered out of a Christmas banquet.

Tiffany Johnson was caught in Murray's fusillade. An affable twenty-four-year-old who said she spent one night every week ministering to adolescent skateboarders involved in "drugs, cutting, branding, and hurting others," Johnson fell and died instantly. A studious twenty-six-year-old named Philip Crouse, who spent part of a summer vacation constructing a house for impoverished residents of the Crow Indian reservation in Montana, was also hit while rushing to stop Murray. Crouse crumpled to the floor and died beside Johnson. Murray fled the blood-soaked complex, fired up his car, and sped away to complete his mission. Days earlier he seethed, "God, I can't wait till I can kill you people. Feel no remorse, no sense of shame, I don't care if I live or die in the shoot-out."

Murray's next stop was the New Life Church.

While police fanned out through Arvada in a frantic search for the still-unidentified YWAM shooter, Murray pulled into the New Life parking lot. At 1 p.m., as worshippers filed out of afternoon services, Murray sprayed a hail of bullets at the crowd with his Bushmaster rifle. He struck two teenaged sisters, Stephanie and Rachel Works, who had recently returned from missionary trips to Brazil and China, killing them instantly. He then charged into the church's main foyer, unaware that Haggard's replacement, Brady Boyd, had authorized as many as thirty parishioners to carry concealed weapons into his spiritual sanctuary, presumably to guard against hell-bent invaders like him. One of Boyd's volunteer guards, Jeanne Assam, an ex-cop who became born again after the Minneapolis police department fired her for lying, sprinted toward Murray, shouting, "Surrender!" again and again. Murray refused to comply. Assam leapt forward, directly in the line of Murray's fire, and peeled off a clip from her pistol, lightly wounding the black-clad shooter in the leg. He retreated. Moments later, he shot himself in the head and died.

All four of Murray's victims were youthful, mostly home-schooled, and extremely idealistic. They could have been his roommates at YWAM or could have joined him in a Christian youth fellowship.

They seemed so much like him, at least on the surface. So did he single them out? Although there is no conclusive answer, Murray's acknowledged grievances hint at his motives. Each of his victims represented to him the obedient, unquestioning religious automaton he was required to be but never could become. They had embarked on the exotic foreign missions he had been rejected for, discovering friendship and even (nonsexual) wholesome romance while he languished in his room—his "buried kennel." The blithe everyday existence of these shiny, happy Jesus people was Murray's "Christian nightmare."

Like the sadistic antagonists of William Golding's *Lord of the Flies* Murray's violent impulses had been constrained only by what Golding called the "invisible yet strong . . . taboo of the old life . . . the protection of parents and school and policemen and the law." When he mowed down his peers, Murray hoped to demonstrate his complete contempt for the civilization of adults, along with all its corruption, cruelty, and internal contradictions. His victims, then, were no more than "littluns" he sacrificed to exact his revenge, to make Colorado Springs weep for the end of innocence long after order returned. Murray's real targets were his rigid parents, their draconian childrearing gurus, and the prying pastor who raided his room—the architects of his "Christian nightmare."

The evangelical hierarchy's handling of the Haggard scandal had hardened Murray's murderous intentions. Both Murray and Haggard were unable to fulfill their essential selves within the strict confines of Pentecostal culture, so each of them sought an escape through drugs and illicit sex. But whereas Murray openly embraced his turn to decadence, Haggard concealed his secret life behind bombastic expressions of religious fervor. After Haggard was unmasked as a fraud, however, he was pronounced "completely heterosexual" by the movement's elders in only three weeks. Murray, who had been irrevocably rejected for abandoning his faith, was stung by this spectacle of cheap grace. "I want to know where was all the love, mercy and compassion for *my* supposed imperfections?" he wrote despairingly.

The mainstream media made little effort to analyze the trauma-wracked mentality that drove Murray to violence, opting instead for a tight focus on the more sensational aspects of his killings. When cable news arrived on the scene of the crime, it sketched a haphazard portrait of Murray hardly distinguishable from that of Eric Harris, Cho Seung-Hui, or John Lee Malvo. He was just another young male nutcase with a gun, or, according to CNN anchor Rick Sanchez, a killer motivated exclusively by "his hate for certain Christians." When Sanchez interviewed Marlene Winell, the psychiatrist who attempted to counsel Murray, her attempts to assess the impact that Murray's religious indoctrination had had in shaping his destructive behavior were brushed aside.

During the brief moments in which Sanchez allowed Winell to speak, she attempted to explain the obvious, that Murray's destructive actions were influenced at least in part by what she called "a crazy-making system that has all sorts of circular reasoning. It's got bottom line rules like, 'Don't think, don't respect your own feelings in any way.' Small children are told they're going to burn in Hell. And if it doesn't work for you . . . [you are told that] it's your fault."

Sanchez crinkled his brow in deep indignation. Finally, he cut in on his guest. "While I disagree with much of what you said as a Christian," he snapped at Winell, "I certainly respect your right to say it." Sanchez suddenly became exasperated. "You're not blaming the faith for this, are you?" he wanted to know. "I mean *a man has free will!*" Before Winell could respond, Sanchez terminated the interview.

By failing to explore the roots of Murray's violence, the mainstream media allowed the far right to seize the narrative. Relying on the insights of Pastor Joe Schimmel, a sixties rock burnout who resolved after becoming born again "to show how Satanism can influence youth through music," the far-right Web magazine *WorldNetDaily* reported that Murray "had sold his soul" to the occult and "another devil: rock and roll." An earlier *WorldNetDaily* report on Murray's killing spree buttressed its analysis with the conclusion of an anonymous commenter on a *Rocky Mountain News* forum: "Two words: DEMONIC POSSESSION."

The *Rocky Mountain News* channeled the movement's version, turning to none other than the evangelical anti-porn crusader Steve Arterburn as the arbiter on the impact of pornography on Murray. The newspaper reported, "Arterburn said Thursday he wasn't surprised to hear that pornography played a role in Murray's life. Not only does pornography dehumanize, but like any addiction, increasing amounts are needed to be satisfied—a deadly recipe for those prone to violence." But if porn breeds violence, then why had Ted Haggard, an avid porn consumer, never engaged in any act of physical brutality beyond lightly spanking the buttocks of a gay bodybuilder?

While the national press clamored for an exclusive interview with Murray's parents, the couple quietly arranged to meet with a psychologist who could help them prepare a satisfactory explanation for their son's acts—and one devoid of the hard truths Winell attempted to tell. On February 27, 2008, the Murrays were escorted onto Focus on the Family's compound, led into its lower recesses, and seated, in an elegantly appointed radio studio, at a table across from James Dobson. Now they poured forth their version of their son's descent into madness. "The lesson is that unforgiveness leads to this bitterness and then opens you up to the spirit of Satan, to the spirit of whatever, and when that occurs, it becomes a power that people cannot control," said Murray's father Ronald, a neurologist.

Dobson was careful not to press the Murrays further for insights into their son's pathology. Blaming Satan was always safer than excessive reflection. "We can't explain it, we can't understand," Dobson declared. "We say, 'Lord, someday we will understand, but today we don't.'"

There was really little else Dobson could say. Murray's parents were not neglectful of their son, nor were they intentionally abusive. By all accounts, they raised him in faithful accordance with the teachings of the Christian right's leading self-help gurus. In their cloistered world, where home-schooling is viewed as an ideal alternative to "government schools," and where the rod is rarely spared, they were model parents. Murray's killing spree thus reflected less on his parents than on the all-encompassing authoritarian culture that Dobson had helped to shape. When practiced in the real world, the movement's "family values" sometimes produced some unusually dysfunctional families. Only by blaming Satan and his minions for Murray's acts could the Christian right avoid acknowledging this absolutely damning indictment of its ideology.

   This sort of reasoning had been seen before, from figures ranging from Ted Bundy to Tom DeLay to Ted Haggard. When confronted with their own crimes and sins, these movement icons found that faulting the prince of darkness was far easier than accepting personal responsibility.

   By the time Colorado Springs completed its mourning period, the Republican primary had begun in earnest. The primary field was a cast of deeply flawed figures, each one less attractive to the conservative movement than the next. Almost none of them boasted culture war bonafides, yet all campaigned as though their ambitions depended on "value voters." Ironically, the Republican politician most despised by the Christian right, Senator John McCain, a sworn enemy of conservative icons from Tom DeLay to Jerry Falwell, secured the nomination. McCain immediately lurched to the right, embarking on a doomed strategy that would ratify the self-destruction of his party.

PART THREE

But mark this: There will be terrible times in the last days. People will be lovers of themselves, lovers of money, boastful, proud, abusive, disobedient to their parents, ungrateful, unholy, without love, unforgiving, slanderous, without self-control, brutal, not lovers of the good, treacherous, rash, conceited, lovers of pleasure rather than lovers of God—having a form of godliness but denying its power. Have nothing to do with them.

2 Timothy 3:1–5

CHAPTER 21

THE PARTY OF DOBSON

The political hopefuls who entered the Republican primary contest each campaigned in the shadow of George W. Bush. Bush was, and still is, the paradigmatic president of the modern Republican Party. Yet few liberals could make sense of his appeal. He was intellectually incurious, inarticulate, and insolent to the point of self-satire. A scion of patrician wealth schooled in the Ivy Leagues, his anti-elitism seemed cynical, if not utterly insincere. Even more, the motives of Bush's seemingly expansive base of supporters mystified the most sagacious pundits. "At one level this election was about nothing," Thomas Friedman wrote the day after Bush's reelection. "None of the real problems facing the nation were really discussed."

Thomas Frank's postelection best-selling book *What's the Matter with Kansas?* asserted that Republican politicians had cleverly exploited culture war issues such as abortion and gay marriage to con low-information middle Americans into voting against their economic interests. This strategy, according to Frank, was honed in Kansas by free-market fanatics such as Senator Sam Brownback and Representative Todd Tiahrt, and it found its apotheosis in Bush's reelection campaign. Frank's analysis was penetrating, refreshing, and even path-breaking, but it was incomplete. Why did evangelical voters feel such a powerful emotional affinity for Bush and his allies? Could his conservative positions on social issues fully explain their enthusiasm? The answers to these questions resided not so much in clever corporate Republican flimflam as in the appeal of Bush's born-again experience—his escape from freedom.

Countless biographies, documentaries, and biopics about Bush begin during his reckless youth. The colorful episodes are well known: Young Bush destroying a Christmas wreath during a drunken prank (one of three known times he was arrested), squandering lucrative business opportunities, failing miserably during a bid for Congress, and compounding a testy relationship with his imperious father. The most essential component of Bush's personality—the character trait that would help define his presidency—developed from his mounting guilt when he submitted himself to a born-again experience.

By embracing Christianity, the alcoholic scion of privilege not only suppressed his urge to drink liquor but also garnered instant cachet in the evangelical movement that increasingly dominated Sun Belt politics. With his willingness to trumpet the personal crises that led him to Jesus, Bush was able to connect to the new Republican base in a way few politicians before him had done. "I've had some personal experience with [drugs and alcohol]. As has been reported, I quit drinking. The main reason I quit was because I accepted Jesus Christ into my life in 1986," Bush told his faith-based initiatives guru, Marvin Olasky. With the help of Michael Gerson, a former speechwriter for the movement's most famous born-again, convicted Watergate felon Chuck Colson, Bush integrated pious confessions into his public addresses and even his answers to questions raised during debates.

But like Tom DeLay, another born-again recovering alcoholic, Bush did not eliminate his addictive tendencies altogether; he simply transmuted them into authoritarian religion. He became what official Alcoholics Anonymous material describes as a "dry drunk"—someone who, by turning sober, develops exaggerated character flaws including "exaggerated self-importance" and "a rigid judgmental outlook."

Bush projected his attitudes into some of his most momentous decisions. "President Bush said to all of us: 'I'm driven with a mission from God,'" said Nabil Shaath, the Palestinian foreign minister at the time of a high-level meeting with Bush in June 2003. "God would tell me, 'George, go and fight those terrorists in Afghanistan.' And I did, and then God would tell me, 'George, go and end the tyranny in Iraq. . . .' And I did. And now, again, I feel God's words coming to me,

'Go get the Palestinians their state and get the Israelis their security, and get peace in the Middle East.' And by God I'm gonna do it."

This account, though denied by a White House spokesman, provided a perfect encapsulation of Bush's tendencies. His God was a stern taskmaster who charged Bush with his historical mission to change the world through force of arms. "You know he is the wrong father to appeal to in terms of strength," Bush said when asked by journalist Bob Woodward whether he had asked his father for advice on Iraq. "There is a higher father that I appeal to." Imbued with divine strength, Bush felt free to project the urges that had been present since his youth into his political behavior. Each evildoer Bush vanquished, from the Afghani taxi driver whose legs were "pulpified" during an "enhanced interrogation" session, to the Democratic senators smeared as treasonous molly-coddlers, bore the consequences of his divinely sanctioned sadism.

None of the candidates in the 2008 Republican primary possessed the psychological traits that animated Bush's radical presidency. Purely from the standpoint of character, the three Republican frontrunners—McCain, Romney, and Giuliani—contrasted with Bush dramatically. Under normal circumstances, this would have been a good thing. After all, by the beginning of the primary Bush was the least popular American president in recent history. However, the 25 percent of the public that still approved of Bush's leadership by the end of his second term represented the backbone of the Republican Party. Indeed, by 2006 the Republican Party had been so thoroughly subsumed by the Christian right, and so well purged of most of its moderate elements, that the insufficiently religious primary frontrunners entered the race with severe handicaps.

Former New York City Mayor Rudy Giuliani's campaign was dead on arrival, even though poll-obsessed Washington pundits and New York–based press wiseguys assumed otherwise. The son of a mafia-linked felon who had made his bones relentlessly prosecuting his targets, Giuliani's own erratic behavior prompted his mayoral campaign in 1993 to commission a "vulnerability study" that highlighted his "raucous social life" and warned that "questions of a weirdness factor" could impede his ambitions. But little could deter the swaggering conquistador from his oddly self-destructive ways. After securing an annulment of his marriage to his second cousin, Giuliani married Donna Hanover, a local television anchor. While he was still with Hanover, Giuliani appeared so frequently with his press secretary, a twenty-eight-year-old woman he handpicked for the job, *Vanity Fair* reported that they were dating. In 1999, Giuliani wooed another mistress, Judith Nathan, by using public funds to chauffeur her to her vacation condo and ordering police detectives to walk her dog. When the scorned Hanover threw Giuliani out of Gracie Mansion, the official mayoral residence, he moved in with two openly gay friends. On at least three occasions, Giuliani appeared in drag in videotaped skits, including once with billionaire Donald Trump, who sniffed his stuffed brassiere and smooched his neck.

In 2000, Giuliani's personal crisis was played out before the media. Along with his health crisis—he developed prostate cancer—the embarrassing revelations caused him to drop his contest for the U.S. Senate against Hillary Clinton. Disgraced and discredited, Giuliani nevertheless resurrected himself during the September 11 terrorist attacks on the World Trade Center. Demonstrating calmness and compassion, he emerged as a national leader, filling the vacuum left by the strange three-day disappearance of President Bush. Rudy the hero was the portrait covering the picture of Rudy the bizarre. Still vigorous at the age of 63, Giuliani was the Republican answer to Dorian Gray.

Among the crisis-addled Christian right, Giuliani's greatest sin was not his "raucous" private life but, rather, his refusal to submit to a born-again process that would have laid his past indulgences to rest. Of course, the evangelical test ran against Giuliani's grain, where piety and hypocrisy lived comfortably side-by-side. When he appeared before the Value Voters Summit in November 2007, Giuliani pleaded for empathy. "You and I know that I'm not a perfect person," he said with a forced chuckle. "I've made mistakes in my life. But I've always done the best that I could to try to learn from them." His confession fell on deaf ears. Outside the conference hall, a group of local movement activists grumbled to me about Giuliani's attempts to win them over. "It's a foundational issue," said Doug Steiger, a Maryland-based anti-abortion organizer. "From our standpoint, three marriages is painful.

He's for abortion, he's for homosexual marriage. It's just evidence of his lack of commitment to our understanding." Giuliani's promise to appoint "strict constructionist" judges—a coded vow to stack the judiciary with anti-gay, anti-abortion figures determined to overturn *Roe v. Wade*—was insufficient as well. So long as he lived outside the rigid social doctrine of evangelical culture, he was unacceptable.

Senator John McCain, already loathed for his defiance of conservative orthodoxy on issues from gay marriage to stem cell research, was also viewed with disdain by the movement. A mainline Episcopalian who claimed suddenly during the 2008 primary to have become a Baptist, McCain was noticeably uncomfortable with overtly religious gestures. Further, he had expressed no remorse for leaving his first wife for a younger, richer woman. McCain attempted to reconcile with his old enemy Jerry Falwell, addressing the graduating class of Liberty University in May 2006, but with negligible results. Before McCain's campaign even began, James Dobson took to the airwaves to condemn him. "Speaking as a private individual, I would not vote for John McCain under any circumstances," Dobson announced in January 2007. Despite Dobson's rebuke, McCain retained the quiet respect of the Republican grassroots, and he was seen by many of the party elite as the GOP's most viable candidate.

Former Massachusetts governor Mitt Romney had never drunk a drop of alcohol and had been married to the same woman for over three decades. But his personal austerity meant little to the self-proclaimed proponents of family values. They preferred someone like themselves, an evangelical who either underwent or understood the born-again process. The sinless, mannequin-like Romney did not fit the mold. His campaign was burdened by evangelical fears about his membership in the Church of Latter Day Saints, the Mormon organization condemned as a cult by the Southern Baptist Convention and Pat Robertson's Christian Broadcasting Network.

James Dobson's wife, Shirley, had excluded Mormons from participation in her 2004 National Day of Prayer, yet Dobson and many of his peers treated Romney respectfully during the campaign. Dobson, for his part, described Romney as "presidential" during a radio broadcast. But behind the scenes at the Value Voters Summit, where Romney introduced himself to Dobson's followers, movement activists attempted to amplify questions about Romney's religion. "Take a look at what he really believes," Janet Folger, an influential Florida evangelical, anti-Mormon activist and founder of a group called Faith2Action, remarked to me after Romney's speech. "He believes that Jesus is Satan's brother! Are you kidding me?"

In the corridors of the summit's exhibition hall, an evangelical film producer accosted attendees, claiming to them that Romney believed in something called the "White Horse Prophecy." According to the producer, Church of Latter Day Saints founder Joseph Smith prophesied that the Constitution would one day "hang by a thread" because of widespread social licentiousness, but that it would be saved by a church elder who had ascended to the presidency. When another Mormon candidate for the Republican nomination, Senator Orrin Hatch, declared during a 1999 appearance on a Salt Lake City radio station, "the Constitution is literally hanging by a thread," he drew unexpected and unwanted attention to his faith, forcing him to deny to reporters any divine motives for seeking the presidency. Romney could not afford similar scrutiny.

Once a proud heir of the liberal Republican tradition bequeathed to him by his father, former Michigan governor George Romney, Romney tacked right. When his father had run for the Republican nomination for president in 1968, his Mormon background had never been raised as an issue. That it now put a question mark over Romney testified to the rise of the religious right.

Romney poured vast sums of his personal fortune into cultivating movement support. In the end, he was only able to entice an avaricious, discredited figure like the Reverend Lou Sheldon into his camp. Sheldon, a fanatically anti-gay preacher dubbed "Lucky Louie" by casino lobbyist Jack Abramoff for his eagerness to line his pockets with gambling industry money, hoped his access to Romney would restore his former influence. "I sat for four hours in Mitt Romney's family room with his wife, Ann," Sheldon told me, "and it became very clear to me that he is clearly with us." (Sheldon then drifted off onto his favorite topic, warning me that I could turn gay at any moment. "Remember, homosexuality could strike you," he said, jabbing a finger in my chest. "You could go into a gender identity confusion because it is a psychological imbalance.")

The unexpected rise of former Arkansas governor Mike Huckabee mortally wounded Romney's campaign. Huckabee brazenly channeled Janet Folger, who now supported his campaign. "Don't Mormons believe Jesus is Satan's brother?" Huckabee remarked to a reporter.

Huckabee's campaign was poorly funded, understaffed, and practically unknown by the time his bid for the Iowa caucus began. Romney, meanwhile, had pumped $17.4 million of his personal fortune into his campaign ahead of Iowa; he would spend $85,000 a day on advertising, much of which was negative. But Huckabee's background as an ordained minister in the Southern Baptist Convention enabled him to compensate for his financial disadvantage, especially in evangelical-heavy primary states.

A longtime confidant of James Dobson, Huckabee had maligned gays well before it was fashionable for Republicans to do so. In 1992, Huckabee called for quarantining AIDS patients to prevent the spread of HIV. To bolster his proposal, he cited the case of Kimberly Bergalis, a woman who said her openly gay dentist infected her with HIV during a routine examination. Bergalis, who claimed she was a virgin, was later diagnosed with two sexually transmitted diseases—genital warts and the human papiloma virus—that she had acquired from sexual encounters prior to contracting HIV. Huckabee's views changed little after the discrediting of Bergalis; when asked about his proposal fifteen years later on the campaign trail, he defiantly stood by it.

Huckabee was not some cynical politician pandering to leaders of the Christian right. He *was* a leader of the Christian right. In ads that his campaign ran in Iowa and South Carolina, Huckabee consolidated his status, ostentatiously billing himself as a "Christian Leader." "I am not coming to you," he told evangelical audiences on the campaign trail, "I come from you."

Romney attempted to neutralize Huckabee's gathering appeal by adopting right-wing positions on gay marriage and abortion, reversing stands he had taken as governor of Massachusetts. Still slipping in the polls with the Iowa caucus only a month away, Romney realized this was not enough. After bunkering with his staff, he resolved to deliver a major speech that would assuage concerns about his Mormon faith. Romney announced his speech to the media with great fanfare, deliberately inviting comparisons to John F. Kennedy's famous 1960 address before an assembly of Southern Methodist ministers, in which he forcefully and defiantly dispelled the notion that his Catholicism disqualified him for the presidency.

"I believe in an America where the separation of church and state is absolute," Kennedy declared, "where no Catholic prelate would tell the president, should he be Catholic, how to act, and no Protestant minister would tell his parishioners for whom to vote; where no church or church school is granted any public funds or political preference; and where no man is denied public office merely because his religion differs from the president who might appoint him or the people who might elect him."

On December 4, 2007, Romney took the rostrum at the George H. W. Bush Library, in College Station, Texas, outside Houston, where JFK delivered his famous speech. Romney opened with a predictable and requisite pledge: "If I am fortunate to become your president, I will serve no one religion, no one group, no one cause, and no one interest." Minutes later, he contradicted his earnest vow to defy religious interest groups. "In recent years," he proclaimed, "the notion of the separation of church and state has been taken by some well beyond its original meaning. They seek to remove from the public domain any acknowledgment of God. Religion is seen as merely a private affair with no place in public life. It is as if they are intent on establishing a new religion in America—the religion of secularism. They are wrong."

Romney's strident attack on separation of church and state was a tacit rebuke of Kennedy, not to mention Thomas Jefferson, and it affirmed the Christian right's control over the Republican Party. Romney went on to mock Europeans "too 'enlightened' to venture inside [their churches] and kneel in prayer;" then he invoked "violent Jihad" as atheism's "other extreme." Finally, he declared, "Freedom requires religion just as religion requires freedom." The line so excited Rush Limbaugh that during his broadcast the following day he falsely attributed it to Founding Father John Adams. But Romney's speech hardly galvanized the party grassroots, especially in Iowa, where Huckabee had already attained the status of a saint.

Huckabee's appeal among the Republican base stemmed from more subtle factors than his positions on social issues. Unlike Romney and the rest of his adversaries, Huckabee demonstrated an intimate understanding of the complexities of the Christian right. Most important, he recognized how the movement's underlying culture of personal crisis animated its politics of resentment. His familiarity with this critical nuance was apparent when he spoke before an assemblage of Iowa's most politically active clergy members, the Pastors and Pews conference, in July 2007. Huckabee's speech was a remarkably coherent disquisition on the nexus between private trauma and political conservatism. Echoing his friend Dobson, he insisted that man is too inherently corrupt to stand against the putrid headwinds of modern culture alone and that he must therefore submit to strict Dominionist guidelines:

> If you want to make the hair on the back of my neck stand up, just tell me that my experience as a pastor lets you know that I don't have a clue about human life and the struggle of it. . . . Name me any profession in this country, on this planet where people touch more the lives of every social pathology today. . . .
>
> To that wife who's trying to use makeup not to enhance her beauty but to hide the scars and the bruises from the abuse of some alcoholic husband who beats the daylights out of her every time he gets drunk—I've talked to her. From the person who's struggling with who he or she may be in the context of a relationship that believes that he's in love with a person of the same gender—I've talked to him. Name any problem, any social pathology, name any issue that's confronting, and I'll tell you who's dealing with them. It's the pastors of America who see the tears pouring out day after day after day . . . who understand life at a level very few people see because these are the men and women who have front row seats to the real struggles of life. . . .
>
> Chuck Colson said it beautifully, he said, "The problem in today's world of this conflict of faith and secularism is that humanists don't

understand humanity, but a lot of Christians don't understand Christianity. In part because we don't understand that the nature of man. . . . The nature of man is not that he's basically good; the nature of man is that he's basically selfish. We have a sin nature, not a God nature. We have a God who made us, but we come into this world broken. We come into this world with a self-centeredness that only grace can fix. And if we fail to understand that, then we will believe as those who are the secularists do, that man's problems are essentially either economic or educational.

Huckabee drew an especially sharp contrast with the signature stump speech of the man who preceded him as Arkansas governor and who was still the standard bearer of the Democratic Party by the time Huckabee entered Iowa: Bill Clinton. Clinton's own campaign for the presidency began in Iowa amid a harsh economic recession. He reassured anxious blue-collar voters there, and later from his Oval Office desk, with a memorable phrase: "I feel your pain." In his Pastors and Pews speech, Huckabee placed the pain of average Americans at the center of his concerns, but he referred to a strikingly different kind of pain than Clinton did.

While another financial crisis loomed on the horizon, Huckabee dismissed economic tinkering as a remedy to the country's hardships. According to Huckabee's pessimistic vision, which was actually a projection of his experiences in evangelical culture, ordinary Americans are totally and naturally depraved. Scholarships and economic aid would do nothing to divert them from their slouch toward Gomorrah. The pain brought on by Americans' "social pathology" could be cured only through "grace," or submission to an omnipotent Jesus. And only Huckabee, with his background as a crude psychologist anointed by God, could lead the serried masses into the Kingdom. His campaign was for a magic helper, not a president.

Huckabee continued his speech by reminding pastors that the next generation was seething with sin. "We've gone from Leave It to Beaver to Beavis and Butthead, . . ." he said. "From a time when teachers carried paddles and ruled the halls to now, where kids carry guns and the teachers are afraid." The only way to heal the nation's pain, Huckabee proclaimed, was to mete it out to the young rebellious ones. Again, he channeled Dobson. "Yes, I do believe that the old-fashioned ways of discipline are good ones," he remarked with a wry smile. "I was the recipient of quite a few. I tell people, 'My father was the most patriotic man I think I knew. Utter patriotism. He laid on the stripes; I saw stars.' True American patriotism!" For the first time, Huckabee's enraptured audience burst into spontaneous applause.

Huckabee's smiling appeals to cultural resentment and anger electrified the Republican base. Soon after his Pastors and Pews address, an ad hoc network of locally influential pastors, many of whom already communicated with one another through Family Research Council President Tony Perkins's weekly conference calls, joined to form the grassroots arm of his campaign. By November 2007, Huckabee was polling even with Romney in Iowa and showed strength across the Bible Belt. Just as his surge in the polls began, Huckabee addressed the student body of the late Reverend Falwell's Liberty University. There, he assured his star-struck audience that his sudden rise was evidence of a holy anointing. "There's only one explanation for [my surge] and it's not a human one," Huckabee insisted, inspiring thunderous applause from the overflow crowd. "It's the same power that helped a little boy with two fish and five loaves feed a crowd of five thousand people."

Huckabee made this remarkable statement in response to a question from a student, not a reporter. Political reporters with access to the candidate shied away from asking him pointed questions about his theological beliefs, focusing instead on what *New York Times* political correspondent Adam Nagourney called his "easy-going, self-effacing, jaunty style." *Times* liberal commentator Frank Rich likened Huckabee to Democratic presidential frontrunner Barack Obama, writing, "both men aspire . . . to avoid the hyper-partisanship of the Clinton–Bush era." With its emotional yearning for postpartisan heroes, the national press corps gave Huckabee all the cover he needed. He would thus remain the "affable," bass-playing Republican counterpart to Obama, not the sectarian ideologue he truly was.

On January 3, 2008, Huckabee scored a stunning upset in Iowa, defeating Romney by eight points. His victory decided the course of the Republican primary. Now, Romney's only hope of salvaging his campaign was to win New Hampshire. But McCain was set to capitalize on substantial residual support from his successful 2000 primary campaign in the Granite State. As Republican voters looked forward to the general election, they were increasingly inclined to vote tactically. With his decades of experience with foreign policy (an Achilles heel for the domestic-minded governors Huckabee and Romney), compelling personal history, and maverick image, McCain seemed strongest in a hypothetical match-up against either Hillary Clinton or Obama.

McCain defeated Romney handily in New Hampshire, then swept into an insurmountable position on Super Tuesday. Huckabee won Alabama, West Virginia, Georgia, Tennessee, and Arkansas on Super Tuesday, all heavily evangelical states (they also are among the nation's leaders in divorce and teen pregnancy rates). But with his campaign funds nearly expended and McCain just inches from securing the nomination, Huckabee could claim only moral victory. His campaign suddenly morphed into a massive publicity stunt made up of paid speeches before Christian-right outfits and talk show appearances full of folksy humor and hearty guffaws.

During this period, a substantial segment of the opinion-making elite resolved to wish away the culture wars. The Christian right of old was dead, they declared, and a new generation of shiny, happy evangelicals had risen from its ashes, ready to scrap their parents' gay-bashing and abortion clinic blockades in favor of feel-good environmental and anti-poverty crusades. Amy Sullivan, a writer for *Time* and self-proclaimed "leading expert on religion and the Democratic Party," first tested this narrative in a lengthy April 2006 profile of Christian-right direct-mail maven Randy Brinson. Over the course of several thousand words, Sullivan detailed Brinson's supposed progressive awakening, concluding he was "proof that some evangelicals are willing to take their chances and cross over to see what Democrats have to offer." By the time the 2008 Republican primary began, however, Brinson had forked over his company's mailing list to Huckabee and cast his lot with the Republican dark horse.

Still, Sullivan would not back down. With the 2008 presidential campaign in full swing, she reiterated her fanciful theory. "Dobson and his colleagues have also been stymied by a new generation of Evangelical leaders who stubbornly refuse to join the political fray," she claimed. ". . . the old lions of the Christian right are suddenly sputtering."

To bolster her point, Sullivan pointed to Rick Warren, author of the best-selling *The Purpose Driven Life* and a California mega-church leader identified by *New York Times* columnist Nicholas Kristof as "an evangelical liberals can love." Warren's press puffers invariably omitted his well-documented history of backing anti-gay crusades (as Sullivan did) and would be caught off guard when he threw his considerable weight behind Proposition 8, a draconian ballot measure designed to nullify already-certified same-sex marriages and civil unions in his home state. In the media-manufactured age of postpartisanship, gays turned out to be collateral damage.

Other like-minded liberal pundits identified Giuliani's presidential campaign as a signal of the Christian right's supposedly imminent destruction. "Merely entertaining Giuliani as a candidate demonstrates that, for many conservatives, political power counts more than Christian values. The religious right is dead," declared columnist Bill Press. Echoing Press, the *Times*'s Rich claimed that Giuliani's early popularity in the GOP primary revealed how "the political clout ritualistically ascribed to Perkins, James Dobson of Focus on the Family, Gary Bauer of American Values and their ilk is a sham. . . . They don't speak for the Republican Party."

But then the Republican Party spoke. Giuliani's campaign strategy, tacitly acknowledging the Christian right's dominance by avoiding any state where the movement held influence, ended where it began, in Florida. Upon his humiliating third-place finish in the Sunshine State, Giuliani flew to the Ronald Reagan Library in Simi Valley to publicly endorse the party's new nominee, McCain. Back in Washington, Tony Perkins danced on Giuliani's political grave. "Giuliani, with his, you know, Big Apple values—abortion rights, gay rights—turned voters sour to him," Perkins said during an appearance on CNN. "That's why he avoided the early states, because conservatives just were, you know, very aggressive in their opposition to him." The GOP may have paraded as the party of Reagan during its national conventions, but the party's grassroots were firmly in the grip of Dobson and his minions.

John McCain loathed the Christian right more than he disliked any Democrat. Ralph Reed and his local allies had sabotaged McCain's campaign in South Carolina in 2000, spreading rumors that he had fathered a black child out of wedlock, when in fact he had adopted a Bangladeshi child whose parents had been killed by land mines. Having surveyed the wreckage of Giuliani's campaign, McCain reluctantly groped for a strategy to energize the elements that once lusted for his destruction.

Dobson, for his part, had endorsed Huckabee just days before he dropped out but refused to campaign for him. He and his allies watched and waited now, scrutinizing McCain's every move. Dobson signaled that if McCain were to select the right vice president, he might reverse his earlier vow to oppose him.

CHAPTER 22

THE PARTY OF DEATH

John McCain's campaign for the White House depended in large part on a parallel campaign he waged for the heart of the Christian right. McCain knew this would be an uphill battle. During the 2000 Republican primary campaign, he damned Christian right leaders as "agents of intolerance," adding, "They are corrupting influences on religion and politics and those who practice them in the name of religion or in the name of the Republican Party or in the name of America shame our faith, our party and our country." So he started early making amends and finding allies, flying off to San Antonio, Texas, in February 2007 to dine with a popular Pentecostal pastor named John Hagee. Hagee was unknown to the national political press corps—and to most Americans, for that matter—but within the Christian right, especially in Pentecostal circles, he was an increasingly influential figure. McCain had been apprised of Hagee's influence, but to his own extreme detriment, never inquired into the source of it.

From the pulpit of his 18,000-member Cornerstone Church in San Antonio, Hagee delivers weekly sermons beamed out over the hundreds of stations owned by evangelical mega-network Salem Communications. His preaching style is hardly different from that of many other Pentecostal televangelists. Hagee routinely assures members of his flock that their terminal diseases, credit card debts, and interpersonal troubles will all be wiped away if only they lavish generous cash donations upon him, donations that he calls "love gifts." By exploiting the desperate and gullible, Hagee and other practitioners of the prosperity gospel, one of the most popular trends in modern Pentecostalism, have raked in more than $1 million a year, making him one of the world's wealthiest preachers.

If this were the extent of Hagee's activities, it would be remarkable enough. But there is more to Hagee than hucksterism. Hagee is a Christian Zionist who preaches that the prophecies of the Book of Revelations will unfold as soon as the Jewish diaspora resettles in "Biblical Israel," meaning all of Israel and the West Bank. A natural ally of Israel's rightist Likud Party and the messianic Jewish settlers colonizing the West Bank, Hagee leveraged his millions to unite dozens of conservative mega-church congregations and some of the Christian right's most prominent figures—including the Reverend Jerry Falwell, Gary Bauer, and Rod Parsley, a Pentecostal preacher with considerable sway in his home state of Ohio—under the banner of Christians United for Israel (CUFI), the largest nationwide evangelical political organization dedicated to supporting Israel, or at least its most right-wing elements. Hagee said he would like to see CUFI become "the Christian version of AIPAC," referring to the vaunted pro-Israel group rated second only to the National Rifle Association as the most effective lobby in Washington. The preacher tapped Republican Senator Arlen Specter's former chief of staff, David Brog, as his Capitol Hill lobbyist and then proceeded to make inroads in influence.

Despite his pretensions to philosemitism, Hagee's interest in Israel was motivated exclusively by his belief in End Times theology, a doctrine that celebrates natural disaster, war, and global pandemics as harbingers of Christ's imminent return. According to Hagee's reading of the Book of Revelations, the lodestar of End Times theology, when Jesus returns to Jerusalem, the Jews must convert to evangelical Christianity or suffer eternal torment in "an everlasting lake of fire." And liberals had better seek cover as well. "As soon as Jesus sits on his throne he's gonna rule the world with a rod of iron," the portly Hagee boomed in a December 2007 jeremiad. "That means he's gonna make the ACLU do what he wants them to. That means you're not gonna have to ask if you can pray in public school. We will live by the law of God and no other law."

Hagee's apocalyptics engulfed more than the ACLU. His vision of the Rapture extended to a Holy War between Israel and its Muslim neighbors. "The coming nuclear showdown with Iran is a certainty," Hagee wrote in 2006 in the Pentecostal magazine *Charisma*. "Israel and America must confront Iran's nuclear ability and willingness to destroy Israel with nuclear weapons. For Israel to wait is to risk committing national suicide." Only through this catastrophic scenario could Hagee's prophecies be realized.

In July 2007, I covered Christians United for Israel's "Washington-Israel" Summit. Staged inside the cavernous halls of Washington, DC's Convention Center, the event was more than a political rally—it was a gigantic vaudeville of doom, despair, and destruction. Speakers from Newt Gingrich to former Israeli Ambassador Dore Gold stoked the anxieties of the nearly three thousand attendees with graphic descriptions of Iran's fearsome Shihab missile, warning that it could strike as far as Israel, into the heart of Europe, and beyond. After the Cornerstone Church chorus belted out a saccharine rendition of the Zionist folk anthem "Jerusalem, City of Gold," and evangelical crowd members, many clad in kippas and tallis, blew supersized shofars and danced in the aisles, Hagee waddled to the rostrum.

"It is time for America to embrace the words of Senator Joseph Lieberman," Hagee rumbled, "and consider a military preemptive strike against Iran to prevent a nuclear Holocaust in Israel!" The crowd leapt to its feet and roared.

When I interviewed summit attendees about their theological views, I was unable to find a single person among them who did not lust for a blitzkrieg of biblical proportions. "I'm looking forward to Armageddon and to the cleansing of the Earth!" exclaimed John G. Rogers, a pastor from California. William Baker, another Californian, told me he was "absolutely" elated about the prospect of "a battle between the Christians and the anti-Christians." "I got a bag packed," a man named Walter Farnham revealed to me. "And when we disappear, you better start to worry. Because if you haven't seen the 'Left Behind' series, it's scary." Two kindly older women standing beside Farnham nodded approvingly at the mention of *Left Behind*.

Written by the Reverend Tim LaHaye, a founder of the Council for National Policy, the *Left Behind* series is the Christian right's most effective recruitment vehicle. Larded from cover to cover with coded anti-Semitic conspiracies about "international bankers" plotting with UN chief Nicholai Carpathia (the evil characters in *Left Behind* all have ethnic names), who represents the anti-Christ, *Left Behind* is replete with descriptions of pornographic violence against unbelievers, whose "bodies burst open from head to toe at every word that proceeded out of the mouth of the Lord."

According to evangelical pollster George Barna, *Left Behind* "represents one of the most widely experienced religious teaching or evangelistic tools among adults who are not born-again Christians." LaHaye's impact on millions of lives cannot be attributed to his storytelling prowess—his prose is painfully turgid—but rather his ability to mesmerize—or terrorize—unbelievers with the prospect of a gruesome death and eternal anguish in the flames of Hell. By literally scaring the devil out of unbelievers, LaHaye and his acolytes have plumbed the country's most panic-prone elements within the ranks of the Christian right and thus have expanded their movement in a startlingly rapid fashion.

Cultural anthropologist Ernest Becker's Pulitzer Prize–winning book *The Denial of Death* offers one explanation for the popular appeal of Hagee and LaHaye's apocalypticism. Published in 1970 and heavily influenced by the work of Erich Fromm, whom Becker credited with offering "the authentic line of cumulative critical thought on the human condition," *Denial* is premised on Becker's theory that the fear of death is the greatest source of human anxiety. To transcend the terror of mortality, people may seek to follow great leaders or dissolve themselves into causes greater than themselves, especially those that literally promise the heavens. As Becker wrote, "The more you fear death and the emptier you are, the more you people your world with omnipotent father-figures, extra-magical helpers." When fearful converts become convinced that outside forces threaten their new cultural sanctuary or its leader, they react with belligerent rage. This symbiosis of submissive and aggressive behavior, first identified by Fromm as the "sadomasochistic trend," is the hallmark of certain right-wing cults.

In 1989, fifteen years after Becker died, a group of psychologists set out to prove his hypothesis. Psychologists Sheldon Solomon, Jeff Greenberg, and Tom Pyszczynski assembled twenty-two municipal court judges from Tucson and divided them into two groups, one of which was required to answer a questionnaire about how its members thought their deaths would occur. Then both groups were asked to set bail for a prostitute who was considered a flight risk. The judges who had been reminded of their impending death set bail at an average of $455, whereas those in the control group set bail at around $80. The greater the fear of death, the more draconian and fearful was the response.

During the next decade, Solomon, Greenberg, and Pyszcynski conducted similar experiments to consolidate their findings. In one test, students from a Christian college were asked to evaluate two essays, one by a Jew and the other by a Christian. Those who performed mortality exercises graded the Jewish author's work far more negatively than the control group did. Subjects asked to offer their opinion on an essay that criticized the United States demonstrated the same effect: those who had the word *death* flashed before their eyes judged the essay more harshly than those who did not.

In the months leading up to the 2004 elections, the psychologists tested the appeal of George W. Bush, showing a group of Rutgers University students an editorial hailing Bush's handling of the so-called war on terror. Rutgers students do not exactly represent Bush's core constituency, but those of them who were subjected to mortality reminders responded favorably to the editorial. Meanwhile, those in the control group reacted negatively, as they would have been expected to.

After studying Solomon, Greenberg, and Pyszcynski's experiments, journalist John Judis of *The New Republic* concluded that the surprising breadth of Republican success during the Bush era could be attributed to a single tactic: mortality reminders. "Mortality reminders not only enhanced the appeal of Bush's political style," Judis wrote, "but also deepened and broadened the appeal of the conservative social positions that Republicans had been running on."

Most candidates in the 2008 GOP primary loaded their rhetorical arsenals with mortality reminders. Rudy Giuliani's entire campaign was based on reminding Americans of 9/11; Fred Thompson, the conservative senator from Tennessee and erstwhile *Law and Order* star, followed Rudy's lead. "Twelve million illegal immigrants later," he warned an audience in California, "we are now living in a nation that is beset by people who are suicidal maniacs and want to kill countless innocent men, women and children around the world." Mike Huckabee also linked immigration to terrorism, commenting darkly the day after Pakistani presidential candidate Benazir Bhutto's assassination by radical Islamic terrorists, "It's interesting that there were more Pakistanis who illegally crossed the border than of any other nationality except for those immediately south of our border." (His claim was immediately contradicted by Immigration and Customs Enforcement officials).

Not to be outdone, Mitt Romney rattled an audience with the horrifying prospect of al-Qaida, China, and Iran teaming up to indoctrinate their offspring—a rhetorical stretch that sounded like a script proposal for *Red Dawn II*. "It's because of America's strength that we don't speak German and that our children don't speak Russian. And it's because of America's strength that our grandchildren won't have to speak Arabic or Farsi or Chinese," he said to raucous applause from the 2007 Conservative Political Action Conference. Colorado Representative Tom Tancredo hammered the death theme the hardest. A fanatical nativist rejected for service in Vietnam on the basis of his claim of "depression and severe anxiety," Tancredo rarely missed an opportunity to detail the invading scourge's murderous capacity. Illegal immigrants are "coming here to kill you and kill me and our families," he told a crowd in Illinois.

John McCain seemed uncomfortable with morbid histrionics. His campaign revolved instead around three themes: his experience, his maverick image, and his honor. Although these themes appealed to many outside the Christian right's sphere of influence, McCain won the nomination only because Romney and Huckabee split the GOP's right-wing base. McCain was convinced he could win over independent voters in the general election—independents had propelled him to victory time and again in states such as New Hampshire—but he needed to expand his appeal to the right to consolidate his weak support within the Republican Party. That meant not only highlighting his conservative record on social issues (to the extent that he had one) but also dialing his tone up to a more hysterical pitch. But because McCain was too dour to pantomime demagogy in a convincing manner—the mannequin-like Romney flopped in his own attempts—he settled on outsourcing his charisma to a most fanatical movement surrogate: Pastor Hagee.

CHAPTER 23

THE HATE BOAT

Hagee was a friend of Huckabee, having paid the ex-governor several thousand dollars to give two sermons at his church in December, after his campaign had collapsed but not officially ended. But Hagee's ambitions overwhelmed his sense of loyalty; he wanted access to the Oval Office, something Huckabee could not deliver. On the evening of February 26, 2008, Hagee called Huckabee, who was prepping for his upcoming appearance on *Saturday Night Live*. Huckabee was stunned by his pal's revelation that he would back McCain. "Have you prayed about this?" Huckabee asked his old friend. "Is this what the Lord wants you to do?" Hagee ducked the question.

The following morning, McCain staged a press conference in San Antonio to accept Hagee's endorsement. After McCain and Hagee exchanged a series of canned complements, a reporter asked McCain whether he was aware of Hagee's conspiratorial End Times prophecies. McCain brushed the question off with boilerplate. "All I can tell you," he said, "is that I'm very proud to have Pastor Hagee's support. He has support and respect from throughout the nation and I continue to appreciate his advocacy for freedom and independence for the state of Israel." Hagee took the microphone, looked the reporter straight in the eye, and declared with all the certitude of a confidence man on the witness stand, "Our support for Israel has nothing to do with an End Times prophetic scenario."

Hagee, in fact, had uttered this disclaimer word for word in a press conference during Christians United for Israel's 2007 Summit. In response, I read to him a passage from his best-selling polemic *Jerusalem Countdown* (the book's cover depicts an atomic mushroom cloud), in which he described anti-Semitism as a divinely ordained phenomenon: "It was the disobedience and rebellion of the Jews, God's chosen people, to their covenantal responsibility to serve only the one true God, Jehovah, that gave rise to the opposition and persecution that they experienced beginning in Canaan and continuing to this very day." Then I asked Hagee to explain his support for Israel in the context of that passage. Moments after my question, which Hagee curtly dismissed, the preacher's wife ordered a team of off-duty police officers to remove me from the premises.

Liberal bloggers seized on the Hagee endorsement moments after it was announced, unearthing his vast catalog of conspiratorial prophesies. Hagee's proclamation that the Vatican was the "Great Whore" of Babylon—a belief shared by most Christian Zionists— gained immediate media traction, mainly because Bill Donohue of the Catholic League denounced it. But Donohue, a strident right-wing apologist for the so-called "Nazi Pope," Pius XII, and assailant of "secular Jews" in Hollywood "who hate Christianity," accepted an apology from Hagee soon after. Like an angel in the whirlwind of the liberal media, McCain stood by Hagee's side, earning effusive praise from Christian-right activists for his loyalty. Perhaps he was not the crypto-liberal traitor they had taken him for.

But when the now notorious footage of Reverend Jeremiah Wright's "greatest hits" emerged in March, first on *ABC News* and then on a feedback loop on Fox News, liberal bloggers resuscitated with renewed passion their campaign to spotlight McCain's own "problem pastor." The bloggers had railed against Hagee with negligible effect, but now, an exceptionally avid researcher of the Christian right named Bruce Wilson provided the weapon they needed.

In a short YouTube video, Wilson reproduced audio of Hagee's declaration in 2006 that Adolf Hitler was used by God to force the Jews to Israel. "Hitler was a hunter," Hagee preached. "That will be offensive to some people. Well, dear heart, be offended: I didn't write it. Jeremiah wrote it. It was the truth and it is the truth. How did it happen?

Because God allowed it to happen. Why did it happen? Because God said, 'My top priority for the Jewish people is to get them to come back to the land of Israel.'"

When Wilson's video exploded online, it generated tens of thousands of hits. McCain, for his part, was shocked by Hagee's animadversions. On May 23, with the *New York Times* poised to report on Wilson's research, McCain cut the preacher loose, calling his remarks about Hitler "crazy and unacceptable" and adding, "I would reject the endorsement of the expression of those kind of views." A frustrated McCain aide excused the campaign's ruinous dance with Hagee as the result of "poor vetting," but it had only taken bloggers a few keystrokes to vet the notorious preacher. Was the McCain campaign truly this incompetent? Or was it naïve about the Christian-right leaders it was courting?

Curiously, even after McCain's embarrassing renunciation of Hagee, his best friend in the Senate and top campaign surrogate, independent Senator Joseph Lieberman, kept a keynote address at Hagee's 2008 Summit on his schedule. Lieberman, an Orthodox Jew, forged ties to the Christian right during a fruitless music censorship campaign in the 1990s and then insinuated himself into neoconservative circles after most congressional Democrats turned against the war in Iraq. He combined these two elements through his alliance with Hagee, who upheld the Christian right's draconian positions on social issues and the neoconservatives' connection to the Israeli right.

During the dinner banquet at Hagee's Summit in 2007, Lieberman had lauded the pastor in Hebrew, as an "Ish Elochim, a man of God. And I have something else," Lieberman added. "Like Moses, he's become the leader of a mighty multitude. Even greater than the multitude that Moses led from Egypt to the Promised Land."

Unlike McCain's, the pious Lieberman's embrace of Hagee seemed genuine. He was very probably the reason why McCain had courted the pastor in the first place. When I first reported Lieberman's scheduled Christians United for Israel speech in June 2008, an appearance that even newspapers in the senator's home state of Connecticut had overlooked, a storm of controversy erupted. In its wake, a liberal pro-

Israel advocacy group called J Street sponsored a poll revealing that only 37 percent of Jews approved of Lieberman's leadership and that a piddling 7 percent approved of Hagee.

Days later, I released more footage on the *Huffington Post*, compiled by Bruce Wilson, this time featuring Hagee identifying the anti-Christ as gay, with "fierce features," and "partially Jewish, as was Adolf Hitler." But even this failed to shake Lieberman's faith. On July 23, he struck a defiant tone in his speech before the gathering of Christians United, likening Hagee once again to the most revered Jewish prophet. "Dear friends," Lieberman said, "I can only imagine what the bloggers of today would have had to say about Moses and Miriam."

The neoconservatives orbiting Lieberman's office had long sought an alliance with the Christian right. As far back as July 1984, Irving Kristol, neoconservative godfather, urged that American Jews, "enmeshed in the liberal time warp," ally with Jerry Falwell's Moral Majority. Kristol's apologia was inspired by the anti-Semitic ravings of a preacher named Bailey Smith. "I don't know why God chose the Jew," Smith had said. "They have such funny noses." When Jewish groups pounced on Smith's remarks and on those of Jerry Falwell, who told his followers that Jews "can make more money accidentally than you can on purpose," Kristol rushed to the preachers' defense.

"Why should Jews care about the theology of a fundamentalist preacher when they do not for a moment believe that he speaks with any authority on the question of God's attentiveness to human prayer?" Kristol wrote. "And what do such theological abstractions matter as against the mundane fact that this same preacher is vigorously pro-Israel?"

In a 2003 essay for his son William's magazine the *Weekly Standard*, Kristol added a new wrinkle to his apologia, claiming that the alliance was formed organically in response to American culture "sinking to new levels of vulgarity." Neoconservatives and the religious right, Kristol wrote, "are united on issues concerning the quality of education, the relations of church and state, the regulation of pornography, and the like, all of which they regard as proper candidates for the government's attention. And since the Republican Party now has a substantial base among the religious, this gives neocons a certain influence and even power."

Neoconservative William Bennett, the Reagan administration's secretary of education and former Bush I drug czar, was a key neocon liaison to the religious right, having led high-profile battles against rap music lyrics, illicit drug use, and gay rights. (William Kristol also served as his chief of staff in the Department of Education.) In his moralistic polemic *The Book of Virtues*, Bennett presented self-control as a panacea for societal problems. "We should know that too much of anything, even a good thing, may prove to be our undoing," he wrote. "[We] need . . . to set definite boundaries on our appetites."

But Bennett had an almost unquenchable appetite of his own, and it wasn't just for catered soufflés on the Washington dinner circuit. Bennett was a "preferred customer" at over a dozen casinos between Atlantic City and Las Vegas. By the time reporters Josh Green and Jonathan Alter revealed his high-stakes hustling in the *Washington Monthly* in 2003, he had gambled away $8 million.

While Bennett faded from the scene momentarily after his gambling addiction came to light, the pantheon of the neoconservative clique fixated on realizing their geopolitical goals in the Middle East, an agenda that dovetailed with the Likud Party, which a few of them had advised. In his original 1984 manifesto for a neoconservative–Christian-right alliance, Irving Kristol insisted that it was essential in order to defend Israel. Under George W. Bush, the neocons cultivated support from the droves of evangelicals who viewed the so-called war on terror as a spiritual war between good and evil. So far as the neocons were concerned, Hagee's occasional anti-Semitic eruptions were inconsequential if the primary target of his vitriol remained the Muslim evildoers surrounding Israel.

When Obama emerged as the frontrunner for the Democratic nomination in the spring of 2008, the neocons urged a slash-and-burn campaign of rumors about Obama's faith and ethnic background. Michael Goldfarb, a young editor for the neocon house organ the *Weekly Standard*, led the charge, proposing that "an unaccountable, right-wing, third-party outfit" create an attack ad highlighting Obama's Islamic heritage. In a blog post, Goldfarb wrote,

Show Obama in Tribal Outfit . . .

Narrator: "Obama wants U.S. forces out of Iraq."

Cut out picture of Obama's head and paste Osama's picture.

Narrator: "Osama wants U.S. forces out of Iraq."

This brand of character attack (essentially a 30-second mortality reminder) still had resonance among the Christian right. However, its appeal among independents and moderate Republicans was questionable so many years after 9/11. McCain pledged that his moderate tendencies would inform the kind of campaign he would run against Obama. "This will be a long and hard and well fought and, I believe, honorable campaign, one that is marked by respect," McCain told the Florida Association of Newspaper Editors in June. But as McCain was joined by neocons such as Goldfarb (who became his deputy spokesman), and as right-wing radio hosts invented and amplified rumors about Obama's background, pressure mounted on the right for McCain to sharpen his tone. When McCain hesitated, movement leaders clamored for a vice presidential candidate who not only shared their values but also demonstrated a willingness to broadcast the attacks they had concocted.

They found their candidate in the unlikeliest of places. In June 2007, three of the movement's leading pundits disembarked from a luxury cruise liner in Juneau, Alaska, for lunch with the state's new governor, Sarah Palin. The pundits were Bill Kristol, the *Weekly Standard*'s editor-in-chief; Fred Barnes, the *Standard*'s executive editor; and Michael Gerson, a former speechwriter for President George W. Bush and Chuck Colson, who was well known for his coded evangelical rhetorical flourishes.

According to the *New Yorker*'s Jane Mayer, Palin began lunch with a lengthy, impassioned grace that left her guests in awe. After an agreeable discussion of local and national politics over a meal of halibut cheeks, Palin invited the pundits for a helicopter journey to a gold mine north of Juneau. On the way, she complained to them about an environmental group's lawsuit that had so far prevented a local mining company from dumping tons of toxic waste into a pristine lake in the Tongass National Forest. They liked the cut of her jib.

By the time they were back at the cruise boat's buffet table, the pundits resolved to promote Palin to their friends inside the Beltway.

Palin was a curious darling for a foreign-policy-oriented figure such as Kristol to choose. She had little knowledge of world affairs and only a faint awareness of the goings-on outside her state. She had traveled outside the country only once, to Kuwait for an official tour during the second U.S. invasion of Iraq, and had spent little time on the east coast. But to Kristol and the neocons, her parochialism was a positive quality. By drawing close a vapid vice president, Kristol—the former chief of staff to Vice President Dan Quayle—and his allies sought to become her Cardinal Richelieu, dictating her agenda from behind a curtain. "She's bright and she's a blank page," said a former White House official working at the neoconservative American Enterprise Institute. "She's going places and it's worth going there with her."

In June 2008, during an episode of *Fox News Sunday*, Kristol gushed praise for Palin, calling her "my heartthrob" and urging McCain to "Go for the gold with Palin." Visibly annoyed by Kristol's cheerleading, moderator Chris Wallace snapped, "Can we please get off Sarah Palin?" But Kristol only amplified his cheerleading in the weeks to come. And soon enough, Palin's name appeared on McCain's shortlist.

CHAPTER 24

A MATTER OF TONE

Hoping to gird himself against the coming storm of character attacks, Obama embarked on his own clumsy foray to co-opt the religious right. Obama's religious outreach strategy was inspired by a Democratic operative named Mara Vanderslice, who had recently formed a political action committee, the Matthew 25 Network, to advocate on his behalf. Vanderslice advised her clients not only to downplay their support for abortion rights and gay rights but also never to use the phrase "separation of church and state." Hired by Senator John Kerry's presidential campaign in 2004, she ultimately found herself sidelined. "She was a little bit overzealous," the late Father Robert Drinan, a liberal Catholic legend and Kerry adviser, told the *New York Times*. Vanderslice claimed results two years later in the congressional midterms. Her clients, she said, citing exit polling, garnered 10 percent more of the evangelical vote than two years before. Widespread uncertainty about whether Democratic gains among so-called "values voters" were a result of Vanderslice's inspired appeals, or simply a reflection of the nationwide backlash against the Republican Congress and Bush's policies, did not deter her from taking credit.

At a 2006 gathering of evangelicals convened by the Reverend Jim Wallis, a moderate figure with close ties to Democratic congressional leaders, Obama put the Vanderslice strategy to the test, attacking unnamed "secularists." "But what I am suggesting is this—secularists are wrong when they ask believers to leave their religion at the door before entering into the public square," he declared. During the South

Carolina Democratic primary, Obama's campaign distributed fliers describing the candidate's supposed born-again experience: "Kneeling beneath that cross on the South Side," the flier quotes Obama, "I felt I heard God's spirit beckon me." In bold type, the words "Committed Christian," appeared beside Obama's profession of faith.

At the same time, the campaign rebuked protests from gay rights groups against a black gospel concert it had organized in South Carolina to generate turnout for Obama. The concert headliner was Donny McClurkin, a Grammy-winning singer who proudly advertised himself as an "ex-gay." "I don't speak against the homosexual. I tell him that God delivered me—from the homo-sex-u-a-li-ty!" McClurkin roared at the concert crowd, skipping across the stage in a flamboyant victory dance that seemed to contradict his claim of deliverance.

With the general election in full swing, Obama took his confessional religious appeals into more hostile territory. On June 10, 2008, he convened a meeting in a law office in downtown Chicago with a wide array of about thirty evangelical leaders. Obama insisted that the gathering remain entirely off the record, forbidding participants to disclose his statements to the press. After acquiring a partial list of attendees, I learned that the meeting included Stephen Strang, founder of the right-wing Pentecostal magazine *Charisma* and a close ally of Pastor Hagee, whose books he publishes. Strang told me that Obama did little to assuage the hostility that many of those assembled—particularly the conservative white evangelicals—harbored toward him and his liberal positions on social issues. (Eager to demonstrate the Christian Zionist fervor for all things Jewish, Strang questioned me about the meaning of my last name—"Is your family from a valley?"—and signed off with "Shalom!")

Franklin Graham, son of the benighted Reverend Billy Graham and head of the international Christian aid organization Samaritan's Purse, was seated next to Obama at the meeting. According to Strang and Graham's spokesman, Mark DeMoss, whom I also interviewed, Graham peppered Obama with pointed questions, repeatedly demanding to know whether the senator believed that "Jesus was *the* way to God or merely *a* way" [italics added]. Graham, who immediately after the 9/11 attacks sparked an international controversy by calling Islam a "very evil and wicked religion," proceeded to inquire about the Muslim faith of Obama's father, suggesting that Obama himself might be a Muslim. After Obama attempted to rebut the canard, one preacher who supported Obama stood up suddenly. Hoping to sour his fellow pastors' opinion of McCain, the preacher reminded them of McCain's bitter divorce, recounted his vulgar tirades on the Senate floor, and claimed that he [McCain] was uncomfortable with outward displays of religiosity.

"He seemed to be saying that if Christians can support a flawed candidate like McCain, the implication was, why couldn't they support a candidate with flawed policies like Obama?" Strang told me. But Strang found the argument unpersuasive. "How I vote is based on whether or not the candidate is for life," he said, explaining why he planned to vote for the anti-abortion McCain.

Obama's attempts to present himself as a "committed Christian" may have endeared him to black Democrats in South Carolina, whose support he had in any case, but his entreaties to conservative white evangelicals floundered. When Obama's religious outreach coordinator, Joshua Dubois, a close associate of Vanderslice, called Focus on the Family's headquarters in June to request a meeting between Obama and James Dobson, he not only was refused but also inflamed Dobson's resentment. On June 24, Dobson took to the airwaves to lash Obama with homophobic rhetoric, accusing him of upholding a "fruitcake interpretation" of the Bible.

After the Dobson debacle, Obama leapt at the opportunity to appear at the "Saddleback Civic Forum on the President," a faith-based Q&A session for both candidates that was televised by CNN and moderated by Pastor Rick Warren, the mega-best-selling author of the self-help manual *The Purpose Driven Life*. Warren, who had maintained a friendly relationship with Obama since the newly elected senator delivered a speech at his Orange County mega-church in 2006, seemed like a refreshing alternative to the hard-right dinosaurs that defined the Christian right's image. Warren preferred jeans and short-sleeved shirts, often with loud, Hawaiian patterns, to the cheap suits familiar to Southern Baptist firebrands. He had a pudgy face and paunch that gave him a teddy-bear-like quality. And Warren favored a measured, almost ponderous preaching style over hectoring or hollering. "I have never been considered a part of the religious right," Warren insisted, "because I don't believe politics is the most effective way to change the world."

The mainstream press was almost universally eager to indulge Warren's image of himself. *New York Times* columnist Nicholas Kristof called Warren "an evangelical liberals can love." *Newsweek* named Warren one of fifteen "people who make America great." And even *The Nation*, a historically left-wing magazine, published an article puffing Warren as a figure who "disassociates himself from the religious right," noting that "he shares its position on social issues but doesn't want to focus on them. He focuses on poverty, disease and aid to Africa." By the time of the 2008 campaign, Warren was ascendant as the twenty-first-century version of Billy Graham, pastor to presidents, and minister of the national soul, and he was hailed for moving away from the hard right. He had constructed an international platform using two powerful constituencies that few figures before him had been able to reconcile: conservative evangelicals hungry for more sophisticated leadership and opinion elites frantically searching for postpartisan heroes.

When I asked the public relations firm responsible for burnishing Warren's image whether the media's worshipful portrayal of its client was accurate, however, a spokesperson reacted with befuddlement. "As far as being America's pastor, or whatever, well, that's just a title the media has given him," Kristin Cole of Larry A. Ross communications told me. For his part, Warren freely admitted to a *Wall Street Journal* reporter that the principal difference between him and Dobson was simply "a matter of tone." Indeed, behind Warren's fuzzy-wuzzy, green-friendly, and altruistic image was a religious-right crusader who opposed abortion, gay rights, and stem cell research. The presence of McCain and Obama at Warren's church for a nationally televised campaign forum was less a testament to the progressive transformation of America's evangelical community than it was proof of the Christian right's continuing hold on the national discourse.

For the first time, at his Saddleback Faith Forum, Warren's right-wing tendencies were on display before a national audience. He began by asking the candidates, "Does evil exist? And if it does, do we ignore it? Do we negotiate with it? Do we contain it? Do we defeat it?" This abstract but loaded question, shot through with Christian Zionist undertones, gave McCain the opportunity to cast the war on terror in terms of spiritual warfare. Meanwhile, Obama rambled on about an array of topics, from Darfur to child abuse. Then Warren asked Obama, "At what point does a baby get human rights, in your view?" Knowing that answering the question directly would only further alienate most evangelicals, Obama replied haltingly, "Answering that question with specificity, you know, is above my pay grade." Few reporters could have—or would have—set a better trap for Obama.

Right-wing radio hosts fulminated for months afterward about Obama's answer to Warren's abortion question. Leading the angry chorus was Dobson, who declared during an indignant radio tirade, "With all due respect, Senator, if this question is above your pay grade, then so is the job attached to it!" Warren chuckled at Obama's response during an appearance on a conservative radio show. Meanwhile, a who's who of religious-right leaders hailed McCain's performance at Saddleback. With the movement beginning to loathe Obama after years of preparing to tear down Hillary Clinton's candidacy, McCain maneuvered to consolidate its support with his vice presidential pick.

On August 31, McCain announced his running mate. Governor Sarah Palin of Alaska, a former beauty queen and ex-mayor of the small town of Wasilla, had met McCain only once, during a fifteen-minute chat at a meeting of the National Governor's Association. While the press scrambled to assemble a profile of the little-known Palin, members of the Council for National Policy gathered secretly at a hotel in downtown Minneapolis to watch her accept the nomination. Tom Minnery, a Focus on the Family operative who accompanied his boss, Dobson, to the meeting, reflected on the CNP's exuberant mood:

> "I was standing in the back of a ballroom filled with largely Republicans who were hoping against hope that something would put excitement back into this campaign," Minnery said during a September

1 Focus on the Family broadcast. "And I have to tell you, that speech by Alaska Governor Sarah Palin—people were on their seats applauding, cheering, yelling . . . That room in Minneapolis watching on the television screen was electrified. I have not seen anything like it in a long time."

When the Republican National Convention began days later, the excitement generated in the CNP's ballroom spread to the throng of Republican delegates assembled in St. Paul's Xcel Center. The Palin that McCain's aides had haphazardly thrust into the national spotlight was an overnight sensation, but like Hagee, she had been subjected to "poor vetting." The real Palin, the Christian-right cadre who subjected herself to an anointing against witchcraft; the Pentecostal "prayer warrior" who could not say which magazines she read; the matriarch of a troubled family who became a paragon for James Dobson's vision of womanhood—this figure would be unveiled to a shocked American public during the weeks ahead.

CHAPTER 25

THE FAMILY THAT PRAYS TOGETHER

f McCain had had his druthers, he would have chosen Senator Joseph Lieberman, the Democrat from Connecticut who had been Al Gore's running mate in 2000 and was a hawkish supporter of the Iraq War, as his running mate. Lieberman would have had some appeal to hawkish Democrats, moderate Republicans, and perhaps older Jewish voters, but his prochoice stance made him anathema on the right. The movement's influence on the party nullified McCain's option.

During a June radio broadcast, James Dobson presented McCain with a stark decision: Pick an anti-abortion politician or lose movement support as Bob Dole had in 1996. "I am not endorsing Senator McCain today," Dobson said. "I don't know who his vice presidential candidate would be. He might even choose a pro-abortion candidate, and it would not be unlike him to do that because he seems to enjoy frustrating conservatives on that account. . . . While I'm not endorsing John McCain, the possibility is there that I might."

Once again, the maverick buckled. McCain's choices were reduced to Mitt Romney, a favorite of the Bush family, and Karl Rove whom he personally disliked; Florida Governor Charlie Crist, an uncharismatic lifelong bachelor who suddenly became engaged to a woman after his name appeared on McCain's VP shortlist; Minnesota Governor Tim Pawlenty, a competent establishment dullard; and the glamorous Sarah Palin. In the end, McCain and his advisors made what they believed to be the "maverick" decision, selecting the woman. But their haphazard vetting of the Alaska governor failed to cover her large family, which turned out to contain enough intrigue for a season's worth of Jerry Springer Show episodes.

Unknown to the national media and possibly to McCain as well, Palin's sixteen-year-old daughter Bristol had been impregnated during the summer by eighteen-year-old Levi Johnston, a local jock who identified himself on his Myspace page:

"I'm a f**kin' redneck who likes to snowboard and ride dirt bikes. But I live to play hockey. I like to go camping and hang out with the boys, do some fishing, shoot some sh*t and just f**kin' chillin' I guess. Ya f*ck with me I'll kick ass." Johnston added that he was "in a relationship" but insisted, "I don't want kids." (The two would split up almost immediately after the campaign ended).

Bristol Palin's pregnancy had been an open secret for months in her hometown. In Wasilla, a community of approximately 10,000, practically every secret is an open one—a northern exposure Peyton Place. When I traveled there in October, I was bombarded by a blizzard of rumors that had not been investigated by the dozens of big-foot journalists who had just blown through town. One local resident told me Bristol (named for Bristol Bay, Alaska, the hometown of Todd Palin) had moved in with her aunt, who lived twenty-five miles from Wasilla, because she resented her mother's imperious, hyperambitious nature.

The oldest Palin child, Track (named for Todd and Sarah's mutual love of track and field), was reputed to be a troublemaking party animal who enlisted in the National Guard to avoid expulsion from high school. In 2005, the progressive Alaska radio station 1080 KUDO reported that Track Palin was among four teenage boys arrested for seriously vandalizing 110 school buses, deflating their tires and unplugging their engine block heaters. Because 1080 only cited an unnamed judicial source and three of the boys were juveniles, only two of the culprits' identities were revealed. However, a local resident told me Track was among the vandals. "The Palin kids really acted out, but that's because their mother's always at work, never around, and their father's up on the North Slope doing business," the local gossiped. "It's actually very sad." (Track Palin joined the National Guard soon after the incident occurred.)

A former classmate of Levi Johnston told me Johnston was expelled from Wasilla High for vandalizing a local liquor store and cutting the brake lines on the school's fleet of buses. Rumors also swirled throughout town about Johnston's mother, Sherry, a reputed dealer in "Hillbilly Heroin," who met her customers in parking lots under cover of darkness. That rumor was confirmed after the campaign was over, although state troopers were prepared to arrest Sherry Johnston much earlier. According to an affidavit signed by a state trooper, they delayed Johnston's arrest and allowed her to continue dealing for several months in order to prevent another embarrassing story from emerging while Palin, the hometown girl, campaigned for vice president.

While Sarah Palin denounced the media's scrutiny of her daughter's pregnancy, she proudly cradled her new son, Trig, in the national press corps limelight. Named by Todd Palin for what he believed was a Norse word for "strength," though no such word exists ("Trygg" means "safe" or "reliable" in Norwegian), the baby was born with Down syndrome. After learning through a sonogram that her child would have Down syndrome, Palin bravely chose to carry him to term.

Her decision excited James Dobson, and he wrote her a letter congratulating her for having what he called "that little Downs Syndrome baby." "What a way to emphasize your pro-life leanings there," Dobson declared on a September 2 radio broadcast. Tony Perkins, who phoned in from the Family Research Council office in Washington, DC, echoed Dobson: "It's one thing to support the policy. It's another to live it out."

Finally, Dobson announced that he was reversing his vow to oppose McCain. "If I went into the polling booth now, I'd pull the lever for John McCain." McCain had suffered torture in a North Vietnamese prison camp and given over thirty years of his life to public service, but he earned James Dobson's vote only for selecting a running mate who decided not to abort her disabled child.

■ ■ ■

Hours before Palin's debut speech at St. Paul's Excel Center, a Christian-right group called Republican Women for Life gathered at a nearby hotel for a pep rally called "The Life of the Party." The octogenarian anti-feminist Phyllis Schlafly had founded Republican Women for Life during a successful battle she initiated with pro-choice moderate Republicans over the 1992 convention plank. Having brought the party's position on abortion squarely in line with that of the movement, Schlafly's group cheered the selection of one of its own, and of a new generation, as an apotheosis.

"You are not welcome here," a young woman working the table at the event's media check-in repeated to me over and over without explanation. She rose and attempted to drag me by my right arm toward an exit, summoning security guards to remove me from the hotel. Visceral hostility to the media instantly became one of Palin's themes.

I learned after my unceremonious ejection that "The Life of the Party" was headlined by Laura Ingraham, a right-wing radio talk show host with a mean-girl shtick, known for her blonde coif, occasional leopard print miniskirt, and anti-elitist harangues. After hailing Palin as the representative of "a new kind of feminism," Ingraham homed in on her favorite target. "But the liberal elites and the media are trashing Sarah Palin. They have all these stamps on their passports because they're so much smarter than we are."

■ ■ ■

Todd Palin and his children filed into the front row of the arena's VIP booth moments before Sarah's prime-time acceptance speech before the Republican National Convention on September 3. Behind a swarm of photographers and cameramen, Bristol Palin and Levi Johnston huddled together, holding hands and whispering asides. Rudy Giuliani and his third wife, Judith, were seated directly behind them. While press photographers swarmed around the Palins, seven-year-old Piper Palin ("It's a cool name," explained her father) cradled the newborn Trig, licked her palm, and smoothed his hair.

John McDonnell, an evangelical blogger for the far-right online community Free Republic, claimed holy significance for Trig's spitshine: "When Piper Palin spat on her hand to wipe down the hair of her brother Trig Palin, it was a touching scene for millions of viewers. I have since discovered some connections between that scene and the story of the blind man in the Gospel of John, chapter 9." McDonnell combined scorn for liberals with scriptural citation. "The ugly suggestion by liberals that Sarah Palin sinned in not having aborted Trig, the spit that Piper wiped across Trig's hair, and the use of 'palon' in the Greek text of John 9, combine in a way that I find interesting."

Palin reveled in the movement's affinity for her family and calibrated her speech to capture its populist spirit. "A writer observed, 'We grow good people in our small towns, with honesty and sincerity and dignity,'" Palin remarked, "and I know just the kind of people that writer had in mind when he praised Harry Truman. I grew up with those people."

After highlighting her background as "an average hockey mom," Palin turned on the liberal media. "I've learned quickly these last few days that, if you're not a member in good standing of the Washington elite, then some in the media consider a candidate unqualified for that reason alone." The crowd erupted in boos and chanting: "NBC! NBC!"

The unnamed "author" whom Palin quoted was Westbrook Pegler, a prominent mid-century columnist and demagogue who became one of the godfathers of right-wing populism. Pegler identified himself in a column defending a lynching in rural California: "I claim authority to speak for the rabble because I am a member of the rabble in good standing." He was a sworn enemy of FDR's New Deal and the Democratic Party's alliance with labor unions, which he portrayed as an international Communist conspiracy designed to undermine the freedom of average working Americans. Pegler loathed FDR so intensely that when an assassin killed the mayor of Chicago, Anton Cermak, in an attempt on FDR's life in early 1933, he lamented that the killer "got the wrong man." During the latter phase of his career, Pegler morphed into a fanatical anti-Semite and open fascist, a curious development considering that he had married a Jew. His screeds grew so extreme even the John Birch Society barred him from the pages of its newsletter. "Some white patriot of the Southern tier will spatter [Robert F. Kennedy's] spoonful of brains in public premises before the snow flies," Pegler wishfully predicted in 1965. Pegler died a year after RFK's assassination.

Had Pegler lived to witness Palin's rise, he probably would have conferred authority upon her to speak for "the rabble." Indeed, her rise to national prominence was remarkable, considering her humble beginnings in southeastern Alaska, where her schoolteacher parents moved from rural Idaho when she was an infant. During hunting season, Palin (born Sarah Heath) learned to fish, shoot, and field dress a moose, then made mooseburgers throughout the winter from the meat her family stored. A star basketball player for Wasilla High, Palin earned the nickname "Sarah Barracuda" for her aggressive playing style. After high school, she zigzagged from Hawaii to Idaho to Alaska and back to Idaho, enrolling in five small colleges before earning her bachelor's degree in journalism.

In 1984, during a break between semesters, Palin won Wasilla's "Miss Congeniality" contest and then gained statewide recognition as runner-up for Miss Alaska, losing to the state's first African American crown winner. Soon after, she eloped with her high school sweetheart, Todd Palin, a part Yu'pik Eskimo and locally famous snowmobile enthusiast. Todd promptly went to earn his fortune in the oil fields on Alaska's North Slope, while in his spare time winning four contests of the Iron Dog, the world's longest and most grueling snowmobile race.

In 2006, Palin scored a stunning victory in the Republican gubernatorial primary, defeating incumbent Governor Frank Murkowski, the corruption-plagued patriarch of one of the state's most powerful families (his daughter Lisa was Alaska's junior senator). Upon inauguration, Palin began referring to her husband as Alaska's "First Dude," a nickname that lent to the couple's populist and distinctly Alaskan charm. She went on to assail the state GOP for its ethical lapses, leading an investigation against party chairman Randy Reudrich for using his position as chair of the Alaska Oil and Gas Commission Pipeline for partisan purposes. Reudrich was forced to resign and pay a $12,000 fine, an outcome that helped Palin consolidate her cutthroat, nonpartisan image. In a state exhausted by corrupt leadership, voters found her style refreshing.

Although she touted herself as a strict fiscal conservative standing against the rising tide of socialism, Palin instituted some relatively liberal fiscal policies. She authorized a 28 percent spending increase in the state budget, doling out checks for $3,269 to every man, woman, and child in Alaska from the Permanent Fund Dividend, a stipend from the state's massive oil investment account. The checks represented a record $1,200 increase from the year before. Alaskans immediately voiced approval for Palin's leadership, giving her a whopping 85 percent approval rating. Her detractors nicknamed her "Moose-o-lini," however, mocking her leveraging of free money into record popularity. *Weekly Standard* editor Fred Barnes omitted mention of the PFD checks in his puff-piece "The Most Popular Governor," which he authored after his magazine's cruise to Alaska.

Within the movement, the personal details of Palin's background—hockey mom, hunter, mother—resonated deeply. She was the antithesis of her running mate, the son and grandson of four-star admirals, whose ancestor served on General George Washington's staff. Beyond her Everywoman image, Palin was a product of the culture of personal crisis and therefore an authentic representative of the movement's true ethos.

"So many families deal with the same issues Sarah Palin is dealing with, so we really can relate to what she is going through," said Grace Van Diest, a Republican delegate from Alaska whom I interviewed on the convention floor. Van Diest, a kindly, middle-aged mother of two from the Mat-Su Valley, Alaska's Bible Belt, was typical of many members I spoke with from her delegation.

"I think that abstinence should be a priority," Van Diest told me. "We have taught our daughters—we have three daughters and a son—and we've taught our daughters to not even date until they're more ready to be married. . . . [All] of our daughters have gone out on a date with their dad and talked about keeping themselves pure until marriage. They each wear a promise ring, a little tiny diamond that they wear constantly to remind them they will keep pure."

In the Last Frontier, where many families live in "the bush," far from roads and public services, sexual trauma is unusually common. The state's rape rate is 2.5 times the national average; it also posted the nation's largest spike in teen birth rates from 2005 to 2006, the year Palin became governor. In addition, Alaskans have America's highest illicit drug use rate and are among the country's leaders in binge drinking. In this harrowing environment, Van Diest and many of her neighbors had turned to the Christian right's crisis industry for relief.

SEASON OF THE WITCH

Prior to her nomination, Palin listed her home phone number in Alaska's yellow pages. She was known to spend hours in her local Wal-mart chatting with constituents. When I traveled to Alaska's Mat-Su Valley, nearly every politically active resident I spoke to had met the governor on at least one occasion. But many of Palin's acquaintances, admirers and critics alike, described her in a dramatically different light from that in which she presented herself to the American public. To those who knew Palin, both her allies and her enemies, she was no ordinary hockey mom, but rather an evangelical foot soldier who spearheaded the movement's takeover of the local government in the Mat-Su Valley. Her power base was the Wasilla Assembly of God, a Pentecostal mega-church where she was baptized and spent over twenty years as a member.

Most Pentecostal congregations are socially conservative, particularly those that are predominantly white, but Wasilla Assembly of God was in thrall to a radical Pentecostal trend once denounced by church authorities as heresy. Ted Haggard's former congregation, New Life Church, was a bastion of this same extreme theology. So was the church that Matthew Murray's parents attended, which the young mass killer described as a hothouse of "charismatic/'fanatical evangelical' insanity."

Called the Third Wave, the theology that informed Wasilla Assembly of God members was rooted in an explicitly anti-intellectual creation myth. According to the Third Wave's founding father, William Branham, a rural Canadian preacher, Satan had sex with Eve and gave birth to Cain—the so-called "Serpent Seed." "Through Cain came all the smart, educated people down to the antediluvian flood—the intellectuals, bible colleges," Branham wrote. "They know all their creeds but know nothing about God."

Despite opposition from inside the Assembly of God's hierarchy, Third Wave congregations won droves of adherents by emphasizing charismatic displays of ecstatic release, including practices such as holy laughter (hysterical giggling that supposedly represents the spirit of God flowing through the bodies of believers) and drunkenness in the spirit, where worshippers emulate the experience of intoxication so melodramatically that Charles Bukowski would reel in embarrassment. Faith healing is also central to Third Wave theology; Todd Bentley, an influential Florida-based Third Wave pastor known for his tattoos, body piercings, and pseudo-punk attitude, once attempted to "explode" a man's tumors by drop-kicking him in the chest. He also kicked an old woman in the face because, he said, "The Holy Spirit spoke to me." One of Bentley's mottoes is "Some people snort cocaine, others snort religion."

Behind the Third Wave's histrionics lies an aggressive brand of Dominionism focused on purging "demon influence" from entire geographic areas through prayer or more forceful means if necessary. Becky Fischer, a Third Wave youth pastor who gained fame as the anti-hero of the 2006 award-winning documentary *Jesus Camp*, urged pastors to indoctrinate an army of spiritual suicide bombers to seize control of the country. "I wanna see young people who are as committed to the cause of Jesus Christ as the young people are to the cause of Islam," Fischer said in the documentary during an unguarded moment. "I wanna see them as radically laying down their lives for the Gospel as they are over in Pakistan and Israel and Palestine and all those different places, you know, because we have . . . excuse me, but we have the truth!"

The Third Wave arrived in Alaska through a "spiritual warfare network" founded by an Anchorage-based Haida Indian named Mary Glazier, who claimed to have converted sixty members of her family, including her formerly alcohol-abusing parents. Seeking a "battle strategy" against the rising tide of sin that consumed her son, who committed suicide in 1990, Glazier tried to gain access to the state's prison system, a pit of desperation. A young female prison chaplain opposed Glazier's Dominionist, evangelizing intentions. Glazier responded by branding the woman a witch and began to utter imprecatory prayers. "As we continued to pray against the spirit of witchcraft," Glazier recalled with glee, "her incense altar caught on fire, her car engine blew up, she went blind in her left eye, and she was diagnosed with cancer."

Sarah Palin was one of the first members of Glazier's spiritual warfare prayer circle in Wasilla. According to Glazier, while Palin prayed with her during the early 1990s, "God began to speak to [her] about entering politics." With Glazier's encouragement, Palin joined other members of the Wasilla Assembly of God in a takeover of Wasilla's government. In 1994, Palin won election to the Wasilla City Council and the local hospital board, a victory that resulted in the ousting of her mother-in-law, Faye Palin. During the first meeting of the new Dominionist-dominated hospital board, Palin and her allies passed a resolution (later overturned by the state Supreme Court) banning abortion in all circumstances, including when the life of the mother was in mortal danger.

While Palin served on the Wasilla city council, a Democrat named Nick Carney befriended her and showed her the ropes. However. when Palin announced her 1996 bid for mayor against Carney, she launched a vicious campaign against her former friend, spewing character attacks utterly foreign to the Mayberry Junction–like atmosphere of Wasilla. "I watched that campaign unfold, bringing a level of slime our community hadn't seen until then," recalled Phil Munger, a local music teacher who counted himself as a close friend of Stein.

Palin supporters from Wasilla Assembly of God touted her sweeping opposition to abortion, distributing fliers hailing her as "The Christian Candidate," a slogan that supporters of Stein, a Lutheran with a Jewish-sounding last name, considered a subtle anti-Semitic ploy. Palin's friend Mark Chryson, then chairman of the Alaskan Independence Party, a secessionist party with close links to anti-government militia groups across the country, claimed that Stein and his wife were not legally married. "So we literally had to produce a marriage certificate," Stein said. "And as I recall, they said, 'Well, you could have forged that.'" Palin easily vanquished Stein.

In 2000, while serving as mayor, Palin asked her pastor at Wasilla Assembly of God for a copy of a video circulating among members called "Transformation," produced by George Otis, an evangelical author who once raised money for former Black Panther Eldridge Cleaver after the latter's conversion to fundamentalist Christianity. (Cleaver went on to found the syncretic pseudo-religion of "Christlam" and to design men's jeans with special codpieces—"Cleaver sleeves," he called them—that prominently displayed the wearer's genitals.) In the video, Otis documented the heroism of a Pentecostal pastor named Bishop Thomas Muthee, who supposedly saved the city of Kiambu, Kenya, from an evil witch named Mama Jane, who supposedly used her otherworldly powers to manipulate top government officials and ordered one death per month by car crash in front of her "divination house." "Mama Jane either gets saved and serves the Lord, or she leaves town!" Muthee proclaimed. "There is no longer room in Kiambu for both of us!"

At the church he "planted" in Kiambu, known as The Prayer Cave, and in the basement of a local grocery story, Muthee organized several weeks of imprecatory prayer against Mama Jane. He led his followers in "spiritual mapping," a technique popularized at Ted Haggard's World Prayer Center that consists of praying around buildings and city blocks occupied by demonic spirits. While cries for Mama Jane's stoning intensified, the local police arrested the evil witch and ordered her never to return to Kiambu. Almost overnight, a golden era of Christian morality descended on the town, churches sprouted in suddenly vacant bars, and criminal activity evaporated like magic. Or so the story goes.

When a reporter from Women's eNews traveled to Kiambu to investigate the story, she discovered that Muthee was a fraud. The reporter found Mama Jane still living in the compound from which Muthee claimed to have had her ousted. A forty-six-year-old woman whose real name was Jane Njenga, Mama Jane is revered by locals for adopting forty abandoned children, including the mechanic who fixed Muthee's car. According to Mama Jane, Muthee paraded around town demanding through a megaphone that locals pray for her death, but nothing happened to her. She concluded that Muthee was a con man. "If I am bad, why haven't people attacked me?" Mama Jane said. "Why haven't they burnt this building down? That is what people here do to witches."

Partly inspired by Muthee's tall tales, Palin initiated her own spiritual battle in Wasilla. Her target was the Reverend Howard Bess, a local Baptist pastor who had opened the doors of his Covenant of the Covenant to openly gay Christians. Bess, an affable eighty-year-old born-again evangelical, had sought refuge in the Mat-Su Valley after infuriating church officials in Anchorage and Santa Barbara, California, with his advocacy for gay rights. Bess's activism culminated in 1995 with the publication of his book-length plea for acceptance of gays in the church, *Pastor, I Am Gay*.

Palin's allies from Wasilla Assembly of God crusaded to ban the book throughout the valley, ensuring that no bookstore—including the national chain Waldenbooks—dared carry it. Palin personally visited the Wasilla public library twice to request that the librarian remove Bess's book from her shelves. When I visited the library, a librarian told me the book had been "moved" to another library out of space concerns. Shelf space, however, was ample enough to accommodate the entire *Left Behind* series.

"Sarah Palin is a true believer," Bess told me over coffee at Vagabond Blues, a café twenty miles from Wasilla in the town of Palmer. "She has a dualistic worldview that divides the world into black and white. She sees it as her mission to destroy evil, whether it is gay people, a foreign government she perceives as an enemy, or a political opponent like Obama." Bess estimated that the Christian right's sabotage cost his ministry at least $200,000. In 2002, while Palin served as mayor, the *Mat-Su Valley Frontiersman* published a cartoon depicting a deranged, drooling child molester rushing into Bess's church to join the homosexuals already inside.

In 2005, with Palin gearing up for a tough campaign for governor against former Democratic Governor Tony Knowles, Muthee paid a special visit to Wasilla Assembly of God to confer his blessing on her candidacy. With Palin seated in the front row, Muthee suggested that Christians like Palin should "invade" government in order to seize the reins of the world's economy from the Jews, to whom he cryptically but clearly referred as "Israelites." "It's high time that we have top Christian businessmen, businesswomen, bankers, you know, who are men and women of integrity running the economics of our nations," Muthee said. "That's what we are waiting for. That's part and parcel of transformation. If you look at the—you know—if you look at the Israelites, that's how they work. And that's how they are, even today."

With that, Muthee summoned Palin to the altar for an anointing. Flanked by Ed Kalnins, the new pastor of Wasilla Assembly of God, and another local Third Wave preacher, Phil Markwardt, Palin bowed her head and closed her eyes. "We are asking you in the name of this Valley, make a way for Sah-rah, even in the political arena!" Muthee exclaimed in his raspy, thickly accented voice. While Kalnins and Markwardt gripped Palin's shoulders, tongue-talking loudly rose from the pews. "Bring finances her way even for the campaign in the name of Jesus!" Muthee shouted, his left palm on Palin's head. "Oh father, use her to turn this nation around . . . so that the curse can be broken. . . . We come against every hindrance of the enemy standing in her way today in the name of Jesus! Every form of witchcraft is what you rebuke in the name of Jesus!"

The experience had a lasting impact on Palin. When she returned to Wasilla Assembly of God in June 2008 to address the graduation ceremony of the Master's Commission, an indoctrination program for the church's college-age members, Palin linked Muthee's anointing to her election as governor. "As I was mayor and Pastor Muthee was here and he was praying over me, and you know how he speaks and he's so bold. And he was praying, 'Lord make a way, Lord make a way,'" Palin said, imitating Muthee's raspy, thickly accented intonations. "And I'm thinking, this guy's really bold, he doesn't even know what I'm going to do, he doesn't know what my plans are. And he's praying not, 'oh, lord if it be your will may she become governor.' No, he just prayed for it. He said, 'Lord make a way and let her do this next step.' And that's exactly what happened."

While Palin barnstormed the country in late September, Muthee returned to the Mat-Su Valley. I was there to observe his activities. Muthee delivered his first sermon at a small house belonging to the Wasilla Assembly of God. When I arrived, members were already in deep prayer, swaying in a trance to a quintet's lilting pop-rock sounds and speaking in tongues. Muthee appeared at the podium half an hour later.

The Kenyan preacher explained the current relevance of Queen Esther, a Jewish beauty queen who married the king of Assyria and then used her seductive wiles to persuade him to save her people from the evil Haman. The resonance was clear: Palin, the former beauty pageant contestant who had chosen Esther as her biblical role model when she first entered politics, would topple the secular tyrants to lead her people, the true Christians, into the kingdom.

Building toward his climax, Muthee summoned the flock to spiritual warfare, invoking Branham's "serpent seed" doctrine. "How do you kill a python?" Muthee asked an adolescent boy in the front row. "Step on its neck!" the boy responded almost instantly. "Right," Muthee replied. "You have to step on the necks of the pythons to crush the enemy." Then Muthee drew the worshippers to their feet for a prayer:

> We come against that python spirit. We come against that spirit of witchcraft as the body of Christ. Right now in the name of Jesus! Ooooh-raba-saka-ta-la. Come on, pray, pray! Raba-sandalalala-bebebebekalabebe. Shanda-la-bebebeka-lelebebe. . . . That's why we come against all forms of witchcraft. All the python spirits that are released against the body of Christ . . . and bring this nation into the Kingdom.

When Muthee finished, a Russian pastor emerged from the pews and took hold of the microphone. In his thick accent, the pastor boomed, "Right now we exercise our power and we put our feet against the heads of the Enemy in the name of Jesus!"

REAL AMERICANS

By the time I returned from Alaska to the lower forty-eight, in early October, Palin's once radiant image had suffered severe damage. Her wounds were mostly self-inflicted. In an interview with Katie Couric, the NBC anchor known for her softball style, Palin proved unable to answer even a basic question about what magazines she read. "All of them," she replied. Palin's insistence to ABC's Charlie Gibson that she was qualified to set national security policy because she could see Russia from her home state (visible from an island called Little Diomede that Palin had never visited) provided weeks of material for late-night TV comedians.

Palin's performance in wide-ranging interviews highlighted not only the gaps in her basic knowledge but also the importance of the Wasilla Assembly of God in the formation of her worldview. She had assimilated her values, philosophy, and outlook not from rigorous study (she attended five colleges in Idaho before earning her communications degree) or from international travel (she had left America only once and did not have a passport) but from the hermetically sealed Third Wave subculture of her church. She was too parochial to withstand heavy media scrutiny and too extreme to cultivate support from anyone other than "the rabble."

Key members of the conservative intelligensia suddenly recoiled at Palin's presence. *New York Times* columnist David Brooks, a neocon who had written glowingly of McCain, said Palin "represented a fatal cancer on the Republican Party." In an interview with the *Dartmouth Review*, former *National Review* editor Jeffrey Hart called Palin "extremely ignorant" and "a religious crackpot." Peggy Noonan, a former speechwriter for Ronald Reagan and a conservative columnist for the *Wall Street Journal*, blasted Palin as "a dope and unqualified from the start." Lincoln Chafee, the liberal Republican senator whose defeat in 2006 signaled the GOP's death knell in the Northeast, described Palin as a "cocky wacko" and said her selection had "thrown this firestorm" into the campaign.

Although Palin's disastrous interviews damaged her credibility, they also obscured her radical religious beliefs. Those were never really investigated. But while the mainstream press generally overlooked details such as Palin's apparent belief in witchcraft, the movement's adulation intensified. For them she had received "the anointing," as former Christian Broadcasting Network director Jim Bramlett said. "I believe

Sarah Palin could not have gotten to where she is without God's backing," a twenty-something male picketer outside an Anchorage abortion clinic remarked to me. "And for whatever reason, God appoints leaders." "I do believe she's anointed for this position," said another protester, a middle-aged woman. The woman added that because Alaska is shaped like a crown, "I really do believe that Alaska's called to a key position to cry out for our nation and to lead our nation."

Instead of the suburban hockey moms the GOP hoped to attract by selecting Palin, those who filled swing-state fairgrounds and arenas to cheer the VP candidate were focused obsessively on social issues and were sometimes openly racist. Not only was this not the portrait of a winning coalition—it was not much of a coalition at all—it became politically combustible. A few words of incitement were all it would take to turn the party base into a virtual lynch mob.

Palin did not hold anything back. Declaring that "the gloves are off," she accused Barack Obama of "pallin' around with terrorists" such as former Weather Underground leader Bill Ayers, who once served on a Chicago nonprofit's board of directors with Obama. "This is a man who launched his political career in the living room of a domestic terrorist," Palin told a crowd in Clearwater, Florida. "This is not a man who sees America the way you and I see America." With these two lines, uttered apparently without the permission of McCain or his top aides, Palin opened up a deep abyss. "Kill him!" a man shouted when Palin linked Obama to terrorism, according to *Washington Post* reporter Dana Milbank.

When Palin mentioned Obama again, another man cried, "Terrorist!" "Treason!" someone else yelled when Palin attacked Obama for supposedly criticizing the U.S. military. "He's a nigger!" a woman screamed during a Des Moines, Iowa, Palin rally. "Go back to Kenya!" a man waiting in line outside a Johnstown, Pennsylvania, rally told Obama supporters across the street. Another man joined the taunting: "Born in Kenya, citizen of Indonesia!" he barked about Obama. And to Obama's supporters, he shouted, "Kill some more babies, you bastards!" "Yeah, you babykillers!" echoed a middle-aged woman. Nearby, a portly old man held a stuffed Curious George monkey with an Obama sticker on its head. "This is little Hussein," he said with a wry smile, using Obama's Muslim middle name for effect. "Little Hussein wanted to see truth and good Americans."

As word spread about the growing atmosphere at Palin's rallies, activists from the right's farthest shores perceived fresh opportunities to recruit new bodies. Outside a Palin rally on October 13 in Virginia Beach, a producer from the anti-Semitic, black-bashing, and avowedly "pro-white" radio show *Political Cesspool*, greeted McCain-Palin supporters with a sign advertising his broadcasts. Just feet away, Randall Terry, the former leader of Operation Rescue, a group responsible at least indirectly for numerous bombings of women's health clinics and for assassinations of abortion doctors in the late 1980s and 1990s, solicited volunteers to canvas for McCain. "We must do whatever it takes to stop Obama!" Terry shouted through a megaphone, inviting cheers from passersby filing into the arena. (Asked by NBC's Brian Williams whether abortion clinic bombers were terrorists, Palin replied, "I don't know.")

Some McCain-Palin supporters unleashed their violent anger against anything they could find. In late October, maintenance workers at Western Carolina University discovered a dead bear cub riddled with bullets in the middle of campus. "It looked like it had been shot in the head as best we can tell," a university spokesman said. "A couple of Obama campaign signs had been stapled together and stuck over its head." Days before the killing of the bear cub, Obama received a report from the Secret Service documenting a dramatic rise in the number of threats against him since Palin linked him to terrorists. "Why would they try to make people hate us?" Michelle Obama plaintively asked her friend and close advisor, Valerie Jarrett.

Under Palin, the self-destructive trend that fueled the movement subsumed the party once and for all. Republican voters could not be restrained from prostrating themselves before Palin's red Naughty Monkey heels, even as the rest of the American public rejected her. They eagerly followed her toward catastrophic defeat with the comforting notion that her repudiation was a form of anti-Christian persecution. To them, she was more than a politician; she was their magic helper, the God-fearing glamour girl who parachuted into their back-water towns to lift them from the drudgery of their lives, assuring them that they were the "good people."

"We believe that the best of America is in these small towns that we get to visit, and in these wonderful little pockets of what I call the real America, being here with all of you hard-working very patriotic, um, very, um, pro-America areas of this great nation," Palin told an audience in Greensboro, North Carolina.

And what about the non-pro-America (read: anti-American) areas of the country? Where was the fake America located? Palin seemed to pinpoint these areas in the coastal cities where transnational elites such as Obama and his latte liberal entourage were grown. To the Palin fol-lowers, Obama was a multicolored piñata stuffed with all the move-ment's most evildoing hobgoblins. But no matter how hard Palin swung, she could not even graze him. Obama remained calmly above the fray, repeating his unifying message—"In times of need there are no red states or blue states"—frustrating and inciting the movement.

WHACKO

In the years since he ended his rancorous tenure as the Bush adminis-tration's secretary of state in 2005, General Colin Powell studiously avoided any confrontation with the right-wing forces that had sought to sabotage him. But when Palin's rhetoric reached its demagogic apogee, Powell, the quintessential good soldier and self-described "Rockefeller Republican," finally broke his monk-like vow of silence, endorsing Obama during an October 19 appearance on *Meet the Press*.

The endorsement stung McCain, who counted Powell as a close friend—so close that Powell had prefaced a phone call delivering Mc-Cain the bad news by telling him, "I love you." But Powell's endorse-ment was not designed to spite McCain. Rather, it was motivated by the general's belief that there was no longer a place for him in a Re-publican Party run according to the movement's sectarian agenda. Powell was a casualty of the movement's machinations, having had his nascent presidential ambitions dashed in 1996 by James Dobson, then having watched while Bush sided with Dobson against his own push to promote reproductive health internationally in 2002. Now that Dobson and his minions spoke through Palin, it was an even more disturbing prospect for Powell.

In explaining his endorsement, Powell singled Palin out. "I don't believe she's ready to be president of the United States, which is the job of the vice president," he said. "And so that raised some question in my mind as to the judgment that Senator McCain made." Calling the McCain campaign's approach "narrower and narrower," Powell noted, "the party has moved even further to the right, and Governor Palin has indicated a further rightward shift. I would have difficulty with two more conservative appointments to the Supreme Court, but that's what we'd be looking at in a McCain administration."

Powell continued with an impassioned repudiation of Palin's concept of "real America." "Mr. Obama, at the same time, has given us a more inclusive, broader reach into the needs and aspirations of our people," Powell said. "He's crossing lines—ethnic lines, racial lines, generational lines. He's thinking about all villages have values, all towns have values, not just small towns have values."

Powell's withering critique of the Republican Party under Palin delivered the coup de grâce to McCain. After withstanding months of attacks on his national security credentials, Obama now had the full-throated support of the former secretary of state and chairman of the Joint Chiefs of Staff. McCain's judgment, once considered his greatest strength, a quality borne from decades of experience, was now in question.

With the stain of a cynical smear campaign tarnishing McCain's once stately image, members of his inner circle turned on Palin, accusing her of "going rogue." "She is a diva," said one top McCain advisor. "She takes no advice from anyone." The advisor added, "She's now positioning herself for her own future. Of course, this is bad for John." Another staffer, who had been privy to discussions of religion and politics with Palin, flatly described her as "a whack job."

Still, the neocons remained loyal. Michael Goldfarb, a *Weekly Standard* editor who went to work in McCain's communications department, invited suspicion from fellow staffers for the "manic zeal" he displayed on Palin's behalf. Randy Scheunemann, a neoconservative foreign policy hand, was fired during the last week of the campaign for "positioning himself with Palin at the expense of John McCain's campaign message," according to an aide. McCain loyalists suspected him of leaking damaging information to Bill Kristol, Palin's original cheerleader. For his part, on October 5, Kristol published in his *New York Times* column an interview with Palin in which she criticized McCain for refusing to attack Obama for his association with Jeremiah Wright—a tactic McCain had foresworn months earlier.

"To tell you the truth, Bill," Palin told Kristol, "I don't know why that association isn't discussed more, because those were appalling things that that pastor had said about our great country, and to have sat in the pews for 20 years and listened to that—with, I don't know, a sense of condoning it, I guess, because he didn't get up and leave— to me, that does say something about character. But, you know, I guess that would be a John McCain call on whether he wants to bring that up." A week later, Kristol publicized information leaked to him from inside the campaign about the growing rancor among McCain's aides and then concluded, "Fire the campaign." The message was a mess indeed.

A close McCain advisor complained to Scott Horton, a human rights lawyer and my colleague at the online site TheDailyBeast.com, that Palin's neocon backers were positioning her to run for president in 2012, and were doing so at McCain's expense. "In the last six weeks there was a remarkable echo," the aide said. "You could listen to arguments made by folks inside of the campaign who were close to Bill Kristol and then open up the *New York Times* and read them in Kristol's columns. It was 'set Sarah free,' coupled with an agenda designed to appeal to the religious right and the more raucous elements of the party. They got their way often enough, and we started noticing that at many of the Palin functions it was nonstop 'Sarah, Sarah,' while John McCain all but vanished. Were they trying to get McCain elected in 2008, or to help Palin on the way to the Republican nomination in 2012? You can't get yourself into a situation in which anyone can credibly ask that question."

With the campaign entering its final stages, Palin phoned in to the Focus on the Family studio for an interview aired on October 22 with

James Dobson, an acknowledged hero of hers. "You have been on the forefront of all of this good for all of these years and your reward will be in heaven," Palin greeted Dobson. "If it were not for you so many of us would be missing the boat in terms of life and of ethics." "I'm just trying to serve the Lord like you are," Dobson humbly replied. Now in her element, Palin could unburden herself in the coded language familiar to her Pentecostal subculture.

When Dobson revealed to Palin how he summoned prayers at the National Day of Prayer for her election victory, she spoke in the special Third Wave vocabulary: "It is that intercession that is so needed. I can feel that strength that is provided through our prayer warriors across this nation." Palin touted herself as "a hardcore pro-lifer" and then falsely assured Dobson's listeners that McCain "absolutely" supported a federal gay marriage ban (he voted repeatedly against it) and a ban on federal funding for stem cell research (his position was exactly the opposite). At the end of the interview, Dobson turned to his audience, reminding them in voice brimming with indignation that Palin's difficulties had nothing to do with her own performance on the campaign trail. "There is hostility to Sarah Palin because she is an unabashed Christian," Dobson yelped. "That's who she is!"

Finally, Dobson pleaded aloud, directing his airwaves heavenward: "We're rather boldly asking for a miracle with regard to the election this year."

Only a miracle could have saved McCain, especially from his running mate. Days before election night, 59 percent of voters surveyed for a *New York Times*/CBS poll said Palin was unqualified to serve as vice president. One-third of those polled said McCain's selection was a major factor influencing whom they would vote for, and nearly all of them planned to vote for Obama. The Obama campaign's final ad— its closing argument—flashed the phrase, "His choice?" on the screen before an image appeared of Palin winking at the camera during the vice presidential debate, an iconic moment that perfectly captured her insouciant charm.

On election night, Virginia and North Carolina, which had voted overwhelmingly Republican since President Lyndon Johnson signed the Civil Rights Act, fell to Obama. The Democrats cut deep into

Republican territory with Senate victories in Virginia, North Carolina, and Palin's home state, where her approval rating had plunged over 15 points since she began her campaign with McCain. (A year earlier, Council for National Policy co-founder Woody Jenkins lost a special congressional election to a Democrat, Don Cazayoux, in one of the most heavily Republican districts in the country.) The last Republican House member from New England, Representative Chris Shays of Connecticut, was defeated as well.

Obama's coalition was formidable, comprising dramatically increased levels of support from white men in every region of the country except the Deep South and in parts of Appalachia. These depopulated, economically depressed, and heavily evangelical regions were now the siege towers of the Republicans' shattered electoral fortress. Was that all that was left of the "real America"?

COLLATERAL DAMAGE

On the day after Obama's victory, a sense of gloom descended on San Francisco's Castro District. After bearing the brunt of anti-gay crusades for the past eight years, residents of the gay boulevard should have been celebrating Obama's victory. Instead, they fashioned signs reading, "No More Mister Nice Gay" and donned the whistle-alert necklaces pioneered by the assassinated gay city council member Harvey Milk during an epidemic of anti-gay violence in the 1970s, preparing to take to the streets for a night of angry demonstrations. Proposition 8, a ballot measure banning same-sex marriage in California, had passed by a narrow margin.

For the movement, ensuring Prop 8's passage was an important consolation once the impending defeat of McCain and Palin became apparent. Not one state ballot measure to ban same-sex marriage had ever been defeated. Prop 8's failure in the country's most populous state would have turned the tide of the decades-long culture war, creating a beachhead for gay rights campaigns in other states. "This vote on whether we stop the gay-marriage juggernaut in California is Armageddon," Charles Colson told the *New York Times*. Tony Perkins echoed Colson's doomsday warning. "It's more important than the presidential election," Perkins said of Prop 8. "We will not survive [as a nation] if we lose the institution of marriage."

With so much on the line, movement backers across the country assembled a massive war chest for Prop 8. Much of the money came from deep-pocketed donors such as the Utah-based Church of Jesus Christ of Latter Day Saints and Focus on the Family, which injected $500,000 into the effort. Prop 8 also received a $450,000 boost from Blackwater matriarch Elsa Broekhuizen Prince.

While these funders received enormous media scrutiny, the involvement of Howard F. Ahmanson Jr., who donated $900,000 to Prop 8 through his unincorporated business entity, Fieldstead and Co., went unnoticed up to election day. For the reclusive Ahmanson, the measure was one more step toward his goal of "the total integration of biblical law into our lives."

Not everyone in Dobson's Colorado Springs mountain kingdom was in a celebratory mood after the historic Prop 8 victory. After pumping enough money into Prop 8 to cover the average annual salary of nineteen Coloradans, Focus on the Family initiated a round of massive layoffs, sending a full 20 percent of its workforce out in the cold just in time for Christmas. Days later, Focus released an online video urging its members to declare "Merry Tossmas," imploring them to trash department store catalogues that used the putatively anti-Christian phrase "Happy Holidays."

Down in Orange County, "America's Pastor" Rick Warren had delivered a purpose-driven message in October to the 22,000 parishioners of his Saddleback mega-church and his millions of followers: "Here's an interesting thing: there are about 2 percent of Americans [who] are homosexual, gay, lesbian people," Warren said in an Internet video posted on his website. "We should not let 2 percent of the population determine—to change—a definition of marriage that has been supported by every single culture and every single religion for 5,000 years. This is not even just a Christian issue. It is a humanitarian and human issue, that God created marriage for the purpose of family, love and procreation. I urge you to support Proposition 8 and to pass that on."

On December 17, several weeks after demonstrators surrounded Warren's church to protest his support for Prop 8, Obama announced that the pastor would deliver the inaugural invocation, a prestigious honor that virtually consolidated his image as the national minister, heir to the Reverend Billy Graham. As outrage from progressive Obama supporters gathered, Warren quietly scrubbed a statement from his website that read, "[S]omeone unwilling to repent of their homosexual lifestyle would not be accepted as a member at Saddleback Church." He also excised declarations banning unmarried couples from his pews and an anti-evolution statement that humans and Brontosauruses once frolicked together like the Flintstones.

At the same time, Warren embarked on a rambling media offensive, claiming, "I happen to love gays" at a gathering of the Muslim Public Affairs Council, then he compared homosexuality to incest and pedophilia in an interview with MSNBC.

Obama's senior political adviser David Axelrod leapt to Warren's defense, suggesting, during an appearance on *Meet the Press*, that criticism of Warren's homophobic politics sowed disunity. "You have a conservative evangelical pastor who's coming to participate in the inauguration of a progressive president," Axelrod said. "This is a healthy thing and a good thing for our country." He added, "We gotta get beyond this sorta politics where . . . we're each on the jagged edge of a great divide, shaking our fists at each other." The Rick Warren prayer moment would go on as scheduled.

Despite Obama's effort to court white evangelicals, he failed to make any inroads. Exit polls showed that Obama earned the votes of only 29 percent of whites who attended church once a week—the same percentage that John Kerry won in 2004—and just 29 percent of white evangelicals, a gain of merely three points despite the Democrats' nationwide gains in nearly every other demographic group.

Amy Sullivan, the *Time* columnist who had signaled that Obama would win record levels of evangelicals' support, concluded in the face of the poor results, "Democrats will need to invest more time to court [young evangelicals] and ask for their votes." But would that constituency ever join the Obama majority? Would the Christian right ever lose its hold?

Looking at the election from the bottom up, the exit poll numbers reflected the completion of the movement's takeover of the Republican Party. In the age of Obama, the movement's impact on public policy would be weaker than at any time since before Reagan entered the White House, but its stranglehold on the party's agenda would be even tighter. And with Obama's inauguration approaching, there were signs that the movement planned to impel the GOP toward the confrontational posture it assumed during the Clinton era, when it leveraged anti-liberal resentment to ramp up donations and recruit new "prayer warriors" for the battles ahead.

When the national economic catastrophe deepened at the beginning of the Obama era, the movement welcomed a new chance to leverage crisis into opportunity. At Mars Hill Church in Seattle, hipster pastor Mark Driscoll grew his congregation by 1,000 members in a year, stirring financially desperate audiences with visions of the all-powerful "Ultimate Fighting Jesus." Pastor John Hagee released his book *Financial Armageddon* just in time for the banking crash, assuring his flock how the dire economic situation was merely a harbinger of Christ's return. According to David Beckworth, an assistant professor of economics at Texas State University, the growth rate of evangelical churches spiked by 50 percent during each recession cycle between 1968 and 2004. With the worst economic crisis since the Great Depression growing more calamitous by the day, the entrepreneurs of personal crisis celebrated ideal market conditions for their next great crusade.

EPILOGUE
THE ANOINTING

On January 7, second-term Republican Representative Paul Broun of Georgia and two friends prayed over a door. It wasn't just any door, but the entranceway beneath the Capitol that president-elect Obama would pass through as he walked onto the inaugural stage to take the oath of office. "I hope and pray that as God stirs the heart of our new president that President Obama will listen and will heed God's direction," Broun proclaimed, while an officer of the Capitol Police stood on the other side of the door, keeping watch over the inaugural stage with his back turned to the ceremony under way on the other side.

Joining Broun were two notorious figures from the abortion wars of the 1990s, the Reverend Rob Schenck and the Reverend Patrick Mahoney. Together, the activists had helped Randall Terry lead the anti-abortion front Operation Rescue from its strategy of "direct confrontation" to its spiraling descent into assassinations and clinic bombings. "There's going to be people wounded," Mahoney declared at a 1993 rally. "It's about whose will shall rule on this planet, God's or man's." Schenck, the Francis Schaeffer acolyte, was arrested over a dozen times outside abortion clinics and was detained twice for threats against President Clinton, including the notorious incident in which he dangled an aborted fetus in his face. Now the two were back, and with unfettered access to a heavily secured area of the Capitol building.

The son of a Democratic state senator from the liberal college town of Athens, Georgia, Broun became born again after a string of failed marriages. He claimed his come-to-Jesus moment arrived while he was watching an NFL game, when he became entranced by a "gentle-man with this big type hair wig on" holding a "John 3:16" sign. (The bewigged "gentleman" was Rollen Stewart, a Christian-right fanatic and fixture at sports events who is currently serving three consecutive sentences in jail on kidnapping charges, as well as several minor sentences for stink bomb attacks.) A medical doctor, Broun was elected in a special election in 2007 after the death of a long-time incumbent.

Although he was only a backbencher, Broun presented himself as the future of the House Republicans. Joining other right-wing members, he opposed the emergency financial bailout, attacked any efforts at immigration reform, and sponsored a bill to protect soldiers from images of unclad women. "Our troops should not see their honor sullied so that the moguls behind magazines like *Playboy* and *Penthouse* can profit," Broun proclaimed. His spokesman testified to his expertise as an "addictionologist" who is "familiar with the negative consequences associated with long-term exposure to pornography." A week after Obama's election victory, Broun took umbrage at the president-elect's call for a national civilian security force, a proposal also backed by George W. Bush.

Acknowledging the possibility that he might be "crazy," Broun said that Obama had revealed himself as a radical Marxist Nazi socialist comparable to Adolf Hitler and Joseph Stalin. "It may sound a bit crazy and off base," Broun told an AP reporter, "but the thing is, he's the one who proposed this national security force. I'm just trying to bring attention to the fact that we may—may not, I hope not—but we may have a problem with that type of philosophy of radical socialism or Marxism. That's exactly what Hitler did in Nazi Germany and it's exactly what the Soviet Union did. When he's proposing to have a national security force that's answering to him, that is as strong as the U.S. military, he's showing me signs of being Marxist."

After seeming to back away from his comments when he was heavily criticized, Broun announced he was "not taking back anything [he] said." "I firmly believe that we must not fall victim to the 'it can't happen here' mentality," he declared in a press release. "I adhere to the adage 'eternal vigilance is the price of liberty.'"

Standing before the inaugural doorway, Broun joined Schenck and Mahoney in deep prayer. He raised his hands to the sky while Mahoney recited a prayer originally delivered by Billy Graham at Nixon's 1969 inauguration. "For too long we have neglected thy word and ignored thy laws," Mahoney preached. "We have sowed to the wind and are now reaping a whirlwind of crime, division, and rebellion. And now with the wages of sin staring us in the face, we remember thy words."

After Mahoney prayed, Schenck dipped his fingers in a jar of oil and painted several crosses on the door's brass framing "as they did the furnishings of the tabernacle in the temple to the use of God and his word." When Obama proceeded down the inaugural walkway thirteen days later, the crosses reflected a faint but ominous mark.

ACKNOWLEDGMENTS

This book would not have been possible without the help of many people. I have been privileged to be edited by Carl Bromley at Nation Books. He guided this book from start to finish with impeccable editorial judgment and kept me sane with his sense of humor. I am extraordinarily grateful for the friendship and unstinting support of Hamilton Fish. No one is more responsible for nurturing my journalistic endeavors. Taya Kitman, Joe Conason, Esther Kaplan, Ruth Baldwin, and everyone at the Nation Institute are great friends and indispensable colleagues. Rita Cant researched complex details of the book, providing essential background information and catching mistakes I would have missed. I look forward to her own endeavors in journalism. John Sherer from Basic Books oversaw a terrific team with confidence and professionalism. I am also grateful to Patrick Lannan and Martha Jessup from the Lannan Foundation, and to my agent, Anna Stein, who nurtured this project from its inception and offered assistance at every stage. Also thanks to Michelle Welsh-Horst at Perseus Books for her meticulous attention to detail.

The *Nation Magazine*, *Media Matters for America*, the *Huffington Post* and the *Daily Beast* provided outlets for much of the reporting contained in this book. Katrina Vanden Heuvel and Betsy Reed at *Nation* offered early and essential support as well as excellent editorial judgment. David Brock inspired my interest in journalism, then made my career possible. I am immensely grateful to him, Darrin Bodner, and everyone at *Media Matters* for their support, especially under very trying circumstances. Thanks to Tina Brown, Edward Felsenthal, and Bryan Curtis at the *Daily Beast* for their innovation and immense generosity. Arianna Huffington at the *Huffington Post* was an aggressive and early supporter of my reporting. Like most books about the Christian right, this one has benefited from the research and insights of Frederick Clarkson and Bruce Wilson at TalkToAction.org.

This book is also the product of the support and influence of countless friends and family members. I dedicated this book to my mother and father, who pushed me to initiate what once seemed like a daunting intellectual undertaking and gave me the support I needed to see it through. My brother, Paul, is a secret weapon on the frontlines of democracy and a natural voice of reason. My grandmother, Claire, has given me her wisdom and humor on an almost daily basis. Steve, Kathy, Jon Michael, and Rebecca Carroll have been like a second family to me, including and especially during this project. With his unique perspective and creative spirit, Jan Frel has been as much an adviser as a friend. I am also grateful for the friendship of Laila Al-Arian, who has thrived under unjust and unfair circumstances with the heart of John Starks. Patricia Valencia urged me to pursue writing and encouraged me when few others did. Also thanks to Jon Jordan, Hillel Schwartz, Dave Tozer, Devon Harris, Ali Gharib, Shama Zerom Davis, Nathan and Tasha Sabatino, David Neiwert, Simon Mayer, Joseph Dunham, Phil Munger and Judy Lundquist, Sandra Harper, Michael Harwin, Chris Hedges, Louis Vandenberg, and Hillel Schwartz.

NOTES

INTRODUCTION: ESCAPE FROM FREEDOM

3   *Mica, head-butted:* ABC's *The World Newser,* September 2, 2008, http://blogs.abcnews.com/theworldnewser/2008/09/rnc-delegate-he.html.

3   *"fuckin' redneck" Levi Johnston:* Dillon, Belenkaya, and Moore, *New York Daily News,* September 2, 2008, http://www.nydailynews.com/news/politics/republican_race/2008/09/01/2008–09–01_bristol_palins_pregnancy_was _an_open_sec.html.

4   *"a man steeped in falsehood":* Richard Halworth Rovere, *Senator Joseph Mc-Carthy* (Berkeley: University of California Press, 1996), p. 15.

4   *"I will not get into the gutter:"* PBS's *The American Experience,* 2002–03, http://www.pbs.org/wgbh/amex/presidents/34_eisenhower/eisenhower_politics .html.

5   *"the paranoid style of politics":* Richard Hofstadter, speech from Herbert Spencer Lecture at Oxford University, November 1963, and "The Paranoid Style in American Politics," *Harper's* (November 1964): 77–86.

5   *Eisenhower clung to a short book:* In 1956, *Look* magazine profiled Eric Hoffer, identifying him as "Ike's Favorite Author."

5   *"hedging and a little uncertainty":* Personal to Robert J. Biggs, February 10, 1959. In *The Papers of Dwight David Eisenhower,* ed. L. Galambos and D. van Ee, doc. 1051. World Wide Web facsimile by The Dwight D. Eisenhower Memorial Commission of the print edition (Baltimore, MD: The Johns Hopkins University Press, 1996), http://www.eisenhowermemorial.org/presidential-papers/second-term/documents/1051.cfm.

7   *"A rising mass movement":* Eric Hoffer, *The True Believer* (New York: Harper & Row, 1951), p. 41.

7   *"Faith in a holy cause":* Hoffer, *The True Believer,* p. 14.

7   *gaining the approval . . . of . . . Bertrand Russell:* Tom Bethell, "The Longshoreman Philosopher," *Hoover Digest,* no. 1, 2003.

7   *"All mass movements are interchangeable":* Hoffer, *The True Believer,* p. 17.

8   *"instead of wanting freedom"*: Erich Fromm, *Escape from Freedom* (New York and Toronto: Rinehart & Company, 1941), p. 3.

8   *"there is no greater mistake"*: Ibid., p. 240.

8   *"security and a feeling of belonging"*: Ibid., p. 4.

9   *"The function of an authoritarian ideology"*: Ibid., p. 238.

9   *"the head of a dreadful company"*: Steve Arterburn, *Wild at Heart* (Nashville, TN: Thomas Nelson, 2006), p. 29.

11   *"hardcore pro-lifer"* and *"prayer warrior"*: Palin interviewed by James Dobson on Focus on the Family radio, Colorado Springs, Colorado, October 22, 2008.

12   *Christie Todd Whitman published:* Christine Todd Whitman and Robert M. Bostock, "Free the GOP: The Party Won't Win Back the Middle As Long As It's Hostage to Social Fundamentalists," *Washington Post,* November 14, 2008.

13   *"military-industrial complex"*: Eisenhower's farewell address to the nation, January 17, 1961.

CHAPTER 1: GOD'S GOVERNMENT

17   *Y. K. Rushdoony and his wife fled:* Speech by Mark Rushdoony at Chalcedon's 40th anniversary, Cumming, Georgia, September 16, 2005, http://www .chalcedon.edu/articles/article.php?ArticleID=185.

17   *reaching back to the year 315:* Ibid.

17   *conservative theological authorities:* Ibid.

18   *"Don't go to the civil courts"*: Interview with R. J. Rushdoony by Joseph McAuliffe, http://forerunner.com/revolution/rush.html. Also see the Bible, Corinthians, 1:6.

18   Rushdoony's friendship with Robert Welch: Chad Bull, "Stalwarts of Freedom: An Inside Look at the John Birch Society," *Faith for All of Life,* September/October 2006, http://www.chalcedon.edu/articles/article.php?ArticleID =2334#_edn1.

18   a *"Master Conspiracy"*: Robert Alan Goldberg, *Enemies Within* (New Haven, CT: Yale University Press, 2001), pp. 22–65.

18   Buckley denounced the John Birch Society: Rick Perlstein, *Before the Storm* (New York, Hill and Wang, 2001), pp. 154–156.

19   Bircher role in JFK assassination: "J.F.K.'s Assassination: Who Was the Real Target?" *Time* (November 28, 1988): 4. Also see William Martin, *With God on Our Side* (New York, Broadway Books, 1996), p. 78, on initial reports blaming the extreme right for the assassination and the right-wing backlash. Erstwhile Francis Schaeffer mentor Carl McIntyre distributed a packet entitled "A Communist Kills Our President But the Right Wing Is Blamed."

19   *"The key to the . . . Society's effectiveness"*: R. J. Rushdoony, *The Institutes of Biblical Law* (Nutley, NJ: The Craig Press, 1973), p. 74.

19   *"Welch always saw things"*: Rushdoony interviewed by Marghe Covino, "Grace Under Pressure: The World According to Rev. R. J. Rushdoony," *Sacramento News and Review* 6, 28 (October 20, 1994).

19   *"humanistic spectrum":* Walter Olson, "Invitation to a Stoning," *Reason Magazine,* November 1999.

20   *"Reconstructionism seeks to replace":* Frederick Clarkson, "Theocratic Dominionism Gains Influence," *Public Eye,* March/June 1994, http://www.public eye.org/magazine/v08n1/chrisre1.html.

20   *"God's government prevails":* Ibid.

20   Ron Paul on the John Birch Society: "Ron Paul Congratulates the John Birch Society on 50th Anniversary," *The New American,* April 28, 2008.

21   *advocated stoning evildoers:* Olson, "Invitation to a Stoning."

21   *"The facilities should be separate":* Martin, *With God on Our Side,* p. 57.

21   Falwell and J. Edgar Hoover: Ibid., p. 69.

21   *"Rushdoony distrusts democracy":* Larry B. Stammer, "The Rev. Rousas John Rushdoony Advocated Rule by Biblical Law," *Los Angeles Times,* March 3, 2001, p. B-7; from Ed Dobson and Ed Hindson, Heritage Foundation Policy Review, 1986.

21   *Rushdoony wrote in response:* Olson, "Invitation to a Stoning."

CHAPTER 2: CREATING A MONSTER

23   *Calvin . . . outlawed cursing:* Jim Bell, James S. Bell, and Tracy Macon Summer, *The Complete Idiot's Guide to the Reformation & Protestantism* (New York: Penguin: 2002), p. 153.

23   Schaeffer and Jacobs: Interview with Frank Schaeffer, January 21, 2009.

24   Schaeffer and Carla: Ibid.

24   *Frank discovered his father sobbing:* Ibid.

24   Schaeffer and Page: Ibid.

24   Schaeffer and Bono: Ibid. Also see "U2Literary.com Reading List," http://www.u2literary.com/ReadingList.htm.

24   Schaeffer and Leary: Michael Hamilton, "The Dissatisfaction of Francis Schaeffer," *Christianity Today* 41, 3 (March 3, 1997): 22.

24   *"The hippies of the 1960s":* Francis A. Schaeffer, *The Complete Works of Francis A. Schaeffer* (Wheaton, IL: Crossway, 1985), p. 14.

25   *Schaeffer appeared beside a suburban sewage drain:* Francis and Frank Schaeffer, DVD of "Dr. Francis Schaeffer's *How Should We Then Live?* (Muskegon, MI: Gospel Communications, 2005).

25   *"I was trying to get those people interested:"* Randall Balmer, *Thy Kingdom Come* (New York: Basic Books, 2006), p. 15.

26   Schaeffer and Ford: Hamilton, "The Dissatisfaction of Francis Schaeffer."

26   Schaeffer and Falwell: Ibid.

26   *the concept of "co-belligerency":* James Risen and Judy Thomas, "Wrath of Angels" (Boulder, CO: Perseus, 1999), p. 129.

26   *"the low IQs":* Interview with Frank Schaeffer. Also see Frank Schaeffer, *Crazy for God* (New York: Carroll & Graf, 2007), p. 300.

27   *"establishment elite":* Schaeffer, *The Complete Works,* p. 71

27 *Schaeffer . . . rebuffed R. J. Rushdoony's requests:* Interview with Frank Schaeffer.
27 *"the nearly verbatim lifting of certain material":* Gary North, *Political Polytheism* (Tyler, TX: Institute for Christian Economics, 1989), p. 196.
28 Schaeffer and LaHaye: Interview with Frank Schaeffer.
28 *once boasted to Schaeffer:* Schaeffer, *Crazy for God,* p. 332.
28 *"Thank God for Francis Schaeffer":* James Dobson, speech at National Religious Broadcaster's Convention, Nashville, Tennessee, February 19, 2002.
29 *"If you want to understand Operation Rescue":* Gary Wills, *Under God* (New York: Simon & Schuster, 1991), p. 324.
29 *Schenck, who had converted:* Interview with Rob Schenck, Washington DC, September 20, 2003.
29 *"God will hold you to account":* Max Blumenthal, "God's Country," *Washington Monthly,* October 2003, http://www.washingtonmonthly.com/features/2003/0310.blumenthal.html.
29 *Kopp, a former resident:* Ibid.
30 *"It's your 'passive' following":* Ibid.
30 *Dobson hosted Frank Schaeffer:* Interview with Frank Schaeffer.
31 *"think-tank of the Christian right":* Gary North, *R. J. Rushdoony, R.I.P.,* (LewRockwell.com, February 10, 2001), http://www.lewrockwell.com/north/north33.html.

CHAPTER 3: WHAT GOD WANTS HIM TO DO

32 *As his wife, Roberta . . . , told me:* Interview with Roberta Green Ahmanson, Los Angeles, California, November 22, 2003.
33 *He burned with resentment toward his father:* Max Blumenthal, "The Avenging Angel of the Religious Right," Salon.com, January 6, 2004, http://dir.salon.com/story/news/feature/2004/01/06/ahmanson/index.html.
33 Ahmanson and Leonetti: Associated Press, "Caroline Leonetti Ahmanson; prominent Southern California philanthropist, 83," June 25, 2005, http://www.signonsandiego.com/uniontrib/20050625/news_1m25ahmanson.html.
33 Leonetti and Clemons: Steve Clemons, "Shame on Howard Ahmanson: California Voters Approve Gay Marriage Ban," *Washington Note,* November 5, 2008, http://www.thewashingtonnote.com/archives/2008/11/california_vote/.
33 *But he was without direction:* Blumenthal, "Avenging Angel."
34 *Ahmanson's physical and psychological problems:* Ibid.
34 *At Occidental College:* Ibid.
34 *the theologian mocked wealthy liberals:* R. J. Rushdoony, *The Politics of Guilt and Pity* (Fairfax, VA: Thoburn Press, [1970] 1978), pp. 3–4. Also see pages 19 and 25 for more on wealthy liberals and "Negroes."
35 *Ahmanson became a full-fledged Calvinist:* Interview with Roberta Green Ahmanson.
35 *Roberta Green Ahmanson explained*: Ibid.
36 *an assignment about the Christian right:* Ibid.

36 Ahmanson and Roberta Green: "Rich in Faith; Part 2, Unconventional couple," *Orange County Register,* August 10, 2005, http://www.ocregister.com/news/2004/ahmanson/.

37 *the first time since 1984:* Blumenthal, "Avenging Angel."

CHAPTER 4: MARCHING THROUGH THE INSTITUTIONS

38 Ahmanson and California Assembly: Ibid.

38 Ahmanson and book banning: Ibid.

39 Stoos and Chalcedon: Jerry Sloan, "John Stoos Reveals . . . a Hidden Agenda?" April 1995, Freedom Writer; Public Eye, http://www.publiceye.org/ifas/fw/9504/stoos.html. Also see Scott Glover, "McClintock Advisor Looks to Bible as Basis for Law," *Los Angeles Times,* September 30, 2003, http://articles.latimes.com/2003/sep/30/local/me-stoos30.

39 Ahmanson's McClintock fundraiser: Daryl Kelley and Megan Garvey, "Isolated at Home, McClintock Finds New Friends," *Los Angeles Times,* September 28, 2003, http://articles.latimes.com/2003/sep/28/local/me-mcclintockmain28.

39 Ahmanson and Prop 209: Blumenthal, "Avenging Angel."

39 Ahmanson and Rice: Ibid.

39 *Rice-Hughes . . . became born-again:* Ramona Cramer Tucker, "Enough Is Enough: Donna Rice-Hughes," *Today's Christian Woman* 18, 5 (September/October 1996): 42, http://www.christianitytoday.com/tcw/1996/sepoct/6w5042.html?start=.

40 Olasky and CPUSA: Marvin Olasky: "Marxism and Me," from Paul M. Anderson, "Professors Who Believe" (Westmont, IL: InterVarsity Press, 1998), p. 173.

40 Olasky and Ahmanson: Blumenthal, "Avenging Angel."

40 Olasky, Rove and Bush: Gary Wills, *Head and Heart* (New York: Penguin Press, 2007), p. 518. Wills calls Olasky "a convert to Rousan John Rushdoony's Christian Reconstruction theology—which is also called Dominion Theology." When I reported the same for Salon.com in "Avenging Angel," Olasky angrily demanded a correction.

41 *"unlikely guru":* T. Christian Miller, "Philosophically, Bush Gets Inspiration from an Unlikely Guru," *Los Angeles Times,* July 27, 2000, http://articles.latimes.com/2000/jul/27/news/mn-60012.

41 *"religion of Zeus":* Jake Tapper, "Bush's 'compassionate' advisor singles out Jews," February 25, 2000, Salon.com, http://dir.salon.com/politics2000/feature/2000/02/25/olasky/index.html.

41 Ahmanson and Chapman: Blumenthal, "Avenging Angel."

42 *John Jones, a Republican judge:* Laurie Goodstein, "Issuing Rebuke, Judge Rejects Teaching of Intelligent Design," *New York Times,* December 21, 2005, http://query.nytimes.com/gst/fullpage.html?res=9C00E6DC1430F932A15751C1A9639C8B63&sec=&spon=&pagewanted=all. Also, for full Jones opinion, see http://msnbcmedia.msn.com/i/msnbc/sections/news/051220_kitzmiller_342.pdf.

42   *"Spying is legitimate":* Rousas J. Rushdoony, *The Independent Republic: Stud-
      ies in the Nature and Meaning of American History* (Thornburg Press, 1978)
      pp. 542–544.

42   *Progressive Methodist minister Andrew Weaver explained:* Frederick Clarkson,
      "The Battle for the Mainline Churches," *The Public Eye Magazine,* Spring
      2006, http://www.publiceye.org/magazine/v20n1/clarkson_battle.html.

43   Ahmanson and IRD: Blumenthal, "Avenging Angel."

43   Hewitt's greatest regret: Interview with Don Hewitt by Larry King, December 2,
      2002, CNN, http://transcripts.cnn.com/TRANSCRIPTS/0212/02/lkl.00.html.

43   *a grant of over $1 million:* Blumenthal, "Avenging Angel."

43   Ahmansons versus Robinson: Ibid.

44   Northern Virginia churches and Akinola: Michelle Boorstein, "Conservative
      N. Va. Priest Installed as Anglican Bishop," Washington Post, May 6, 2007,
      http://www.washingtonpost.com/wp-dyn/content/article/2007/05/05/
      AR2007050501215_pf.html.

44   Akinola's anti-gay bill: The Most Rev. Peter J. Akinola, "Standing Committee
      Meeting Held at the Cathedral Church of St. Peter," February 22–25, 2006,
      Aremo, Nigeria, http://www.anglican-nig.org/communique_ibadan2006
      .htm.

44   the IRD and Karsh: John Dorhauer, "The IRD's Next Front Line: Gambling on
      Your Xenophobia," *Talk2Action,* September 12, 2007, http://www.talk2action
      .org/story/2007/9/12/164049/560/shadow_war.

44   Rushdoony on freedom: R. J. Rushdoony, "The Fear of Freedom," *California
      Farmer,* February 1, 1975, reprinted on The American View, http://www.the
      americanview.com/index.php?id=914.

46   *"Such symptoms result:"* Fromm, *Escape from Freedom,* p. 4.

46   Ahmanson and Focus on the Family: People for the American Way, "Buying a
      Movement: Individual Donors," 1996, http://67.192.238.59/multimedia/pdf/
      Reports/buyingamovement.pdf. The report notes that Ahmanson and former
      California State Senator Rob Hurtt co-founded Capitol Resource Institute, the
      California arm of Focus on the Family, bankrolling it with $1 million.

CHAPTER 5: THE PERSONAL CRISIS INDUSTRY

47   *Half of his original employees followed him:* Dale Buss, *Family Man* (Carol
      Stream, IL: Tyndale House, 2005), p. 119.

48   Dobson repelled by Pomona's racial diversity: Gil Alexander-Moegerle, *James
      Dobson's War on America* (Amherst, NY: Prometheus Books, 1997), p. 154.

48   Dobson's radio following: Dan Gilgoff, *The Jesus Machine* (New York: St. Mar-
      tin's Press, 2007), p. 7.

48   Dobson invited to meeting on Iran: Max Blumenthal, "Bush Met with Dob-
      son and Conservative Christian Leaders to Rally Support for Iran Policy,"
      Raw Story, May 14, 2007, http://rawstory.com/news/2007/Bush_meets_with
      _Dobson_Christian_right_0514.html.

48   Dobson's approval rating: "Poll: America's Evangelicals More and More Mainstream But Insecure," *Religion & Ethics Newsweekly,* April 13, 2004, http://www.pbs.org/wnet/religionandethics/episodes/by-faith/evangelical/poll-americas-evangelicals-more-and-more-mainstream-but-insecure/939/.

49   Fagerstrom on Dobson: Alexander-Moegerle, "James Dobson's War," p. 53.

49   *250,000 visitors:* Jen Mulson, "Focus on the Family/Institute Receives 250,000 Visitors a Year," *Colorado Springs Gazette,* September 27, 2002.

50   Dobson on Nazi experiments: Max Blumenthal, "Dobson Likened Embryonic Stem Cell Research to Nazi Experiments," *Media Matters for America,* August 3, 2005, http://mediamatters.org/items/200508030007.

50   Adventures in Odyssey memo: Buss, *Family Man,* pp. 137–138.

50   *Visitors are invariably told:* Visit to Focus on the Family, Colorado Springs, Colorado, October 13, 2006.

50   Dobson and Prince: Buss, *Family Man,* pp. 111–112.

50   *described by journalist Jeremy Scahill:* Jeremy Scahill, "Bush's Shadow Army," *The Nation,* March 15, 2007, http://www.thenation.com/doc/20070402/scahill.

51   *a vast security apparatus:* Cara Degette, "How Focus on the Family Deals with 'Difficult Guests,'" *Colorado Confidential,* October 29, 2006, http://www.coloradoconfidential.com/showDiary.do?diaryId=901.

51   *a bullet still remains lodged:* Visit to Focus on the Family, October 13, 2006.

51   Focus correspondence department: Gilgoff, *The Jesus Machine,* pp. 28–29, and Buss, *Family Man,* p. 52.

51   Dobson and Neil Clark Warren: Buss, *Family Man,* pp. 278–279.

52   *in order to sidestep the lawsuit:* Joshua Rhett Miller, "eHarmony to Provide Gay Dating Service After Lawsuit," FoxNews.com, November 20, 2008, http://www.foxnews.com/story/0,2933,454904,00.html.

52   Dobson and O'Reilly: "Dr. James Dobson Talks with Bill O'Reilly," Fox News Channel, February 16, 2006, http://www.foxnews.com/story/0,2933,185121,00.html.

53   Dobson on "the secular media": Focus on the Family, "Focus Clarifies Dr. Dobson's Comments on Sen. Thompson," Citizenlink.org, March 30, 2007, http://www.citizenlink.org/focusaction/pressreleases/A000006865.cfm.

53   Dobson and Fineman: Howard Fineman, "Living Politics: Daddy Dobson," *Newsweek,* May 4, 2005, http://www.newsweek.com/id/51655 Also see "*Newsweek*'s Fineman Wrong About Dobson, Who's No Political Newcomer," *Media Matters for America,* http://comediamatters.com/items/200505060002.

CHAPTER 6: THE KING OF PAIN

54   On Dobson Sr.: Buss, *Family Man,* pp. 11–12.

54   "Dad-gummit!": Eileen Welsome, "And on the Eight Day, Dr. Dobson Created Himself," 5280.com, July, 2006, http://www.5280.com/issues/story_for_print.php?pageID=400.

54   *"I learned very early"*: James Dobson, *Dare to Discipline* (New York: Bantam Books, 1977), pp. 18–19.

55   *Dobson formed a close bond*: Welsome, "And on the Eighth Day," 5280.com; and Buss, *Family Man*, p. 18.

55   Dobson and Nazarenes: Alexander-Moegerle, "James Dobson's War," pp. 94–95.

55   "Entire Sanctification" doctrine: Alexander-Moegerle, "James Dobson's War," p. 98.

55   Dobson born again at age three: Paul Apostolidis, *Stations of the Cross: Adorno and Christian Right Radio* (Durham, NC: Duke University Press), p. 22.

56   *"overindulgence, permissiveness, and smother-love"*: Dobson, *Dare to Discipline*, p. 11.

56   *"My father was a gentleman"*: Barbara T. Roessner, "Obedience, Diligence, and Fun: Bush's 'Extraordinary Family Life Recalled by Brother Prescott,'" *Jacksonville Times-Courier*, January 15, 1989.

56   Agnew on Spock: Ann Hulbert, "Dr. Spock's Baby: Fifty Years in the Life of a Book and the American Family," *New Yorker*, May 20, 1996, pp. 82–91.

56   Dobson vs. Spock: Buss, *Family Man*, pp. 44–45.

57   *"Farmer John could take his sassy son"*: James Dobson, "Relating to Teens," Focus on the Family, "Focus on Your Child" section of website reprinted in *Cornerstone Connection Christian Magazine*, October 21, 2005, http://www.cornerstone-osceola.com/archive/2005/10–21–2005/featured.php.

57   *"A little bit of pain"*: Dobson, *Dare to Discipline*, p. 23.

57   *"There is a muscle"*: Ibid., p. 26.

57   Dobson's *Dirty Harry* moment: Ibid., pp. 27–28.

58   Dobson beats Siggie: James Dobson, *The Strong-Willed Child* (Mount Pleasant, MI: Living Books, 1992), excerpted by Chris Dugan, http://www.geocities.com/cddugan/DobsonsDog.html.

58   *"paralleled the decline in authority"*: Dobson, *Dare to Discipline*, p. 99.

59   Dobson's ten-point plan: Ibid., pp. 96–98.

59   Hard-hat riot: *New York Times*, May 7, 1970, p. A19, and May 8, 1970, p. A16. Also, for police encouragement of rioters, see *Washington Post*, May 19, 1970, and *Washington Star*, May 17, 1970.

59   *"brown shirts of Hitler's Germany"*: Emanuel Perlmutter, "Heads of Buildings Trade Unions Here Says Response Favors Friday's Action," *New York Times*, May 12, 1970, p. 18.

59   Colson instigated attack: Seymour Hersh, "1971 Tape Links Nixon to Plan to Use 'Thugs,'" *New York Times*, September 24, 1981, pp. 1 and (excerpts) 26.

60   Colson and Philips: Max Blumenthal, "Born Again, Again," *Washington Monthly*, July/August 2005, http://www.washingtonmonthly.com/features/2005/0507.blumenthal.html.

60   Colson, Schaeffer, and Dobson: Ibid.

60   *"a socially approved way"*: Jonathan Aitken, *Charles W. Colson: A Life Redeemed* (New York: Continuum International Publishing Group, 2005), p. 291.

61   Colson and Rushdoony: Colson interviewed by Bill Moyers in "God and Politics: On Earth As It Is in Heaven," Pacific Arts Video, April 8, 1992.

61   *Gideon's Torch* on Army of God site: ArmyofGod.com, http://www.armyofgod
      .com/CharlesColson.html.

62   *"The persistent 'conservatism' of American politics"*: Philip Greven, *Spare the
      Child* (New York: Vintage Books), 1990, p. 187. Psychiatrist Alice Miller as-
      serts links between child abuse and anti-Semitism in *"For Your Own Good:
      Hidden Cruelty in Child-Rearing and the Roots of Violence* (New York: Farrar,
      Straus and Giroux), 1990.

62   *"Pain is a marvelous purifier"*: Dobson, *Dare to Discipline,* p. 16.

63   *"Whenever children suffer"*: Greven, *Spare the Child,* p. 186.

63   *"The essence of the authoritarian character"*: Fromm, *Escape from Freedom,*
      p. 221.

CHAPTER 7: SATAN IN A PORSCHE

67   *blamed for eroding the country's moral character:* Political Research Associates,
      Gary Bauer Right-Web Profile, Right-Web, June 27, 2007, http://rightweb.irc
      -online.org/profile/1022.html.

67   Bauer and Dobson: Sara Diamond: *Not by Politics Alone* (New York: Guilford
      Press), 1998, p. 32.

67   *Focus hired 200 new staffers:* Buss, *Family Man,* p. 68.

68   *"sex between women and bulls"*: James Dobson and Gary Bauer, *Children At
      Risk* (Nashville, TN: Thomas Nelson, 1994), cited by Nathan Callahan, "Cor-
      porate Vulture," *OC Weekly,* May 8, 2003, http://www.ocweekly.com/2003-05
      -08/news/corporate-vulture/1.

68   ChristiaNet.com porn survey: ChristiaNet, "Evangelicals Are Addicted to
      Porn," 2007, http://christiannews.christianet.com/1154951956.htm.

68   *25 percent of calls:* Jane Lampman: "Churches Confront an 'Elephant in the
      Pews,'" *Christian Science Monitor,* August 25, 2005, http://www.csmonitor.com/
      2005/0825/p14s01-lire.html.

68   Sears and South Africa: Philip Nobile and Eric Nadler, *United States of Amer-
      ica vs. Sex* (New York: Minotaur Press, 1986), p. 289.

69   *"their precious erections"*: Cathy Young, "Bizarre Bedfellows: Andrea Dworkin's
      Intercourse with the Right," *Reason Magazine,* July 2005, http://findarticles
      .com/p/articles/mi_m1568/is_3_37/ai_n15998571.

69   *"skull-fucking"*: Nobile and Nadler, *United States,* p. 149.

69   *They pored over "evidence"*: Ibid., pp. 141, 158, 227.

70   field trip to Times Square: Ibid., p. 95.

70   Sears and enemas: Ibid., p. 321.

70   *In their final report*: Ibid., p. 290.

70   *"I couldn't figure out why"*: Ibid., p. 289.

71   Sears's divorce: Interview with Rev. Barry Lynn, Washington DC, October 26,
      2007.

71   *"Pornography's greatest harm"*: Nobile and Nadler, *United States,* p. 284.

71   Ritter and Kite: Mary Cronin, "Bleak Days for Covenant House," *Time,* February
      19, 1990 http://www.time.com/time/magazine/article/0,9171,969410,00.html.

71   Dobson at NRB: Nobile and Nadler, *United States,* p. 278.

72   *"river of smut":* Ibid., p. 214.

72   *"We urge that many of the recommendations":* Hendrik Hertzberg, *Politics,* (New York: Penguin, 2005), p. 406.

72   Bundy read the Meese Commission report: Buss, *Family Man,* p. 92.

CHAPTER 8: THE KILLER AND THE SAINT

73   *one man, whom he proclaimed a hero:* Ibid.

74   rumor about grandfather as biological father: Ted Bundy case background, Mystery Crime Scene, http://www.mysterycrimescene.com/ted-bundy.html.

74   Grandfather's abuse: Ibid. Also see Paula Bentley, "10 Weird Facts About Ted Bundy's Childhood," http://www.bukisa.com/articles/16246_10-weird-facts -about-ted-bundys-childhood.

74   Bundy idolized his grandfather: Ann Rule, *The Stranger Beside Me* (London: Signet, reprinted 2001), p. 29.

74   Bundy at crisis hotline: Ibid., p. 10.

74   Bundy and Evans: Ibid., pp. 41, 44.

74   Bundy and rape prevention pamphlet: Ibid., p. 44.

74   *"I just mingled with the crowds":* Rule, *The Stranger Beside Me,* p. 41.

75   Bundy and Brooks: Ibid., pp. 26–27.

75   Bundy and Tanner: Buss, *Family Man,* p. 92.

75   *to teach his children "spiritual things":* Derek Catron, "Your State Attorney: Man of God, Man of Law," News-Journalonline.com, June 24, 2007, http:// www.news-journalonline.com/special/flaglerpolice/frtHEAD01062407.htm.

76   *"bones-for-time scheme":* Michael Mello, *Dead Wrong* (Madison, WI: University of Wisconsin Press, 1997), p. 108.

76   *"For [Bundy] to be negotiating":* Stephen G. Michaud and Hugh Aynesworth, *The Only Living Witness* (Irving, TX: Authorlink Press, 2000), pp. 335–336.

76   Jackson on Bundy: Buss, *Family Man,* p. 92.

76   *"So should I":* Ibid., p. 99.

76   *the Bundy tapes reaped a windfall profit:* Ibid., p. 99.

CHAPTER 9: A DANGEROUS WOMAN

78   *whipped her with a belt:* Marlee Macleod, "Aileen Wuornos: Killer Who Preyed on Truck Drivers," TruTV Crime Library, http://www.trutv.com/library/ crime/notorious_murders/women/wuornos/2.html.

79   Wuornos and Mallory: Phyllis Chesler, "Sexual Violence and a Woman's Right to Self-Defense," *Criminal Practice Law Report* 1, 9 (October 1993), http:// 76.12.0.56/index.php?option=com_content&task=view&id=274&Itemid=97.

79   *"his emotional disturbance":* Ibid.

79   *"That's his favorite time":* Catron, "Your State Attorney."

79   *Wuornos finally lost her composure:* Chesler, *Sexual Violence.*

79   *"She liked to be in control"*: "Florida Executes Female Serial Killer," News Channel2000.com, October 9, 2002, http://www.wesh.com/sh/news/stories/ nat-news-171041320021009–071054.html.

80   Chesler on Wuornos: Chesler, *Sexual Violence.*

81   Wuornos and Merchant: "Merchant Allows Her song 'Carnival' to Be Included in a Film About a Notorious Serial Killer," Natalie Merchant official fan site, September 2003, http://www.nataliemerchant.com/news/?paged=3.

81   *her huckster lawyer, Stephen Glazer:* Nick Broomfield, "Aileen Wuornos: The Selling of a Serial Killer," *First Look,* February 4, 1994.

81   Robertson supports Tucker: Teresa Malcolm, "Tucker's Death Affected Robertson Views," *National Catholic Reporter,* April 23, 1999, http://findarticles .com/p/articles/mi_m1141/is_25_35/ai_54527745.

81   Robertson against Barkett: John W. Kennedy, "When Killers Become Christians," *New Man,* November/December 2002, http://www.newmanmag.com/ display.php?id=6767.

81   Tanner and Moorehead: Alex Fryer, "Florida Arrest Was Followed by Suspicions—His Lawyer's Election as Prosecutor Ignited Newspaper Scrutiny, Had Repercussions Here," *Seattle Times,* May 18, 1998, http://community .seattletimes.nwsource.com/archive/?date=19980518&slug=2751424 also see factually accurate editorial account with satirical commentary "Anti-gay pastor finds cumfort fondling 'the staff and rod,'" Totalbull.com, http:// www.martinhiggins.com/PAGES/SACREDBURGERS/newbull/bull/masturb minister.html.

82   *"to inappropriately touch somebody"*: Carol M. Ostrom and Alex Fryer, "Church Hires Private Investigator in Moorehead Case—More Sexual Misconduct Allegations Surface Against Overlake Pastor," *Seattle Times,* February 19, 1998, http://community.seattletimes.nwsource.com/archive/?date=19980219&slug =2735280.

82   *"Satan likes none of this!"* Ostrom and Fryer, "Church Hires Private Investigator."

82   Berkowitz and Dobson: Charlie Brennan, "Killer Now Listens to Son of God," *Rocky Mountain News,* June 23, 2004.

83   *"I was there when we interviewed Berkowitz"*: Ibid.

83   *"I'm just incredulous"*: Paul Asay, "Focus Denies Profiting from Son of Sam Recording," *Colorado Springs Gazette,* June 25, 2005.

CHAPTER 10: CHEAP GRACE

84   Talent's conversion: Safir Ahmed, "Talent for Deception," *The American Prospect,* November 4, 2002, http://www.prospect.org/cs/articles?article =talent_for_deception.

84   Largent a Family member: Michael J. Gerson, Major Garrett, and Carolyn Kleiner, "A Righteous Indignation," *U.S. News & World Report,* April 26, 1998, http://www.usnews.com/usnews/news/articles/980504/archive_003835.htm.

85   *quietly committed himself to their ouster:* Gilgoff, *The Jesus Machine,* pp. 111–112.

85 *"Contract with America"*: Jeffrey Gayner, *The Contract with America: Implementing New Ideas in the U.S.*, The Heritage Foundation, October 12, 1995, http://www.heritage.org/Research/PoliticalPhilosophy/HL549.cfm; for House document: http://www.house.gov/house/Contract/CONTRACT.html.

85 *Dobson grumbled in 1995:* Buss, *Family Man*, p. 159.

85 Colin Powell polled highest: Max Blumenthal, "The Man Who Helped Drive Powell Away from His Party," *The Daily Beast*, October 22, 2008, http://www.thedailybeast.com/blogs-and-stories/2008–10–22/the-bitter-back-story-behind-powells-defection/1/.

85 Dobson's war against Powell: Ibid.

86 Phillips and Rushdoony: Michelle Goldberg, "In Theocracy They Trust," *Salon*, April 11, 2005, http://dir.salon.com/story/news/feature/2005/04/11/judicial_conference/index.html.

86 AIDS and the gold standard: U.S. Taxpayers Party platform, ConstitutionParty.com, undated, http://www.constitutionparty.com/party_platform.php.

87 Trewhella's address: Melinda Liu, "Inside the Anti-Abortion Underground," *Newsweek*, August 29, 1994, http://www.newsweek.com/id/115829.

87 Dobson's influence: *1996 Presidential General Elections Results*, US Elections Atlas, http://uselectionatlas.org/RESULTS/national.php?year=1996&minper=0&f=1&off=0&elect=0.

87 DeLay on Gingrich: Robert Novak, "The Wrath of Tom DeLay," *Washington Post*, March 15, 2007. http://www.washingtonpost.com/wp-dyn/content/article/2007/03/14/AR2007031402179.html.

87 *"I think you can write"*: Gail Sheehy, "The Inner Quest of Newt Gingrich," *Vanity Fair*, September 1995, posted to PBS.org http://www.pbs.org/wgbh/pages/frontline/newt/vanityfair4.html.

87 *Newt Gingrich was born Newt McPherson:* Ibid.

87 Gingrich's abusive childhood: Jacob Weissberg, "Battered-Republican Syndrome," *Slate Magazine*, March 23, 1997, http://www.slate.com/id/2269/.

87 *Gingrich, fascinated with zoos and dinosaurs:* Jerry Gray, "Speaker Gingrich Mixes Politics and Paleontology," *New York Times*, August 29, 1997, http://query.nytimes.com/gst/fullpage.html?res=9A0CE3DC1331F93AA1575BC0A961958260&n=Top/Reference/Times%20.

88 *"Soon after his first extramarital tryst"*: Gail Sheehy, "The Inner Quest of Newt Gingrich," *Vanity Fair*, September 1995, posted to PBS.org http://www.pbs.org/wgbh/pages/frontline/newt/vanityfair4.html.

88 *"She wasn't pretty enough"*: Ibid.

89 *his national approval rating plummeted:* Richard Berke, "Clinton's Ratings Over 50% in Poll as G.O.P. Declines," *New York Times*, December 14, 1995, http://query.nytimes.com/gst/fullpage.html?res=9504E5DF1739F937A25751C1A963958260&sec=&spon=&pagewanted=all.

89 Bisek affair: Ben Evans, "Gingrich Had Affair During Clinton Probe," Associated Press, March 8, 2007, http://www.washingtonpost.com/wp-dyn/content/article/2007/03/08/AR2007030801847.html.

89   Attempted coup: James Carney and Karen Tumulty, "Ready, Aim, Misfire," *Time*, July 28, 2007, http://www.cnn.com/ALLPOLITICS/1997/07/21/time/gingrich.html.

89   Dobson addresses CNP: Ben Winton, "Dobson Declares War on GOP," *Freedom Writer*, March 1998, http://www.publiceye.org/ifas/fw/9803/dobson.html. See also Laurie Goodstein, "Conservative Christian Leader Accuses Republicans of Betrayal," *New York Times*, February 12, 1998.

90   *"He immediately launched into a jeremiad"*: James Dobson's CNP address, February 7, 1998, Arizona Biltmore resort, Phoenix, Arizona, posted to PublicEye.org: http://www.publiceye.org/ifas/cnp/dobson.html.

90   *"Armey confronted Dobson"*: D. Michael Lindsay, Pew Forum's Faith Angle Conference, Key West, May 2008, published at PewResearch.org June 30, 2008, pewresearch.org/pubs/883/american-evangelicalism.

90   *"was never so wrongfully and viciously attacked"*: D. Michael Lindsay, *Faith in the Halls of Power* (New York: Oxford University Press, 2007), p. 65.

90   ACLU rumor: Dick Armey, "Why Faith Requires Freedom," *FreedomWorks*, October 12, 2006, http://www.freedomworks.org/publications/christians-and-big-government.

90   *"in a pool of my own blood"*: Dick Armey, Jenny Woo interview, *Gambling911*, December 8, 2008, http://www.gambling911.com/maintest/gambling-news/jenny-woo-interviews-former-house-majority-leader-dick-armey-120808.html.

91   *Gingrich promptly resigned from Congress:* "Gingrich Calls It Quits," CNN.com, November 6, 1998, http://www.cnn.com/ALLPOLITICS/stories/1998/11/06/gingrich/.

91   Gingrich's second divorce: *New York Post*, July 18, 2000; Ann Gerhart, "The Gingrich Divorce and Its Repercussions on the Right," *Washington Post*, December 18, 1999, http://mediamatters.org/altercation/200703090003.

91   *a trilogy of "alternative" historical novels:* Newt Gingrich and William Forstchen, *Never Call Retreat* (New York: St. Martin's Press, 2005).

91   *"before we actually lose a city"*: Riley Yates, "Gingrich Raises Alarm at Event Honoring Those Who Stand Up for Freedom of Speech," *New Hampshire Union Leader*, November 26, 2006, http://www.unionleader.com/article.aspx?headline=Gingrich+raises+alarm+at+event+honoring+those+who+stand+up+for+freedom+of+speech&articleId=d3f4ee4e-1e90–475a-b1b0-bbcd5baedd78.

91   *"drive God out of America's public life"*: Newt Gingrich, *Rediscovering God in America* (Nashville, TN: Thomas Nelson, 2006), Foreword.

92   *"He is yesterday's man"*: Jeffrey Kuhner, *Insight*. *Insight*'s archives were scrubbed during *Washington Times* site redesign; an excerpt is available at http://blogs.whereistand.com/adamelijah/724.

92   Gingrich on "Focus": Gingrich interviewed by Dobson, Focus on the Family radio, March 9, 2007, Colorado Springs, Colorado. Also see Bill Schneider, "Gingrich Confession: Clearing the Way for a 2008 Run?" CNN, March 9, 2007, http://www.cnn.com/2007/POLITICS/03/09/gingrich.schneider/index.html.

93   *"richly satisfied by what he heard"*: Jerry Falwell, "Why I Invited Gingrich to Give a Speech at Liberty," *WorldNetDaily,* March 10, 2007, http://www.world netdaily.com/index.php?pageId=40560.

94   Falwell's funeral: Max Blumenthal, "Diary of a Christian Terrorist," *Huffington Post,* March 23, 2007, http://www.huffingtonpost.com/max-blumenthal/ diary-of-a-christian-terr_b_49167.html.

94   Liberty University commencement: James Klattel, "Gingrich: Confront 'Radical Secularism,'" Associated Press, May 19, 2007, http://www.cbsnews.com/stories/ 2007/05/19/politics/main2828219.shtml?source=RSSattr=HOME_2828219.

94   Gingrich at Value Voters: Max Blumenthal, *Theocracy Now!* Value Voters Summit, Washington, DC, YouTube, October 21, 2007, http://www.youtube .com/watch?v=nvhn43BmdWM.

95   *He called it "cheap grace"*: Dietrich Bonhoeffer, *The Cost of Discipleship* (New York: Touchstone, 1959), p. 43.

CHAPTER 11: THE ADDICT AND THE ENABLER

97   *"on December 20, 1998, Livingston resigned"*: Howard Kurtz, "Larry Flynt, Investigative Pornographer," *Washington Post,* December 19, 1998, http://www .washingtonpost.com/wp-srv/politics/special/clinton/stories/flynt121998.htm.

97   *"We are all pawns on the chessboard"*: Bob Livingston, "Excerpts from Livingston's Resignation Speech," *New York Times,* December 20, 1998, http://query.ny times.com/gst/fullpage.html?res=9A05E2D7173CF933A15751C1A96E958260.

97   *DeLay turned Congress into his fiefdom*: John Dean, *Conservatives Without Conscience* (New York: Viking Penguin, 2006), pp. 127–128.

98   *"But while Gingrich was autocratic"*: Ibid.

98   DeLay's profile: Peter Perl, "Absolute Truth," *Washington Post Magazine,* May 13, 2001, http://www.washingtonpost.com/wp-dyn/content/article/2006/11/ 28/AR2006112800700_pf.html.

98   *"there was only one topic: deregulation"*: Lou Dubose interviewed by NPR, "Texas Journalist Lou Dubose on Tom DeLay," *Fresh Air,* September 29, 2004, http://www.npr.org/templates/story/story.php?storyId=4052979.

99   *"Where's Dad?"*: Ibid., p. 55.

99   *"I've been walking with Christ"*: Tom DeLay, Gary Schneeberger interview, "The Lord Has Had a Major Part in Developing Who Tom DeLay Is," *CitizenLink,* March 23, 2007, http://www.citizenlink.org/CLtopstories/A000004195.cfm.

99   *"intensity in their dependence upon religion"*: Robert Minor, *When Religion Is an Addiction* (St. Louis, MO: HumanityWorks!, 2007), p. 46.

100   *"DeLay's faith has solidified his political base"*: Peter Perl, "Absolute Truth," *Washington Post Magazine,* May 13, 2001, http://www.washingtonpost.com/ wp-dyn/content/article/2006/11/28/AR2006112800700_pf.html.

100   *"unconscious suffering of the average automatized person"*: Fromm, *Escape from Freedom,* p. 255.

100   Norquist's analogies: Grover Norquist profile, Media Transparency, undated, http://www.mediatransparency.org/personprofile.php?personID=52.

100 K Street Project: Nicholas Confessore, "Welcome to the Machine," *Washington Monthly*, July/August 2003, http://www.washingtonmonthly.com/features/2003/0307.confessore.html.

101 *"As Republicans control more and more"*: Ibid.

101 DeLay and the 2002 Texas elections: R. Jeffrey Smith, "DeLay's Corporate Fundraising Investigated," *Washington Post*, July 12, 2004, http://www.washingtonpost.com/ac2/wp-dyn/A43219–2004Jul11?language=printer.

101 *holing up in a motel in Oklahoma:* Andrew Nelson, "Democrats Stage a Lone Star Revolt," *Salon*, May 15, 2003, http://dir.salon.com/story/news/feature/2003/05/15/texas/print.html.

101 *force them back to Texas:* "Lieberman: Federal Authority Misused by Texas Republicans," Senate Committee on Homeland Security and Governmental Affairs, August 22, 2003, http://hsgac.senate.gov/public/index.cfm?FuseAction=PressReleases.Detail&Affiliation=C&PressRelease_id=e96bcc0b-8a5d-43d3–8fbe-1a2dc58c885f&Month=8&Year=2003.

101 *DeLay's elaborate schemes had finally attracted scrutiny:* Sheryl Gay Stolberg, "House Ethics Panel Admonishes Rep. DeLay for Second Time in a Week," *New York Times*, October 7, 2004, http://query.nytimes.com/gst/fullpage.html?res=9C01E0DA173BF934A35753C1A9629C8B63&sec=&spon=&pagewanted=all.

102 *Joel Hefley was unceremoniously removed:* Carl Hulse, "New Chairman for House Ethics Panel," *New York Times*, February 3, 2005, http://www.nytimes.com/2005/02/03/politics/03ethics.html?_r=1.

102 Investigative bombs: Jack Newfield, "DeLay on the Hot Seat," *The Nation*, September 23, 2004, http://www.thenation.com/doc/20041011/newfield.

102 Abramoff and the Family: Jamie Dean, "Focus on the Finances," *World*, February 4, 2006, http://www.worldmag.com/articles/11489.

102 Dobson's ire: Max Blumenthal, "Abramoff Splits the Christian Right," *Huffington Post*, March 7, 2006, http://www.huffingtonpost.com/max-blumenthal/abramoff-splits-the-chris_b_16933.html.

CHAPTER 12: CASINO JACK, THE FACE PAINTER, AND THE SAUSAGE KING

103 *He was murdered execution style:* Curt Anderson, "Three Charged in Gangland-style Murder of Suncruz Founder 'Gus' Boulis," Associated Press, September 27, 2005, http://www.sun-sentinel.com/news/local/southflorida/sfl-927boulis murder,0,6594337.story?coll=sfla-home-headlines.

103 Kidan and the other Family: Timothy Appleby, "Boulis Investigation Dredges Up Big Names," *Globe and Mail*, October 10, 2005, http://www.commondreams.org/headlines05/1010–06.htm.

104 *where he conferred more than eighty times:* Philip Shenon, "Abramoff and Rove Had 82 Contacts, Report Says," *New York Times*, September 29, 2006, http://www.nytimes.com/2006/09/29/washington/29abramoff.html?hp&ex=1159.

104 *sought to keep Abramoff's visits secret:* "Judge OKs Scrutiny of Abramoff Visits to White House," Associated Press, October 2, 2008, http://www.usatoday.com/news/washington/2008–10–02-abramoff-white-house_N.htm.

104 *Their good times rolled*: Committee for Government Reform staff report, prepared for Tony Davis and Henry Waxman, September 29, 2006, oversight .house.gov/abramoff/docs/abramoff.pdf.

104 *laundered through DeLay's U.S. Family Network:* R. Jeffrey Smith, "The DeLay–Abramoff Money Trail," *Washington Post,* December 31, 2005, http:// www.washingtonpost.com/wp-dyn/content/article/2005/12/30/AR2005 123001480.html.

104 *an inveterate bully:* The God Blog, "Jack Abramoff the Bully," *Jewish Journal,* October 4, 2007, http://www.jewishjournal.com/thegodblog/item/jack_abramoff _the_bully/.

104 *the same sort of sadistic tendencies*: Christopher Brauchli, "Tom DeLay and His Friends of Distinction," *Boulder Daily Camera,* November 28, 2004, http://www.commondreams.org/views04/1128–27.htm.

105 Abramoff–Scanlon e-mails: Michael Crowley, "A Lobbyist in Full," *New York Times Magazine,* May 01, 2005, http://query.nytimes.com/gst/fullpage.html ?res=9B01E3DE1231F932A35756C0A9639C8B63.

105 *manipulating "the wackos"*: Michael Scherer, "Abramoff–Scanlon School of Sleaze," *Salon,* November 3, 2005, http://dir.salon.com/story/news/feature/ 2005/11/03/abramoff/index.html.

105 Reed and the Christian right: Max Blumenthal, "Abramoff's Evangelical Soldiers," *The Nation,* February 2, 2006, http://www.thenation.com/doc/2006 0220/blumenthal/single?rel=nofollow.

105 *"Ninny of the 20th Century"*: Doug Monroe, "The Baby Jesus vs. Gandhi," *Creative Loafing Atlanta,* June 15, 2005, http://atlanta.creativeloafing.com/ gyrobase/Content?oid=oid%3A19515.

106 Yellow Pages salvation: Ryan Werder, "Know Your Right-Wing Speakers: Ralph Reed," August 8, 2006, http://74.125.47.132/search?q=cache :D_Wg26CDKdoJ:www.campusprogress.org/tools/1058/know-your-right -wing-speakers-ralph-reed+%22simply+demanded+that+I+come+to+ Jesus%22&cd=1&hl=en&ct=clnk&gl=us&client=safari.

106 Reed's entry into politics: Nina Easton, *Gang of Five: Leaders at the Center of the Conservative Ascendancy* (New York: Touchstone, 2000), pp. 205–208.

106 *"schizoid tendencies"*: Sidney Blumenthal, *Pledging Allegiance: The Last Campaign of the Cold War* (New York: HarperCollins, 1990), pp. 101–102.

107 *Abramoff wrote to Rabbi Daniel Lapin:* Mary Curtius, "A Lobbyist's E-Mail Train of Billing, Status, Charity," *Los Angeles Times,* June 25, 2005, http:// articles.latimes.com/2005/jun/25/nation/na-jack25

107 *"I do guerrilla warfare"*: James Carney, "The Rise and Fall of Ralph Reed," *Time,* July 23, 2006, http://www.time.com/time/magazine/article/0,9171 ,1218060,00.html.

107 *"The Right Hand of God"*: "The Right Hand of God: Ralph Reed of the Christian Coalition," *Time,* May 15, 1995.

107 *His own consulting firm, Century Strategies: Joshua Green,* "Second Coming," *The Atlantic,* April 2004, http://www.theatlantic.com/doc/200404/green.

107   *"humping in corporate accounts"*: Max Blumenthal, "Abramoff's Evangelical
       Soldiers," *The Nation*, February 2, 2006, http://www.thenation.com/doc/
       20060220/blumenthal.

107   *"a cancer on the American body politic"*: Jack Newfield, "Once a Foe, Now a
       Casino Lobbyist," *New York Sun*, September 8, 2004, http://www.nysun.com/
       national/once-a-foe-now-a-casino-lobbyist/1396/.

110   *"good to see Gary Bauer"*: Bruce Reed, "A Ralph by Any Other Name," *Slate*,
       May 25, 2007, http://www.slate.com/id/2166674/.

111   Olasky exposed Reed and Abramoff: Blumenthal, "Abramoff Splits the Chris-
       tian Right."

111   Minnery defended Focus: Max Blumenthal, "Focus on the Family's Minnery
       Contradicted Himself Regarding Group's Involvement with Abramoff Associate
       Reed in Casino Scheme," *Media Matters*, March 2, 2006, http://mediamatters
       .org/items/200603020007.

111   *"added fuel to the fire"*: James Dobson, "Dr. Dobson's Response to the DefCon
       Attack," CitizenLink.org, April 5, 2006, http://www.citizenlink.org/focusaction/
       fofafeatures/A000006832.cfm.

111   *ordered its members to cancel their subscriptions:* "Set Straight," Mailbag, *World
       magazine*, May 27, 2006.

111   Defcon ads: http://www.afa.net/pdfs/defcon_religiousright.pdf.

112   *firing off a mass e-mail:* Leftwing group uses lies to slander Dr. James Dobson,
       http://www.soulforce.org/forums/archive/index.php/t-322.html. Also see
       "Show your support to Dr. Dobson by signing this letter of appreciation: Text
       of letter to Dr. Dobson," https://secure.afa.net/afa/afapetition/signpetition
       .asp?id=1530.

112   *"the symbiotic [sadomasochistic] drives"*: Fromm, *Escape from Freedom*, p. 174.

CHAPTER 13: TALK TO HER

114   Schindlers and Randall Terry: Barbara Miner, "Randall Terry Resurfaces," *In
       These Times*, November 24, 2003, http://www.inthesetimes.com/article/369/
       randall_terry_resurfaces/.

114   *"modern-day crucifixion"*: Phil Long, "Parents Appeal Ruling Refusing to
       Reinsert Schiavo's Feeding Tube," Knight Ridder, March 22, 2005, http://
       www.mcclatchydc.com/190/story/11313.html.

114   *"more than just Terri Schiavo"*: Karen Tumulty, "Tom DeLay: 'It Is More Than
       Just Terri Schiavo,'" *Time*, March 23, 2005, http://www.time.com/time/nation/
       article/0,8599,1040968,00.html.

115   *Soros and the "do-gooder organizations"*: Ibid.

115   *"the pro-life base will be excited"*: Mike Allen, "Counsel to GOP Senator Wrote
       Memo on Schiavo," *Washington Post*, April 7, 2005, http://www.washington
       post.com/wp-dyn/articles/A32554–2005Apr6.html.

115   *President Bush rushed back:* "House Passes Schiavo Bill," CNN.com, March 21,
       2005, http://www.cnn.com/2005/LAW/03/20/schiavo/index.html.

115 *nullified by Judge Greer's final ruling:* Abby Goodnough and Maria Newman, "Schiavo's Feeding Tube Removed at Judge's Order," *New York Times*, March 18, 2005, http://www.nytimes.com/2005/03/18/national/18cnd-schiavo.html ?pagewanted=all&position=.

115 Charlie Ray DeLay's death: Walter F. Roche Jr., and Sam Howe Verhovek, "De-Lay's Own Tragic Crossroads," *Los Angeles Times*, March 27, 2005, http:// articles.latimes.com/2005/mar/27/nation/na-delay27.

116 Delay's frivolous lawsuit: Sheryl Gay Stolberg, "Years Ago, DeLay's Father Was Taken Off Life Support," *New York Times*, March 28, 2005, http://www .nytimes.com/2005/03/28/politics/28delay.html.

116 *Congress's public approval rating:* Bootie Cosgrove-Mather, "Poll: Keep Feeding Tube Out," CBS News, March 23, 2005, http://www.cbsnews.com/stories/ 2005/03/23/opinion/polls/main682674.shtml.

116 *a March 23 CBS News poll:* Joel Roberts, "Political Fallout over Schiavo," CBSNews.com, March 23, 2005, http://www.cbsnews.com/stories/2005/03/ 23/politics/main682619.shtml.

117 *"pure, blatant pandering to James Dobson":* Dick Armey, Ryan Sager interview, "Dick Armey on the Direction of the GOP," Sager's blog, September 15, 2006, http://www.ryansager.com/blog/index.php/2006/09/15/qa-with-dick-armey/.

117 *the Constitution Restoration Act:* James Pfander, "Federal Supremacy, State Court Inferiority, and the Constitutionality of Jurisdiction-Stripping Legislation," *Northwestern University Law Review*, 101, 1 (2007): 191–238, http:// www.law.uchicago.edu/files/pfander.pdf.

117 *"The judges need to be intimidated":* Bob Herbert, "In America, a Plan to Intimidate Judges," *New York Times*, December 4, 2000, http://query.nytimes .com/gst/fullpage.html?res=9902E2DD173CF937A35751C1A9669C8B63& sec=&spon=&pagewanted=all.

118 the "Judicial War on Faith" conference: Max Blumenthal, "In Contempt of Courts," *The Nation*, April 11, 2005, http://www.thenation.com/doc/2005 0425/blumenthal.

118 *In Defense of Mixing Church and State:* Rick Scarborough, *In Defense of Mixing Church and State* (Lufkin, TX: Vision America, 1999).

118 *How to Dethrone the Imperial Judiciary:* Edwin Viera: *How to Dethrone the Imperial Judiciary* (San Antonio, TX: Vision Forum Ministries/The Conservative Caucus, 2004).

118 *"Death solves all problems":* Stalin quoted by Robert Conquest, *Stalin Breaker of Nations* (New York: Viking, 1991).

119 *abortion doctors should be executed:* Ron Jenkins, "Coburn Different Kind of Political Cat," Associated Press, July 10, 2004. Coburn posted Jenkins's article featuring his remarkable quote on his own 2004 campaign website. The website and article can still be viewed at http://www.coburnforsenate.com/press21.shtml.

119 *"I want to impale them!":* Blumenthal, "In Contempt of Courts."

119 *"some form of strangulation":* Ibid.

120 *"malignant aggression":* Erich Fromm, *The Anatomy of Human Destructiveness* (New York: Henry Holt, 1973), pp. 366–369.

121 Fromm and Maccoby study: Ibid., p. 380.

121 *"They are the haters"*: Ibid., p. 409

122 Dannemeyer's list: The Clinton Body Count, Snopes.com, http://www.snopes .com/politics/clintons/bodycount.asp.

122 *"This isn't Colombia"*: William Levesque, "Quiet Judge Persists in Schiavo Maelstrom," *St. Petersburg Times,* March 6, 2005, http://www.sptimes.com/ 2005/03/06/Tampabay/Quiet_judge_persists_.shtml.

122 *Houston Chronicle* poll: Associated Press, "'Houston Chronicle' poll: Support for DeLay Falling in His District," April 4, 2005, http://www.editorand publisher.com/eandp/news/article_display.jsp?vnu_content_id=1000865613.

122 *"salute" to DeLay*: Mark Leibovich, "A Heaping Helping of Devotion," *Washington Post,* May 13, 2005, http://www.washingtonpost.com/wp-dyn/content/ article/2005/05/13/AR2005051300045.html.

123 *DeLay set the tone*: Juliet Eilperin and Mark Leibovich, "In Texas, The Hammer Runs into an Anvil," *Washington Post,* October 6, 2005, http://www.washington post.com/wp-dyn/content/article/2005/10/01/AR2005100101471.html.

123 Dobson's statement: "Dobson Speaks Up for DeLay; Focus Action Chairman Praises Majority Leader's 'Reason and Clarity,'" U.S. Newswire, September 28, 2005, http://www.encyclopedia.com/doc/1P2–13205353.html.

123 *"I hope the Rapture comes tomorrow"*: Max Blumenthal, *Rapture Ready, Christians United for Israel Tour,* Washington, DC, July 16, 2007, posted on YouTube July 26, 2007, http://www.youtube.com/watch?v=mjMRgT5o-Ig.

123 *"Enabling thereby helps the addict remain in denial"*: Robert Minor, *When Religion Is an Addiction*, p. 40

CHAPTER 14: THE BAD COP

125 his personal qualities as critical assets: "The most influential US conservatives: 81–100," *London Daily Telegraph,* April 24, 2008, telegraph.co.uk/news/main .jhtml?xml=/news/exclusions/uselection/nosplit/ uscons.xml.

125 *To Jenkins, Perkins was like a son:* Max Blumenthal, "Justice Sunday Preachers," *The Nation,* April 26, 2005, http://www.thenation.com/doc/20050509/ blumenthal.

126 *"Ronald Reagan, both George Bushes"*: Craig Unger, *The Fall of the House of Bush* (New York: Scribner, 2007), p. 171.

126 *Davis's name exploded into national headlines:* Mark Gribben, "Murder at Mockingbird Lane," Tru TV Crime Library, http://www.trutv.com/library/ crime/notorious_murders/not_guilty/t_cullen_davis/index.html.

126 *Born to a rape victim:* Robison biography, http://www.jamesrobison.org/. Also see Robison, Scott Ross interview, "James and Betty Robison: Life Today . . . and Yesterday," Christian Broadcasting Network, August 2, 2004, http:// www.cbn.com/700club/guests/interviews/JamesBetty_Robison_080204.aspx.

126 Robison on Christians "coming out of the closet": "God's People" speech, posted to YouTube March 27, 2007, http://www.youtube.com/watch?v=AV n3SEHYU2o.

126   *Robison submitted to an exorcism:* Edmond Cohen, "The Religiosity of George W. Bush," *Free Inquiry,* 24, 4 (2004).

127   *Evangelical minister from Arkansas named Mike Huckabee:* Michael Kranish, "Huckabee's Views on Gays Under Greater Scrutiny," *Boston Globe,* December 12, 2007, http://www.boston.com/news/nation/articles/2007/12/12/huckabees _views_on_gays_under_greater_scrutiny/?page=2.

127   *Davis's sins:* David Gates with Nikki Finke Greenberg, "Mockingbird Lane's Born-Again Baron," *Newsweek,* October 17, 1983.

127   *Woody Jenkins made a bold prediction:* Max Blumenthal, "Justice Sunday Preachers."

127   Bush's pledge to CNP: Marc Ambinder, "Inside the Council for National Policy," ABC News, May 2, 2007, http://abcnews.go.com/Politics/story?id=121170.

128   Tony Perkins's *Washington Post* op-ed: "It's About Religious Belief," *Washington Post,* May 14, 2005. http://www.washingtonpost.com/wp-dyn/content/article/2005/05/13/AR2005051301389.html.

128   Perkins and the "Summer of Purpose": Max Blumenthal, "Good Cop, Bad Cop," *The Nation,* May 23, 2005, http://www.thenation.com/doc/20050606/blumenthal.

130   *Jenkins's quixotic 1996 campaign for the U.S. Senate:* Max Blumenthal, "Justice Sunday Preachers."

131   CofCC "Statement of Principles": Sam Francis, adopted 2005, http://cofcc .org/?page_id=71.

131   Lott and the CofCC: Anthony York, "A Whole Lott of Trouble," *Salon,* December 12, 2002, http://dir.salon.com/story/politics/feature/2002/12/12/lott/index.html.

131   Barbour and the CofCC: Max Blumenthal, "Beyond Macaca: The Photograph That Haunts George Allen," *The Nation,* Aug 29, 2006, http://www.thenation .com/doc/20060911/george_allen/1.

132   *Yet Perkins remained unable to explain:* Max Blumenthal's blog, June 05, 2005, http://maxblumenthal.com/2005_06_01_maxblumenthal_archive.html.

133   Christian right concerns about Bauer's alleged behavior: "Eavesdropping: An Open Door Policy," *Christianity Today,* November 1, 1999. http://www.ct library.com/ct/1999/novemberweb-only/41.0a.html.

133   Bauer and the FRC: Tony Carnes, "Gary Bauer Can't Go Home Again," *Christianity Today,* February 1, 2000, http://www.christianitytoday.com/ct/2000/februaryweb-only/21.0.html.

133   *Dobson . . . was livid:* Thomas Edsall and Hanna Rosin: "Bauer Says He Did Not Have Affair," *Washington Post,* September 30, 1999, http://www.washington post.com/wp-srv/WPcap/1999–09/30/012r-093099-idx.html.

133   *broke off all contact:* Buss, *Family Man,* p. 171.

134   *"America's increasing decadence":* Charles Colson and Anne Morse, "The Moral Home Front," *Christianity Today,* October 1, 2004, http://www.christianity today.com/ct/2004/october/18.152.html.

134   *St. Augustine's Just War doctrine:* "US Bishops Say Preemptive Strike on Iraq Not Justified," January 29, 2003, www.nds.edu/NDS%20Documents/U.S.% 20bishops%20say.pdf.

134 Stanley attacks anti-war movement: Max Blumenthal, "Onward Christian Soldiers," *Salon,* April 15, 2003, http://dir.salon.com/story/news/feature/2003/04/15/in_touch/index.html.

135 *Christian-right leaders shrank into the shadows:* Wolf Blitzer, "The Republican National Convention," CNN.com, Aug 30, 2004, http://edition.cnn.com/2004/US/08/30/rnc/index.html.

135 *"Lining up with Hitler":* Sheri Dew, adapted from a February 28, 2004 address, "Defenders of the Faith," which appeared in *Meridian* magazine, March 10, 2004, posted to FreeRepublic.com, http://www.freerepublic.com/focus/f-religion/1095244/posts.

136 *The destiny of the nation:* David Kirkpatrick, "Club of the Most Powerful Gathers in Strictest Privacy," *New York Times,* August 28, 2004, http://query.nytimes.com/gst/fullpage.html?res=9C0CE3DA1E3EF93BA1575BC0A9629C8B63.

136 *Donation was made two years after Perkins's campaign:* Max Blumenthal, "Justice Sunday Preachers."

136 Bush's filibuster strategy: "Bush to Resubmit Blocked Judicial Nominees," CNN.com, December 24, 2004, http://www.cnn.com/2004/ALLPOLITICS/12/23/bush.judiciary/index.html.

136 Perkins recruited Frist to rally: "Frist speaks to Christian anti-filibuster rally," CNN.com, April 25, 2005, http://www.cnn.com/2005/POLITICS/04/24/justice.sunday/index.html.

136 *"Liberal racism":* "Perkins Accused Opponents of Bush's Judicial Picks of Anti-Christian bigotry," April 22, 2005, http://mediamatters.org/items/200504220005.

CHAPTER 15: BOLDLY AFFIRMING UNCLE TOM

137 California bar opposed Rogers-Brown: "Perkins Accused Opponents of Bush's Judicial Picks of Anti-Christian bigotry," *Media Matters,* April 22, 2005, http://mediamatters.org/items/200504220005.

138 *"It is the opiate"* Janice Rogers-Brown, "Fifty Ways to Lose Your Freedom" speech, Institute for Justice, August 12, 2000, *The Best of Janice Rogers-Brown,* NeoPerspectives.com, http://www.neoperspectives.com/janicerogersbrown.htm.

138 *"the liberal plantation":* Judicial Race," *Mother Jones,* October 24, 2003, http://www.motherjones.com/politics/2003/10/judicial-race.

138 *"too qualified—and black":* "Brown Gets Borked," *Wall Street Journal,* October 30, 2003, http://www.opinionjournal.com/editorial/feature.html?id=110004235.

138 *"race-traitor, Uncle Tom sellout":* Sean Rushton, "Inaccurate Radio," NPR.org, October 30, 2003, http://www.nationalreview.com/comment/rushton200310300857.asp.

138 Allen on "the queers": Siobhan Roth, "Lost in the Mix: Who Is Claude Allen?" *Legal Times,* November 5, 2003, http://www.law.com/jsp/article.jsp?id=1067350986917.

138   Allen and Clarence Thomas: Michael A. Fletcher and Joshua Partlow, "Arrest
       of Ex-Bush Aide Shocks Associates," *Washington Post,* March 12, 2006.

139   *ordered the removal of information about condoms:* "Dems Slam HHS for Se-
       lective Information-Sharing," Associated Press, October 22, 2002, http://www
       .foxnews.com/story/0,2933,66359,00.html. Also see Doug Ireland, "Bush's
       War on the Condom," *L.A. Weekly,* December 12, 2002, http://www.laweekly
       .com/2002–12–12/news/bush-s-war-on-the-condom/1; and Doug Ireland,
       "Condom Wars," *L.A. Weekly,* June 24, 2004, http://www.laweekly.com/2004
       -06-24/news/condom-wars/1; and Henry Waxman, Representative, Los An-
       geles, to Claude Allen, domestic policy advisor, Washington DC, October 12,
       2005, oversight.house.gov/documents/20051012160222–41619.pd.

139   *"I love you and appreciate you":* Focus on the Family "stem cell" interview, August
       4, 2005, posted on *Media Matters,* "White House Adviser Allen Appeared on
       Dobson Show, Failed to Repudiate Stem Cell/Nazi Comparison While Joining
       in Frist Attack," August 4, 2005, http://mediamatters.org/items/200508050001.

139   *he nominated Charles Pickering Sr:* Sean Wilentz, "The Racist Skeletons in
       Charles Pickering's Closet," *Salon,* May 12, 2003, http://dir.salon.com/story/
       news/feature/2003/05/12/pickering/index.html.

139   *Pickering's son, Charles Jr., dispatched campaign staffers:* The *Citizens Informer,*
       33, 3 (May-June 2002) notes that Pickering Jr. and Ronnie Snow sent repre-
       sentatives to a July 25 CofCC meeting at Bo-Don's seafood restaurant in Jack-
       son, Mississippi. See Edward Sebesta, http://newtknight.blogspot.com/
       2008/01/chip-pickering-and-council-of.html.

139   *"a radical minority in the U.S. Senate":* "Perkins Accused Opponents of Bush's
       Judicial Picks of Anti-Christian Bigotry," *Media Matters,* April 22, 2005,
       http://mediamatters.org/items/200504220005.

140   *A flier for Justice Sunday:* Jill Lawrenson, "Dems' Filibusters Cast as Attack on
       'People of Faith,'" *USA Today,* April 17, 2005, http://www.usatoday.com/
       news/washington/2005–04–17-filibuster_x.htm.

140   On Justice Sunday: Max Blumenthal, "Justice Sunday Preachers."

141   *he grew despondent:* Focus on the Family radio, May 25, 2005, Colorado
       Springs, Colorado.

143   *"the most brilliant man":* David Frum, "Justice Miers?" *National Review,* Sep-
       tember 29, 2005, http://frum.nationalreview.com/post/?q=MjliZWZlOWJh
       NjQ0ZjA0MmQyYThiMTBlNjhjYmE3ZTg=.

143   *"Miers is more a leap of faith":* Gilgoff, *The Jesus Machine,* p. 273.

143   *Dobson hyped her to his radio audience:* David Kirkpatrick, "Endorsement of
       Nominee Draws Committee's Interest," *New York Times,* October 10, 2005,
       http://www.nytimes.com/2005/10/10/politics/politicsspecial1/10confirm
       .html?_r=1.

144   *"increasingly concerned about her conservative credentials":* "Harriet Miers
       calls it quits," *WorldNetDaily,* October 27, 2005, http://www.worldnetdaily
       .com/news/article.asp?ARTICLE_ID=47080.

144   *"relied on the word of Karl Rove":* Gilgoff, p. 273.

144 Alito and CAP: Eyal Press, "Alito's CAP Connection," *The Nation,* November 22, 2005, http://www.thenation.com/doc/20051212/press.

145 *a subpoena for Concerned Alumni's records:* Transcript of the Senate Judiciary Committee Hearing of Alito's nomination, *Washington Post,* January 11, 2006, http://www.washingtonpost.com/wp-dyn/content/article/2006/01/11/AR2006011101335.html.

145 Congressional Black Caucus statement: *Norton Explains Strong Opposition to Alito,* Norton.House.gov, December 8, 2005, http://www.norton.house.gov/index.php?option=com_content&task=view&id=58&Itemid=79.

145 *masterminded by a white Republican operative:* Joshua Holland, "Blackwashing," *AlterNet,* July 26, 2004, http://www.alternet.org/story/19331/.

145 Project 21 press release: David Almasi, *Black Activists Criticize Congressional Black Caucus Rush to Judgment on Alito Nomination and CBC's Call for Filibuster,* National Leadership Network of Conservative African-Americans, December 9, 2005, http://www.nationalcenter.org/P21PRCBCAlitoFilibuster1205.html.

146 *"no factual or logical bases":* Peter Kirsanow, "Alito Accuracy," *National Review,* January 6, 2006, http://www.nationalreview.com/comment/kirsanow200601060712.asp.

146 *"Kirsanow had shocked an audience of Arab Americans":* Max Blumenthal, "Alito's Pro-Internment Witness: 'You Can Forget About Civil Rights,'" *Huffington Post,* January 12, 2006, http://www.huffingtonpost.com/max-blumenthal/alitos-prointernment-wi_b_13670.html.

146 *"Colson, who once burned a cross":* Jonathan Aitken, Stan Guthrie interview, "From Disgrace to Sage," *Christianity Today,* August 8, 2005, https://www.christianitytoday.com/ct/2005/augustweb-only/132–22.0.html?start=1. Also see Max Blumenthal, "Born Again, Again," *Washington Monthly,* July/August 2005, http://www.washingtonmonthly.com/features/2005/0507.blumenthal.html.

146 Colson on MLK: "Colson Misrepresented Martin Luther King Jr. As 'a Great Conservative' Who Would Have Supported Alito Nomination," *Media Matters,* January 18, 2006, http://mediamatters.org/items/200601180011.

146 *"We need to boldly affirm Uncle Tom":* Wellington Boone, *Breaking Through* (Nashville, TN: Broadman & Holman [Bible] Publishers, 1996). Also see Max Blumenthal, "Who Are Justice Sunday's Ministers of Minstrelsy?" *Huffington Post,* January 6, 2006, http://www.huffingtonpost.com/max-blumenthal/who-are-justice-sundays-_b_13348.html.

147 *"we're making funeral arrangements":* Michelle Goldberg, "We Shall Overcome . . . Liberals," *Salon,* January 9, 2006, http://www.salon.com/news/feature/2006/01/09/justice_sunday/.

147 Lusk's faith-based federal grants: Laurie Goodstein, "Minister, a Bush Ally, Gives Church as Site for Alito Rally," *New York Times,* January 5, 2006, http://www.nytimes.com/2006/01/05/politics/politicsspecial1/05church.html.

147 *yet another historical revisionist:* William Martin, *With God on Our Side,* p. 57.

147 *Her appearance at Justice Sunday III:* Michelle Goldberg, "We Shall Overcome . . . Liberals."

147   *A. D. King drowned*: Ester Kaplan, "Justice Sunday, All Dressed Up," Talk to Action, January 2, 2006, http://www.talk2action.org/story/2006/1/2/181050/5012.

148   *A self-described post-abortive mother: Alveda's Testimony*, Silent No More, undated, http://www.silentnomoreawareness.org/testimonies/alveda-king.html.

148   Alveda King's speech: Kyle-Anne Shiver, "What Would MLK Do?" *National Review*, August 22, 2008, http://article.nationalreview.com/print/?q=ZmNm Nzg2M2QzMzkzJQ2OTY2ZWI4ZjMyNTJjNWJhZWI=.

149   *Alito personally thanked Dobson*: Max Blumenthal, "Alito Sends James Dobson a Valentine," *Huffington Post*, March 1, 2006, http://www.huffingtonpost .com/max-blumenthal/alito-sends-james-dobson-_b_16596.html.

149   *Thomas remarked bluntly in his majority opinion*: Bill Mears, "Divided Court Rejects School Diversity Plans," CNN, June 28, 2007, http://www.cnn.com/2007/LAW/06/28/scotus.race/index.html?eref=rss_topstories.

149   Justice Steven Breyer's dissent: Linda Greenhouse, "Justices Limit the Use of Race in School Plans for Integration," *New York Times*, June 29, 2007, http://www.nytimes.com/2007/06/29/washington/29scotus.html?ref=todays paper&pagewanted=all.

150   *Allen liked to go shopping*: Mike Allen, "Former Bush Adviser Arrested in 'Theft Scheme,'" *Time*, March 11, 2006, http://www.time.com/time/nation/article/0,8599,1172159,00.html.

150   *the president's sensitive side*: William Douglas, "10th Anniversary of March Marked," Knight Ridder, October 16, 2005, http://www.signonsandiego.com/uniontrib/20051016/news_1n16rights.html.

151   *Allen wept to the judge*: "Ex-adviser to Bush Gets 2 Years Probation, Fine," Associated Press, August 4, 2006, http://www.msnbc.msn.com/id/14189452.

151   *"The masochistic 'solution'"*: Fromm, *Escape from Freedom*, p. 152.

CHAPTER 16: FEEDING BABY MONSTERS

153   *we have aborted more than a million people*: Max Blumenthal, *Theocracy Now!*

154   *"women whose husbands were hooked on pornography"*: Buss, *Family Man*, p. 256.

155   *Let's Talk!*: Danae Dobson, *Let's Talk! Good Stuff for Girlfriends About God, Guys, and Growing Up* (Carol Stream, IL: Tyndale House, 2003).

155   *"ski on one day and drink the next"*: Danae Dobson, "God Is Cool!" Spiritual Health, *Brio*, 2004, excerpt from *Let's Talk!*, 2003, http://www.briomag.com/briomagazine/spiritualhealth/a0005186.html.

155   Danae Dobson's letter and Thomas's column: "Danae Dobson Letter About Mel Gibson Movie 'The Passion,'" http://www.real-world-solutions.org/calvin/html/danae.htm.

155   *"or passing his muster"*: Buss, *Family Man*, p. 257.

155   *"she wants to go on with her life"*: Ibid.

156   *"their system of double standards"*: Paola Bacchetta and Margaret Power, *Right-Wing Women: From Conservatives to Extremists Around the World* (New York: Routledge, 2002), Introduction.

157   *"Purity balls":* Neela Banerjee, "Dancing the Night Away, with a Higher Purpose," *New York Times*, May 19, 2008, http://www.nytimes.com/2008/05/19/us/19purity.html.

157   *The fathers rise and read a pledge:* Randy Wilson and family, New Horizon Foundation, Colorado Springs, Colorado, http://www.generationsoflight.com/html/ThePledge.html.

157   *highest rates of sexually transmitted diseases:* Peter Bearman and Hannah Brückner, "After the Promise: The STD Consequences of Adolescent Virginity Pledges," *Journal of Adolescent Health*, 36 (2005): 271–278, www.yale.edu/ciqle/PUBLICATIONS/AfterThePromise.pdf.

157   *the rate of gonorrhea has risen:* Ceci Connolly, "Texas Teaches Abstinence, with Mixed Grades," *Washington Post*, January 21, 2003, http://www.washingtonpost.com/ac2/wp-dyn/A19148–2003Jan20?language=printer.

157   *lose their virginity on average at age sixteen:* Margaret Talbot, "Red Sex, Blue Sex," *The New Yorker*, November 3, 2008, http://www.newyorker.com/reporting/2008/11/03/081103fa_fact_talbot?currentPage=all.

158   *"Once you begin feeding baby monsters":* Shannon Ethridge and Stephen Arterburn, *Every Young Woman's Battle* (Colorado Springs, CO: WaterBrook Press, 2004), p. 46.

158   *Leslee Unruh, a leading female culture warrier:* Myra Batchelder, "Who Is Leslee Unruh?" *Planned Parenthood*, May 10, 2006, http://www.plannedparenthood.org/issues-action/sex-education/leslee-unruh-6248.htm.

158   *"You carry an empty crib":* Unruh to Maria Hinojosa, PBS, "No Right to Choose?" April 14, 2006, http://www.pbs.org/now/transcript/transcriptNOW215_full.html.

158   *"allegations about improper adoptions":* Cristina Page, *How the Pro-Choice Movement Saved America* (Jackson, TN: Basic Books, 2006), p. 74.

159   *a bill she authored banning abortion:* "South Dakota Bans Most Abortions," CNN.com, March 06, 2006, http://www.cnn.com/2006/POLITICS/03/06/sd.abortion/index.html.

159   *a "pesticide," she called it:* Unruh to Neil Cavuto, Fox News Channel, "Your World with Neil Cavuto," posted to YouTube, May 23, 2007, http://www.youtube.com/watch?v=xOVhyXHmuS4.

159   *"This is true feminism":* Unruh to Maria Hinojosa, PBS, "No Right to Choose?" April 14, 2006, http://www.pbs.org/now/transcript/transcriptNOW215_full.html.

159   *Unruh's abortion ban was overturned:* "South Dakota Abortion Ban Rejected," *USA Today*, November 8, 2006, http://www.usatoday.com/news/politicselections/vote2006/SD/2006–11–08-abortion-ban_x.htm.

159   *Men's versus women's success:* Cristina Page, *How the Pro-Choice Movement Saved America*, p. 74.

159   *80 percent false or misleading:* "The Content of Federally Funded Abstinence-Only Education Programs," prepared for Henry Waxman, House Committee on Government Reform, December 2004, oversight.house.gov/documents/20041201102153–50247.pdf.

160   *Judith Reisman has affected my life personally:* Max Blumenthal, "Her Kinsey Obsession," *AlterNet,* December 15, 2004, http://www.alternet.org/story/20744/her_kinsey_obsession/?page=entire.

161   *Reisman recalled in a short memoir:* Judith Reisman, "A Personal Odyssey to the Truth," DrJudithReisman.com, http://www.drjudithreisman.com/about_dr_reisman.html#journey.

161   *the grant was a mistake:* Max Blumenthal, "Her Kinsey Obsession," *AlterNet,* December 15, 2004, http://www.alternet.org/story/20744/her_kinsey_obsession/?page=entire. Also from interview with Al Regnery, CPAC 2009, Washington DC, February 12, 2009.

162   *Regnery retreated into his conservative publishing empire:* Murray Waas, "Al Regnery's Secret Life," *The New Republic,* June 23, 1986, http://www.tnr.com/politics/story.html?id=5d5ed82c-aa0d-4cac-b514-efdb892649c8. Also see Nobile and Nadler, *United States,* p. 266.

163   *a proselytizing homosexual movement*: Max Blumenthal, "Her Kinsey Obsession."

164   Stockman and militias: Nina Burleigh, Hilary Hylton, and Richard Woodbury, "The Movement's Sympathetic Ears on Capitol Hill," *Time,* May 8, 1995, http://www.time.com/time/magazine/article/0,9171,982917,00.html.

164   *Stockman, a former drifter:* "Wacko, Texas," *Mother Jones,* September/October 1996, http://www.motherjones.com/politics/1996/09/wacko-texas.

164   *H.R. 2749:* Judith Reisman, sponsored by Steve Stockman, "Child Protection and Ethics I Education Act of 1995," introduced July 12, 2009, posted to Library of Congress website, http://rs9.loc.gov/cgi-bin/bdquery/z?d104:HR02749:@@@L&summ2=m&.

164   *over seven hundred obscenity cases:* Taylor, *Frontline* interview transcript, PBS.org, June 2001, http://www.pbs.org/wgbh/pages/frontline/shows/porn/interviews/taylor.html.

164   *serial killer Joseph Paul Franklin:* Donald Altschiller, "Hate Crimes," ABC-CLIO, p. 69.

164   *jailing pornographers such as Paul Little:* Ben Montgomery, "Pornographer Sentenced to Nearly 4 Years in Prison," *St. Petersburg Times,* October 4, 2008, www.tampabay.com/news/courts/criminal/article838305.ece.

164   *"We should probably call her Detective Reisman":* Bruce Taylor, "Comments on Dr. Reisman and Her Work," DrJudithReisman.com, April 2000, http://www.drjudithreisman.com/about_dr_reisman.html.

164   *Reisman testified*: Max Blumenthal, "Her Kinsey Obsession."

165   *Camp American*: Ibid.

165   Larry Pratt and militias: Southern Poverty Law Center, "False Patriots," *Intelligence Report* (Summer 2001): 9, http://www.splcenter.org/intel/intelreport/article.jsp?pid=365. Also see original source: Larry Pratt, *Armed People Victorious* (Springfield, VA: Gun Owners Foundation, 1990).

165   Camp American statement of purpose: http://www.campamerica.org/.

165   *"Pornography is training all your sex educators":* Max Blumenthal, "Her Kinsey Obsession."

165 *Goeglein resigned his White House post:* Sheryl Gay Stolberg, "Bush Aide Resigns After Admitting Plagiarism," *New York Times*, March 1, 2008, http://www.nytimes.com/2008/03/01/us/01aide.html?em&ex=1204520400&en=43c14d789352578f&ei=5087.

166 Unruh and allies form lobbying front: Kevin Freking, "Abstinence Groups Try to Maintain Funds," Associated Press, April 10, 2007, http://www.usatoday.com/news/washington/2007–04–10-abstinence-funding_N.htm.

166 *easier for states to opt out:* "States Opt Out of Millions in Federal Abstinence Education Grants," FoxNews.com, June 24, 2008, http://www.foxnews.com/politics/2008/06/24/states-opt-millions-federal-abstinence-education-grants/.

166 Vitter finally exposed: "New Orleans Madam Says Sen. David Vitter Used Her Brothel," Associated Press, July 11, 2007, http://www.foxnews.com/story/0,2933,288868,00.html.

CHAPTER 17: HUMAN TOOLS

167 2004 marriage bans: Sarah Kershaw, "Gay Marriage Bans Gain Wide Support in 10 States," *New York Times*, November 3, 2004, http://www.nytimes.com/2004/11/03/politics/campaign/03gay.html?scp=3&sq=same-sex%20marriage%202004%20election&st=cse.

167 *"marriage between a man and his donkey":* "Dobson: Same-sex marriage would lead to 'marriage between daddies and little girls . . . between a man and his donkey'," *Media Matters*, October 7, 2005, http://mediamatters.org/items/200510070004.

167 No homosexual teachers or single female teachers: DeMint, Tim Russert interview, *Meet the Press*, NBC, October 17, 2004, http://www.msnbc.msn.com/id/6267835/.

167 *another gay-baiting Senate hopeful:* Robert Schlesinger, "Medicine Man," Salon, September 13, 2004, http://dir.salon.com/story/news/feature/2004/09/13/coburn/index.html.

167 *his declaration that "abortionists" should be executed:* Jenkins, "Coburn Different Kind of Political Cat."

167 *a "servant leader" for Jesus:* Maureen Dowd, "The Red Zone," *New York Times*, November 4, 2004, http://query.nytimes.com/gst/fullpage.html?res=9E02EFD9173CF937A35752C1A9629C8B63.

168 Vitter's gubernatorial withdrawal: Glenn Greenwald, "Sen. David Vitter, a Leading Christian Social Conservative," *Salon*, July 10, 2007, http://www.salon.com/opinion/greenwald/2007/07/10/vitter/.

168 *"There are no skeletons in my closet":* http://righthandthief.blogspot.com/2007/07/senator-vitter-lied-to-christian.html.

168 Barna survey: Christine Wicker, "Survey Inspires Debate over Why Faith Isn't a Bigger Factor in Marriage," *Dallas Morning News*, undated, http://www.adherents.com/largecom/baptist_divorce.html.

169   Louisiana marriage law: Kevin Sack, "Louisiana Approves Measure to Tighten Marriage Bonds, *New York Times*, June 24, 1007, http://query.nytimes.com/ gst/fullpage.html?res=9800E2DF1631F937A15755C0A961958260&n=Top/ Reference/Times%20Topics/Subjects/L/Law%20and%20Legislation. Also see Tony Perkins and Elizabeth Farnsworth *The NewsHour* interview, "Bound by Love?" PBS.org, August 20, 1997, http://www.pbs.org/newshour/bb/law/ july-dec97/marriage_8–20.html.

169   *converted their own marriage to covenant status:* Michelle Goldberg, "A Dispatch from the Culture War," *Salon,* February 15, 2005, http://dir.salon .com/story/news/feature/2005/02/15/covenant/index.html.

169   Ryan Dobson's website: http://www.korministries.com.

169   *his ghostwritten book:* Ryan Dobson: *Be Intolerant: Because Some Things Are Just Stupid* (Colorado Springs, CO: WaterBrook Press/Multnomah, 2003).

170   Ryan Dobson on Terri Schiavo: "The Plight of Terri Schiavo," Kor podcast, March 28, 2005, http://www.korministries.com/podcast.html.

170   *the "Be There" talk:* Buss, *Family Man,* pp. 23, 186.

170   Ryan struggled in school: Ibid., p. 258.

171   *"I just didn't care if I got another one":* Ibid., p. 259.

171   *Ryan divorced Cezanne:* Dobson v. Dobson, #00D010621, Superior Court of the State of Orange County, September 11, 2001. Also see Stipulated Judgment on Reserved Issues in re marriage of James Ryan Dobson and Cezanne Dobson, Superior Court of the State of California for the County of Orange, October 2, 2001.

171   *he was ordered to pay Cezanne $80,000:* Buss, *Family Man,* p. 324.

171   *"a disaster for the family":* James Dobson, "Handling Stress Is All About Attitude," Focus on the Family, August 5, 2001, http://www.uexpress.com/focusonthefamily/?uc_full_date=20010805.

171   *Dobson fired his radio sidekick, Mike Trout:* "Focus on the Family Official Resigned Over Affair," Associated Press, October 17, 2000, http://www.belief net.com/Faiths/Christianity/Protestant/Evangelical/Focus-On-The-Family -Official-Resigned-Over-Affair.aspx.

172   *a newfound sense of direction*: Buss, *Family Man,* p. 259.

172   *"our enemy is deadly":* Ryan Dobson, *2Die4: The Dangerous Truth About Following Christ* (Colorado Springs, CO: WaterBrook Press/Multnomah, 2004).

172   *"pay a price in four years":* David Kirkpatrick, "Some Bush Supporters Say They Anticipate a 'Revolution,'" *New York Times,* November 4, 2004, http:// www.nytimes.com/2004/11/04/politics/campaign/04conserve.html?page wanted=all&position.

172   Dobsons at National Religious Broadcasters convention: Max Blumenthal, "Air Jesus: With the Evangelical Air Force," *Media Matters,* February 27, 2005, http://www.mediatransparency.org/storyprinterfriendly.php?storyID=16.

174   *"as advertised as a husband and father":* Buss, *Family Man,* p. 251.

174   *"St. Jim Dobson":* Albert Tremaine, personal e-mail, March 17, 2006, http:// maxblumenthal.com/2006_03_01_maxblumenthal_archive.html.

174 *"a giant influx in gay marriage":* Ryan Dobson interview, Pulling Weeds out of Potholes blog, June 21, 2004, http://regansravings.blogspot.com/2004/06/interview-with-ryan-dobson.html.

175 *Vitter's culture war rant*: Vitter Statement on Protecting the Sanctity of Marriage, Vitter2004.com, undated, http://www.vitter2004.com/News/Read.aspx?ID=20.

175 *New Orleans newspapers reported allegations:* Cain Burdeau, "Vitter Latest of Louisiana's Bad Boys," Associated Press, July 10, 2007, http://www.usatoday.com/news/washington/2007-07-10-1608672327_x.htm.

175 *the city's notorious Canal Street:* Chuck Hustmyre, "The Story of a Canal Street Brothel," TruTV, undated, http://www.trutv.com/library/crime/gangsters_outlaws/cops_others/fbi_brothel/4.html.

175 *a call from David Bellinger:* David Vitter, "Ringside," July 25, 2002, aired on MSNBC, September 11, 2007, http://www.youtube.com/watch?v=fxlqiDn2zM8.

176 *pledged total loyalty to his host:* Bill Walsh, "Vitter Earmarks Funds for Religious Groups," *New Orleans Times-Picayune*, September 3, 2007, http://www.nola.com/timespic/stories/index.ssf?/base/news-9/1190529501310280.xml&coll=1.

176 *a bill to ban gay marriage:* "Senate Set to Reject Gay Marriage Ban," CNN.com, June 06, 2006, http://www.cnn.com/2006/POLITICS/06/06/same.sex.marriage/index.html.

177 *Tobias resigned his position:* "Senior Official Linked to Escort Service Resigns," ABC News, April 27, 2007, http://blogs.abcnews.com/theblotter/2007/04/senior_official.html.

177 *an anti-prostitution "loyalty oath":* Nico Pitney, "Official Caught Using Escort Service Demanded Anti-Prostitution 'Loyalty Oaths,'" *Think Progress,* April 28, 2007, http://thinkprogress.org/2007/04/28/tobias-prostitution/.

177 *a call from David Vitter:* "'Hustler' Call May Have Prompted Vitter Admission," ABC News, July 10, 2007, http://blogs.abcnews.com/theblotter/2007/07/hustler-call-pr.html.

177 *Hustler's Vitter story:* Interview with Wendy Cortez, *Hustler,* January 2008.

178 *When Vitter made his grand confession:* Shailagh Murray, "Senator's Number on 'Madam' Phone List," *Washington Post,* July 10, 2007, http://www.washingtonpost.com/wp-dyn/content/article/2007/07/09/AR2007070902030.html.

178 *"this 'modern day lynching'":* "'D.C. Madam's Suicide Notes Released," CBS News, May 05, 2008, http://www.cbsnews.com/stories/2008/05/05/national/main4071471.shtml.

178 *Vitter's predecessor Bob Livingston:* Edward Walsh and Eric Pianin, "Now Livingston's Past Becomes an Issue," *Washington Post*, December 18, 1998, http://www.washingtonpost.com/wp-srv/politics/special/clinton/stories/livingston121898.htm.

179 *Perkins rushed to Vitter's defense:* Statement on Sen. David Vitter, Family Research Council, July 11, 2007, http://www.frcblog.com/2007/07/statement_on_sen_david_vitter.html.

179   *a defender in Gene Mills:* Bill Walsh, "Vitter Earmarks Funds."

179   McCormack, Duke and *Mein Kampf:* William Moore, Elizabeth Rickey, and
      Lance Hill, *The Emergence of David Duke and the Politics of Race*, ed. Douglas
      Rose (Chapel Hill: University of North Carolina Press, 1992), pp. 44–95.

179   *"I will continue to support him fervently":* Andrew Purcell, "A Right Madam,"
      Sunday Herald, undated, http://www.sundayherald.com/international/sh
      international/display.var.1546321.0.0.php.

179   *HETERPOPHOBIA!:* Mac Johnson, "Sen. Vitter Outed As Heterosexual: Het-
      erophobia Feared," *Human Events*, July 13, 2007, http://www.humanevents
      .com/article.php?id=21505&page=3&viewID=811984.

180   *federal money to the Louisiana Family Forum:* Bill Walsh, "Vitter Shifts
      $100,000 from Religious Group," *New Orleans Times-Picayune*, October 10,
      2007, http://www.nola.com/timespic/stories/index.ssf?/base/news-9/119052
      9501310280.xml&coll=1.

180   *a supposed expert, Kent E. Hovind:* Kent Hovind, "A Battle Plan Practical Steps
      to Fight Evolution," Creation Science Evangelism blog, undated, http://www
      .drdino.com/read-article.php?id=52.

180   *"the governments of the world":* Kent Hovind, "Man-Made Plagues," *Informed
      Christians,* undated. http://www.informedchristians.com/articles/ART-man
      -made-plauges.htm.

180   *Hovind was sentenced to ten years:* Michael Stewart, "Kent Hovind—Dr. Dino—
      Sentenced to 10 Years in Prison," *Pensacola News Journal*, January 19, 2007,
      http://www.religionnewsblog.com/16426/kent-and-jo-hovind-deny-having
      -income.

181   *banned federal grants to women's health centers:* Bruce Alpert, "Abortion Plan Is
      Defeated in Senate," *New Orleans Times-Picayune*, October 19, 2007, http://www
      .nola.com/timespic/stories/index.ssf?/base/news-2/1192804244133220.xml
      &coll=1.

181   *Thus they become "human tools":* Czeslaw Milosz, *The Captive Mind* (New
      York: Vintage, 1953), p. 75.

183   *the link between homophobia and repressed homosexuality:* Henry Adams,
      Lester Wright Jr., and Bethany Lohr, "Is Homophobia Associated with Homo-
      sexual Arousal?" *Journal of Abnormal Psychology*, 105, 3 (1996): 440–445.

183   *"the shriller you are":* Glenn Feldman, *Politics and Religion in the White South*,
      ed. Glen Feldman (Lexington: The University Press of Kentucky, 2005), p. 303.

184   *"like a Jew in Germany in 1934":* Marvin Liebman, *Coming Out Conservative:
      An Autobiography* (San Francisco: Chronicle Books, 1992). Also see David
      Brock, *Blinded by the Right: The Conscience of an Ex-Conservative* (New York:
      Crown Publishers, 2002), p. 162.

184   *Liebman renounced the conservative movement:* Marvin Liebman, "Indepen-
      dently Speaking," *The Advocate*, February 7, 1995, http://www.cs.cmu.edu/
      afs/cs.cmu.edu/user/scotts/bulgarians/marvin-liebman.txt.

184   *"A little bit nutty and a little bit slutty":* David Brock, "The Real Anita Hill,"
      The American Spectator, March 1992. See also David Brock, *The Real Anita
      Hill* (New York: The Free Press, 1993).

184 *"I knew I didn't belong behind that podium":* David Brock, *Blinded by the Right,* p. 162.

185 *an anonymous letter:* Ibid., p. 163.

185 *"deflect legitimate criticism that it was anti-gay":* David Brock, Ibid., p. 174.

185 *promoting "ex-gay" therapy:* Andrew Sullivan, "Going Down Screaming," *New York Times Magazine,* October 11, 1999, http://query.nytimes.com/gst/fullpage .html?res=9505E2DD163BF932A25753C1A96E958260&n=Top/Reference/ Times%20Topics/People/C/Clinton,%20Bill.

185 *Brock's final rift with the movement:* David Brock, *The Seduction of Hillary Clinton* (New York: The Free Press, 1993).

185 *"the Road Warrior of the Right":* David Brock, "Confessions of a Right-Wing Hit Man," *Esquire,* July 1997.

185 *his "spiritual and moral conversion":* Howard Kurtz, "David Brock: The Genuine Article?" *Washington Post,* March 10, 1998, http://www.washingtonpost .com/wp-srv/politics/special/clinton/stories/brock031098.htm.

185 *letters of apology:* David Brock, Open letter, *Esquire,* April 1998.

185 *vowed to "firebomb" his house:* Howard Kurtz, "Author Who Trashed Anita Hill Now Confesses to Lies," *Los Angeles Times,* July 3, 2001, http://articles .latimes.com/2001/jul/03/news/cl-18003?s=o&n=o&rd=www.google.com &sessid=90d6f54d6d8def54aa279ef208ad18141732dbe0&pg=2&pgtp= article&eagi=&page_type=article&exci=2001_07_03_news_cl-18003.

185 *doubted the sincerity of his conversion:* Kerry Lauerman, "The Apostate," *Salon,* March 8, 2002, http://dir.Salon.com/story/books/feature/2002/03/08/brock/ index.html. In reviewing *Blinded by the Right,* Lauerman warned readers to "take Brock's insinuations with a grain of salt."

186 the *Media Matters* Don Imus report: "Imus Called Women's Basketball Team 'Nappy-Headed Ho's,'" *Media Matters,* April 4, 2007, http://mediamatters .org/items/200704040011.

186 *"the most vicious element in our society":* "O'Reilly on 'Assassins Who Work for *Media Matters* and Move On,'" *Media Matters,* Sept 6, 2007, http://media matters.org/items/200709060006.

186 *"I want Media Matters deported":* "Bill O'Reilly on *Media Matters:* 'Any of the presidential candidates who can deport those swine—I'm voting for them,'" *Media Matters,* March 20, 2008, http://mediamatters.org/items/200803200008.

187 *bureau chief for Talon News:* "Lights Out for Talon News," Chris Hawke, CBS/ Associated Press, Feb 25, 2005, http://www.cbsnews.com/stories/2005/ 02/25/politics/main676503.shtml.

187 *breezed through a White House security check:* Frank Lautenberg press release, *Lautenberg Requests All Documents from White House Relating to Discredited "Journalist" James D. Guckert, A.K.A. Jeff Gannon,* February 10, 2005, http://lautenberg.senate.gov/newsroom/record.cfm?id=254468.

187 *Gannon delighted the embattled president:* "Talon News 'Reporter' Lobs Bush Another Softball; Is Talon a News Organization or an Arm of the Republican Party?" *Media Matters,* January 26, 2005, http://mediamatters.org/items/ 200501260015.

187   *"so divorced from reality"*: transcript, "President Bush's News Conference,"
       New York Times, January 26, 2005, p. 8, http://www.nytimes.com/2005/01/26/
       politics/26TEXT-BUSH.html?pagewanted=8.

187   *he had literally cut and pasted*: "Talon News 'Reporter' Lifts from GOP Docu-
       ments Verbatim for 'News Reports,'" *Media Matters*, January 27, 2005,
       http://mediamatters.org/items/200501260015.

188   *a high-priced male prostitute*: David Margolick and Richard Gooding, "Jeff
       Gannon: Wrong Man, Wrong Place," *Vanity Fair*, June 2005, http://www.van-
       ityfair.com/politics/features/2005/06/gannongate200506?currentPage=2.

188   *access to highly sensitive CIA documents*: Mike Allen and Dana Milbank,
       "Leaks Probe Is Gathering Momentum," *Washington Post*, December 26,
       2003, http://www.washingtonpost.com/ac2/wp-dyn?pagename=article&con-
       tentId=A30842–2003Dec25.

188   *an October 2003 interview with Joseph Wilson:* Jeff Gannon, "Wilson Talks
       About Niger Mission; Blasts Bush Foreign Policy," *Talon News*, October 28,
       2003, http://mensnewsdaily.com/archive/newswire/nw03/talonnews/1003/
       102803-wilson.htm.

188   Slaughter and Conyers wrote to Fitzgerald: FoxNews.com, February 24, 2005,
       http://www.foxnews.com/story/0,2933,148588,00.html.

188   *conviction of Libby for perjury:* Neil Lewis, "Libby Guilty of Lying in C.I.A.
       Leak Case," *New York Times*, March 06, 2007, http://www.nytimes.com/
       2007/03/06/washington/06cnd-libby.html?pagewanted=1.

189   *"more macho than their straights"*: Ann Coulter, "Republicans, Bloggers and
       Gays, Oh My!" Coulter's blog, February 23, 2005, http://www.anncoulter
       .com/cgi-local/printer_friendly.cgi?article=43.

189   *"the guy at the end of 'American Beauty'"*: Margolick and Gooding, "Jeff Gannon."

189   *filled his blog posts with anti-gay vitriol:* Jeff Gannon, "Gay Marriage Is a Lost
       Cause," *Washington Blade,* September 1, 2006, http://www.washblade.com/
       2006/9–1/view/columns/gannon.cfm.

190   *"There is somebody who's living my life"*: Luigi Pirandello, quoted in Gwyneth
       Cravens, "Past Present," *The Nation*, June 24, 1991.

190   *"a bit like a religious experience"*: Matt Sanchez, Randy Thomas interview,
       Randy Thomas's blog, April 9, 2007, http://www.kimtragedy.info/OT18/.

190   *a "baby-killer" and "stupid minority"*: "A Firm Stance: CU Marine Reservist Tar-
       getedin Angry Confrontation; No Disciplinary Action Taken," Columbia Daily
       Spectator, April 4, 2007.

190   *Sanchez was shuttled to the Fox News:* Matt Sanchez, Hannity and Colmes in-
       terview, posted on YouTube, January 4, 2007, http://www.youtube.com/watch
       ?v=3jy6CJvEmCs, and O'Reilly interview, posted on YouTube, Jan 04, 2007:
       http://www.youtube.com/watch?v=DFYSmjIUrY0.

190   *the anti-Americanism of Columbia's latte liberals*: Matt Sanchez, "Diversity Dou-
       ble Talk: Ivy's 'Inclusion' Excludes Military," *New York Post,* December 4, 2006,
       http://www.nypost.com/seven/12042006/postopinion/opedcolumnists/
       diversity_double_talkivys_inclusion_excludes_military_opedcolumnists_matt
       _sanchez.htm?page=0.

190   Sanchez presented with award: Max Blumenthal, *CPAC PART DEUX: Conflicted Conservatives in Crisis*, Conservative Political Action Conference, Washington, DC, YouTube, March 5, 2007, http://www.youtube.com/watch?v=nvhn43BmdWM.

191   *a light went on:* Andy Towle, "Conservatives Laud Gay Porn Star Marine," *Towleroad,* March 6, 2007, http://www.towleroad.com/2007/03/conservatives _l.html; and "Jeff Gannon Redux," Joe.My.God, March 06, 2007, http://joe mygod.blogspot.com/2007/03/jeff-gannon-redux.html.

191   *Finally Sanchez came out:* Matt Sanchez, "Porn Free," *Salon,* March 8, 2007, http://www.Salon.com/opinion/feature/2007/03/08/matt_sanchez/print .html.

191   *instantly exorcised his homosexual tendencies:* Matt Sanchez, Jack E. Jett interview, "Strife of the Party," *Radar,* March 30, 2007, http://www.radaronline .com/features/2007/03/matt_sanchez_2.php.

192   *challenged him to produce a marriage license:* See *http://cplsanchez.info/*: "None of the claims has been backed up by marriage records or statements from wives, fiancees, or girlfriends."

192   *"Gay men are like fundamentalist Muslims":* Matt Sanchez, Jack E. Jett interview.

192   *gay-bashers were delighted:* Michelle Malkin, "A Message for and from Matt Sanchez," Malkin's blog, March 8, 2007, http://michellemalkin.com/2007/ 03/08/a-message-for-and-from-matt-sanchez/.

192   *the honor of meeting Sanchez at CPAC:* Max Blumenthal, "CPAC's Gay Porn Star Honoree, Ann Coulter, and the Politics of Personal Crisis," *Huffington Post,* March 7, 2007, http://www.huffingtonpost.com/max-blumenthal/ cpacs-gay-porn-star-hono_b_42842.html.

192   *"a very cunning strategy":* Matt Sanchez, "The Press's War," *National Review,* July 5, 2007, http://article.nationalreview.com/?q=NzQ3ODUyNGZmNT AxODJkYjMxOWU2MTRlN2UxY2ZiNmU=.

192   *Sanchez's war cheerleading:* Matt Sanchez, "Which to Trust: Media or Vets?" *WorldNetDaily,* August 20, 2008, http://www.worldnetdaily.com/index.php? fa=PAGE.view&pageId=72809.

192   *an exhaustive four-part series:* Jim Rutz, "Soy Is Making Kids 'Gay,'" *WorldNet Daily,* December 12, 2006, http://www.worldnetdaily.com/news/article.asp ?ARTICLE_ID=53327.

193   *likening them to pedophiles:* Matt Sanchez, Randy Thomas interview, Thomas's blog, April 9, 2007, http://www.kimtragedy.info/OT18/.

193   *"Gay Jihad":* Matt Sanchez blurb, Matt Sanchez, "Hypocrisy or Decency? The Left's Dirty Little Secret," *Right Wing News,* November 6, 2007, http://www .rightwingnews.com/mt331/2007/11/hypocrisy_or_decency_the_lefts.php.

193   *"the gay lifestyle":* Jeremy Duboff, "Open Letter to Matt Sanchez," *Jeremayakovka,* March 20, 2007, http://jeremayakovka.typepad.com/jeremayakovka/ 2007/03/an_open_letter_.html.

193   *Alberto Moravia's novel:* Alberto Moravia, *The Conformist* (New York: Farrar, Straus & Giroux, 1951); Bernardo Bertolucci, director, *The Conformist,* 1970.

193   *"I intend to construct my normality":* Bertolucci, *The Conformist.*

195   *"Once maybe I touched him or so"*: Joel Roberts, "Priest Admits Foley Rela-
      tionship," CBS/Associated Press, October 19, 2006, http://www.cbsnews.com/
      stories/2006/10/19/national/main2104978.shtml.

195   *the Christian right's mounting anti-gay crusade:* Jean O'Leary and Bruce
      Voeller, "Anita Bryant's Crusade," *New York Times,* June 7, 1977.

195   Green accused: Kathie Lee Gifford, *I Can't Believe I Said That!: An Autobiogra-
      phy* (London: Pocket Books, 1992), cited by Gavin Elster at "They Always Come
      Back," http://theyalwayscomeback.blogspot.com/2008/03/anita-bryant.html.

195   *"people who sleep with St. Bernards":* David Jefferson, "How Getting Married
      Made Me an Activist," *Newsweek,* November 15, 2008, http://www.newsweek
      .com/id/169195/page/2.

195   *Bryant summoned local right-wing forces:* Morton Kondracke, "Anita Bryant Is
      Mad About Gays," *The New Republic,* May 7, 1977.

196   the Miami Archdiocese's role: John Tanasychuk, "Exhibit Marks 30th An-
      niversary of How Anita Bryant Fought and Helped Gay Rights," *South Florida
      Sun-Sentinel,* June 4, 2007.

196   law against homosexuals adopting children in Florida: *Angela Gilmore et al.
      vs. Charlie Crist, Robert Pappas and the Department of Children and Family
      Services,* 99-10058-CV-JLK, Appeal from the United States District Court for
      the Southern District of Florida, January 28, 2004, caselaw.findlaw.com/
      data2/circs/11th/0116723p.pd.

196   *"Why Certain Sexual Deviations Are Punishable by Death":* Bob Moser, "Holy
      War," Southern Poverty Law Center, Spring 2005, http://www.splcenter.org/
      intel/intelreport/article.jsp?pid=863.

196   *South Florida's culture war was a microcosm:* Tina Fetner, "Working Anita
      Bryant: The Impact of Christian Anti-Gay Activism on Lesbian and Gay
      Movement Claims," *Social Problems,* 48, 3 (2001): 411–428, http://caliber.uc-
      press.net/doi/abs/10.1525/sp.2001.48.3.411?cookieSet=1&journalCode=sp.

196   *"It's vile":* Bill Adair, "Congress Sees Through Party-Colored Glasses," *St. Peters-
      burg Times,* September 12, 1998, http://www.sptimes.com/Worldandnation/
      91298/Congress_sees_through.html.

197   *Foley's lifelong passion:* R. Jeffrey Smith, "Foley Built Career as Protector of
      Children," *Washington Post,* October 1, 2006, http://www.washingtonpost
      .com/wp-dyn/content/article/2006/09/30/AR2006093001177.html.

197   *fellow Republican lawmakers, who said nothing:* Carl Hulse and Jeff Zeleny, "Re-
      view of Messages Sent by Congressman Begins," *New York Times,* October 2,
      2006, http://www.nytimes.com/2006/10/02/washington/02foley.html?ex=131
      7441600&en=05964d30032a0385&ei=5090&partner=rssuserland&emc=rss.

197   *"watch out for Congressman Mark Foley":* Brian Ross, "Foley's Behavior No
      Secret on Capitol Hill," ABC News, October 1, 2006, http://abcnews.go.com/
      WNT/story?id=2514770.

197   Alexander went to RNC chair Tom Reynolds: Carl Hulse and Raymond Her-
      nandez, "G.O.P. Aides Knew in Late '05 of E-Mail," *New York Times,* October 1,
      2006, http://www.nytimes.com/2006/10/01/washington/01foley.html?hp=
      &pagewanted=all.

197 *Foley donated $100,000:* Jennifer Hoar, "Candidates Unload Money from Foley," Associated Press, October 3, 2006, http://www.cbsnews.com/stories/2006/10/03/politics/main2059264.shtml.

197 *"What's at stake here":* Bob Moser, "Holy War," Southern Poverty Law Center, Spring 2005, http://www.splcenter.org/intel/intelreport/article.jsp?pid=865.

197 *"kill him and tell God he died":* "Swaggart Apologizes for Talk of Killing Gays," Associated Press, September 23, 2004, http://www.msnbc.msn.com/id/6074380/.

197 *avoided making any public statement:* Adrian Brune, "Outed Hill Staffer Condemns Campaign," *Washington Blade,* July 9, 2004, 200http://washington blade.com/2004/7–9/news/localnews/outed.cfm?page=2.

198 *involving Kirk Fordham:* Peter Wallsten and Noam N. Levey "Aide at Center of the Controversy," *Los Angeles Times,* October 4, 2006, http://articles.latimes.com/2006/oct/04/nation/na-fordham4.

198 *"but not in the press":* Alex Koppelman, "The Glass Closet," *Salon,* October 20, 2006, http://www.Salon.com/news/feature/2006/10/20/outing/print.html.

198 Trandahl alerted Van Der Meid and Fordham: Jonathan Weisman, "Hastert Aides Interest Ethics Panel," *Washington Post,* October 12, 2006, http://www.washington post.com/wp-dyn/content/article/2006/10/11/AR2006101101639_pf.html.

198 *"these slaps on the wrist":* Chris Crain, "Trandahl Finally Speaks," *Citizen Crain,* October 19, 2006, http://citizenchris.typepad.com/citizenchris/2006/10/trandahl_speaks.html.

199 *Foley fired off a breathless letter:* Mark Foley, Florida Member of Congress, to Jeb Bush, Florida Governor, June 18, 2003, posted by CNSNews.com, June 20, 2003, http://www.cnsnews.com/public/Content/Article.aspx?rsrcid=5633.

199 *"Foley has a point":* John Cloud, "Nude Family Values," *Time,* June 25, 2003, http://www.time.com/time/magazine/article/0,9171,1101030630–460225,00.html.

199 Foley's instant messaging with page: ABCNews, posted February 2, 2003, abcnews.go.com/images/WNT/02–02–03b.pdf.

200 *outing Foley as gay:* Mark Meenan, "Is He Gay or Not? US Rep. Mark Foley Calls Press to Say He Won't Talk About His Sexual Orientation," *Gay City News,* May 30, 2003.

200 *suggestive e-mail entreaties:* Hulse and Hernandez, "G.O.P. Aides Knew."

201 *Ross refused the deal:* John Nichols, "The House Republican Leadership Scandal," *The Nation,* October 03, 2006, http://www.thenation.com/blog/the-beat/126922/the_house_republican_leadership_scandal.

201 Hudson on Foley: Lev Grossman, "Lane Hudson," *Time,* December 16, 2006, http://www.time.com/time/magazine/article/0,9171,1570716,00.html.

201 *the story gathered momentum and exploded:* David Folkenflik, "Foley Story Wasn't Reported, Until It Was," *All Things Considered,* NPR.org, October 6, 2006, http://www.npr.org/templates/story/story.php?storyId=6211216.

201 Drudge's proposition: David Brock, *Blinded by the Right,* p. 283.

201 *"a piece of fiction":* Nolan Clay and Michael McNutt, "Istook Aide to Cooperate with Inquiry," *The Oklahoman,* October 6, 2006, http://www.newsok.com/article/2951710.

201 *headed off Pelosi's investigation:* Charles Babington and Jonathan Weisman, "Rep. Foley Quits in Page Scandal," *Washington Post*, September 30, 2006, http://www.washingtonpost.com/wp-dyn/content/article/2006/09/29/AR2006092901574.html.

202 *Father Mercieca had molested him:* Abby Goodnough, "Foley Was Sexually Abused as a Youth, His Lawyer Says," *New York Times*, October 4, 2006, http://www.nytimes.com/2006/10/04/washington/04foley.html?scp=8&sq=congress%202006%20foley%20election&st=cse.

202 *the vicious cycle often continues:* Pamela Cooper White, "Soul Stealing: Power Relations in Pastoral Sexual Abuse," *Christian Century,* February 21, 1991, pp. 196–199, http://www.anandainfo.com/soul_stealing.html.

202 *"Punch Foley for Joe":* Brit Hume, "Negron's New Campaign Slogan: Punch Foley for Joe," FoxNews.com, October 27, 2006, http://www.foxnews.com/story/0,2933,226007,00.html.

202 *elected Democrat Tim Mahoney:* "Democrat Tim Mahoney Wins Race to Replace Mark Foley," Associated Press, November 7, 2008, http://www.usatoday.com/news/politicselections/vote2006/FL/2006–11–07-FL-US-house_x.htm.

203 Hastert refused to resign: Mike Dorning and Rick Pearson, "Hastert Vows to Hold On," *Chicago Tribune*, October 5. 2006, http://archives.chicagotribune.com/2006/oct/05/news/chi-0610050132oct05.

203 *Tony Perkins vented the movement's rage:* Max Blumenthal, "The Coming Gay Republican Purge," *The Nation*, October 12, 2006, http://www.thenation.com/doc/20061030/blumenthal.

203 *the old reverend was furious:* Ibid.

204 On *Washington Confidential:* Jack Lait and Lee Mortimer, *Washington Confidential* (New York: Crown Publishers, 1951), p. 116. Also see David Johnston, *The Lavender Scare: The Prosecution of Gays in the Federal Government* (Chicago: University of Chicago Press, 2004).

204 *the ruthless Roy Cohn:* Tom Wolfe, "Dangerous Obsessions," *New York Times*, April 3, 1998, http://query.nytimes.com/gst/fullpage.html?res=940DE6D9163BF930A35757C0A96E948260.

204 *"defended fags":* "Right-wing Gay-baiting Queers," Democratic Underground, October 2, 2006, http://www.democraticunderground.com/discuss/duboard.php?az=view_all&address=364x2287207.

204 *"Roy [Cohn] was not gay":* Jeffrey Toobin, "The Dirty Trickster," *The New Yorker*, June 2, 2008, http://www.newyorker.com/reporting/2008/06/02/080602fa_fact_toobin?currentPage=all.

204 *"Hot, insatiable lady":* Ibid.

205 Lee LaHaye outed: Michael Rogers, "They MUST be kidding at Concerned Women for America! Write or Call Lee LaHaye Today," blogActive, http://www.blogactive.com/2004/08/action-they-must-be-kidding-at.html. Rogers referred to LaHaye as "openly gay." LaHaye has never denied the designation.

205 *son of Tim LaHaye:* Tim LaHaye, *The Unhappy Gays* (Carol Stream, IL: Tyndale House, 1978).

205 Phyllis Schlafly's gay son: Yvonne Abraham, "At 80, Schlafly Is Still a Conservative Force," *Boston Globe*, September 2, 2004, http://www.boston.com/news/nation/articles/2004/09/02/at_80_schlafly_is_still_a_conservative_force/.

205 *Robert Traynham:* Sean Loughlin, "Two Republicans Criticize Santorum for Remarks About Gays," CNN.com, April 24, 2003, http://www.cnn.com/2003/ALLPOLITICS/04/24/santorum.gays/; and "Spokesman for Antigay Senator Says He's Gay," *The Advocate*, July 16, 2005, http://www.advocate.com/news_detail.asp?id=18876.

205 *Wildmon interrupted me mid-sentence, and backpedaled:* Blumenthal, "The Coming Gay Republican Purge."

205 *nothing but "siege and suspicion":* Mark Leibovich, "Foley Case Upsets Balance of Gay Republicans," *New York Times*, October 8, 2006, http://www.nytimes.com/2006/10/08/washington/08culture.html?pagewanted=1.

CHAPTER 18: THE WIDE STANCE

207 *allegations about his homosexual tendencies:* Dan Popkey, "Men's Room Arrest Reopens Questions About Sen. Larry Craig," *Idaho Statesman*, August 28, 2007, http://www.idahostatesman.com/localnews/story/143801.html.

207 *honorably discharged in 1972 after six months:* Ibid.

207 *Craig felt compelled to deny his involvement:* ABC News, July 2, 1982, posted on YouTube October 17, 2006, http://www.youtube.com/watch?v=0RntWGPEjoo.

207 *Craig married Suzanne Scott:* Dan Popkey, "Men's Room Arrest."

208 *"Just ask my wife":* Dan Popkey, "More Gay Men Describe Sexual Encounters with U.S. Sen. Craig," *Idaho Statesman*, December 3, 2007, http://www.idahostatesman.com/eyepiece/story/226703.html.

208 *"a nasty, bad, naughty boy":* Larry Craig, Matt Lauer interview, *Today*, NBC, October 16, 2007, http://www.msnbc.msn.com/id/21303825/page/2/.

208 *"stand up now and protect traditional marriage":* "Senator Pleaded Guilty, Reportedly After Bathroom Stall Incident," CNN.com, August 27, 2007, http://www.cnn.com/2007/POLITICS/08/27/craig.arrest/index.html.

208 *"a lifestyle I don't agree with":* Larry Craig, Matt Lauer interview, p. 6.

208 *Statesman* investigation: Dan Popkey, "More Gay Men."

209 *"the best place for anonymous action":* Andy Birkey, "Minneapolis Airport Restroom Sting Nabs Idaho Senator," *Minnesota Monitor*, August 27, 2007, http://www.minnesotamonitor.com/showDiary.do?diaryId=2309.

209 Karsnia's bathroom sting report: David Karsnia, "Lewd Conduct," June 11, 2007, posted to Smoking Gun June 12, 2007, http://www.thesmokinggun.com/archive/years/2007/0828071craig1.html#Reporthere.

209 *"wide stance":* Dan Popkey, "Idaho Senator Larry Craig Arrested in Airport Men's Room," *Idaho Statesman*, August 28, 2007, http://www.idahostatesman.com/eyepiece/story/143517.html.

209 *Craig appeared before a mob of reporters:* Boise, Idaho, August 28, 2007, *The Situation Room*, CNN, posted to YouTube August 28, 2007, http://www.youtube.com/watch?v=Y8C3tR9Yl4g.

210   *the wrath of his peers:* William Yardley, "Craig Defends Decision to Stay in Senate and Attacks Romney," *New York Times,* October 16, 2007, http://www.nytimes.com/2007/10/16/us/politics/16craig.html.

210   Perkins condemned Craig: Tony Perkins, Chris Matthews *Hardball* interview transcript, MSNBC.msn.com, August 28, 2000, http://www.msnbc.msn.com/id/20496581/.

211   *compare gays to alcoholics and kleptomaniacs:* Lott to Williams, *NewsHour with Jim Lehrer,* July 22, 1998, http://www.pbs.org/newshour/bb/congress/july-dec98/gop_7–22a.html.

211   *"we don't know the whole story":* Armstrong Williams, "Sex, Lies, and Video-tapes," *Townhall,* September 3, 2007, http://townhall.com/columnists/ArmstrongWilliams/2007/09/03/sex,_lies,_and_videotapes.

211   *accepting a $240,000 bribe:* Greg Toppo, "Education Dept. Paid Commentator to Promote Law," *USA Today,* January 7, 2005, http://www.usatoday.com/news/washington/2005–01–06-williams-whitehouse_x.htm.

211   *accused of sexual harassment:* John Cloud, "He Said/He Said," *Washington City Paper,* 17, 24 (June 13, 1997), http://www.washingtoncitypaper.com/display.php?id=12891.

211   *"false, baseless, and completely without merit":* Deborah Mitchell and Beth Landman, "A Lott of Irony for Trent Interviewer," *New York Magazine,* July 6, 1998, http://nymag.com/nymetro/news/people/columns/intelligencer/2902/.

211   *"wholly unrelated" to his official duties:* "Sen. Larry Craig Vows to Stay in Office," CBS/AP, September 5, 2007, http://www.cbsnews.com/stories/2007/09/05/politics/main3235652.shtml.

212   *the Idaho Hall of Fame:* "Craig to Be Inducted into Idaho Hall of Fame," Associated Press, October 7, 2007, http://www.idahostatesman.com/1264/story/177526.html.

212   *nabbed outside a men's bathroom:* CNN, July 11, 2007, posted on YouTube, August 8, 2007, http://www.youtube.com/watch?v=pmeGpAzPIho.

212   *arrested for performing oral sex:* Larry Thomas, "Murphy Resigns Political Posts; Cooperating with Police in Apparent Criminal Investigation," Jeffersonville *News and Tribune,* August 8, 2007, http://www.news-tribune.net/breakingnews/local_story_219210228.html.

212   *arrested after calling the police:* Joe Peterson, Spokane Police Department Additional Report, October 27, 2007, posted by Dan Savage, *The Stranger,* October 30, 2007, http://slog.thestranger.com/2007/10/richard_curtis_more_shocking_details.

213   Curtis resigned: "Rep. Richard Curtis Resigns over Gay Sex Scandal," Associated Press, King5.com, October 31, 2007, http://www.king5.com/localnews/stories/NW_103107WAB_curtis_resignation_LJ.1c5c1238f.html.

213   *Spokesman-Review* exposé: Bill Morlin, "Mayor West Offered Perks, Internship to Expert Posing as 18-Year-Old During Web Chats," *Spokesman-Review,* May 5, 2005, http://www.spokesmanreview.com/jimwest/story.asp?ID=050505_online_relationships.

213   West accused of molestation: David Postman, "Even the Mayor Wonders: Who
        Is the Real Jim West?" *Seattle Times*, December 2, 2005, http://seattletimes
        .nwsource.com/html/localnews/2002649195_west27m.html.

213   *Despite his privately acknowledged bisexuality:* Jim West, Matt Lauer interview,
        "Jim West on 'The Today Show,'" *The Today Show,* NBC, May 31, 2005, http://
        www.spokesmanreview.com/jimwest/story.asp?ID=053105_transcript
        _today.

214   *"The authoritarian character worships the past":* Fromm, *Escape from Free-
        dom,* p. 169.

CHAPTER 19: PASTOR TED'S EXCELLENT ADVENTURE

216   *the concept of "creation care":* Laurie Goodstein, "Evangelical Leaders Swing In-
        fluence Behind Effort to Combat Global Warming," *New York Times*, March 10,
        2005, http://www.nytimes.com/2005/03/10/national/10evangelical.html?th.

216   *to denounce the notion of global warming:* "Global Warming Gap Among
        Evangelicals Widens," CNN.com, March 14, 2007, http://www.cnn.com/2007/
        POLITICS/03/14/evangelical.rift/index.html.

216   *an "evil and wicked religion":* Jarrett Murphy, "Pentagon's Preacher Irks Mus-
        lims," CBSNews.com, April 16, 2003, http://www.cbsnews.com/stories/2003/
        04/16/national/main549684.shtml.

216   *Haggard was restrained, even criticizing Graham:* Laurie Goodstein, "Top Evan-
        gelicals Critical of Colleagues over Islam," *New York Times,* May 8, 2003, http://
        query.nytimes.com/gst/fullpage.html?res=9B0CE7DB163FF93BA35756C0A9
        659C8B63.

216   Haggard and the loudmouths: Nicholas Kristof, "Giving God a Break," *New
        York Times*, June 10, 2008, http://query.nytimes.com/gst/fullpage.html?res
        =9C01E5D71239F933A25755C0A9659C8B63.

217   *more than a place of worship:* "Ted Haggard Pastor of the New Life Church,"
        YouTube, http://www.youtube.com/watch?v=M63ULXRLPtE&feature=PlayList
        &p=340DF149E37C1099&index=0&playnext=1.

217   *"I have an interest in satanic meetings":* Michael Lewis, Campaign Journal,
        The New Republic, July 8, 1996, p. 20.

217   *a vision of demons:* Eric Gorski, "Reality Stems from Pastor's Vision," Col-
        orado Springs *Gazette,* December 22, 2002, http://www.gazette.com/articles/
        haggard_18942___article.html/church_life.html.

218   *he learned to speak in tongues:* Ibid.

218   *a stadium throbbing with men:* David Kelly, "In Colorado, a Wellspring of
        Conservative Christianity," *Los Angeles Times*, July 06, 2004, http://articles
        .latimes.com/2004/jul/06/entertainment/et-kelly6.

218   *a "spiritual NORAD":* Dan Harris, "Calling for Prayer in Internet Age," ABC
        News.com, December 16, 2004, http://abcnews.go.com/WNT/story?id
        =337032; and Ted Olsen, "Prayer Center Construction Begins," *Christianity To-
        day,* May 20, 1996, http://www.ctlibrary.com/ct/1996/may20/6t678b.html.

219   *retreated to the center's Praise Mountain:* Paul Asay, "There Are No Secrets,"
        Colorado Springs *Gazette,* January 7, 2007.

219   Haggard and Amendment 2: Paul Asay and Dave Phillips, "Haggard's Mecca
        Materialized, But Vision May Now Be Fading," Colorado Springs *Gazette,* De-
        cember 31, 2006.

219   *informal advisor to President George W. Bush:* Eric Gorski, "Haggard Profile:
        Man of Cloth and Clout," *Denver Post,* October 30, 2005, http://www.denver-
        post.com/search/ci_3165558.

219   *Haggard was on the front lines:* Tim Egan, "State of the Union: The Evangelical
        Vote," News.BBC.co.uk, November 4, 2004, http://news.bbc.co.uk/1/hi/
        programmes/3992067.stm.

219   *contemplating a run for Congress:* Paul Asay, "Pastor May Step Up If Hefley
        Steps Down," Colorado Springs *Gazette,* August 5, 2005, http://findarticles
        .com/p/articles/mi_qn4191/is_20050805/ai_n14852030.

219   *"Justice Sunday II":* Max Blumenthal, "Preaching Justice, Slaying Demons,"
        The Nation, August 19, 2005, http://www.thenation.com/doc/20050829/
        blumenthal2.

219   *support of Supreme Court nominee John Roberts:* "Others Weigh In on Roberts,"
        U.S. News & World Report, July 20, 2005, http://www.usnews.com/usnews/
        news/articles/050720/20courtquotes.htm.

219   *writing a weight loss handbook:* Ted Haggard, *The Jerusalem Diet* (Colorado
        Springs: WaterBrook Press, 2005).

219   *"I'm a fat guy":* Ibid. Also see Paul Asay, "New Life Pastor Touts Diet," Col-
        orado Springs *Gazette,* December 31, 2005, http://www.gazette.com/articles/
        diet_6194___article.html/haggard_pastor.html.

220   *"Seven Promises of a Promise Keeper":* Mike Allen, "Male Bonding for the
        Evangelical Set," *New York Times,* August 23, 1999, http://query.nytimes.com/
        gst/fullpage.html?res=950CEEDE1138F930A1575BC0A96F958260; also see
        James Dobson et al., *Seven Promises of a Promise Keeper* (Nashville, TN:
        Thomas Nelson, 1999).

220   *"the feminization of men":* Johnette Howard, "For Coach McCartney, a Leap
        of Faith," *Washington Post,* October 25, 1994, http://www.washingtonpost
        .com/wp-srv/local/longterm/library/PK/mccartney/leap1094.htm.

220   *"the men feel uninhibited and free":* Steve Rabey, "The New Christian Man,"
        Colorado Springs *Gazette,* April 4, 2003, http://www.believersweb.org/
        view.cfm?ID=503.

221   *The Promise Keepers was founded in 1990:* Howard, "For Coach McCartney."
        Also see Bill McCartney, *From Ashes to Glory* (Nashville, TN: Thomas Nelson,
        1995).

221   McCartney's quarterback Aunese: Bruce Weber, "Bill McCartney, Away from
        the Sideline, Brings His Inspirational Message to the Bowery," *New York
        Times,* June 20, 1997, http://query.nytimes.com/gst/fullpage.html?res=9E03
        E1DB123EF933A15755C0A961958260&sec=&spon=&pagewanted=2.

221   *Bible verses inscribed on index cards:* Howard, "For Coach McCartney."

221 *"so focused on winning football games"*: Weber, "Bill McCartney."

221 *warned Jews that they are "toast"*: Louis Sahagun, "Plotting the Exit Strategy," *Los Angeles Times*, June 22, 2006, http://articles.latimes.com/2006/jun/22/local/me-endtimes22.

221 *"A man's man, a real man"*: Weber, "Bill McCartney."

222 *"Ultimate Fighting Jesus"*: Brandon O'Brien, "A Jesus for Real Men," *Christianity Today*, April 18, 2008, http://www.christianitytoday.com/ct/article_print.html?id=55035.

222 *"raw and uninhibited"*: Ibid.

222 *the men's movement's seminal tract*: John Eldredge, *Wild at Heart: Discovering the Secret of a Man's Soul* (Nashville, TN: Thomas Nelson, 2001).

223 *the "Farm Belt Fuhrer"*: Camille Jackson, *Fightin' Words*, Southern Poverty Law Center Intelligence Report, Fall 2004, http://www.splcenter.org/intel/intelreport/article.jsp?aid=490.

223 *proposed torpedoing boatloads of African migrant workers:* Celestine Bohlen, "Italy Rebuked by Vatican over Migrants," *New York Times*, November 20, 1995, http://query.nytimes.com/gst/fullpage.html?res=9D04E3DE1339F933A15752C1A963958260&n=Top/Reference/Times%20Topics/People/B/Bossi,%20Umberto.

223 Bossi's "Braveheart" poster: Allan Brown, "Braveheart and the Nazis," *Sunday Times of London*, May 5, 2002.

223 Nazis recruit *Braveheart* fans: *Sunday Mail*, July 7, 1996.

223 *a pre–Vatican II Catholic traditionalist:* Michael Paulson, "Cherishing an Older Catholicism," *Boston Globe*, February 22, 2004, http://www.boston.com/news/local/articles/2004/02/22/cherishing_an_older_catholicism/.

223 *penchant for anti-Semitic rants*: "Gibson's Anti-Semitic Tirade—Alleged Cover Up," TMZ.com, July 28, 2006, http://www.tmz.com/2006/07/28/gibsons-anti-semitic-tirade-alleged-cover-up/.

225 *"I make all things new"*: Book of Revelation 21:5.

225 *"sacrificial love"*: Ted Haggard, "What's the Point of Focusing on Anti-Semitism?" *BeliefNet*, September 2003, http://www.BeliefNet.com/Faiths/Christianity/2003/09/Whats-The-Point-Of-Focusing-On-Anti-Semitism.aspx.

226 *Arterburn's come-to-Jesus moment:* Stephen Arterburn and Fred Stoeker, *Every Man's Battle* (Colorado Springs: WaterBrook Press, 2005). Also see Jeff Sharlet, "Sex as a Weapon," *Nerve,* undated, http://www.nerve.com/dispatches/sharlet/sexasaweapon/.

226 Stoeker "wash[ed] clean": Fred Stoeker bio, Editorial Unilit, undated: http://www.editorialunilit.com/pages/eng/_autores1.php?vAut=359.

227 *a dystopian 1973 sci-fi novel:* J. G. Ballard, *Crash* (New York: Farrar, Straus & Giroux, 1973).

227 *In an online video that Arterburn produced:* "Every Man's Battle" promotional video, posted to YouTube April 14, 2007, http://www.youtube.com/watch?v=hV5kurZ_Yz0.

228 *Jesus Camp:* Directors: Heidi Ewing and Rachel Grady. Magnolia Pictures, 2006.

228 *"It's written in the Bible!"*: Ibid.

229 *"endless succession of orgasms"*: Jeff Sharlet, "Sex as a Weapon," *Nerve*, April 25, 2005, http://www.nerve.com/dispatches/sharlet/sexasaweapon/.

229 Haggard outed: "Haggard Admits 'Sexual Immorality,' Apologizes," Associated Press, Nov 5, 2006, http://www.msnbc.msn.com/id/15536263/.

229 *excursions to the Mile High City*: Mike Jones and Sam Gallegos, *I Had to Say Something* (New York: Seven Stories Press, 2007), p. 73.

229 *"6 to 8 college age guys"*: John Aravosis, "Signorile Interviews Fallen-Evangelical-Leader Ted Haggard's Male Hooker," AmericaBlog.com, November 6, 2006, http://www.americablog.com/2006/11/signorile-interviews-fallen.html.

230 *"evangelicals have the best sex life"*: Director: Alexandra Pelosi, "Friends of God," HBO, January 25, 2007, http://www.hbo.com/docs/programs/friends _of_god/index.html.

230 *documentarians*: "Ted Haggard Says Evangelicals Have the 'Best Sex Life,'" ABC News, January 22, 2007, http://abcnews.go.com/GMA/Story?id=2813 078&page=1.

230 *a "combat nurse" tending to "wounded men"*: Mike Jones and Sam Gallegos, *I Had to Say Something*, p. 24.

230 *"When a man cries"*: Ibid., p. 25.

230 *"the last generation"*: Ibid., p. 138.

231 *"I had to say something"*: Ibid., p. 153.

231 *"I threw it away"*: "Rev. Ted Haggard Admits Buying Meth," KUSA-TV/CNN, November 3, 2006, http://www.youtube.com/watch?v=OHXQIyeE7Ak.

231 *a fabrication of the Enemy*: "Ted Haggard Accused of Gay Affair, Steps Down," TheDenverChannel.com, November 2, 2006, http://www.thedenverchannel .com/news/10227610/detail.html.

231 *"This is clearly a political stunt"*: Cara DeGette, "Pastor Ted: 'The Farthest Thing from a Homosexual . . . '" *Colorado Confidential*, November 2, 2006, http://www.coloradoconfidential.com/showDiary.do?diaryId=923.

231 *New Life Church organized a rally*: Ibid.

231 *He was one of them, after all*: Jean Torkelson, "Purity of Pastors Questioned," *Rocky Mountain News*, November 18, 2006, http://m.rockymountainnews .com/news/2006/Nov/18/purity-of-pastors-questioned/.

231 *In a letter read aloud*: "Ted Haggard: 'I Am a Deceiver and a Liar,'" posted on *BeliefNet*, November 5, 2006, http://www.BeliefNet.com/News/2006/11/Ted-Haggard-I-Am-A-Deceiver-And-A-Liar.aspx.

232 Dobson, Zacharias, and Mohler on Haggard: Max Blumenthal, "The Ted Haggard Movement Airs Its Shame," *Huffington Post*, November 7, 2006, http://www.huffingtonpost.com/max-blumenthal/the-ted-haggard -movement-_b_33481.html.

232 *"so repulsive and dark"*: "Ted Haggard: 'I Am a Deceiver and a Liar.'"

233 *Everything appeared to go swimmingly*: Eric Gorski, "Haggard Says He Is 'Completely Heterosexual,'" *Denver Post*, February 6, 2007, http://www.denverpost .com/ci_5164921.

233   *a payout of $130,000:* Eric Gorski, "Rise and Fall of Ted Haggard Documen-
       tary to Air," Associated Press, December 18, 2008, http://www.christianpost
       .com/Ministries/Figures/2008/12/rise-and-fall-of-ted-haggard-documentary
       -to-air-18/index.html.

233   *never disclose details of his scandal:* "Haggard Agrees Not to Discuss Scandal
       Publicly," TheDenverChannel.com, February 7, 2007, http://www.thedenver
       channel.com/news/10958240/detail.html.

233   *the dawning of a new era:* "Haggard's Former Church Holds 'Day of Hope,'"
       Associated Press, February 19, 2007, http://www.christianpost.com/church/
       Megachurches/2007/02/haggard-s-former-church-holds-day-of-hope-19/
       index.html.

233   *fired for "sexual misconduct with an adult":* Jean Torkelson, "New Life Direc-
       tor Admits Misconduct," *Rocky Mountain News,* December 19, 2006, http://
       www.rockymountainnews.com/drmn/local/article/0,1299,DRMN_15_52230
       16,00.html.

233   *New Life sacked at least thirty more employees:* Dan Frosch, "Layoffs Follow
       Scandal at Colorado Megachurch," *New York Times,* March 6, 2007, http://
       www.nytimes.com/2007/03/06/us/06church.html.

234   *the well-worn massage table:* Cary Leider Vogrin, "Massage Table in Haggard
       Scandal Pulled by eBay," Colorado Springs *Gazette,* March 20, 2007, http://
       findarticles.com/p/articles/mi_qn4191/is_20070320/ai_n18763641.

234   *what Haggard called "broken people":* Cara DeGette, "A Year Ago: 'Ted Hag-
       gard Is the Farthest Thing from a Homosexual,'" *Colorado Independent,* No-
       vember 2, 2007, http://coloradoindependent.com/2930/a-year-ago-ted
       -haggard-is-the-farthest-thing-from-a-homosexual.

234   *the Phoenix Dream Center, a "deliverance ministry":* Rick Ross, Skipp Porteous
       interview, "Exclusive Interview Exit-counselor Rick Ross," *Walk Away,* Sum-
       mer 1990, http://www.rickross.com/reference/about/about2.html.

234   *"rewarded in heaven":* Cara DeGette, "Ted Haggard's Cash-for-Heaven Offer,"
       Colorado Confidential, August 23, 2007, http://www.coloradoconfidential
       .com/showDiary.do?diaryId=2630.

234   Sex offender at FWAM: Dan Savage, "Ted Haggard and the Man Behind
       'Families with a Mission,'" *The Stranger,* August 24, 2007, http://slog.the
       stranger.com/2007/08/families_with_a_mission.

235   *a last desperate media blitz:* Pelosi, Logan Hill interview, "Alexandra Pelosi on
       Ted Haggard's 'I'm-Super-Sorry' Publicity Tour," *New York magazine,* January
       29, 2009, http://nymag.com/daily/intel/2009/01/alexandra_pelosi_on_ted
       _haggar.html.

CHAPTER 20: THE NIGHTMARE OF CHRISTIANITY

236   *his "nightmare of Christianity":* "Demons Haunted Colo. Gunman," Associated
       Press, December 12, 2007, http://www.msnbc.msn.com/id/22221432/print/1/
       displaymode/1098/.

236 *Murray heaped contempt on his mother:* Matthew Murray discussed Gothard homeschooling under the user ID "Chrstnghtmr" at http://independent spirits.net/e107_plugins/forum/forum_viewtopic.php?750, September 4, 2006.

237 *the home-schooling regimen:* Berny Morson, "Gunman Railed Against Home-school Christian Curriculum," *Rocky Mountain News*, December 12, 2007, http://www.rockymountainnews.com/news/2007/dec/12/gunman-railed -against-home-school-christian-curric/.

237 Bill Gothard: *Bill Gothard General Teachings/Activities*, Biblical Discernment Ministries, February 2004, http://www.rapidnet.com/~jbeard/bdm/exposes/ gothard/general.htm.

237 *an all-consuming environment:* Ron Henzel, *Bill Gothard and the Institute in Basic Life Principles*, Midwest Christian Outreach, http://www.midwestoutreach .org/02-Information/02-OnlineReference/02-UnorthodoxyGuide/105-IKnow Something/Gothard-IBLP/index.html.

237 *a devastating exposé:* Ron Henzel, Joy Veinot, and Don Veinot, *A Matter of Basic Principles* (Lombard, IL: Midwest Christian Outreach, 2003).

237 *receives $800,000 in state funds each year:* "'Little Soldiers in the Culture Wars': Evangelical Radical Bill Gothard's Character First! Curriculum Teaches Students in Fort Lauderdale to Obey His Will," *New Times Broward-Palm Beach*, February 18, 1999.

237 Charter School for Excellence anthem: Bob Norman, "Obedience School," *Orlando Weekly*, March 11, 1999, http://www.orlandoweekly.com/features/ story.asp?id=1159.

238 Huckabee attended Basic Seminar: Joe Conason, "Holy Constitution!," *Salon*, January 18, 2008, http://www.Salon.com/opinion/conason/2008/01/18/ huckabee/.

238 *"instilling character into people":* Mike Huckabee, *Prison Ministry*, Institute in Basic Life Principles, undated, http://iblp.org/iblp/about/whatwedo/ community/prison/.

238 Murray and Oral Roberts University: "Demons Haunted Colo. Gunman."

238 *under the weight of scandalous revelations:* "Oral Roberts President Faces Corruption Lawsuit," Associated Press, October 5, 2007, http://www.msnbc.msn .com/id/21156263/.

238 *a cocaine-addicted closet homosexual:* Interview with Jerry Sloan, January 6, 2004. Sloan is a Sacramento, California–based gay rights activist and former Baptist minister who won $5,000 from Jerry Falwell after Falwell offered that sum to anyone who could prove he called gays "brute beasts." When Sloan produced a videotape of Falwell's denunciations, Falwell refused to pay. Only after Sloan sued Falwell did the reverend cough up the money. See Max Blumenthal, "Agent of Intolerance," *The Nation*, May 16, 2007, http://www.thenation .com/doc/20070528/blumenthal.

238 *committed suicide in 1982:* "Oral Roberts's Son, 37, Found Shot Dead in Car," Associated Press, June 10, 1982, http://query.nytimes.com/gst/fullpage.html ?res=9503E3D61F38F933A25755C0A964948260.

239   *"cult mind-controlling techniques"*: Max Blumenthal, "ABC 9/11 Docudrama's Right-Wing Roots," *The Nation*, September 11, 2006, http://www.thenation.com/doc/20060925/path_to_911.

239   *Murray became paranoid:* Alan Gathright, "Roommate Recalls Bizarre Times, Said He Knew 'It Was Matthew,'" *Rocky Mountain News*, December 11, 2007, http://www.rockymountainnews.com/news/2007/dec/11/roommate-recalls-bizarre-times-said-he-knew-it-was/.

239   Sex and drugs at YWAM: Matthew Murray, "Chrstnghtmr," in the discussion thread "Growing Up in the Nightmare of Bill Gothard and Charismatic Christianity," at http://independentspirits.net/e107_plugins/forum/forum_viewtopic.php?750, September 4, 2006.

239   *"could be planning violence"*: Jeff Kass and Sara Burnett, "Rejection Fueled Church Gunman's Hatred, Psychologist Says," *Rocky Mountain News*, December 14, 2007, http://www.rockymountainnews.com/news/2007/dec/14/the-pattern-of-the-avenger/.

239   *After the trauma-inducing raids:* Murray, "Chrstnghtmr."

239   *a flamboyant, self-proclaimed Satanist:* Ibid.

239   *L. Ron Hubbard and Jack Parsons:* George Pendle, "Strange Angels," *Frieze* magazine, April 3, 2002, http://www.frieze.com/issue/print_article/strange_angels/.

240   *a confusing new world of cheap thrills:* "Chrstnghtmr."

240   *Winell immediately posted a response:* Jeremy Reynalds, "Coroner: Colorado Gunman Killed Himself," Assist News Service, December 11, 2007, http://www.assistnews.net/Stories/2007/s07120075.htm.

241   *"here in a buried kennel"*: Murray, "Chrstnghtmr."

241   *"rejected sheltered Christian boy"*: Ibid., September 24, 2007.

241   *"necrophilious character"*: Erich Fromm, *The Anatomy of Human Destructiveness* (New York: Henry Holt, 1973), p. 303.

242   *"maybe I'll just OD on stuff"*: Matthew Murray, "Chrstnghtmr," July 22, 2007, http://www.thoughttheater.com/2007/12/murray_had_confrontation_at_new_life_church_in_200.php.

242   *"You Christians brought this on yourselves"*: "Reports: Colorado Gunman Posted Anti-Christian Writings," CNN.com, December 11, 2007, http://www.cnn.com/2007/US/12/11/shooter.youth/.

242   *a fearsome arsenal of assault rifles:* Howard Pankratz, "Murray Obsesses with Guns, Shootings," *Denver Post*, March 28, 2008, http://www.denverpost.com/headlines/ci_8723969.

242   *"Do as thou wilt"*: Aleister Crowley, *The Book of the Law* (York Beach, ME: Red Wheel/Weiser, 1976), p. 50.

242   Murray and *The Book of the Law*: Kevin Vaughan, "Autopsy: Gunman Matthew Murray Killed Himself," *Rocky Mountain Times*, January 8, 2008, http://www.rockymountainnews.com/news/2008/jan/08/autopsy-gunman-matthew-murray-killed-himself/.

242   Murray and *I Had to Say Something*: "Book on Serial Killers in Church Gunman's Car," *Denver Post*, January 16, 2008, http://www.denverpost.com/breakingnews/ci_7989014.

243   *"I don't care if I live or die":* Jace Larson, Nicole Vap, and Paula Woodward, "Gunman's Web Writings Warn of Shootings," 9News.com, December 12, 2007, http://www.9news.com/news/article.aspx?storyid=82548.

244   *"Invisible yet strong":* William Golding, *Lord of the Flies* (New York: Penguin Putnam, 1954), p. 62.

244   *"where was all the love":* Matthew Murray, "Chrstnghtmr," at http://independent spirits.net/e107_plugins/forum/forum_viewtopic.php?750, November 06, 2006.

245   *"his hate for certain Christians":* Marlene Winell, Rick Sanchez interview, "Church Shooting Tragedy," CNN, YouTube, http://www.youtube.com/watch ?v=HY1ZJb5tZwU.

245   *"had sold his soul" to the occult:* "Gunman Boasted of Following 'Wickedest Man in the World,'" *WorldNetDaily*, December 14, 2007, http://www.wnd .com/index.php?fa=PAGE.view&pageId=45061.

245   *WorldNetDaily*'s analysis: "Attacker's Diatribe Copied Columbine Killer," *WorldNetDaily*, December 11, 2007, http://www.WorldNetDaily.com/news/ article.asp?ARTICLE_ID=59148.

246   *"Not only does pornography dehumanize":* Jean Torkelson, "'Wow 500,000 images' of porn," *Rocky Mountain News*, March 28, 2008, http://www.rocky mountainnews.com/news/2008/mar/28/wow-500000-images-of-porn/.

246   *"unforgiveness leads to this bitterness":* Ronald and Loretta Murray interviewed by James Dobson, Focus on the Family radio, Colorado Springs, Colorado, February 28 and 29, 2007.

CHAPTER 21: THE PARTY OF DOBSON

251   *"This election was about nothing":* Thomas Friedman, "Two Nations Under God," *New York Times*, November 4, 2004, http://www.nytimes.com/2004/ 11/04/opinion/04friedman.html?hp.

251   *voting against their economic interests:* Thomas Frank, *What's the Matter with Kansas?* (New York: Metropolitan Books, 2004).

252   *"I accepted Jesus Christ into my life":* Marvin Olasky, *Compassionate Conservatism* (New York: The Free Press, 2000), p. 192.

252   *With the help of Michael Gerson:* Laurie Goodstein, "A President Puts His Faith in Providence," *New York Times*, February 9, 2003, http://query.nytimes .com/gst/fullpage.html?res=9800E7DE133BF93AA35751C0A9659C8B63.

252   *even his answers to questions raised during debates:* George Bush to John Bachman, UCSB transcript, Republican Presidential Candidates Debate, Des Monies, Iowa, December 13, 1999, http://www.presidency.ucsb.edu/ws/ index.php?pid=76120.

252   *Alcoholics Anonymous material describes as a "dry drunk":* Gary L. Fisher and Nancy A. Roget, "Dry Drunk Syndrome," *Encyclopedia of Substance Abuse Prevention, Treatment, and Recovery* (Thousand Oaks, CA: Sage Publications, 2008), p. 345.

252 *"'I'm driven with a mission from God'"*: Ewan MacAskill, "George Bush: 'God Told Me to End the Tyranny in Iraq,'" *The Guardian*, October 7, 2005, http://www.guardian.co.uk/world/2005/oct/07/iraq.usa.

253 *though denied by a White House spokesman:* "White House Denies Bush God Claim," BBC.co.uk, October 6, 2005, http://news.bbc.co.uk/1/hi/world/americas/4317498.stm.

253 *"a higher father that I appeal to":* Bob Woodward, *Plan of Attack* (London: Simon & Schuster, 2004), p. 421.

253 *Afghani taxi driver whose legs were "pulpified":* Alex Gibney, director, *Taxi to the Dark Side*, 2007: Also see Jane Mayer, *The Dark Side* (New York: Random House, 2008), p. 312, http://query.nytimes.com/gst/fullpage.html?res=9D02 EFD8113CF931A25751C0A9649C8B63&sec=&spon=&pagewanted=1.

253 *the least popular American president in recent history:* Susan Page, "Bush Approval Rating Hits Record Low," *USA Today*, October 6, 2008, http://www .cnn.com/2008/POLITICS/05/01/bush.poll/.

253 Harold Giuliani's past: Wayne Barrett: *Rudy! An Investigative Biography of Rudolph Giuliani* (New York: Basic Books, 2000), pp. 8–9, 43–67.

253 a *"vulnerability study":* Ibid., or "Rudy Giuliani's Vulnerabilities," *The Smoking Gun*, February 12, 2007, http://www.thesmokinggun.com/archive/years/2007/0212072giuliani1.html.

253 *"questions of a weirdness factor":* Christopher M. Lyon and Ronald A. Giller, "Rudolph W. Giuliani Vulnerability Study," Giuliani for New York, April 8, 1993. http://www.thesmokinggun.com/archive/years/2007/0212072giuliani11.html.

254 *appeared so frequently with his press secretary:* Jennet Conant, *Vanity Fair*, September 1997.

254 *another mistress, Judith Nathan:* Michael Saul and David Saltonstall, "City Taxpayers Picked Up Tab for Judith Giuliani's Visit to Kin in Pennsylvania," *New York Daily News*, December 1, 2007, http://www.nydailynews.com/news/politics/2007/12/01/2007–12–01_city_taxpayers_picked_up_tab_for_judith_-1.html; and Judy Bachrach, "Giuliani's Princess Bride," September 2007, http://www .vanityfair.com/fame/features/2007/09/giuliani200709?currentPage=1.

254 *moved in with two openly gay friends:* Frank Rich, "1 Mayor, 2 Guys, 1 Shih Tzu," *New York Times*, August 4, 2001, http://query.nytimes.com/gst/fullpage .html?res=9804E1DA133CF937A3575BC0A9679C8B63.

254 *appeared in drag in videotaped skits:* Inner Circle press dinner, March 11, 2000: "Rudy Giuliani in Drag Smooching Donald Trump," YouTube, http://www.youtube.com/watch?v=4IrE6FMpai8.

254 *drop his contest for the U.S. Senate:* Adam Nagourney, "Conflicting Advice at City Hall Complicates Giuliani's Decision," *New York Times*, May 15, 2000, http://query.nytimes.com/gst/fullpage.html?res=9B05E2D9103BF936A2575 6C0A9669C8B63&sec=&spon=&pagewanted=all.

254 *Rudy the hero was the portrait:* Susan Page, "Giuliani: Can Hero of 9/11 Win Over His Own Party?" *USA Today*, January 31, 2007, http://www.usatoday .com/news/washington/2007–01–31-giuliani-cover_x.htm.

254 *"I'm not a perfect person":* Max Blumenthal, *Theocracy Now!*

255 *promise to appoint "strict constructionist" judges:* Rudy Giuliani, "Presidential Commitments," *National Review*, July 13, 2007, http://article.nationalreview .com/?q=NDA1ZGZmOGU1OTE1ZmQ4NDE5YzQyYzM3NzFjYjc1YzU=.

255 McCain the Baptist: Bruce Smith, 'Episcopalian' McCain Is a Baptist, Really," *Chicago Sun-Times*, September 17, 2008, http://www.suntimes.com/news/ elections/560477,CST-NWS-mccain17.article.

255 *no remorse for leaving his first wife:* Nicholas Kristoff, "P.O.W. to Power Broker, a Chapter Most Telling," *New York Times*, February 7, 2000, http://query .nytimes.com/gst/fullpage.html?res=9B02EFDF1439F934A15751C0A9669C8 B63; see also: http://blogs.wsj.com/washwire/2008/08/15/christian-pac-to-air -pro-obama-ad/.

255 *McCain attempted to reconcile with his old enemy:* Jerry Falwell, "An Invitation, Not an Endorsement," *New York Times*, May 07, 2006, http://www.nytimes .com/2006/05/07/opinion/07falwell.html.

255 *Dobson's rebuke:* Bob Unruh, "Dobson Says 'No Way' to McCain Candidacy," WorldNetDaily.com, January 13, 2007, http://www.WorldNetDaily.com/ news/article.asp?ARTICLE_ID=53743.

255 *the Mormon organization condemned as a cult:* David Van Biema, "What Is Mormonism? A Baptist Answer," *Time*, October 24, 2007, http://www.time .com/time/nation/article/0,8599,1675308,00.html.

255 Christian Broadcasting Network on Mormons: *Frequently Asked Questions: How Do I Recognize a Cult?* CBN.com, http://www.cbn.com/spirituallife/CBN TeachingSheets/FAQ_cult.aspx.

255 *excluded Mormons from participation:* Robert Marus, "Bush Salutes National Day of Prayer, But Some Christians Decry Politicization," Associated Baptist Press, May 06, 2004, http://www.abpnews.com/index.php?option=com_content &task=view&id=2302&Itemid=117.

255 *described Romney as "presidential":* Michael Kranish, "Romney Increases Overtures to Disenchanted Evangelicals," *Boston Globe*, October 5, 2007, http://www.boston.com/news/nation/articles/2007/10/05/romney_increases _overtures_to_disenchanted_evangelicals/.

256 *"Jesus is Satan's brother!":* Blumenthal, *Theocracy Now!*

256 *"hang by a thread":* Bill McKeever, *When the Constitution "Hangs by a Thread": The White Horse Prophecy in Modern Mormonism*, Mormonism Research Ministry, undated, http://www.mrm.org/topics/joseph-smith/when -constitution-hangs-thread-white-horse-prophecy-modern-mormonism.

256 *appearance on a Salt Lake City radio station:* Ibid.

256 *to deny to reporters any divine motives:* John Heilprin, "Did Hatch Allude to LDS Prophecy?" *Salt Lake Tribune*, November 11, 1999.

256 *Romney poured vast sums:* David D. Kirkpatrick, "Romney Used His Wealth to Enlist Richest Donors," *New York Times*, April 6, 2007, http://www.nytimes .com/2007/04/06/us/politics/06romney.html.

256   *Reverend Lou Sheldon into his camp: Favorable Statements and Endorsements
       from Evangelicals*, aboutMittRomney.com. http://www.aboutmittromney
       .com/evangelicals_part2.htm#LouSheldon.

256   *a fanatically anti-gay preacher:* Scott Moxley, "Lou Sheldon's Nightmare," *OC
       Weekly*, March 9, 2000, http://www.ocweekly.com/2000–03–09/news/lou
       -sheldon-s-nightmare/; also see *Jewish Week* interview with Sheldon, "Sur-
       prise Surprise, They Knew About Pastor Ted All Along," posted on Talk to
       Action, November 10, 2006, http://www.talk2action.org/story/2006/11/10/
       153452/07.

256   *his eagerness to line his pockets:* Susan Schmidt and James V. Grimaldi, "How a
       Lobbyist Stacked the Deck," *Washington Post*, October 16, 2005, http://www
       .washingtonpost.com/wp-dyn/content/article/2005/10/15/AR2005101501
       539.html.

256   *"he is clearly with us":* Blumenthal, *Theocracy Now!*

257   *Janet Folger, who now supported his campaign:* Janet Folger, "Huckabee's Con-
       sistency," *WorldNetDaily*, December 11, 2007, http://www.WorldNetDaily
       .com/news/article.asp?ARTICLE_ID=59136.

257   *"Don't Mormons believe Jesus is Satan's brother?":* Zev Chafets, "The Huckabee
       Factor," *New York Times Magazine*, January 12, 2007, http://www.nytimes
       .com/2007/12/12/magazine/16huckabee.html?pagewanted=2&_r=1.

257   *poorly funded, understaffed, and practically unknown:* Holly Bailey and
       Michael Isikoff, "A Pastor's True Calling," *Newsweek*, December 17, 2007,
       http://www.newsweek.com/id/74469/page/8.

257   *$17.4 million of his personal fortune:* Jake Tapper, "Romney Surpasses Steve
       Forbes' Self-Funding Pace," ABCNews.com, October 10, 2007, http://abcnews
       .go.com/Politics/story?id=3714738.

257   *$85,000 a day on advertising:* Mark Preston, "Romney Spending $85,000-plus
       a Day on TV Ads," CNN.com, November 13, 2007, http://www.cnn.com/
       2007/POLITICS/11/13/romney.ads/.

257   *quarantining of AIDS patients:* Andrew DeMillo, "Huckabee Wanted to Isolate
       AIDS Patients," Associated Press, December 8, 2007, http://www.time.com/
       time/nation/article/0,8599,1692878,00.html.

257   *the discrediting of Bergalis:* Mike Wallace, "Kimberly's Story," *60 Minutes*, CBS,
       June 19, 1994.

257   *he defiantly stood by it:* Dana Bash and Evan Glass, "Huckabee Refuses to Re-
       tract '92 Remarks on AIDS Patients," CNN.com, December 10, 2007, http://
       www.cnn.com/2007/POLITICS/12/10/huckabee.aids/index.html.

257   *billing himself as a "Christian Leader":* "Believe" ad, Mike Huckabee cam-
       paign, http://www.youtube.com/watch?v=BjtGgfhKIvo&feature=PlayList&p
       =6BC86473F77ED120&index=3&playnext=3&playnext_from=PL.

257   *"I come from you":* Warren Cole Smith, "Divided We Stand," *World*, April 5,
       2008, http://www.worldmag.com/printer.cfm?id=13894.

257   *reversing stands he had taken as governor:* Blumenthal, *Theocracy Now!*

258   *he resolved to deliver a major speech:* Kenneth L. Woodward, "Mitt Romney Is No Jack Kennedy," *New York Times*, December 5, 2007, http://www.nytimes .com/2007/12/05/opinion/05woodward.html.

258   *John F. Kennedy's famous 1960 address:* Transcript, *JFK's Speech on His Religion, Sept. 12, 1960*, available at NPR.org, http://www.npr.org/templates/ story/story.php?storyId=16920600.

258   *he contradicted his earnest vow:* Scott Horsley, "Romney: Church to Guide Him, Not the Presidency," NPR.org. December 6, 2007, http://www.npr.org/ templates/story/story.php?storyId=16982216.

258   *The line so excited Rush Limbaugh:* Rush Limbaugh, "Mitt Romney's Inspiring Speech," *Rush Limbaugh Show,* December 6, 2007, http://www.rushlimbaugh .com/home/daily/site_120607/content/01125106.guest.html.

259   Mike Huckabee's speech: Pastors and Pews conference, West Des Moines, Iowa, June 28, 2007, http://www.youtube.com/watch?v=gP0g4T-Egqk.

260   *Americans are totally and naturally depraved:* Ibid.

261   *Huckabee was polling even with Romney:* Dan Balz and John Cohen, "Huckabee Gaining Ground in Iowa," *Washington Post*, November 21, 2007, http:// www.washingtonpost.com/wp-dyn/content/story/2007/11/20/ST2007 112002497.html?hpid=topnews.

261   *showed strength across the Bible Belt:* Anthony Salvanto, "Analysis: Iowa Polls Drove Huckabee Surge," CBSNews.com, December 13, 2007, http://www .cbsnews.com/stories/2007/12/13/politics/main3615334.shtml.

261   *"There's only one explanation":* John Nichols, "Playing the God Card," *The Nation*, December 13, 2007, http://www.thenation.com/doc/20071231/ Nichols.

261   *"easy-going, self-effacing, jaunty style":* Adam Nagourney, "For a Joke-Telling Candidate, a Second-Place Finish," *New York Times*, August 13, 2007, http:// www.nytimes.com/2007/08/13/us/politics/13huckabee.html.

261   *its emotional yearning for postpartisan heroes:* Frank Rich, "The Republicans Find Their Obama," *New York Times*, December 9, 2007, http://www.nytimes .com/2007/12/09/opinion/09rich.html?ref=opinion.

261   *the sectarian ideologue he truly was:* Max Blumenthal, "The Real Mike Huckabee," *The Nation*, January 11, 2008, http://www.thenation.com/doc/ 20080128/Blumenthal.

262   *a stunning upset in Iowa:* Iowa Caucus Results, *New York Times*, January 3, 2008, http://politics.nytimes.com/election-guide/2008/results/states/IA.html.

262   *Huckabee could claim only moral victory:* "Huckabee Bows to 'Inevitable,' Ends GOP Run," CNN.com, March 5, 2008, http://www.cnn.com/2008/POLITICS/ 03/05/huckabee/index.html.

262   *resolved to wish away the culture wars:* Peter Beinart: "The End of the Culture Wars," *The Daily Beast,* January 26, 2009, http://www.thedailybeast.com/ blogs-and-stories/2009-01-26/the-end-of-the-culture-wars/.

262   *self-proclaimed "leading expert" on religion:* Amy Sullivan, Biography, Progressive Faith Media, http://therespublica.org/progressivefaithmedia.com/Bios/ sullivan.htm.

262 Randy Brinson profile: Amy Sullivan, "When Would Jesus Bolt?" *Washington Monthly*, April 2006, http://www.washingtonmonthly.com/features/2006/0604.sullivan.html.

263 *forked over his company's mailing list:* Chris Cillizza and Shailagh Murray, "The Man Who Helped Start Huckabee's Roll," *Washington Post*, December 2, 2007, http://www.washingtonpost.com/wp-dyn/content/article/2007/12/01/AR2007120101569.html.

263 *"Dobson and his colleagues have also been stymied":* Amy Sullivan, "Is Dobson's Obama Hit Backfiring?" *Time*, June 26, 2008, http://www.time.com/time/politics/article/0,8599,1818313,00.html.

263 *Rick Warren:* Rick Warren, *The Purpose Driven Life* (Philadelphia: Running Press, 2003).

263 *"an evangelical liberals can love":* Nicholas Kristof, "Evangelicals a Liberal Can Love," *New York Times*, February 3, 2008, http://www.nytimes.com/2008/02/03/opinion/03kristof.html.

263 *history of backing anti-gay crusades:* Max Blumenthal, interview with Amy Goodman, The War and Peace Report, *Democracy Now!* New York, December 23, 2008, http://i1.democracynow.org/2008/12/23/max_blumenthal_on_rick_warrens_double.

263 *"political power counts more than Christian values":* Bill Press, "The Death of the Religious Right," WorldNetDaily.com, November 23, 2007, http://www.WorldNetDaily.com/index.php?pageId=44688.

263 *"They don't speak for the Republican Party":* Frank Rich, "Rudy, the Values Slayer," *New York Times*, October 28, 2007, http://query.nytimes.com/gst/fullpage.html?res=980DE7DE1430F93BA15753C1A9619C8B63.

263 Giuliani's run ended: Kelley Beaucar Vlahos, "Giuliani to Quit Republican Presidential Race," FoxNews.com, January 29, 2008, http://www.foxnews.com/politics/elections/2008/01/29/giuliani-to-quit-republican-presidential-race/.

264 *"Big Apple values":* Tony Perkins interviewed by Wolf Blitzer, *The Situation Room*, January 30, 2008, CNN, http://transcripts.cnn.com/TRANSCRIPTS/0801/30/sitroom.02.html.

264 *had sabotaged McCain's campaign:* Eric Pooley, "Read My Knuckles," *Time*, February 28, 2000, http://www.time.com/time/magazine/article/0,9171,996191-5,00.html.

264 *Dobson, for his part, had endorsed Huckabee:* "Christian Leader James Dobson Endorses Huckabee for GOP Nod," Associated Press, February 7, 2008, http://www.foxnews.com/politics/elections/2008/02/07/christian-leader-james-dobson-to-endorse-mike-huckabee/.

264 *scrutinizing McCain's every move:* Lisa Miller interview, "'More Comfortable with McCain,'" *Newsweek*, July 22, 2008, http://www.newsweek.com/id/148126.

CHAPTER 22: THE PARTY OF DEATH

265 *"agents of intolerance":* David Barstow, "McCain Denounces Political Tactics of the Christian Right," *New York Times*, February 29, 2000, http://query

.nytimes.com/gst/fullpage.html?res=9A0DE2DA1239F93AA15751C0A9669 C8B63&sec=&spon=&pagewanted=all.

265   *making amends and finding allies:* "U.S. Pro-Israel Evangelical Leader Hagee Endorses McCain," Reuters, February 28, 2008, http://www.haaretz.com/ hasen/spages/959110.html.

266   *one of the world's wealthiest preachers:* Sarah Posner, "John Hagee's Controversial Gospel," *The American Prospect*, March 12, 2008, http://www.prospect .org/cs/articles?article=john_hagees_controversial_gospel. Also see Analisa Nazareno, "Critics Say John Hagee's Compensation Is Too High," *San Antonio Express*, June 20, 2003, http://www.rickross.com/reference/tv_preachers/tv _preachers7.html.

266   *ally of Isreal's rightist Likud Party:* "Likud: Christian Zionists Israel's Best Friends," Christian Broadcasting Network, April 7, 2007,

266   *"the Christian version of AIPAC":* Max Blumenthal, "Birth Pangs of a New Christian Zionism," *The Nation*, August 8, 2006, http://www.thenation .com/doc/20060814/new_christian_zionism/single?rel=nofollow.

266   *"an everlasting lake of fire":* The Bible, Revelation 19:20.

266   Hagee on Jesus and the ACLU: Max Blumenthal, "The Real Mike Huckabee," *The Nation*, January 11, 2008, http://www.thenation.com/doc/20080128/ blumenthal.

267   *"coming nuclear showdown with Iran":* John Hagee, "The Coming Holy War," *Charisma*, January 31, 2006, http://www.charismamag.com/index.php/ component/content/article/545-israel-the-middle-east/12391-the-coming -holy-war.

267   *"Washington-Israel" Summit:* Max Blumenthal, "Rapture Ready."

268   *"bodies burst open from head to toe":* Tim LaHaye and Jerry B. Jenkins, *Left Behind* (Carol Stream, IL: Tyndale House, 1996), pp. 226, 286.

268   *widely experienced religious teaching or evangelistic tools: Different Groups Follow Harry Potter, Left Behind and Jabez,* Barna Group, October 22, 2001, http://www.barna.org/barna-update/article/5-barna-update/61-different -groups-follow-harry-potter-left-behind-and-jabez.

268   *"the authentic line of cumulative critical thought":* Ernest Becker, *The Denial of Death* (New York: The Free Press, 1973), p. 134.

268   *"omnipotent father-figures, extra-magical helpers":* Ibid., p. 147.

269   *psychologists set out to prove his hypothesis:* Abram Rosenblatt, Sheldon Solomon, Jeff Greenberg, Tom Pyszczynski, and Deborah Lyon, "Evidence for Terror Management Theory I: The Effects of Mortality Salience on Reactions to Those Who Violate or Uphold Cultural Values," *Journal of Personality and Social Psychology*, 57, 4 (1989), pp. 681–690.

269   *mortality reminders:* John B. Judis, "Death Grip," *The New Republic*, August 27, 2007, http://www.tnr.com/politics/story.html?id=9e9af105–6745–497a- b5f8–4f304749eed4&p=5.

270   *"Twelve million illegal immigrants later":* "Ex-Senator Faults '86 Law on Immigrants," Associated Press, May 26, 2007, http://www.nytimes.com/2007/05/

26/us/politics/26thompson.html?scp=1&sq=Ex-Senator%20Faults%20 '86%20Law%20On%20Immigrants&st=cse.

270 *Huckabee also linked immigration to terrorism:* Adam Aigner-Treworgy and Ben Weltman, "Huckabee Ties Pakistan, Immigration," MSNBC.msn.com, December 28, 2007, http://firstread.msnbc.msn.com/archive/2007/12/28/ 537063.aspx.

270 *His claim was immediately contradicted:* Adam Aigner-Treworgy, "Huck's Pakistani Immigration Numbers," MSNBC.msn.com, December 28, 2007, http:// firstread.msnbc.msn.com/archive/2007/12/28/537385.aspx.

270 *"Arabic or Farsi or Chinese":* Mitt Romney, transcript of CPAC speech, *The American Conservative,* http://www.conservative.org/pressroom/2007/speech _romney.asp. Also see Max Blumenthal, "CPAC 2007: The Unauthorized Documentary," Washington, DC, March 2, 2007, posted to YouTube: http:// www.youtube.com/watch?v=ByLqJD36F7E.

270 *"kill you and kill me and our families":* Max Blumenthal, "Republicanizing the Race Card," *The Nation,* March 23, 2006, http://www.thenation.com/doc/ 20060410/blumenthal.

CHAPTER 23: THE HATE BOAT

272 Hagee paid for Huckabee speeches: "Huckabee Still Getting Paid for Political Speeches," CNN, December 27, 2007, http://politicalticker.blogs.cnn.com/ 2007/12/27/huckabee-still-getting-paid-on-the-speech-circuit/.

272 *"Have you prayed about this?":* Michael Sherer, "Huckabee Finally Settles His Campaign Scores," *Time,* November 16, 2008.

272 *McCain brushed the question off:* Peter J. Boyer, "Party Faithful," *The New Yorker,* September 8, 2008, http://www.newyorker.com/reporting/2008/09/ 08/080908fa_fact_boyer?currentPage=all.

272 *had uttered this disclaimer word for word:* Ibid.

273 Donohue and Hagee: Bill Donohue, *"McCain Embraces Bigot,"* Catholic League statement, February 28, 2007, http://www.catholicleague.org/release .php?id=1393.

273 *apologist for the so-called "Nazi Pope":* Dave Gibson, "Catholic Firebrand Bill Donohue Attacks ABC Priest, Backs Pope," November 16, 1997, http://www .observer.com/node/39868.

273 *"secular Jews" in Hollywood "who hate Christianity":* Bill Donohue to Pat Buchanan, "Scarborough Country," MSNBC, December 8, 2004, transcript posted to MSNBC.msn.com; December 9, 2004, http://www.msnbc.msn .com/id/6685898.

273 *accepted an apology from Hagee:* Bill Donohue on "Fox and Friends," *Fox News,* May 13, 2008, http://www.youtube.com/watch?v=91TfmnKl3hQ.

273 *"Hitler was a hunter":* Bruce Wilson, "Audio Recording of McCain's Political Endorser John Hagee Preaching Jews Are Cursed and Subhuman," Talk to Action, May 15, 2008, http://www.talk2action.org/story/2008/5/15/141520/281;

and Sam Stein, "McCain Backer Hagee Said Hitler Was Fulfilling God's Will," *Huffington Post,* May 21, 2008, http://www.huffingtonpost.com/2008/05/21/mccain-backer-hagee-said_n_102892.html?redux.

274   *"crazy and unacceptable":* CNN video pool, CNN ImageSource, May 23, 2008, http://imagesource.cnn.com/imagesource/ViewAsset.action;jsessionid=9A94 6D4F957CD6E7E8474F4E59F10A78?viewAsset=&_sourcePage=%2FWEB -INF%2Fpages%2Fbrowseaction%2FsearchResults.jsp&cnnId=05506609& searchResultsActionBeanClass=com.cnn.imagesource.action.search.Browse ActionBean.

274   *the result of "poor vetting":* Holly Bailey, "A Turbulent Pastor," *Newsweek,* May 12, 2008, http://www.newsweek.com/id/135385/output/print.

274   *a fruitless music censorship campaign:* "A Campaign Against 'Degrading' Rock Lyrics," Associated Press, March 31, 1996, http://query.nytimes.com/gst/fullpage .html?res=9506E5DB1E39F932A05756C0A960958260&n=Top%2FReference %2FTimes%20Topics%2FPeople%2FB%2FBennett%2C%20William%20J.

274   *Lieberman had lauded the pastor in Hebrew:* Blumenthal, "Rapture Ready."

274   Lieberman at CUFI: Max Blumenthal, "Joseph Lieberman to Headline Upcoming Pastor Hagee Summit," *Huffington Post,* May 27, 2007, http://www .huffingtonpost.com/max-blumenthal/joseph-lieberman-to-headl_b _103624.html.

275   *J Street sponsored a poll:* "CNN's Schneider Asserted That Lieberman Speech at RNC Could Draw Jewish Voters, But Did Not Mention Polling Showing Low Approval Among Jews," *Media Matters,* August 22, 2008, http://media-matters.org/items/200808220012.

275   *Hagee identifying the anti-Christ as a gay:* Max Blumenthal, "Pastor Hagee: The Antichrist Is Gay, Partially Jewish, As Was Adolph Hitler (Paging Joe Lieberman!)" *Huffington Post,* June 2, 2008, http://www.huffingtonpost .com/max-blumenthal/pastor-hagee-the-antichri_b_104608.html.

275   *ally with Jerry Falwell's Moral Majority:* Irving Kristol, "The Political Dilemma of American Jews," *Commentary Magazine,* July 1984.

275   *"They have such funny noses":* Hackensack *Sunday Record,* June 21, 1981, http://www.sullivan-county.com/id3/right_jews.htm.

275   Jews *"can make more money accidentally":* "Politicizing the Word," *Time,* October 1, 1979, http://www.time.com/time/magazine/article/0,9171,947467–2,00 .html.

275   *"Why should Jews care":* Kristol, 1984.

275   *"sinking to new levels of vulgarity":* Irving Kristol, "The Neoconservative Persuasion," *Weekly Standard,* August 25, 2003, http://www.weeklystandard .com/Content/Public/Articles/000/000/003/000tzmlw.asp?pg=2.

276   *self-control as a panacea for societal problems:* William Bennett, *The Book of Virtues: A Treasury of Great Moral Stories* (New York: Simon & Schuster, 1993), cited by Joshua Green in "The Bookie of Virtue," *Washington Monthly,* June 2003, http://www.washingtonmonthly.com/features/2003/0306.green.html.

276   *"preferred customer" at over a dozen casinos:* Green, "The Bookie of Virtue."

276 *a neoconservative–Christian-right alliance:* Kristol, 1984.

276 Goldfarb led the charge: Michael Goldfarb, "McCain/McSame/McStupid" blog entry, *Weekly Standard*, March 6, 2008, http://www.weeklystandard .com/weblogs/TWSFP/2008/03/mccainmcsamemcstupid.asp.

277 *"one that is marked by respect":* "Polls Show Obama–McCain Race Tight As Campaign Begins," CNN.com, June 5, 2008, http://www.cnn.com/2008/ POLITICS/06/05/campaign.wrap/index.html.

277 *lunch with the state's new governor, Sarah Palin:* Jane Mayer, "The Insiders," *The New Yorker,* October 27, 2008, http://www.newyorker.com/reporting/ 2008/10/27/081027fa_fact_mayer?currentPage=all.

278 *"she's a blank page":* Tim Shipman, "Neoconservatives Plan Project Sarah Palin to Shape Future American Foreign Policy," London *Telegraph*, September 16, 2008, http://www.telegraph.co.uk/news/newstopics/uselection2008/ sarahpalin/2827217/Neoconservatives-plan-Project-Sarah-Palin-to-shape -future-American-foreign-policy.html.

278 *Kristol gushed with praise for Palin:* Mayer, "The Insiders."

CHAPTER 24: A MATTER OF TONE

279 Vanderslice's political action committee: Michael Luo, "New PAC Seeks to Court Christians for Obama," *New York Times*, June 10, 2008, http://thecaucus .blogs.nytimes.com/2008/06/10/new-pac-seeks-to-court-christians-for-obama/.

279 *"She was a little bit overzealous":* David Kirkpatrick, "Consultant Helps Democrats Embrace Faith, and Some in Party Are Not Pleased," *New York Times*, December 26, 2006, http://www.nytimes.com/2006/12/26/us/politics/26faith .html?_r=1&ref=politics&oref=slogin.

279 *10 percent more of the evangelical vote:* Max Blumenthal, "Inside Obama's Christian Crusade," *The Nation*, July 1, 2008, http://www.thenation.com/doc/ 20080714/blumenthal.

279 *"secularists are wrong":* Barack Obama, speech at Call to Renewal conference, June 26, 2006.

280 *"Committed Christian":* Obama's "Committed Christian" campaign brochure, available at http://www.talkingpointsmemo.com/images/2008–01–21_obama _faith_2.jpg.

280 *The concert headliner was Danny McClurkin:* "Obama Supporter: 'God Delivered Me from Homosexuality,'" CNN.com, October 29, 2007, http://political ticker.blogs.cnn.com/2007/10/29/obama-supporter-god-delivered-me-from -homosexuality/.

280 Obama's off-the-record meeting: Blumenthal, "Inside Obama's Christian Crusade."

281 *a "fruitcake interpretation" of the Bible:* Amy Chozick, "Young Clergyman Leads Obama's Drive to Attract 'Faith Voters,'" *Wall Street Journal*, August 16, 2008, http://online.wsj.com/article/SB121883753433545501.html?mod=google news_wsj.

282 *"I have never been considered a part"*: Max Blumenthal, "Rick Warren's Double Life," *The Daily Beast,* November 14, 2008, http://www.thedailybeast .com/blogs-and-stories/2008–11–14/how-rick-warren-became-a-media -darling-in-spite-of-himself/.

282 Warren *"an evangelical liberals can love"*: Nicholas Kristof, "Evangelicals a Liberal Can Love," *New York Times,* February 3, 2008, http://www.nytimes.com/ 2008/02/03/opinion/03kristof.html?scp=1&sq=Warren%20evangelical%20li berals%20can%20love&st=cse.

282 *"people who make America great"*: "The Giving Back Awards," *Newsweek,* July 3, 2008, http://www.newsweek.com/id/46165/page/8.

282 *"disassociates himself from the religious right"*: Wendy Kaminer, "Rick Warren, 'America's Pastor,'" *The Nation,* August 25, 2005, http://www.thenation.com/ doc/20050912/kaminer.

282 *"a title the media has given him"*: Blumenthal, "Rick Warren's Double Life."

282 *"a matter of tone"*: Naomi Schaefer Riley, "What Saddleback's Pastor Really Thinks About Politics," *Wall Street Journal,* August 23, 2008, http://online.wsj .com/public/article_print/SB121944811327665223.html.

282 *a nationally televised campaign forum: Saddleback Presidential Candidates Forum* transcript, CNN.com, August 16, 2008, http://transcripts.cnn.com/ TRANSCRIPTS/0808/16/se.02.html.

283 *"above my pay grade"*: Jonquil Frankham, "Dr. James Dobson Explains McCain Endorsement: America Needs a 'Pro-family, Pro-life President,'" *Life-SiteNews,* October 22, 2008, http://www.lifesitenews.com/ldn/2008/oct/ 08102211.html.

283 *Warren chuckled at Obama's response:* Blumenthal, "Rick Warren's Double Life."

283 *religious-right leaders hailed McCain's performance:* Jennifer Riley, "Evangelicals Praise McCain's Performance at Saddleback," August 18, 2008, http:// www.christianpost.com/Society/Church-state/2008/08/evangelicals-praise -mccain-s-performance-at-saddleback-18/index.html.

283 Minnery on Palin's CNP unveiling: Max Blumenthal: "Secretive Right-Wing Group Vetted Palin," *The Nation,* September 1, 2008, http://www.thenation .com/blogs/state_of_change/352178/secretive_right_wing_group_vetted_palin.

CHAPTER 25: THE FAMILY THAT PRAYS TOGETHER

285 *"I am not endorsing Senator McCain today"*: Dobson, "Focus on the Family," *Focus Action,* July 21, 2008, http://mediamatters.org/items/200807230009.

285 *whom he personally disliked:* Ana Marie Cox, "The 'I Hate Romney' Club," *Time,* February 3, 2008, http://www.time.com/time/politics/article/0,8599 ,1709507,00.html.

285 *his name appeared on McCain's VP shortlist:* "Florida Gov. Charlie Crist Engaged," Associated Press, July 3, 2008, http://www.foxnews.com/politics/ elections/2008/07/03/florida-gov-charlie-crist-engaged/.

285 *Pawlenty, a competent establishment dullard:* "State of Minnesota Too Polite," *Onion,* February 23, 3005, http://www.theonion.com/content/node/30916.

286   *Unknown to the national media:* Michael D. Shear and Karl Vick, "No Sur-
       prises from Palin, McCain Team Says," *Washington Post*, September 2, 2008,
       http://www.washingtonpost.com/wp-dyn/content/article/2008/09/01/
       AR2008090100710.html; and Elisabeth Bumiller, "Palin Disclosures Raise
       Questions on Vetting," *New York Times*, Septmber 1, 2008, http://www
       .nytimes.com/2008/09/02/us/politics/02vetting.html.

286   *"I'm a f**kin' redneck":* Luisa Yanez, "Sarah Palin's Future Son-in-Law Says
       He's an Alaska 'Redneck,'" *Miami Herald*, September 2, 2008, http://www
       .mcclatchydc.com/homepage/story/51459.html.

286   *bombarded by a blizzard of rumors:* see Max Blumenthal, interview with Amy
       Goodman, The War and Peace Report, *Democracy Now!* New York, October
       13, 2008, http://www.democracynow.org/2008/10/13/max_blumenthal_on
       _sarah_palins_radical; and Blumenthal, "How Sarah Palin Excluded African-
       Americans in Alaska," Anchorage, Alaska, YouTube, October 18, 2008, http://
       www.youtube.com/watch?v=pVMpOoegxQU&feature=channel_page; and
       Blumenthal, "In the Land of Queen Esther: The Unauthorized Sarah Palin
       Story," Wasilla and Anchorage, Alaska, YouTube, October 7, 2008, http://www
       .youtube.com/watch?v=Lpe_lOEn0VY&feature=channel_page.

287   *Johnston's mother, Sherry, a reputed dealer:* Zaz Hollander, "Levi Johnston's
       Mother Hit with Drug Charges," *Anchorage Daily News*, December 18, 2008,
       http://www.adn.com/news/alaska/crime/story/628010.html.

287   *they delayed Johnston's arrest:* "Trooper Says Election Delayed Alaska Drug
       Case," Associated Press, December 26, 2008, http://www.washingtonpost
       .com/wp-dyn/content/article/2008/12/25/AR2008122500930.html.

287   *a Norse word for "strength":* TurabianNights, "Alaska's First Family," The Bad
       Baby Names Blog, August 31, 2008, http://turabiannights.blogspot.com/
       2008/08/alaskas-first-family.html.

287   *"that little Downs Syndrome baby":* James Dobson and Tony Perkins, "Focus on
       the Family," *Focus on the Family Action,* September 2, 2008, http://focusfamaction
       .edgeboss.net/download/focusfamaction/c4daily/2008–09–02-daily-c4.mp3.

288   *"You are not welcome here":* Also see Francis X. Clines, "Lives of the Party,"
       New York Times, September 3, 2008, http://www.nytimes.com/2008/09/04/
       opinion/04thu4.html?partner=rssnyt&emc=rss.

288   *"It's a cool name":* Sandra Sobieraj Westfall, "John McCain & Sarah Palin on
       Shattering the Glass Ceiling," *People*, August 29, 2008, http://www.people
       .com/people/article/0,,20222685_2,00.html.

288   *licked her palm, and smoothed his hair:* John McDonnell, "Piper Palin, Spit,
       Trig Palin, and John Chapter 9," *Free Republic,* October 9, 2008, http://www
       .freerepublic.com/focus/f-religion/2079674/posts.

289   *"We grow good people in our small towns":* Palin's acceptance speech, Republi-
       can National Convention, St. Paul, Minnesota, http://elections.nytimes.com/
       2008/president/conventions/videos/20080903_PALIN_SPEECH.html.

289   *Pegler, a prominent mid-century columnist and demagogue:* William F. Buckley Jr.,
       "Rabble-Rouser," *The New Yorker*, March 1, 2003, http://www.newyorker
       .com/archive/2004/03/01/040301fa_fact_buckley?currentPage=2.

289   the killer *"got the wrong man"*: Alden Whitman, "Free-Swinging Critic," *New York Times*, June 25, 1969, http://select.nytimes.com/gst/abstract.html?res =F40F15FD385E1B7493C7AB178DD85F4D8685F9&scp=5&sq=pegler%20 and%20jewish&st=cse.

290   Sarah Palin's background: William Yardley, "Sarah Palin, an Outsider Who Charms," *New York Times*, August 30, 2008, http://www.nytimes.com/2008/ 08/30/us/politics/30palin.html?_r=1&pagewanted=1&hp.

290   *she eloped with her high school sweetheart*: Kate Zernike and Kim Severson, "A Low-Key Outdoorsman and Family Man Now Faces a National Role," *New York Times*, September 2, 2008, http://www.nytimes.com/2008/09/03/us/politics/ 03todd.html.

290   *victory in the Republican gubernatorial primary*: "Alaska Gov. Murkowski Concedes Defeat in GOP Gubernatorial Primary," Associated Press, August 23, 2008, http://www.foxnews.com/story/0,2933,209918,00.html.

290   *investigation against party chairman Randy Ruedrich*: Sean Cockerham, *Anchorage Daily News*, "Ruedrich Resigns Post As Regulator on State Oil and Gas Commission," November 9, 2003, http://www.adn.com/sarah-palin/background/ story/513772.html.

290   *a 28 percent spending increase*: Wesley Loy, "Legislature Passes $1,200 Rebate," *Anchorage Daily News*, August 08, 2008. Also see Matt Volz, "Palin Has Mixed Record As Fiscal Conservative," Associated Press, October 12, 2008, http:// www.usatoday.com/news/politics/2008–10–12–413514155_x.htm.

291   *a whopping 85 percent approval rating*: Sabra Ayres, "Alaska's Governor Tops the Approval Rating Charts," *Anchorage Daily News*, May 30, 2007, http://dwb.adn.com/front/story/8931726p-8831940c.html.

291   Weekly Standard*'s puff-piece*: Fred Barnes, "The Most Popular Governor," *Weekly Standard*, July 16, 2007, http://www.weeklystandard.com/Content/ Public/Articles/000/000/013/851orcjq.asp.

291   *his magazine's cruise to Alaska*: Jane Mayer, "The Insiders: How John McCain Came to Pick Sarah Palin," *The New Yorker*, October 27, 2008, http:// www.newyorker.com/reporting/2008/10/27/081027fa_fact_mayer?current Page=all.

291   *"we really can relate"*: Max Blumenthal, *Sarah Palin's Daughter, Republican Values and the RNC '08*, Value Voters Summit, St. Paul, Minnesota, YouTube, September 1, 2008.

299   Palin's magazine reading: Sarah Palin, interview with Katie Couric, "Palin Opens Up on Controversial Issues," CBSNews.com, September 30, 2008, http:// www.cbsnews.com/stories/2008/09/30/eveningnews/main4490618.shtml.

299   *could see Russia from her home state*: Gary Tuchman, "You CAN see Russia from here!" CNN.com, September 30, 2008, http://ac360.blogs.cnn.com/ 2008/09/30/you-can-see-russia-from-here/.

299   *not from rigorous study*: Nicholas K. Geranios, "Palin Switched Colleges 6 Times in 6 Years," Associated Press, September 4, 2008, http://abcnews.go .com/Politics/wireStory?id=5728215.

299   *a "fatal cancer" on the Republican Party:* David Brooks, interview with Jeffrey Goldberg, Le Cirque, New York, October 6, 2008, http://www.huffington post.com/2008/10/08/david-brooks-sarah-palin_n_133001.html.

299   *"extremely ignorant"and "a religious crackpot":* Jeffrey Hart, interview with Mostafa Heddaya, "TDR Exclusive Interview: Obamacon Jeffrey Hart," *Dartmouth Review*, October 21, 2008, http://dartreview.com/archives/2008/10/21/tdr_exclusive_interview_obamacon_jeffrey_hart.php.

299   *"a dope and unqualified from the start":* Peggy Noonan, "Palin's Failin,'" *Wall Street Journal*, October 17, 2008, http://online.wsj.com/article/SB1224192 10832542317.html.

299   *a "cocky wacko":* Lincoln Chaffee, speech "What Does Patriotism Look Like?" New America Foundation, Washington, DC, September 9, 2008, http://www.newamerica.net/video/chafee/chafee-on-palin-naf090908a.mov.

299   Muthee anoints Palin against witchcraft: Thomas Muthee address at Wasilla Assembly of God, Wasilla, Alaska, May 2005, http://www.youtube.com/watch?v=jl4HIc-yfgM&eurl=http://www.thenation.com/blogs/state_of_change/363724/the_witch_hunter_anoints_sarah_palin.

299   *For them she had achieved "the anointing":* Jim Bramlett, "Barack, Sarah, and the Bible," InJesus.com, September 1, 2008, http://www.injesus.com/index.php?module=message&task=view&MID=YB007F5G&GroupID=2A004N9G.

300   *"God appoints leaders":* Max Blumenthal, "In the Land of Queen Esther," posted to YouTube October 18, 2008, http://www.youtube.com/watch?v=Lpe_lOEn0VY.

300   *Declaring that "the gloves are off":* Jim Kuhnhenn, "Palin Defends Terrorist Comment Against Obama," Associated Press, October 5, 2008, http://www.foxnews.com/wires/2008Oct05/0,4670,PalinRecharged,00.html.

300   *"the living room of a domestic terrorist":* Julie Bosman, "Palin Plays to Conservative Base in Florida Rallies," *New York Times*, October 7, 2008, http://www.nytimes.com/2008/10/08/us/politics/08palin.html.

300   McCain/Palin crowd rage: Sarah Baxter, "McCain Tussles with Palin over Whipping Up a Mob Mentality," Sunday *Times*, October 12, 2008, http://www.timesonline.co.uk/tol/news/world/us_and_americas/us_elections/article49262 83.ece http://www.cnn.com/2008/POLITICS/10/10/mccain.crowd/index.html.

300   *"Kill him!":* Dana Milbank, "Unleashed, Palin Makes a Pit Bull Look Tame," *Washington Post*, October 7, 2008, http://www.washingtonpost.com/wp-dyn/content/article/2008/10/06/AR2008100602935.html.

300   *"Terrorist!" "Treason!":* Russell Goldman, "Is Negative Rhetoric a License to Taunt?" ABCNews.com, October 8, 2008, http://abcnews.go.com/Politics/Vote2008/Story?id=5987004&page=1.

300   *"He's a nigger!":* Epithet screamed by a Palin supporter at Des Moines, Iowa, rally, "Ballot Bowl 08," CNN, October 25, 2008, http://www.youtube.com/watch?v=KF5ZkgNNBQE.

300   *"Go back to Kenya!":* "Racism and Vitriol at Palin Rally in Johnstown, PA," Salon.com, October 13, 2008, open.Salon.com/content.php?cid=28870.

300 *"Born in Kenya, citizen of Indonesia!":* Ibid.

301 *"This is little Hussein":* Palin supporter displayed monkey doll at rally in Johnstown, Pennsylvania, October 11, 2008, http://www.youtube.com/watch? v=bKUovpF9LWU.

301 *Political Cesspool* and Operation Rescue recruit Palin supporters: Max Blumenthal, "Guess Who Came to the Palin Rally?" *The Daily Beast,* October 13, 2008, http://www.thedailybeast.com/blogs-and-stories/2008–10–30/guess -who-came-to-the-palin-rally/.

301 *whether abortion clinic bombers were terrorists:* Brian Williams interview, *NBC Nightly News,* NBC, October 22, 2008, http://www.youtube.com/watch? v=bBv88ixx74k.

301 *a dead bear cub riddled with bullets:* Dale Neal, "Dead Bear Dumped at WCU," *Asheville Citizen-Times,* October 21, 2008.

301 *a report from the Secret Service:* Jon Meacham, "How He Did It, 2008," *Newsweek,* November 17, 2008.

301 *Palin's red Naughty Monkey heels:* "Sarah Palin Likes Naughty Monkeys," Sarah Palin Blog, January 29, 2009, http://www.thesarahpalinblog.com/ 2009/01/sarah-palin-likes-naughty-monkeys.html.

301 criticism of Palin as anti-Christian phenomenon: "Christophobe Attacks Palin," Christian Anti-Defamation Commission, September 3, 2008, http:// www.christianadc.org/news-and-articles/116-christophobes-attacks-palin.

302 *"what I call the real America":* Elizabeth Holmes, "Palin Touts the 'Pro-America' Areas of the Country," WSJ.com, October 17, 2008, http://blogs.wsj.com/ washwire/2008/10/17/palin-touts-the-pro-america-areas-of-the-country/, and Rosa Brooks, "The 'Real' America, Really," *Los Angeles Times,* October 23, 2008, http://www.latimes.com/news/opinion/sunday/la-oe-brooks23–2008 oct23,1,7763246.column.

302 *above the fray, repeating his unifying message:* "Obama Says No Red States [or] Blue States in Times of Need," WisPolitics, September 2, 2008, http://www .midwestpolitics.com/blog/2008/09/wi-obama-says-no-red-states-bluestates .html.

302 *endorsing Obama during an October 19 appearance:* Tom Brokaw interview, *Meet the Press,* NBC, October 19, 2008, *http://www.youtube.com/watch? v=efv3Vr8T9MA*; and Colin Powell, *Meet the Press* transcript for October 19, 2008, MSNBC.msn.com. http://www.msnbc.msn.com/id/27266223/.

302 *no longer a place for him:* Tom Brokaw interview, *Meet the Press,* NBC, October 19, 2008 (0:40, 2:39, 4:12/7:09), http://www.youtube.com/watch?v=efv 3Vr8T9MA.

302 *a casualty of the movement's machinations:* Max Blumenthal, "The Man Who Helped Drive Powell Away from His Party," *The Daily Beast,* October 22, 2008, http://www.thedailybeast.com/blogs-and-stories/2008–10–22/the-bitter -back-story-behind-powells-defection/1/.

303 *"She is a diva":* Dana Bash, Peter Hamby, and John King, "Palin's 'Going Rogue,' McCain Aide Says," CNN.com, October 26, 2008, http://www.cnn .com/2008/POLITICS/10/25/palin.tension/.

303 *"positioning herself for her own future"*: Ginger Adams Otis and Carl Campanile, "Pit Bull Turns on McMaverick," *New York Post*, October 26, 2008, http://www.nypost.com/seven/10262008/news/politics/pit_bull_turns_on _mcmaverick_135366.htm.

303 *"a whack job"*: Mike Allen, *Playbook*, Politico, October 28, 2008, http://www.politico.com/playbook/1008/playbook476.html.

303 *"manic zeal"*: Scott Horton, "Palin's Mole at The Times," *The Daily Beast*, November 7, 2008, http://www.thedailybeast.com/blogs-and-stories/2008–11–07/palins-mole-at-the-times/.

303 Scheunmann's firing: Dana Bash, "Sources: McCain Aide Fired for 'Trashing' Staff," CNN.com, November 5, 2008, http://politicalticker.blogs.cnn.com/2008/11/05/soruces-mccain-aide-fired-for-trashing-staff/.

303 *Scheunemann, a neoconservative foreign policy hand:* Elisabeth Bumiller, "Internal Battles Divided McCain and Palin Camps," *New York Times*, November 5, 2008, http://www.nytimes.com/2008/11/06/us/politics/06mccain.html ?pagewanted=2.

304 *"To tell you the truth, Bill"*: William Kristol's Palin interview, "The Wright Stuff," *New York Times*, October 5, 2008, http://www.nytimes.com/2008/10/06/opinion/06kristol.html.

304 *The message was a mess indeed:* Bill Kristol, "Fire the Campaign," *New York Times*, October 12, 2008, http://www.nytimes.com/2008/10/13/opinion/13kristol.html.

304 *McCain all but vanished:* Scott Horton, "Palin's Mole."

304 *interview aired on October 22 with James Dobson:* "Focus on the Family," Focus on the Family, October 19, 2008, http://www.citizenlink.org/dailybroadcast/A000008476.cfm.

305 *supported a federal gay marriage ban:* Ed Henry and Craig Broffman, "McCain: Same-Sex Marriage Ban Is Un-Republican," CNN.com, July 14, 2004, http://www.cnn.com/2004/ALLPOLITICS/07/14/mccain.marriage/.

305 *ban on federal funding for stem cell research: Health Care: Funding Medical Research*, 2008 Republican Platform, Republican National Committee, http://www.gop.com/2008Platform/HealthCare.htm#4.

305 *New York Times*/CBS poll: Michael Copper and Dalia Sussman, "Growing Doubts on Palin Take a Toll, Poll Finds," *New York Times*, October 30, 2008, http://www.nytimes.com/2008/10/31/us/politics/31poll.html?_r=1&partner =rssnyt&emc=rss&oref=slogin.

305 *The Obama campaign's final ad:* "His Choice," October 28, 2008, http://www.youtube.com/watch?v=5eUz13-pmTY.

306 *her approval rating had plunged:* Chris Adams, "Even in Alaska, Palin's Popularity Is Taking a Tumble," McClatchy, September 30, 2008, http://www.mcclatchydc.com/staff/chris_adams/story/53299.html.

306 *Woody Jenkins lost a special congressional election:* Alex Mooney, "Democrats Emboldened by Louisiana Win," CNN.com, May 5, 2008, http://www.cnn.com/2008/POLITICS/05/05/congress.democrats/index.html.

306 Chris Shays's defeat: Richard C. Dujardin, "Rep. Shays Still 'Shell-Shocked' over Election Defeat," *Providence Journal*, November 11, 2008, http://www

.projo.com/news/politics/content/shays_speaks__11–11–08_MRC8230
_v13.3c72ede.html.

306 Colson's Armageddon: Laurie Goodstein, "A Line in the Sand for Same-Sex Marriage Foes," *New York Times*, October 26, 2008, http://www.nytimes.com/2008/10/27/us/27right.html?ref=us.

306 *"It's more important than the presidential election":* Ibid.

307 Broekhuizen Prince donation: Ted Roelofs, "Local Money Fights Gay Marriage in Florida, California," *Grand Rapids Press*, October 27, 2008, http://www.mlive.com/news/grand-rapids/index.ssf/2008/10/local_money_fights_gay_marriag.html.

307 *Howard F. Ahmanson Jr., who donated $900,000:* Max Blumenthal, "The Man Behind Proposition 8," *The Daily Beast*, November 3, 2008, http://www.thedailybeast.com/blogs-and-stories/2008–11–03/the-man-behind-proposition-8/1/.

307 *a round of massive layoffs:* Cara Degette, "More Layoffs at Focus on the Family," *Colorado Independent*, November 17, 2008, http://coloradoindependent.com/15287/after-pumping-money-into-prop-8-focus-on-the-family-announcing-layoffs.

307 *imploring them to trash department store catalogues:* Stuart Shepard, "Merry Tossmas 2008," Focus on the Family Action, November 13, 2008, http://www.citizenlink.org/Stoplight/A000008654.cfm.

307 *an Internet video posted on his website:* "Pastor Rick's News and Views," SaddlebackFamily.com, October 23, 2008, http://www.saddlebackfamily.com/blogs/newsandviews/index.html?contentid=1502.

308 *Warren quietly scrubbed a statement:* See the original statement at http://1.bp.blogspot.com/_1xQeOPE9ePU/SUv9WdHa8EI/AAAAAAAADBg/rjsnxsln4gY/s1600-h/warrenchurchbansgays.jpg.

308 *"I happen to love gays":* Rick Warren, "I love gays" speech, Muslim Public Affairs Council, December 23, 2008, http://www.swamppolitics.com/news/politics/blog/2008/12/rick_warrens_i_love_gays_speec.html.

308 *he compared homosexuality to incest and pedophilia:* Steve Waldman, "Rick Warren's Controversial Comments on Gay Marriage," *BeliefNet*, December 17, 2008, http://blog.BeliefNet.com/stevenwaldman/2008/12/rick-warrens-controversial-com.html.

308 *"a good thing for our country":* Mike Allen, "Axelrod: Warren Prayer 'a Good Thing,'" Politico, December 28, 2008, http://www.politico.com/news/stories/1208/16884.html.

308 *Despite Obama's efforts to court white evangelicals:* David Paul Kuhn, "No Gain for Obama with Religious Whites," Politico, November 17, 2008, http://www.politico.com/news/stories/1108/15604.html.

308 *"Democrats will need to invest more time":* Amy Sullivan, "Obama: Bringing (Some) Evangelicals In," *Time*, November 5, 2008, http://www.time.com/time/nation/article/0,8599,1856819–2,00.html.

309 *the all-powerful "Ultimate Fighting Jesus":* Molly Worthen, "Who Would Jesus Smack Down?" *New York Times,* January 6, 2009, http://www.nytimes .com/2009/01/11/magazine/11punk-t.html?_r=1&pagewanted=all.

309 *merely a harbinger of Christ's return:* John Hagee, "Financial Armageddon," *Front Line,* 2008.

309 *market conditions for their next great crusade:* Paul Vitello, "Bad Times Draw Bigger Crowds to Churches," *New York Times,* December 13, 2008, http:// www.nytimes.com/2008/12/14/nyregion/14churches.html?_r=2&pagewanted =1&hp.

EPILOGUE

311 *prayed over a door:* Max Blumenthal, "Inaugural Freak Show," *The Daily Beast,* January 14, 2009, http://www.thedailybeast.com/blogs-and-stories/ 2009–01–14/inaugural-freak-show/full/.

312 Paul Broun's come-to-Jesus moment: Broun address on House floor, November 11, 2007, Washington, DC; C-SPAN footage posted to YouTube November 11, 2007, http://www.youtube.com/watch?v=IUKnAaPvyNo&feature=Play List&p=17E1588640CCE833&playnext=1&playnext_from=PL&index=7.

312 *The bewigged "gentleman" was Rollen Stewart:* J. Michael Kenyon, "Real Action in '79 Was Outside the Lines," *Seattle PI,* July 6, 2001, http://seattlepi .nwsource.com/allstar/30179_1979game06.shtml?rand=80222.2.

312 *opposed the emergency financial bailout:* Carl Hulse and David Herzenhorn, "Defiant House Rejects Huge Bailout; Next Step Is Uncertain," *New York Times,* September 30, 2008.

312 *protect soldiers from images of unclad women:* Karen Jowers, "Bill: Stop Selling *Playboy, Penthouse* on Base," *Army Times,* April 24, 2008, http://www .armytimes.com/news/2008/04/military_pornography_stores_042208w/.

312 *"philosophy of radical socialism or Marxism":* Ben Evans, "Georgia Congressman Warns of Obama Dictatorship," Associated Press, November 7, 2008.

313 *announced he was "not taking back anything":* Blake Aued, "Broun Defends Remarks," Morris News Service, November 12, 2008, http://chronicle.augusta .com/stories/111208/met_483105.shtml; and Max Blumenthal, "Inaugural Freak Show."

313 *Broun joined Schenck and Mahoney in deep prayer:* Blumenthal, "Inaugural Freak Show."

INDEX